INCOMPREHENSIBLE!

The legal system is awash in excessive and incomprehensible information. Yet many of us assume that the unrelenting torrent of information pouring into various legal programs is both inevitable and unstoppable. We have become complacent; but it does not have to be this way. *Incomprehensible!* argues that surrendering to incomprehensibility is a bad mistake. Drawing together evidence from diverse fields such as consumer protection, financial regulation, patents, chemical control, and administrative and legislative process, this book identifies a number of important legal programs that are built on the foundational assumption that "more information is better." Each of these legal processes has been designed in ways that ignore the imperative of meaningful communication. To rectify this systemic problem, the law must be redesigned to pay careful attention to the problem of incomprehensibility.

WENDY WAGNER is the Richard Dale Endowed Chair in Law at the University of Texas at Austin, School of Law. She is the author of two books: *Bending Science: How Special Interests Corrupt Public Health Research* with Tom McGarity (Harvard University Press, 2008), which received the Hamilton Grand Prize for the best book published at University of Texas in 2009, and *Rescuing Science from Politics: Regulation and the Distortion of Scientific Research* with Rena Steinzor (Cambridge University Press, 2006).

Incomprehensible!

A STUDY OF HOW OUR LEGAL SYSTEM ENCOURAGES INCOMPREHENSIBILITY, WHY IT MATTERS, AND WHAT WE CAN DO ABOUT IT

WENDY WAGNER

University of Texas School of Law

WITH
WILL WALKER

Harvard Divinity School

CAMBRIDGE
UNIVERSITY PRESS

CAMBRIDGE
UNIVERSITY PRESS

University Printing House, Cambridge CB2 8BS, United Kingdom

One Liberty Plaza, 20th Floor, New York, NY 10006, USA

477 Williamstown Road, Port Melbourne, VIC 3207, Australia

314–321, 3rd Floor, Plot 3, Splendor Forum, Jasola District Centre, New Delhi – 110025, India

79 Anson Road, #06–04/06, Singapore 079906

Cambridge University Press is part of the University of Cambridge.

It furthers the University's mission by disseminating knowledge in the pursuit of education, learning, and research at the highest international levels of excellence.

www.cambridge.org
Information on this title: www.cambridge.org/9781107008472
DOI: 10.1017/9781139051774

First published 2019

Printed and bound in Great Britain by Clays Ltd, Elcograf S.p.A.

A catalogue record for this publication is available from the British Library.

Library of Congress Cataloging-in-Publication Data
NAMES: Wagner, Wendy (Wendy Elizabeth), author. | Walker, Will, 1995- author.
TITLE: Incomprehensible! : a study of how our legal system encourages incomprehensibility, why it matters, and what we can do about it / Wendy Wagner, University of Texas School of Law with Will Walker, Harvard Divinity School.
DESCRIPTION: Cambridge, United Kingdom ; New York, NY, USA : Cambridge University Press, 2019. | Includes bibliographical references and index.
IDENTIFIERS: LCCN 2018061719 | ISBN 9781107008472 (hardback : alk. paper) | ISBN 9781107400887 (pbk. : alk. paper)
SUBJECTS: LCSH: Law–United States–Interpretation and construction. | Law–United States–Language. | Comprehension. | Law reform–United States.
CLASSIFICATION: LCC KF425 .W34 2019 | DDC 349.73–dc23
LC record available at https://lccn.loc.gov/2018061719

ISBN 978-1-107-00847-2 Hardback
ISBN 978-1-107-40088-7 Paperback

To: Becky, Mice, and Mike

Contents

Figures

Table

Boxes

Acknowledgments

The very best part of working on this project was engaging with a number of generous, talented people who were willing to give comments, read drafts, talk about issues, and otherwise contribute to the effort.

Two colleagues – Peter Gerhart and Rena Steinzor – committed to the project at an early stage. Both read virtually every chapter, often several times, and their questions helped shape the arguments and form the substance of the book.

Terri LeClercq also read the entire book multiple times as well as engaging with the project well before pen met paper. Her encouragement, direction, and substantive writing suggestions offered over the years (and sometimes compressed into hectic months) were critical to the book's direction and content. We only wish we had still more energy to follow through on all of her many brilliant suggestions.

Kasia Solon Cristobal, Chris Bond, and Dottie Lee were the grease in the wheels for the project. Kasia, a crackerjack librarian at the University of Texas School of Law, engaged in the project at an early stage and was on constant lookout for material relevant to the project. In addition to sending out regular alerts on topics of interest (many of which ultimately formed the basis for individual chapters), she located vital information on short notice that immediately made its way into the final product. Chris Bond, our meticulous Cambridge University Press copy editor, was exceptional in all respects. Not only did he identify every misplaced semicolon and incomprehensible passage, but he cheerfully accommodated more than a few of our eleventh-hour adjustments. Dottie managed the entire project. She hired and oversaw research assistants and contracts, managed drafts and mailings, and otherwise kept the project on track.

Our editor at Cambridge University Press, John Berger, patiently extended our contract more times than we can count. Had he called in the book, the project would have ended, and we are most grateful that he allowed this book to finally see the light of day. Dean Ward Farnsworth at the University of Texas School of Law made it clear that whatever resources or time we needed for this project was ours. He provided generous financial assistance for research assistants and allowed the project to drift over years without once inquiring "when it might be finished." He even volunteered to help edit the text.

A number of colleagues, particularly from Wendy's home institution – the University of Texas School of Law – offered extremely helpful comments, sources, and general ideas on individual chapters. While all remaining errors fall on us, their comments made a substantial difference in our knowledge of various specialty areas and our ability to comfortably apply arguments to these topics. Specific thanks go to:

> Chapters 1–3: David Adelman, Bob Bone, Neil Komesar, and participants in the law and economics workshop at the University of Bonn
>
> Chapter 4: Juliet Kostritsky, Andrew Kull, Angela Littwin, David Rabban, Alan Rau, David Sokolow, Lauren Willis, and participants in the Advanced Contracts seminar at Case Law School
>
> Chapter 5A: Mira Ganor, Henry Hu, and James Spindler
>
> Chapter 5B: John Golden and Jori Reilly-Diakun
>
> Chapter 5C: Bernie Goldstein
>
> Chapter 6: Lynn Blais, Michael Livermore, Richard Pierce, Sid Shapiro, and the faculties at the University of Minnesota and University of Virginia Law Schools
>
> Chapter 7: Lisa Bressman, Jesse Cross, and James Curry

A small army of research assistants from the University of Texas School of Law also provided research assistance on various facets of the book. They include Elizabeth Esser-Stuart, Kelvin Han, Gabriel Jerome, Joshua Kelly, Jae Won Kim, and Kiran Vakamudi.

One final, particularly warm thank you (from Wendy) to her husband, Mike. He was not only the project's biggest cheerleader, but rolled up his sleeves to see the project to completion. Mike read multiple versions of virtually every chapter, providing intricate line edits, substantive suggestions, and general reactions. Since the project also took its toll at times on the time left for family, Mike also quietly and without complaint picked up the slack there as well. Mike's selflessness and dedication is a testament to what a true partnership really is.

PART I

The Concept

1

Introduction

Who worries about the substance of the convoluted contract they sign when they buy a mobile phone? Or is kept awake late at night because Congress passed an omnibus bill that is 1,000 pages long that even the congressmen involved concede they do not understand? How much unintelligible or overwhelming information do we ignore every day – from the pages of safety warnings and instructional inserts in consumer products, to the convoluted boilerplate that permeates every aspect of American daily life?

The simple fact of the matter is that excessive, incomprehensible information is everywhere. Lawyers are particularly well acquainted with it. Unnecessary complexity and incomprehensibility complicate efforts to extract meaning from long, convoluted statutes; overwhelm more than a few advocates who try to participate in public rulemaking proceedings; and infiltrate corporate disclosures documenting various financial and environmental activities.

And, for the most part, we have become resigned to that situation. The incomprehensibility that infiltrates so many of our legal, economic, and even personal relationships is accepted as a given. We shrug our shoulders when large segments of the public sign legally binding contracts or are bombarded with intricate product warnings they can never hope to understand, or when participation in complicated rulemakings consists only of industry experts who have the resources to navigate the morass of technical details, without equally savvy public-interest representatives. The assumption is that this unrelenting torrent of undigested information pouring into the legal system is inevitable and unstoppable. And so, many of us – perhaps especially in the legal field – have become complacent. We accept that incomprehensibility is a necessary feature of our contemporary world and conclude that nothing can be done about it.

But it doesn't have to be this way. And in this book, we argue just the opposite – that to surrender to incomprehensibility is a bad mistake. Incomprehensibility is *not* inevitable. Information overload is *not* just a force of nature or the price to be paid for entering the information age.

On the contrary, incomprehensibility is to some extent a self-inflicted wound that results from clumsy legal design. Legal architects have become quite adept, over the years, at devising rules that discourage privileged parties from hiding information. But they have neglected the corresponding imperative that this shared information must also be comprehensible and useful. Some of the deluge of incomprehensible information exists, in other words, because we have invited and even encouraged it.

Nobel prize-winning economist Herbert Simon warned way back in the 1940s that if we did not get ahead of the constant flood of information and figure out a way to manage it, we would find ourselves swept away and unable to make sense of it. He warned that legal and social institutions must be carefully structured to anticipate and ensure that the deluge of information that continues to inundate our markets and public institutions is understandable and usable.[1]

In this book, we argue that legal architects failed to heed Simon's warning and, as a result, the integrity of a number of legal programs has been compromised. Drawing together evidence from cutting edge work in diverse fields such as consumer protection, financial regulation, patents, chemical control, and administrative and legislative process, we identify a number of important legal programs that depend on vigorous communication and yet are afflicted with this same structural flaw. These legal programs are not designed to ensure that the incoming information is usable. Instead, the programs are built on a foundational assumption that, when it comes to information, "more is better" and that the problem of usefulness will take care of itself.

This oversight is not a fine detail or niggling technicality. On the contrary, when the effectiveness of a legal program depends on facilitating the communication of critical information, but that program neglects to ensure the information is also comprehensible, the system is poised for breakdown. Indeed, in extreme cases, if the imperative of comprehensibility is ignored, legal interventions initially intended to correct market failures or social inequities can actually make problems worse.

I SCOPING OUT THE PROBLEM

Return to the examples of information deluge at the start of this chapter. Contracts, financial forms, package inserts – each of these features of everyday life is highly regulated by laws, common law principles, and public and private enforcement – and each has been tweaked, adjusted, and amended for decades. These programs exist to *ensure* effective communication by the speakers and other actors. Large financial entities must explain their financial arrangements rigorously and clearly so investors can evaluate and compare them. Sellers need to ensure the average consumer understands the nature of their product so that the competitive market works and products are used safely.

But these programs (and, as we will soon see, many others) stop short of insisting on comprehensible communications. Yes, they require all information to be shared. And yes, an itemized list of facts is singled out for disclosure to make sure the transparency is complete. Indeed, in some programs, actors are even forced to fit their communications into user-friendly templates, draft in plain English, and place main messages in ALL CAPS or yellow highlights.

Despite these gestures, however, many legal programs do not close the circle and ensure that the speaker is eager to communicate meaningfully with the audience. Instead, if we step back and trace the incentives structure, we see the speaker in these situations is often better off remaining incomprehensible. Indeed, in some cases the speaker's profits increase in lockstep with the speaker's resourcefulness in confusing the target audience, rather than engaging and illuminating them.[2]

Take disclosure requirements. In the United States, we have hundreds of disclosure laws intended to ensure that various audiences are not misled.[3] The very point of the disclosure requirement is to facilitate meaningful communication of key information. But most mandated disclosures stop short of ensuring that the resulting information is actually comprehensible to the intended audience.[4] A firm eager to manipulate its consumers to gain an edge in the market need apply only a little creativity to devise a way around a required disclosure while still complying with the letter of the law. Indeed, firms may find themselves compelled to do this in order to survive.[5] As Lauren Willis observes: "Even without any intent to deceive, firms not only *will* but *must* leverage consumer confusion [in the consumer market] to compete with other firms that deceive customers."[6]

This same story is replayed in other important legal environments. After more than 40 years of regulating chemical manufacturers, we still know next to nothing about the toxicity of most of their chemicals. Indeed, most of what we do learn comes after the fact, once thousands of gallons of a chemical spill into a river or leach into the environment and jeopardize the survival of an endangered species. The spectacular failure of this regulatory design is explained, in part, by the fact that manufacturers bear almost no responsibility for understanding or communicating the hazards of their chemicals.[7] Instead, manufacturers' legal incentives are pointed in the reverse direction: encouraging strategic ignorance and obfuscation of what is known about product hazards. The more onerous the regulator's burden to assess the chemical, the less likely the regulator will be able to develop binding regulatory requirements.

Likewise, the patent process has been the topic of reform for decades since inventors regularly obtain patents that they do not deserve. Here again, however, we see the same story: a structural flaw in the design of the patent process itself. In patent law, the burden is on the patent examiner to understand the novelty of each invention. When the examiner is not sure about the invention's value, she is encouraged – by law – to grant, rather than reject, the claim. From this legal design, inventors discover that one way to obtain a patent is to craft a description that is so complicated that it outstrips the examiner's resources to make sense of it.[8] It is not worth the trouble (or money) to draft a concise, clear application since the burden is on the examiner to process it, with all errors cutting in favor of patent approval.

Even institutional processes intended to ensure rigorous democratic deliberation are designed in ways that miss the key step of encouraging decision-makers to be comprehensible. Congress has developed intricate procedures, rules, and practices governing how it can pass laws. But none of these institutional controls require that a bill be comprehensible to other members of Congress. Indeed, for some controversial laws, a powerful sponsor's net incentives can encourage the crafting of incomprehensible legislation that moves a bill through the process so quickly that it cannot be analyzed by members who might disagree with it.[9]

II THE CENTRAL ARGUMENT

Each of these institutional examples occupies a very different part of the legal system. But they all reveal the same essential lesson: Expert actors are often not required to master or effectively communicate the information they load into the system. Instead, the gears are set in reverse: to encourage more and more information, regardless of whether it is understood by those generating it. Even the most dedicated, public-minded company or civil servant can find themselves guided by rules that lead them away from ensuring their audience can reasonably understand their communications. Their effort is directed toward generating long paper trails that frequently lead nowhere, rather than ensuring their audience's overall comprehension. Instead of encouraging information that is useful, the design of many legal programs attracts undigested information like a gravitational force and passes it along to an unequipped, disadvantaged audience.

However, each example yields an additional lesson as well. Not only is excessive information detrimental to communication, but because our legal designs ignore this simple fact, some actors exploit this oversight. Savvy actors sometimes derive a significant advantage in the market or political process from imposing excessive processing costs on their disadvantaged audiences. Companies make money, patent applicants are rewarded with patents, and members of Congress gain power by deploying strategies that exploit their audience's limitations in processing voluminous and unduly complicated content. In fact, in some cases, extraneous information can serve as a kind of intimidation tactic: causing audiences to give up, even if they really want to understand the information in front of them.

Thus, as we connect the dots in each of these programs, we consistently find, at the end of the causal chain, a legal structure that sets up the wrong incentives. The law is unilaterally focused on the enlightening power of information – more is almost always better. Yet in their zeal for transparency and complete information, legal architects neglect the equally important, dual objective of ensuring that information is also comprehensible to its target audience. By erring on the side of too much information – without any provisions for ensuring that information is meaningful – the functioning of many legal programs is deeply compromised.

This state of affairs results in what we call "comprehension asymmetries." Comprehension asymmetries are similar to the familiar "information asymmetries" in adversely impacting communications, but the two concepts differ in the nature of their impediments. "Information asymmetries," which have been factored into institutional analyses for decades, occur when one actor in a conversation has superior access to relevant information that he or she does not share with the other party (e.g., a land negotiation where the sellers know there is a hazardous landfill buried under the farmhouse, while the buyers do not). By contrast, "comprehension asymmetries," a term that we introduce in this book, arise when one party has a greater ability to understand or process the relevant information relative to his or her conversational partner. A large financial entity, for example, might have significant advantages in processing and understanding important information about the risks of its investments relative to the purchaser. That's not to say that the consumers know nothing; in fact, in many cases, the seller, company, or agency will have to go to great lengths to make sure that the audience has access to all relevant data. But, ultimately, if that information isn't comprehensible to the audience – either because there's too much to be reasonably digestible, or it's too complicated, or it's made purposely confusing – a comprehension asymmetry exists. Even though all relevant information is on the table, the competitive situation remains deeply unbalanced.

As a consequence, comprehension asymmetries mimic incomplete information. They can undermine the functioning of the market or institutional program and make the audience vulnerable to the risks of manipulation. But comprehension asymmetries create communication challenges that are different from those of standard information asymmetries. In fact, as we will see throughout this book, attempting to redress information asymmetries often provides the foundation for burgeoning comprehension asymmetries. The two are thus related in complicated but not always supportive ways.

From this backdrop our central argument takes shape. We advance three sequential propositions in the chapters that follow:

1 When legal programs depend on, or try to force, communication – for example, by requiring disclosures to improve market functioning – legal design should not stop at requiring complete information. It is essential to ensure that the key information being communicated is also comprehensible to the target audience.

2 When significant comprehension asymmetries are not rectified, the target audience will operate largely in the dark, without informed choices or meaningful opportunities to engage. This communication failure may, in turn, embolden some speakers to take advantage of the situation since they can now exploit their audience's limited processing capacity by playing information games.

3 When the audience is at a significant disadvantage in processing key information relative to the speaker, but the speaker is not inclined to invest time and energy in communicating effectively, legal intervention may be necessary to correct the underlying "comprehension asymmetries." In effect, legal reform must introduce incentives so that the speakers face more benefits than costs to engage in meaningful communication with their target audiences.

Of course, when speakers face strong incentives to communicate meaningfully with their target audience, all confusion and complexity will not magically disappear. Even when a speaker succeeds in making a message reasonably comprehensible to its target audience, some fraction of the audience may still not understand the message. Additional problems on the audience side may thus also deserve intervention, but these challenges lie outside of the reach of our analysis. We focus here only on the first, crucial step in a communication: ensuring the speaker is held responsible for being reasonably comprehensible.

III A ROADMAP OF THE BOOK

To make this argument work, however, the concept of incomprehensibility must be sufficiently defined and specified so that it can serve as a viable, diagnostic probe. To that end, we dedicate Part I, the first third of the book, to delineating the concept of a comprehension asymmetry. In the next two chapters we construct a model for how to think about comprehensibility in a number of different legal programs that depend for their success on meaningful communication. The model synthesizes existent work on information overload with basic economic concepts to identify a point at which – in an individualized setting – communications become incomprehensible. From this, we then identify a simple conceptual test for assessing when a legal program is poised to encourage effective or cooperative communication: examining the speaker's net incentives to be comprehensible. Comprehensibility in communications is costly, and in some cases, incomprehensibility reaps more benefits than costs for the speaker. An assessment keyed to assessing the speakers' incentives also provides a way to sidestep difficult optimization problems that otherwise plague the measurement of incomprehensibility.

Part II (Chapters 4–7) applies this model to assess a variety of very different legal programs with respect to how well those programs encourage comprehensible communications. Given the vast and decentralized nature of the law, generalizing across diverse areas is treacherous. But in the six chapters that comprise Part II, we will notice that, from program to program, our current legal architecture typically focuses on demanding that the information is complete, while neglecting the equally important requirement that it be comprehensible to its target audience.

We also see through a study of diverse legal programs that the "incomprehensibility" problem is not simply one that afflicts the masses in consumer markets who are preyed upon by payday lenders and credit card companies. Rather, incomprehensibility's victims can include powerful Wall Street investors, expert regulators, and elected officials who run our country.

Moreover, and perhaps more strikingly, the effects of incomprehensibility are uniquely bipartisan. We will see instances where this design flaw cuts to the heart of what Republicans value most – efficient regulations that do not drain needless resources from important economic actors. And we will see how this omitted structural element also undermines the Democratic platform of providing greater government support for those at the bottom of the socioeconomic ladder and the protection of collective goods, such as public health and environmental protection.

The individual application chapters in Part II are written to be self-contained. Each chapter provides evidence in support of our argument, and each chapter closes with individualized proposals for reform based on the analysis. Readers can thus select individual chapters of interest within Part II, rather than reading all of them front to back, without losing the central argument of the book.

In Part III, the last chapter of the book, we summarize the key lessons for institutional design and reform emerging from our close-up study of individual legal programs in Part II. We underscore that, at its core, reform must involve turning the focus of legal architects to an oft-overlooked step in legal design – the speaker's responsibility for effective communication. And even though our diagnosis of a systemic structural weakness may initially seem discouraging, in this final chapter we argue that its pervasiveness may ultimately be an advantage for enacting meaningful reform. Rather than trying to patch up a dilapidated legal infrastructure, afflicted with hundreds of loopholes and defects, we will identify a single, foundational element that – once corrected – can begin to right the collapsing building.

Of course, existing economic and political elites will attempt to keep the status quo in place since they generally benefit from this architectural oversight. However, if we are right – and neglected comprehension asymmetries *do* explain some of our legal failures – then the ubiquity of this structural flaw will become an important focal point for reform. In effect, despite the protestations of certain entrenched actors, the *best* way to address the problem of comprehension asymmetries will be through a large-scale overhaul of the current incentive structure. Rather than employing dispersed, fragmented groups to address inequities and inefficiencies in isolated specialty areas, reformists can join forces behind a shared project: ensuring comprehensible, as well as accurate and complete, communication.

Clearly, a study of legal programs pitched at such high altitude necessarily entails taking liberties with nuances and details. And some of the simplifications may go too far. However, evidence amassed from a diverse group of scholars recounted in the pages that follow exposes a recurring foundational instability. Thus, even if our effort to map comprehension asymmetries misses important particulars, one must start somewhere. And the cumulative evidence suggests that, with respect to this specific neglected and important structural feature, such a conversation is long overdue. Phrased differently: Even if we miss some key elements, it is our hope that, by bringing the skeletal structure of this problem to light, we will spark a conversation about the role and importance of ensuring comprehensible communications within our legal system.

The first crucial step, however, requires elucidating the underlying problem of incomprehensibility. It is to that discussion we now turn.

2

Modeling Comprehension Asymmetries

The issue of communication has always been at the center of matters of law, order, and justice. As Herbert Simon observes, "It is obvious that without communication there can be no organization, for there is no possibility then of the group influencing the behavior of the individual."[1] In other words, effective communication is the essential lubricant that facilitates all transactional, political, and social relationships.

Consequently, for around the last half-century, legal analysts have turned their attention to the impediments to communication that arise when information is imperfect or unequally held. In particular, economic and legal scholars have zeroed in on the difficulties posed by *asymmetrical information*: an imbalanced communicative situation where information is not perfect because one party holds more information than the other.[2] The basic idea is that, when information is asymmetrically held, the participants in a legal proceeding do not operate on a level playing field. Instead, actors use this hidden information – like any other resource – as a strategic asset: It is withheld to provide advantages at the expense of the other party in the conversation.

In response to pioneering work on asymmetrical information, judges and lawmakers have developed a variety of rules that seek to encourage full disclosure of relevant information between parties. By promoting transparency and comprehensiveness, these reforms seek to level the playing field to ensure that all parties have access to the same information.[3] While reformers appreciate that redressing information asymmetries will not necessarily lead to perfect communication between two parties on its own, most seem to assume that one cannot have too much transparency, only too little. As a result, transparency and complete information are viewed as a one-way rachet that consistently improves the quality of communications. The greater the flow of information and transparency, the more confidence we can place in the resultant communication.

Yet this single-minded pursuit of information access – done without equivalent attention to the end goal of meaningful communication – is what leads to the "the fallacy of thinking that 'more information is better.'"[4] In some settings, complete information may not only fail to ensure effective communication, but when pursued too far, it can even get in the way of this goal.

If equivalent efforts are not in place to ensure that the "perfect" information is also comprehensible to the target audience, then complete access to information accomplishes much less than it sets out to do. Clever actors, for example, can comply with requirements to share all information, while investing energy in ensuring that this information is nevertheless incomprehensible. But even obedient parties may conscientiously load information into a transaction without being reminded (or encouraged) by the law to ensure it is also comprehensible.

By focusing too thoroughly on *one* kind of asymmetry, then, legal architects can sometimes exacerbate another kind of asymmetry. This other kind of asymmetry – comprehension asymmetry – applies *not* to access to information but instead to the actual *communicative value* of that information. Comprehension asymmetries can result even when actors are completely compliant in providing information that is exhaustive, complete, and ostensibly perfect.

Therefore, if we are going to fully come to grips with ensuring rigorous communication, we need to fundamentally expand the way that we think about the problem.

The purpose of this chapter is to break down, take apart, and investigate the pernicious problem of comprehension asymmetries. By synthesizing work from economics, communications theory, and information theory, we provide a simple model for understanding comprehension asymmetries. This simple model – our main melody – is then embellished and elaborated as it is applied to various legal programs in the chapters that make up Part II.

This introductory chapter unfolds in three parts. In the first two sections, we isolate the most important feature underlying comprehension asymmetries – processing costs. We define that critical feature and explore the way excessive processing costs, when left unchecked, can lead to comprehension asymmetries. We then address the dual impediments to resolving the problem of comprehension asymmetries: misplaced speaker incentives and an inability to optimize processing costs. We also introduce the model that we will use to evaluate comprehension asymmetries throughout the rest of the book. In the final section, we offer a general template for reform – a way of thinking that might lead us toward rectifying the problem of comprehension asymmetries.

I UNDERSTANDING PROCESSING COSTS

The first step to incorporating the phenomenon of comprehension asymmetries into our institutional and legal structures is to gain some understanding of how they work. That, in turn, involves accounting for the fundamental component that leads to comprehension asymmetries: "processing costs."

FIGURE 2.1 Processing Costs are Needed to Transform Raw Information into Knowledge

Raw information, like data or "bytes," does not necessarily result in knowledge or understanding. If that were the case, merely holding a contractual agreement in one's hands would provide the reader with the central messages. Instead, in the real world, understanding text and data entails an investment of time and energy. Phrased differently, the recipient or audience must incur a processing cost to turn data into practical knowledge or usable information. See Figure 2.1.

Processing costs are the costs a speaker or the audience must invest to unlock and make sense of information. In some transactions, processing costs can constitute a central bottleneck to effective communication. Legally requiring a bank to report its assets and liabilities to investors is worthless if the report is not also comprehensible to the investors. Mandating disclosure of workplace risks by employers accomplishes nothing if the disclosures are not reasonably comprehensible to the workers themselves. The purpose of information is not to exist, but to be *understood* by a group of individuals or an organization. Therefore, until the information can be reasonably processed by the target audience, it is effectively useless.

Even when information is complete, communication of that information could fail miserably. When processing costs are too high, the target audience may not be able to understand the message. Indeed, when the audience does not have sufficient leverage to sanction a speaker for incomprehensible communications, the audience may not only end up confused, but actively exploited as a result of its disadvantaged position.

Yet despite the centrality of processing costs to communication in general and the law's aims in particular, processing costs are rarely acknowledged in legal design. Instead, they are regularly ignored as a discrete and vital component of establishing deliberative and transactional processes that are fair and efficient.

Box 2.1 Definition of Key Terms

Information asymmetry:	When a speaker has superior access to information relevant to a communication, but that information is not shared with the audience.
Comprehension asymmetry:	When a speaker has a greater ability to understand and/or process information relevant to a communication as compared to the audience, but the speaker does not provide this information in a way that a reasonable or median member of the audience would understand.

Processing costs:	The costs needed to make reasonable sense of information so that it can be used.
Cooperative communication:	When a speaker and audience are highly motivated to ensure that the key messages are transmitted effectively and efficiently in a conversation.
Incomprehensibility (and information overload):	When the costs of processing information are greater than the perceived benefits of investing in the processing.
Speaker:	The party sending a message in a communication.
Audience:	The target recipient(s) for a message in a communication.

How could such an obvious step in communication be overlooked? At least in part, the neglect of processing costs is likely due to the way that information has changed over the course of the twentieth and twenty-first centuries.

Up until recently, the primary challenge associated with information has been its scarcity, not its comprehensibility.[5] As Mark Andrejevic notes, this history helps explain an assumption running through the laws and legal processes explored here that generally equates "access to information with empowerment."[6] The common perception is that transparency and information produce meaningful communication and accountability; after all, "sunlight is . . . the best disinfectant."[7]

Today, access to information no longer poses the challenge it once did. On the contrary, the supply of information is abundant and growing.[8] See Figure 2.2.[9] "It is estimated that one weekday edition of today's New York Times contains more information than the average person in seventeenth-century England was likely to come across in a lifetime."[10] "[M]ost branches of science show an exponential growth of [information] of about 4–8 percent annual(ly), with a doubling period of 10–15 years."[11] And that's without even mentioning the internet, which has provided the most dramatic increase in "enhancing public access to information" and effectively countered many "attempts by the state or the private sector to hoard, control, or otherwise monopolize access to information."[12]

However, in this new age of abundant information, the scarce resource has shifted from the information itself to something more transient: the *attention of the audience*. As Nate Silver warns, "We face danger whenever information growth outpaces our understanding of how to process it. The last forty years of human history imply that it can still take a long time to translate information into useful knowledge, and that if we are not careful, we may take a step back in the meantime."[13]

In effect, then, while the twentieth century (and the preceding millennium) might have struggled to overcome barriers posed by access to information, the twenty-first century must deal with more pernicious information problems: among

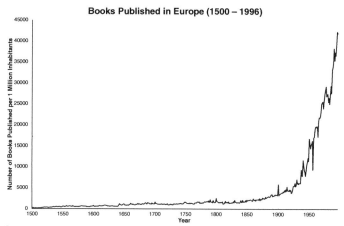

Data source: Fink-Jensen, Jonathan, 2015, "Book Titles per Capita", http://hdl.handle.net/10622/AOQMAZ, IISH Dataverse, V1

*The figure draws from data limited to Austria, Belarus, Belgium, Bulgaria, Croatia, Cyprus, Denmark, Estonia, Finland, France, Georgia, Germany, Greece, Hungary, Iceland, Ireland, Italy, Latvia, Lithuania, Macedonia, Malta, Moldova, Netherlands, Norway, Poland, Portugal, Romania, Russia (including USSR), Slovenia, Spain, Sweden, Switzerland, United Kingdom, and Yugoslavia.

FIGURE 2.2 Books Published in Europe over Time
Data drawn from Jonathan Fink-Jensen, "Book Titles per Capitata," http://hdl.handle.net/10622/AOQMAZ, IISH Dataverse, V1

them, excessive information and the resultant, high processing costs. If we want to use this plentiful information effectively, we have to design legal and organizational systems that focus on preserving and maintaining meaningful communication and comprehension.[14] And yet, as Herbert Simon cautioned, too many information systems are designed in ways that neglect to "conserve the critical scarce resource – the attention of managers."[15]

II THE EFFECTS OF INFLATED PROCESSING COSTS

Processing costs – standing alone – are not necessarily a problem; effective processing of information has always been a feature of the information landscape. The serious challenges begin to arise only when processing costs become so high that they actually become an impediment to communication. This impediment occurs when the *cost* of processing a given message outweighs the *perceived benefit* the audience would receive from actually understanding the data.[16]

A *The Bottleneck*

In its simplest form, this results in something called the "bottleneck" phenomenon – an informational situation where processing costs become so high that they prevent communication altogether.[17] Eli Noam describes how these bottlenecks result from "the limited ability of individuals and institutions to mentally process, evaluate, and use information."[18] Therefore, in bottlenecks, when the volume and technicality of information is unreasonably high, individuals and entities would rather give up than spend hours parsing the difficult, lengthy, or obtuse information in front of them. In these settings, more information perversely forecloses, rather than facilitates, genuine communication.

But even when processing costs are high, but not so high as to create a bottleneck, they can still take a toll on comprehension and the successful extraction of key messages. More than a half-century ago, researchers began examining ways that "information loads" – information that requires processing by an audience – affect the audience's overall ability to comprehend it.[19] In general, an inverse "U" shape describes comprehension relative to the size of the data-load. See Figure 2.3. In circumstances where the supply of information is very low, the audience's comprehension of the information is also low, because key messages are missing altogether.[20] But, counterintuitively, when the data-load is too high, comprehension is also very low – in some circumstances, even lower than it would be were the information load insufficient. The lesson of this finding is clear: Even when comprehension isn't totally prevented by excessively high processing costs, it is often reduced significantly when processing costs are inflated.

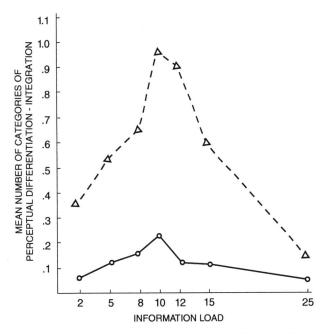

FIGURE 2.3 Processing Capabilities of Individuals over Differing Information Loads
Siegfried Streufert and Michael J. Driver, "Conceptual Structure, Information Load, and Perceptual Complexity," 3 *Psychon Science* 249, 250 (1965) © Used with permission from Springer Nature

We see this inverted "U" play out frequently in the real world. In consumer markets, for instance, excessive information can lead to "product choice errors" where consumers pick the wrong products because of their limited capacity to make sense of too much information.[21] In some of these cases, "[t]he psychological reaction to such an overabundance of information and competing expert opinions is simply to avoid coming to conclusions."[22] This is a kind of paralysis by analysis that prevents any sort of meaningful decision-making. In other cases, audience members forge on in the dark despite their imperfect grasp of the information landscape,[23] working on gut instinct and intuition so that "affect and emotion" rather than logic and clearheaded analysis "[become] decision-making drivers – means of cutting through the clutter."[24] Some participants even exit the scene prematurely – preventing themselves from even trying to engage in the vital processes of discernment and intellectual investigation. What's clear, though, is that in all of these cases, *too much information* leads to confusion and failed communications, rather than heightened comprehension.

And the consumer market is not the only area where we see processing costs occasionally factored into institutional analyses. In the area of organization, for example, Mark Casson dedicates a book to exploring how "the costs of collecting information and communicating it" influence the organizational structure of institutions.[25] Henry Smith discusses the excessive processing costs that result from unclear title documents in property law; the costs of this lack of clarity fall in part on the courts and owners who seek to penalize violators.[26] And, in their work on administrative process, Cynthia Farina and Mary Newhart refer to cumulative processing costs as the "information load" that participants must bear to participate in a deliberation, drawing from the term used in consumer marketing studies. They helpfully define information load as "the amount and complexity of the substantive information that commenters must understand in order to make useful comments on issues of importance to them."[27]

Unfortunately, though, while the effects of processing costs crop up sporadically throughout the legal and sociological literature, they are not rigorously accounted for in designing and modeling institutional processes more generally. In most cases, as already noted, legal analysts do not distinguish between access and comprehension challenges. Instead, they sometimes try to resolve communication problems by adding even more information to the mix, hoping that "transparency" or "comprehensiveness" will facilitate more meaningful communications.[28] And, also as noted, that solution can be counterproductive, leading to a condition of information or "data smog" that audiences have neither the ability nor the inclination to work their way through.[29]

Therefore – due both to their significance and their general neglect in institutional analyses and design – developing theoretical models that account for processing costs becomes all the more important. To adequately diagnose and counteract bottlenecks and resulting comprehension asymmetries, we must begin with a more detailed understanding of what they are and how to measure them. It is to this task that we now turn.

B When Is There a Bottleneck?

Thus far, we have shown that processing costs can be an underappreciated, but still significant feature of the communications landscape. However, if we want to construct our own model for incorporating processing costs into contemporary scholarship, we have to start by answering one vital question: At what point are processing costs *actually* an impediment to communication? In other words, when do processing costs lead to the larger problem of comprehension asymmetry?

One of the most difficult features of processing costs is that they're almost entirely context-driven. Unlike other impediments to communication, which may be more or less constant (a bad radio signal is a bad radio signal, regardless of who is trying to talk to whom, or what they're trying to say), "processing costs" vary greatly with the particular audience that is being targeted and the particular message that is trying to be conveyed.[30] In bureaucratic agencies, for example, researchers have discovered that broader, more accessible reports ("high-impact" reports, well-written with active voice, etc.) are assimilated by expert bureaucrats no differently from "low-impact" reports (densely written memos, laden with highly technical, expert terminology).[31] The processing costs are essentially the same because the audience's background and expertise allow for quick assimilation of complex and highly technical messages. However, in other settings, such as consumer markets, the audience sometimes foregoes processing information – for example, technical inserts on product risks – because the way that information is communicated makes the key messages impenetrable. As a result, the audience effectively learns to live without information – giving up on any sort of meaningful comprehension because the processing costs have become higher than they deem acceptable.

Consequently, every individual – whether she is a member of the general public, an expert regulator in an agency, or someone in between – has a price point: a point at which she will give up on understanding a message and proceed in ignorance. In some settings, that reasonable price point is very low. However, for even the most determined and expert participants, the costs of processing complicated information might be high enough in some cases to keep them out of the conversation.

But how do we determine this price point for the processing capacity of a person in any given setting? Neil Komesar has developed a simple participation-based formula that can be adapted to determine the point at which processing costs may become unreasonably high:[32]

> Processing costs are too high (results in incomprehensibility/overload) when:
> Benefits of understanding < Costs involved in unlocking the message.

The great virtue of this formula is its sensitivity to different individuals and varying contexts. After all, what is incomprehensible to most lay people may be easy for an expert to understand. An expert's "processing costs" will be much lower than the "processing costs" of the general public. Alternatively, if a given audience member has some sort of added benefit associated with trying to process information – for example, he or she hopes to master the information to impress a future employer in an interview – the *value* of understanding that information becomes much higher. That person is now more willing to invest resources in understanding the information, even when doing so is costly.[33]

So, to return to our initial question: How high, for processing costs, is too high? When do processing costs stop being an annoyance or a nuisance and start crystalizing into an impediment we call a comprehension asymmetry? The answer is, unfortunately: it depends.

And, it is undoubtedly this ephemeral feature of processing costs that explains why they are often neglected in institutional design and analyses. Because processing costs cannot be measured, much less optimized reliably given their contextual and individualized qualities, they generally tend to be ignored completely. Indeed, in the limited cases where processing costs are considered, they are generally lumped in with other types of information costs. Processing costs, for example, are sometimes categorized as a subset of transaction costs[34] or even swept in with problems of asymmetrical information.[35] Yet by including excessive processing costs with these other information costs that involve very different properties, we not only lose track of their unique features but risk embracing reforms that create perverse interaction effects between these very different types of informational challenges.

If we are going to try to address comprehension asymmetries, then, we need to take these contextual features head-on.

III THE CRITICAL ROLE OF THE SPEAKER

Up until this point, the discussion of processing costs has underscored the role of the audience. Comprehension asymmetries arise when the target audience is unable or unwilling to process key information because the investment in doing so is greater than the perceived benefits to understanding. A straightforward (and, as we discuss later, the prevailing) solution to minimize these comprehension asymmetries is thus to provide the audience with more support in terms of expert assistance, resources, and formats for communication keyed to the audience's comprehension level. Comprehension asymmetries will disappear, so this thinking goes, once the audience has more resources and/or expertise to make sense of the information. Supplementing the audience's ability to process information seems to provide a ready answer.

But as the preceding discussion makes clear, this is not so easy, given the contextual nature of communication. Identifying what constitutes "reasonable" processing costs will vary from one contract or transaction to the next and will also vary over time, sometimes wildly.

In any communication, however, there is not only an "audience" but a "speaker."[36] Both parties must grapple not only with accessing but also making sense of, or processing, the relevant information to the communication.

So, what about this speaker? Shouldn't the speaker bear significant responsibility for processing information as well, particularly when the speaker is the one creating the message? Indeed, not only does the speaker construct and package the message, he or she also, implicitly or explicitly, determines the processing costs that will be associated with understanding that message. In particular, treating incomprehensibility as a function of *fixed* processing costs that can be overcome by supplementing audience resources mistakenly assumes away the speakers' role in creating a garbled message in the first place.

In fact, much like the audience, speakers also face a cost–benefit problem at the start of any given conversation. In particular, this cost/benefit informs whether the speaker should invest time and energy in creating a digestible, comprehensible message for her audience, or whether she should pass information along in raw, or incomprehensible, form.

Speaker will Invest in Cooperative Communication when
Benefits of Cooperative Communication > Costs

As a result, it is important to be just as attentive, if not more, to a speaker's incentives and resources as to an audience's processing capacity. For instance, if the speaker's only incentive is to collect and convey complete information – and not comprehensible or useful information – it is unlikely that he or she will invest many resources in making the message accessible. The result is to effectively shift most of the processing costs to the audience by kicking the can down the line of communication. A speaker may even be incentivized against meaningful communication and invest resources to artificially *inflate* the audience's processing costs.[37] As long as processing costs are not the speaker's responsibility, he can shift them to the audience.

Ines Macho-Stadler and J. David Perez-Castrillo, in their *Introduction to the Economics of Information*, corroborate the importance of considering a speaker's incentives to communicate a key message effectively. As they state: "An agent is never interested in revealing private information if he obtains greater utility by keeping it secret. In the same way, he will also not want to signal the information if the signal is costly, and if the signaling act does not end up covering this cost."[38]

Take, as an example, a legal transaction in which a speaker benefits by reducing audience comprehension – confusing or misdirecting the consumer or contracting party. In such a case, even when full disclosure is mandatory, the transaction can be loaded with so much extraneous information and unanalyzed data that the audience has no practical way to parse the technical nuance of the document. Even if the audience is "captive" (eager to proceed) and well-educated, they can sometimes find themselves at the mercy of a highly motivated speaker determined to confuse or mislead them.

And the problem is not just limited to producer–consumer relationships. In a book published four decades ago, Bruce Owen and Ronald Braeutigam discussed the same phenomenon in their work on regulation. Specifically, they trace how – by "flood[ing] the agency with more information than it can absorb," raising endless (but ultimately fruitless) concerns, and using a variety of other obfuscatory techniques – participants in legal processes can prosper or even reap rewards by strategically manipulating the agencies' processing costs.[39] Like in producer–consumer relationships, participants in regulatory processes sometimes have an incentive to *manipulate* processing costs and exacerbate comprehension asymmetries between themselves and the regulators, all for the purpose of advancing their own self-interest.

Of course, not all communications work this way. There are settings in which speakers work tirelessly to bring processing costs down to a level where even the most disadvantaged audience can comprehend their key messages. Educators spend a good portion of their day learning techniques to reach their students – to convey the key messages in ways that eliminate superfluous facts and simplify complex topics. Public relations firms specialize in finding ways to communicate succinctly – in the form of advertisements, pamphlets, and sales pitches (although these messages are not always intended to be accurate, as we discuss later). And, of course, in most social communications the speaker's sole purpose is to convey a particular message or idea to her audience.

Yet, note that the only difference between these *optimal* communicative conversations and the problematic exchanges that can create bottlenecks for the audience are the speaker incentives. In these ideal circumstances, comprehension really *is* the objective. Teachers, PR firms, and advertisers are *rewarded* when they communicate effectively – when they make their message as clear and comprehensible as possible. But unfortunately, as we shall see, many other speakers – in some regulatory processes, consumer markets, areas of patent law, and even the US Congress – may face the opposite incentives, leaving an unfair, incomprehensible, and imbalanced informational landscape in their wake.

This insight then lets us return to the task set out at the start of this section – how to address the contextual nature of processing costs that vary in different communicative settings. If processing costs are not assessed and managed, it is difficult to ensure that the audience is adequately equipped to overcome comprehension asymmetries. Yet the role of the speaker may provide an answer to this dilemma. If the speaker faces strong incentives to communicate a message to the audience, then excessive processing costs that impede the audience's understanding may disappear simply because the speaker is poised to take on this responsibility and communicate meaningfully. Tracking the speakers' incentives, then, becomes at least as important as identifying excessive processing costs on the audience side of the conversation.

With these critical insights about the significance of the speaker's role in processing information in place, we can finally begin to construct the model we will use in the chapters that follow.

So far in our consideration of comprehension asymmetries, we have taken two critical steps. The first was descriptive: We boiled comprehension asymmetries down to their most essential feature and showed that overwhelming the audience with processing costs renders an unfair advantage to the speaker. The second was analytical: We showed how processing costs in a communication are impacted by the speakers' incentives. Now we build on these two steps to construct a conceptual approach we use throughout the rest of the book to locate comprehension asymmetries.

Before we construct that approach, though, we need to acknowledge three, simplifying assumptions. First, we assume that the audience's only impediments to understanding a message are the costs associated with information processing; the audience is perfectly rational. Of course, in the real world, this is not always the case. Audiences are afflicted with numerous heuristics, biases, and other cognitive and psychological features that affect their processing ability, even when they have the time and energy to dedicate to understanding a communication. Even when messages are delivered in a way that in theory should allow for reasonable processing by the audience, those messages may still be ignored or misunderstood for a host of complex reasons that we must bracket for the sake of analysis.[40]

Second, we assume that any message in a given conversation can ultimately be decoded and deciphered. Again, in the real world, there may be some settings where this isn't true – where audience members or speakers simply cannot make sense of information they are presented with, even given high motivation and considerable resources. A speaker can't communicate clearly what they are unable to reasonably understand, for example. However, for our purposes here, we assume that all messages *can* be processed, given a reasonable investment of time and energy, by either the audience or the speaker.

Finally, in order to expose the neglected significance of processing costs in legal process, we include in our analysis some situations where a speaker enjoys both information asymmetries as well as advantages in processing capacity relative to the audience. A speaker, for example, may enjoy some limited inside information related to the risks of his investments, as well as greater resources to process the significance of those risks. Nonetheless, this speaker will be included in our analysis since he or she enjoys asymmetries in processing capacity, along with some modest advantages in information access. Until there is a way to cleanly separate out the information asymmetry side of the speaker's informational advantage, we must lump these two types of asymmetries together. After all, if we tried to value these duel advantages as purely the result of information access, we would lose track of the unique harms inflicted by processing cost asymmetries, which is precisely the issue we hope to illuminate in this book.

With that preliminary work out of the way, we offer a simple, four-step approach that seeks to identify comprehension asymmetries within any legally established process for which meaningful communication is essential.

Step 1: Isolate the "speaker" and "audience" in a given market or legal setting. The speaker is producing the message; the audience is receiving it.

Step 2: Evaluate the audience's ability to process the central message in front of them. Think of this step as a rough, qualitative measure: Are the audience's available resources and expertise sufficient and their perceived benefit to investing in understanding the message high? Or is the audience's processing capacity comparatively low (for example, a busy consumer trying to find a safe and effective shower cleaner).

Step 3: Evaluate the speaker's net, aggregate incentives to communicate the central message. Again, this measure is qualitative and crude, but can often be quite informative. In particular, we consider whether the speaker's incentives to communicate cooperatively are high (as they would be in the case of a firm touting the virtues of a new, superior product) or low, nonexistent, or *negative*, where the speaker actually derives *benefits* from miscommunicating key information (a firm marketing a product that is of objectively lower quality and higher price than competitor products).

Step 4: Compare the speaker's incentives to communicate with the audience's ability to process the information. This is the step that identifies important comprehension asymmetries in institutional processes.

Again, given the qualitative nature of the analysis, this four-step inquiry will not be algebraically rigorous. And yet, by exploring audience-speaker processing capacities and incentives, we should be able to identify the most blatant comprehension asymmetries. For instance, if there is a situation where the audience's processing power is very low, and the speaker's incentive for cooperative communication is also very low (or even negative), it will likely be an area where some comprehension asymmetries exist. Conversely, if the audience's ability to process a message is very high, and the speaker's incentive to communicate is also very high, it's unlikely that comprehension asymmetries will be present.

What about the other two combinations, where the audience's ability to process is high but the speaker's incentive to communicate is low, or where the audience's processing power is low, but the speaker's incentives to communicate are high? Unfortunately, in these cases, we can't make generalizations quite so comfortably. However, it would be safe to say that, in general, the speakers' incentives dictate the success of the communication more than the audience's ability to process. In other words, if a speaker really wants to communicate effectively, it's more likely than not that he or she will find some way to deliver key messages to the audience.[41] However, if a speaker has very low or negative incentives to communicate accurately and effectively, it will be very difficult for even the most expert audience to process the full meaning of the speaker's message.

It is our hope, then, that by cataloguing and tracing the communication transactions in this way, we will be better able to detect and understand the presence of comprehension asymmetries in the legal and economic landscape. Although this model is rudimentary, it still provides an illuminating first step for properly diagnosing communicative imbalances and asymmetries whenever they start to appear in the real world.

V THE PRINCIPLES OF REFORM

Now that we've taken apart the problem, explored its component parts, and created a workable diagnostic tool to detect the presence of imbalanced communications, what might we do to eliminate comprehension asymmetries when we locate them? Or, more technically, how can we reform institutional systems to optimize processing costs so they don't overwhelm their audiences or unduly tax their speakers?

This section examines popular proposals for reform – audience and technology support – and explains their limitations. We then build our own general blueprint for reform, one that will more systemically deal with the problems posed by comprehension asymmetries.

A *Ineffective Reforms: Audience and Technology-Based Support*

In many fields, including anthropology and psychology, the preferred approach to addressing information "gluts" is to shore up the audience's processing capacity. The assumption incorporated into these approaches is that the audience will be able to comprehend a message if one of two things occurs. Either the audience is given more resources or support, or, alternatively, the messages themselves are subjected to some kind of restrictions under which excessively convoluted communications are not allowed.

Consistent with these approaches, some legal reformers advocate for requiring that contracts be drafted with the central and unexpected provisions up front and in bold to alert consumers to messages that might otherwise be lost in the fine print.[42] Disclosure requirements are similarly designed with the objective of forcing complex communications into pre-set scripts. Moreover, a variety of speakers, including federal agencies and regulated corporations, are required to communicate in "plain language" rather than legalese and other technical speak.[43] And there is clamoring for the use of greater ombuds, expert intermediaries, and consumer support groups to help reduce the processing burden of disadvantaged audiences.[44] All of these examples focus on providing needed support for audiences, however. Much less attention is given to the possibility that the speaker may still be motivated to work around the mandated audience supports to be purposely incomprehensible.

Given this emphasis on shoring up the audience – and lack of accounting for addressing speaker incentives – it is not terribly surprising that the results of these reforms have been generally disappointing. In *More Than You Wanted To Know*, Omri Ben-Shahar and Carl Schneider make a compelling case for the widespread failure of mandated disclosures.[45] Moreover, even some proponents of audience-focused disclosures concede that there are significant shortcomings with these approaches.[46] These accounts suggest that, even in the best case, audience-based approaches sometimes offer only a temporary salve – a stopgap that briefly reduces but never actually eliminates the excessive processing costs that impede effective communication in some settings.

The popularity of audience-targeted reform has found particular purchase in the growing field of technology studies, an area that many futurists see as the solution to the problem of comprehension asymmetries. After all, if technology largely solved the problem of access to information, why couldn't it eliminate comprehension asymmetries as well? Why can't we simply develop search engines, filters, and other information-processing tools that audiences can use to digest information without investing significant time and effort? As the power of technology grows exponentially, so the thinking goes, excessive processing costs can be readily eliminated by computer chips and cloud-based search engines.[47]

While substantial strides have been and continue to be made in using technological innovations to address a number of information overload problems, these technology-based approaches face more severe limitations when they are deployed to overcome the comprehension asymmetries we explore in this book. Most obvious, technological tools do not emerge out of thin air; they are produced by experts who have the resources to develop them. So, when a technological processing tool is needed to impede resourceful and powerful actors from earning profits at their audience's expense, exactly who will pay for the tool's development? It seems unlikely that the audience will be in a position to provide the financing, and it seems far from a sure thing that governments will provide the funding if it runs against the interests of powerful political constituencies.

Second, there are concerns about whether search engines, filters, and processing algorithms will in fact be trustworthy. In his book, *Infoglut*, Mark Andrejevic explores the dark sides of technological fixes – where information "processing" technologies may be manipulated by powerful parties.[48] To ensure these technological tools are not used for nefarious ends, some type of neutral geek squad may be needed to review them and make sure they are on the up-and-up. Assembling, overseeing, and supporting this geek squad, however, will require not only public dollars, but political oversight as well.

A more practical challenge is ensuring that these technological tools can keep up with speakers who are determined to take advantage of their audiences. The technological tools that seek to process complicated information will necessarily be reactive. As soon as one algorithm or information-processing approach is developed, persistent speakers will already be busy developing a work-around. When speakers have significant motivations and resources, they may be able to outflank these technological innovations as soon as they are made public.

There are other challenges as well, none of which are trivial. Technology is not available to everyone, and these processing tools may not be useful to or even accessible to those most in need of using them. On the flip side of the access concern, it is not clear that viable technological processing tools can in fact be developed in the first place. Variations in the processing needs of multiple types of audiences;[49] in the nature of the text that needs processing – e.g., specialized, scientific, legal, etc.; and in specifying concrete endpoints for what it means to truly "understand" or synthesize information are each very complicated challenges in their own right. To put these challenges together into one assignment and expect technologists to solve them seems unrealistic.[50]

Therefore, despite its apparent promise, the solution posed by technology – like the solution posed by more standard, "audience-focused" regulation – is ultimately unsatisfying. If we focus our attention only on audience resources without addressing the speaker's inclination to artificially inflate processing costs, we won't be able to provide a long-term solution to comprehension asymmetries. Indeed, no matter how much technology or audience reinforcements we throw at this problem, the audience will almost always be outplayed by an advantaged speaker who doesn't want to communicate cooperatively with them.

B *Effective Reform: Re-Calibrating Speaker Incentives*

How, then, would we go about creating a more promising solution for comprehension asymmetries? A successful reform would have to satisfy two distinct criteria. First, it would have to address the problem we just identified in the last section – to effectively manage speaker incentives to ensure a speaker faces net benefits to communicating cooperatively. Second, it would have to overcome the challenges of figuring out what "reasonable" processing costs for an audience should be given the wide variation and contextual nature of communications. While we need some means of ensuring that audiences take responsibility for reasonable processing, finding and optimizing these processing costs is an analytical nightmare. Given these complications, it's easy to understand why processing costs are ignored in legal analysis and reform.

Yet, a second look at the theoretical literature on communication suggests a simple solution that has been in front of us the whole time. This literature assumes "cooperative communication," where both the speakers and audiences are reasonably motivated to communicate and receive the message. Much of the foundational work on communications is in fact quite explicit in assuming that the entire reason for a communication is because the speaker is eager to get the message across; the major challenges occur in enabling that effective communication to happen despite noisy channels and other transmission problems.[51] Since information theory seeks to minimize interference in the communications channels, and communication theory focuses on ways that speakers enhance the receptivity of the audience to a message in different settings, both bodies of work necessarily begin from the premise that effective communication is an end goal of all participants.[52]

"Cooperative communication" – drawn from this theory – thus serves as the goal in designing legal programs and processes. If speakers are encouraged to communicate their messages in a way that the "reasonable or median target audience" will understand, then both the incentives and optimization problems should be naturally corrected. Speakers will be motivated to communicate. And a reasonable audience will take responsibility for processing information that is appropriate under the circumstances. If audience memberd don't invest this effort, then the lack of understanding is their own fault.

Cooperative communication does not mean, however, that the conversation will be comprehensible to everyone; to be successful, the message need only be comprehensible to the target audience. If the target audience consists exclusively of technical experts, as it sometimes does in the case of a complicated administrative rule or the review of a patent application, for example, the speaker need ensure only that his particular elite audience can reasonably process the message.[53] As Part II will make clear, this means that many communications that satisfy our test for comprehensibility will still be effectively incomprehensible to the average person.

But how to actually require this "cooperative communication" in practice? In settings afflicted with the types of comprehension asymmetries we explore in this book, the audience is the primary loser. Incomprehensibility deprives these audiences of market choices, opportunities for deliberation, and the ability to oversee powerful actors. As a result, target audiences (or at least a subset of these audiences) are generally motivated to engage in cooperative communication because most of the losses fall on them.

The same is not true on the speaker side, however. Incomprehensibility typically insulates speakers from accountability and that insulation can sometimes be used to the speaker's advantage. Even when speakers aren't acting strategically, as long as the costs of incomprehensible communications fall primarily on the audience, speakers have little reason to make an investment in clearer communications.

The best place to focus reform for this subset of programs, therefore, is on the speaker, with a *speaker*-centric rather than *audience*-centric approach to reform. As we saw in the previous discussion, building up audience support systems to temporarily reduce the effect of processing costs will rarely resolve the problem of comprehension asymmetries as long as speakers are not equally motivated to enage with their audience. Ill-incentivized speakers can always find a way to further inflate processing costs; as long as the speakers have a net incentive to miscommunicate and misinform their audiences, they'll find a way of doing it.

By establishing a communicative situation that changes the speakers' incentives – that actually *encourages* the speakers to communicate to their audience effectively – we make headway against this problem of comprehension asymmetries. In particular, if a speaker has some financial or economic reason to communicate his message clearly (avoiding tort liability, for example, or expensive, audience-based fines), he or she has fewer reasons to seek out legal loopholes or deploy obfuscatory techniques. On the contrary, rather than expending resources "getting around" the rules, speakers would focus on alerting their audience to the actual, underlying issues at stake without burying them in technical jargon or long-winded, unnecessary exposition. An incentive-based approach to reform, then, endeavors not only to discourage speakers from manipulating their audience, but endeavors to change the ways that speakers deploy their resources – aligning the speakers' own self-interest with successful communication and the public good.

Insisting on cooperative communication from the speaker also addresses the problem of "optimization" – ensuring that processing costs are set at the exact right level for each specific communicative situation. After all, one of the major sticking points for successful reform of comprehension asymmetries is the context-uality. How should an external agency or regulatory body provide a "bright line" for effective communication that applies to *all* different communicative situations and speaker/audience combinations? How can we define and legislate universally "effective" communication?

As we've discovered, we can't; but by incentivizing speakers to communicate effectively to their target (reasonable or median) audience, the problem essentially disappears. Rather than imposing some external and universally applicable standard to all communications, incentive-based reform gives speakers the ability to set the level of processing costs needed for effective and efficient audience comprehension in each distinct communication setting. We do not need to consider what processing costs are acceptable in different settings – they necessarily vary. Instead, we need to be concerned only with whether a speaker's success depends on the effective communi-cation of an accurate and clear message to the target audience. And it is up to the speaker to prove that he has engaged in this cooperative communication.

If success turns on whether a reasonable audience understands the message, the speakers' energies will be focused in a much more productive direction.

Of course, how to create incentives for cooperative communication within our current legal system raises new questions that we will address in more detail in the chapters ahead. For the time being, however, suffice it to say that the best way to limit comprehension asymmetries and ensure that processing costs are fairly minimized is to focus on the speaker's incentives. This is the controlling feature that, in many ways, determines the success of a communication.

3

The Implications of Comprehension Asymmetries
for the Law

So far in our investigation into comprehension asymmetries, we have uncovered what we might call the fundamental schematic of incomprehensible conversations. In particular, we have identified the significance of audience processing power, the critical importance of speaker incentives, and the unholy mess that results when the two meet in an uncooperative setting. We have attempted to situate our understanding of comprehension asymmetries within the existent, yet fragmented literature; created a diagnostic framework that can be used to probe and detect the existence of incomprehensibility; and, at the end, even sketched out a generalized (and generalizable) plan for future reform.

However, if we are going to understand the concept of comprehension asymmetry in all of its accompanying intricacy, we must turn away from generalized models and toward specific applications. We look to the law – the system of rules and processes that structure our collective civic experience – and explore how it interacts with, and often intensifies, the problems of comprehension asymmetries.

The purpose of this chapter is to provide a preliminary overview of the ways in which the legal system may perpetuate, if not exacerbate, the problem of incomprehensibility. This chapter is, in a sense, the concrete counterpart of Chapter 2. Where that discussion was devoted to conceptually outlining incomprehensibility and introducing the vocabulary of "processing costs," this chapter attempts to explain the way incomprehensibility is neglected and intensified by the legal system – often gliding "under the radar" in a way that aggravates asymmetries in information processing and makes legally regulated conversations even more impenetrable. It is our hope that this exploration then provides a springboard for how the concept can be deployed in each of the subsequent, topic-based chapters that follow.

This tour of incomprehensibility and the law unfolds in three parts. First – and most substantially – we consider how a poorly designed legal system that does not account for comprehension asymmetries in its mandated communications may actually make these asymmetries and resulting inequities worse. A wide range of perverse speaker behaviors can arise in these poorly designed systems. We then attempt to triage our analysis, focusing our attention on those areas of the legal system where comprehension asymmetries are likely to be the most egregious, and offer preliminary explanations for why these asymmetries exist. We close by applying the conceptual reforms of the last chapter to the narrower area of law and regulation to consider how we might redesign the legal system to counteract comprehension asymmetries in the future.

I LEGAL STRUCTURE AND PERVERSE SPEAKER BEHAVIORS

A *The Structure of the Law*

As Justice Oliver Wendell Holmes observed more than 120 years ago, it is not the job of the legal system to turn fundamentally "bad men" into "good men" – to propel or instigate some sort of genuine moral transformation. Instead, all we can hope is that the law might encourage "bad men" to *act* more like "good men." Phrased differently (and in language we might be more familiar with): The law should ensure that the *incentives* of all actors – regardless of their underlying qualities of righteousness or greed – are oriented toward the public good.[1]

Over most of the American legal landscape, we see Holmes's theory play out fairly cleanly. A criminally inclined person, for instance, might be dissuaded from committing theft in our society because the law punishes that behavior with fines and prison time. In other words, by rewarding good actions and punishing bad behavior, the legal system acts as a corrective – adjusting the incentives of individual actors to reflect the public interest.

But suppose there are laws that don't work that way. Suppose, for example, that the law ignored incentives all together; the government stopped attempting to adjust the behavior of burglars and home-invaders through felony statutes and instead advocated that victims install better alarm systems to protect against theft, perhaps providing subsidies for the purchase of these alarms by homeowners in high crime communities. We can predict, without too much speculation, that Holmes – or, for that matter, any pragmatically minded legal theorist – would dismiss those laws as woefully inefficient, unfair, and ineffective.

Unfortunately, this problematic approach is the one taken in addressing comprehension asymmetries in a number of major legal programs. The vital step of ensuring that actors (speakers) have strong incentives to communicate cooperatively with their audiences is skipped. Instead, the speaker can turn raw, unsorted but potentially relevant information over to its relatively disadvantaged audience without regard to the audience's ability to understand this information. Indeed, if speakers *do* attempt to synthesize this information for the audience, they may face a greater, rather than lower, risk of being in violation of the law. And, if that weren't bad enough, in some legal programs the speaker – after loading excessive processing costs onto the audience – then enjoys a legal right to contest the audience's efforts to make sense of it.

It doesn't take much expertise to see how structuring legal processes in this way is problematic. Just by following the law, many speakers – in a range of different fields – become more incomprehensible. Furthermore, these legal designs not only allow the "bad" speakers in society to act without constraint; they inadvertently encourage the "good" speakers to act in negative or detrimental ways. These adverse behaviors, moreover, occur not *in spite of the law*, but *because of it*.

In the chapters that follow, we will see dozens of concrete examples of these mis-designed legal programs, but for now, we resist delving into these case studies and focus on finishing our orientation to comprehension asymmetries. Our next stop in this orientation is to consider the range of behaviors we can expect when speakers are not eager to communicate meaningfully. To make this analysis more useful, we consider two, very different types of speakers, which parallel the pair of actors contemplated by Holmes. The first set of speakers we consider are *Rule-Benders* who are eager to exploit audience weaknesses and legal loopholes to advance their own interests; they are the archetypical "bad men." The second group of speakers are well-meaning *Rule-Followers* who endeavor to be upstanding, public-spirited actors. These "good men" rationally follow the law wherever it leads them and always act in good faith. Of course, there is no bright line that separates the good from the bad, as Arthur Leff so aptly demonstrated in *Swindling and Selling*.[2] Yet, by considering caricatured versions of both sets of actors positioned at opposite ends of the continuum, we gain a greater understanding of how existing legal requirements might affect a broad range of behaviors.

B Rule-Benders: Exploitive Actors

The Rule-Benders will always be willing to use their superior processing advantages to exploit less capable audiences when doing so earns them profits, power, or prestige. In doing this, however, Rule-Benders will hardly ever violate the law.[3] On the contrary, Rule-Benders – true to their name – stay within the letter of the law, while still advancing their own narrow private ends.[4]

The Rule-Benders thus walk a tightrope – advancing their own self-interest while remaining highly attuned to staying within legal constraints. Balancing these two very different goals requires considerable acumen, and Rule-Benders can be quite scientific in their strategies. In his book, *Fraud*, Ed Balleisen quotes from an 1878 book (aptly named *How 'Tis Done*) that analyzes the art of con games: These "most adroit practitioners of economic deceit had reduced their endeavors to 'a science.' Every possible weakness of human nature, every loophole of ignorance, every assailable point where advantage may be gained, is studied with utmost care."[5]

Given this "science" of Rule-Bending, it is thus not surprising that some of the Rule-Bender's techniques have become so established that they have been given names.[6] Familiar tactics include:

Databombing: Databombing is the well-worn technique of providing so much information that the target audience can no longer make sense of it.[7] In the Urban Dictionary, "databomb" includes situations when one "purposely provide[s] too much information either out of spite, CYA, or to slow them down."[8] A sample use of the term: "I'm not sure what report [the boss] wants; just databomb him."[9]

We will see many examples of databombing in the chapters that follow. In the regulatory arena, as just one example, Bruce Owen and Ronald Braeutigam tracked a number of the information games played by industry in the 1970s to gain control of the rulemaking process. Which strategy was most common? "[F]lood the agency with more information than it can absorb."[10] And, predictably, when a regulator seeks a particularly damaging piece of information, industries' "best tactic is to bury [him/her] in a mountain of irrelevant material."[11] Today, databombing continues to provide a tried-and-true way to overwhelm a target audience.

Technical Complexification and Obfuscation: Technical complexification is accomplished by obscuring key messages with unduly technical information so that even the most dedicated audience cannot crack the technical barrier. But unlike databombing, in "complexification" it is not the volume so much as the density of information that inflates processing costs. For example, if a doctor did not offer a patient an expert diagnosis, but simply provided the patient with his MRIs, x-rays, and blood tests, leaving him to figure out his maladies on his own, it would be a form of technical complexification. The audience (patient) must bear the costs of processing the information, while the speaker (doctor) is relieved of the burden that might ordinarily be assigned to him or her.

Obfuscation overlaps with technical complexification, but involves more concerted efforts to confuse and obscure key messages. One form of obfuscation is what William Lutz calls "gobbledy-gook" communications. Here the speaker inevitably appreciates that a message is way too complicated for the target audience in its current, unprocessed form, and yet makes no effort to communicate the message in a way the target audience could ever hope to understand. Lutz offers Alan Greenspan's congressional testimony as an illustration. Greenspan advised Congress that in financial markets, "[i]t is a tricky problem to find the particular calibration in timing that would be appropriate to stem the acceleration in risk premiums created by falling incomes without prematurely aborting the decline in the inflation-generated risk premiums."[12] President Eisenhower used this same technique as a way to dodge press questions about the Formosan Strait crisis in 1955. He reassured his Press Secretary, "Don't worry Jim, if that question comes up, I'll just confuse them."[13]

Of course, not every instance of obfuscation and technical complexification is intentional; sometimes it just involves lazy or resource-constrained speakers who choose not to invest time demystifying complicated material for their audiences. However, in other cases – such as when firms "build complex products ... to confuse consumers [so] ... that consumers will not bother to spend the time and effort ... to eliminate confusion" – complexification is the result of conscious manipulation.[14]

Fine Print Manipulations: Fine print manipulations provide speakers with a way of conveying parts of core messages clearly, while loading other, equally important parts of the message in tiny font where these equally critical assertions are likely to be ignored. The result is deceptive communication where the good news is headlined up front and the bad news is buried at the bottom of page 13.[15] In his book, *Seduction by Contract*, Oren Bar-Gill traces how, in practice, sellers can "hook" purchasers with come-on features (such as inexpensive cell phones) and bury the costs of those features (such as high late fees and excessive penalties for going over data limits) in the fine print.[16]

Deliberate Ambiguity: Deliberate ambiguity is the technique of crafting claims or passages that are intentionally designed to remain open to multiple interpretations. Particularly in uncertain legal environments, this deliberate ambiguity helps the speaker keep his or her options open. To be truly useful to the Rule-Bender in creating incomprehensible messages, however, all adverse consequences that result from deliberate ambiguities must fall on the disadvantaged audience. Only then can the Rule-Bender enjoy a processing edge.

As discussed in greater detail in Chapter 5B, patents offer a particularly notable illustration of how Rule-Benders deploy deliberate ambiguities to their advantage; indeed, in patent law the phenomenon of "deliberate ambiguity" is so well established that it is a term of art.[17] Burk and Lemley observe, for example, how the deployment of deliberative ambiguities woven throughout patent specifications "to cover things the patentee did not invent" is "legion."[18] Patent applicants sue other inventors for infringing "not on what they actually designed or described in the patent but on the fact that the language of their patent claims can be read in hindsight to cover those later-developed technologies.'"[19] Deliberate ambiguities, then, apparently provide one of the main drivers of a lucrative subfield of patent litigation.[20]

Contextualization Games. Contextualization games are used by Rule-Benders to misrepresent the scale and significance of a mandated communication. In other words, a speaker will communicate all relevant information but leave out the context that would help the information be understood. The marketing of some processed foods provides a concrete example of this kind of manipulation. Consider a cereal company that is required to provide information on the type and amount of sugar that is included in each serving (an example we pick up again in the next chapter). Without also explaining how each gram of sugar compares to the maximum recommended daily intake, that information is largely useless unless the consumer invests energy in searching out that information on his own. Consequently, even though individual details are presented and catalogued, without some context or frame of reference, the information isn't useful. A gullible audience member might think that 12.3 grams of sugar per serving of cereal is low and eat accordingly – a decision that seems all well and good, until obesity and heart problems set in.

C Rule-Followers: Well-Meaning Rational Actors

Not every speaker who contributes to incomprehensibility is malicious, willful, or even cognizant of his or her actions. In fact, one of the most perverse features of some legal designs is the way that the law can sometimes encourage well-intentioned, compliant speakers to inflate processing costs for the target audience and, in so doing, increase incomprehensibility.

These well-meaning speakers – termed Rule-Followers – are not trying to strategically overwhelm their audience with unnecessary processing costs. But Rule-Followers do abide by the directions of the law, wherever it leads them. Thus, because of the law's misplaced emphasis – for example, encouraging complete and transparent information over comprehensible information – Rule-Followers may be encouraged to be incomprehensible. In contrast to Holmes's hoped-for role of law, then, some legal designs create a situation where well-intentioned "good men" become indistinguishable from malicious or self-interested "bad men" with respect to the comprehensibility of their communications.

Common ways that the law encourages Rule-Followers to become less comprehensible include:

More Information Is Better (Innocent Databombing). If the law insists only on full transparency and comprehensiveness – and severely sanctions any speaker who leaves information out – then it makes sense for a rational, law-abiding speaker to err on the side of providing too much information, even if it undermines the comprehensibility of the message. A compliant Rule-Follower may overload his audience with so much detail and minutiae that the audience's processing capabilities are overwhelmed. Even though the speaker's only goal is compliance, the Rule-Follower inadvertently has databombed his audience with information, inhibiting, rather than facilitating, genuine communication.

Shifting Processing Costs. As we mentioned in the last chapter, some processing costs are fixed, and therefore must be absorbed in any given conversation by either the speaker or the audience. Consequently, we can fairly easily imagine a situation in which a rational speaker decides not to invest added resources to process information at the beginning of the conversation if this is not required by law. Rather than take the time to understand the key risks of their own activities, for example, these speakers will essentially pass the buck or kick the can down the road to their audience, shifting the entire burden of processing onto them. When the law places priority on ensuring that a document is thorough, complete, or compliant with other requirements (having nothing to do with comprehensibility), the law-abiding Rule-Follower will elevate those legal requirements over communicating cooperatively. In a world where time and energy are in short supply, Rule-Followers typically focus their energy on complying with the letter of the law instead of creating the most comprehensible document when the latter is not specifically required.

Prescribed Communication. By prescribing certain types of communication, the law may even impede the efforts of Rule-Followers to be comprehensible. Some disclosure requirements demand that speakers include certain line items in a given public filing or legal document, even if doing so might be misleading or confusing. In these cases, however, the Rule-Follower is without recourse even if he or she is frustrated by the result. If the law mandates inclusion of certain misleading or ambiguous phrases that get in the way of meaningful communication, the conscientious Rule-Follower has no choice but to comply.

Avoiding Accusations of Bias. Some legal programs do not stop at simply encouraging speakers to share every potentially relevant detail with the audience, but actually discourage speakers from summarizing or synthesizing this information for their audience. In the patent process, for example, some inventors worry that preparing a summary that explains the novelty of their invention (which is not required by the law) may backfire as a legal matter. If the patent examiner perceives the summary to be incomplete, this could lead to accusations that the inventor provided misleading information.[21] Providing raw information *without* contextual summaries is thus both a legally safer and a less expensive course of action.[22]

II TRIAGING INCOMPREHENSIBILITY

Thus far we have explored how speakers might behave in perverse ways to make messages incomprehensible, but we have left open-ended when and where in our legal institutions these behaviors are most likely to occur. Surely the manipulation of audiences with limited processing capacity is not ubiquitous. In this section we attempt to gain purchase on this question; we try to understand *when* comprehension asymmetries become a serious impediment to the effective functioning of a legal program. Of course, since the focus is on improving communications, we consider only those legal programs for which meaningful communication is central to the law's successful functioning. We will see that in these settings, comprehension asymmetries become more than the practical friction of real-world communication and become an intractable problem that requires active intervention. We also explore preliminarily some of the reasons for differences in the severity of comprehension asymmetries among different legal regimes.

A *Locating Where Comprehension Asymmetries Are at Their Worst*

Legal systems are hardly uniform or even coherent, so we can expect in practice that comprehension asymmetries will vary on a number of dimensions. For example, speakers and audiences can include a variety of private actors and governmental decision-makers who can end up at either end of the communication channel – in some cases as a privileged speaker or in other cases as a disadvantaged audience. The law itself also arises from a variety of sources, including legislation, regulation, common law, and even congressional process rules, and each legal program will impact a speaker's incentive system in different ways. And finally, in some of these settings, multiple audiences may exist in a single communication.

However, while each problematic comprehension asymmetry will have its own distinct setting, actors, and accompanying complications, there are two primary variables that – once the speaker and target audience are identified – help isolate the very worst problems.[23]

Variable #1: Imbalance in Processing Ability. The first variable is an intrinsic imbalance in processing ability between a speaker and the audience. We specifically consider imbalanced communication when the audience is at a significant processing disadvantage relative to the speaker (the reverse is outside the scope of this study). These imbalances occur in a number of settings and relationships, including doctor–patient, manufacturer–consumer, bank–homeowner, and regulator–public communications. The key in all cases is that – objectively – the average target audience member has a much lower processing capacity relative to the average speaker. Because the audience's resources and often the benefit/cost ratio is much lower than that of the speaker, the audience sometimes lacks the processing horsepower to keep up.

Variable #2: Speaker Incentives for Cooperative Communication. The second variable is whether the speaker faces net positive incentives to communicate the message effectively. Of course, as with the "imbalance" variable, generalizations are required. But, with that caveat, for this variable the speaker's success in the transaction hinges on whether his communication will reasonably be understood by an average audience member. As we shall see, in some legal and market settings, the average speaker's incentives stop well short of this cooperative communication goal. Indeed, in some settings, the speaker himself does not benefit from comprehending the message and prefers to operate in the dark.

Table 3.1 places these variables into context to spotlight the one quadrant where comprehension asymmetries are most significant. Note that the 2x2 is a gross simplification, intended at this point as a conceptual model. In fact, and as discussed subsequently, there is significant gray in the lines separating these boxes.

TABLE 3.1: *Locating the Worst-Case Quadrant for Comprehension Asymmetries*

		Speaker Incentives to Communicate Comprehensibly	
		YES: Incentives for Comprehensible Communication	NO: Lack of Incentives for Comprehensible Communication
Balance in speaker–audience processing power	YES: Processing Balance between Speaker and Audience	Social settings; appellate arguments	Discovery in litigation
	NO: Imbalance between Speaker and Audience	Tort labels; informed consent; jury trials	THIS BOOK (complex consumer market; financial, patent, health and environmental regulation; some complicated deliberative processes)

Moreover, the 2x2 requires considerable abstraction from complex realities in order to track comprehension asymmetries through transactions and deliberations. For example, to simplify the analysis, we identify the primary speaker and the primary target audience(s). We also consider only settings in which the audience is attentive and on balance wants to be informed, rather than preferring ignorance.

In this conceptual model, only one of the four quadrants – shaded in gray – is of concern to our analysis here. While several other quadrants are sub-optimal and could be rife with inefficiencies and inaccurate information, they are less problematic than the worst-case quadrant where imbalances and misplaced incentives come into play. Therefore, after a brief review of the other three quadrants, we focus our attention on the lower right quadrant: these are the most significant comprehension asymmetries that deserve special attention.

It is clear from Table 3.1 that not every conversation results in incomprehensible communications. Instead, the upper left quadrant shows us the opposite case: those "ideal" situations where the audience and speaker are relatively balanced and the speaker generally faces strong net incentives to communicate his or her key message. Consider, as an example, professional situations in which employees want to communicate what they've been working on to their superiors. Or appellate arguments, where lawyers attempt to explain sophisticated legal arguments to a highly trained judge. In these cases, the operating dynamics consist of the desire and ability to communicate meaningfully. Consequently, in "ideal" situations, relatively little slippage in understanding is likely to occur.

In the upper right quadrant, we have what we call adversarial communications. Here a perverse incentive to play information games exists, but the games are played and understood by parties who are relatively equal in processing capacity. Litigation provides a standard example. Opponents may seek to sink opponents with excessive information in document production. Or they might try to throw their opposition off with cagey responses to interrogatories. But the playing field between speaker and audience is relatively level.[24] An adversary receiving an incomprehensible mess is generally willing and able to process the incoming information despite the high costs of doing so. Thus, while these conversations can be hugely inefficient, the ultimate communication will often be successful. The message – hidden in the haystack of documents – can still be located (albeit after dozens of hours have been billed to the client).

The lower left quadrant consists of communications in which there are substantial imbalances in processing abilities and resources between speaker and audience, yet the speaker faces strong net incentives in favor of effective communication. Outside of the legal system, examples could include teachers trying to communicate complex concepts to their students. Within the legal system, we include informed consent provisions for medical care, which ensure audiences with lower processing power are educated about their medical options. In all examples, whether the ultimate communiqué is successful or unsuccessful, the speakers are still *incentivized* to deliver the message as clearly as possible. As a result, the comprehension asymmetries are overcome by the speakers themselves.

It is the lower right box where we confront the worst of all possible worlds. Here the legal and market system often work together to perversely relieve a speaker of responsibility for communicating in a reasonable and comprehensible way. Rational speakers are instead encouraged to externalize processing costs on to their already disadvantaged audience. Not only are speakers' incentives off track, but in this quadrant, there are profound asymmetries between the processing power of speakers and audience members – with a resource-rich and technically adept speaker lording over an educationally limited or time-strapped audience. As a result, in this quadrant, the audience is generally at the mercy of the speaker.

But what of the gray that inevitably surrounds the lines that separate the quadrants? Aren't there in-beween cases? Certainly, but those gray areas can be incorporated into the existent model. Take a liminal issue such as the informed consent requirements in tort law. Under this rule, a medical doctor is obliged to share with her patient the significant risks of treatment and any reasonable alternatives. But the careful reader will note that this legal directive does *not* always mean that the doctor is incentivized to communicate her message clearly to the patient in every case. On the contrary, there may be a whole host of individual settings in which a doctor's net incentives may move her to the right lower quadrant. Perhaps a pharmaceutical

company or surgical procedure offers payouts for prescribing a particular treatment.[25] If the benefits of these payouts exceed the risks of violating the spirit of
informed consent, it would be in the doctor's economic best interest to fudge his or
her communication and manipulate the patient's choice by exploiting the patient's
limited processing capacity.

And yet, the fuzziness of the lines separating the quadrants does not undermine
our model. Instead, it serves only to further illustrate the usefulness of the variables
for sorting cases into problem and non-problem categories. In the case of informed
consent, for example, which quadrant best captures a situation may depend in part
on the speaker's unique incentives. Perhaps there are no rewards to the doctor for
picking one treatment over another. Or perhaps the patient is litigious and likely to
challenge the doctor, causing the doctor to bend over backwards to communicate
effectively.

Therefore, the key feature of our charting exercise has less to do with making
absolute distinctions between different communicative situations and more to do
with tracking key variables. Our goal, in effect, is to think more clearly about those
conversations where incomprehensibility runs rampant – where the absence of
incentives for comprehensible communication by the speaker are combined
with a disadvantaged audience in processing information relative to the speaker.
Therefore, while we might not be able to cleanly and permanently place something
like informed consent requirements in one spot in our matrix, we can *use* our matrix
illustratively to demonstrate the value of tracing comprehension asymmetries.

B *Why the Legal Variation in Attending to Comprehension Asymmetries?*

Before moving on, we pause briefly to consider *why* we might see such different
treatment of comprehension asymmetries among different legal programs, particularly in the lower two quadrants. Doesn't this hit-or-miss record suggest there is some
kind of system in place both to detect and rectify comprehension asymmetries?

One of several likely explanations for the differences between legal programs with
respect to comprehension asymmetries arises from the very different nature of the
laws that tend to populate these two quadrants. At a very general level, it appears that
the common law and judicial processes (lower left quadrant) do a better job taking
comprehension asymmetries into account than the general and abstracted, top-
down programs codified in regulation and legislation (lower right quadrant). In tort
law, for example, consumer warnings are built on a foundation that considers the
adequacy of the warning from the standpoint of the reasonable consumer. In this
legal setting, communication is evaluated on an ad hoc basis – e.g. "did this
particular warning label communicate effectively to its particular audience?" (As
an aside, this model seems remarkably similar to the mode of "comprehension
reform" we advocate throughout the rest of this book.)

Property rules follow a similar audience-centric reference point. Henry Smith describes how, for example, in property law, "[c]ourts' decisions seem to reflect a concern with the processing burden on the 'audience' of dutyholders, who must process rights in order to respect them."[26] The law is therefore designed to ensure that "the message communicated to potential violators is kept simple and the law is sensitive to the amount and type of background knowledge that such messages require in those processing them."[27] Put differently: In order for property rules to hold, they must be *communicated* to their audience reasonably and effectively.

Most litigation at the appellate level also involves explicit limits on the time allocated for oral argument, the number of pages of attachments, and even the pages, margins, and font size of briefs.[28] These limits occur as an organic matter – the judges find themselves limited in time and impose limits to address their own, audience-based handicaps. Trials before juries similarly require counsel to distil and abbreviate key messages for a group of lay people with average attention spans and educational levels. Trial courts impose a number of important filters on evidence to ensure that counsel, rather than the judicial system, bears the cost of processing information prior to trial.[29] In effect, since the focus in judicial proced-ures is on a "fair trial" (and not, for example, an exhaustive trial), the emphasis is necessarily on comprehension and understanding. Of course, this goal can be undermined in practice. For example, a jury's comprehension of pattern jury instructions is notoriously poor, a phenomenon explained in part by the fact that these instructions are generally written "by legal scholars who were concerned with developing instructions which would withstand scrutiny if challenged in court" rather than with jury comprehension.[30] However, in general, judicial procedures are adversarial and hence provide stronger incentives for speakers to communicate meaningfully with their audience.

Although it requires considerably more research, one possible reason that these common law and judicial approaches may be more attuned to comprehension asymmetries is that their analyses are more grounded in real life disputes. They require judges and juries to put themselves in the shoes of individual litigants in specific cases or face excessive processing burdens themselves.

The problematic programs we explore in this book, by contrast, are generally a product of the legislative, rather than the common law, process. Rather than implementing a bottom-up, organic approach to solving social problems, it is easy to understand why at least some top-down legislative and regulatory programs might be designed without viewing the problems primarily from the perspective of the audience. Instead, legislative approaches generalize away from practical details.

Further reinforcing the occasional legislative and regulatory neglect of compre-hension asymmetries is the fact that this neglect tends to benefit already-advantaged actors in political decision-making. As long as the privileged groups are the benefi-ciaries of comprehension asymmetries, it seems likely that this problem of incomprehensibility will proliferate in legislation and regulation where lobbying can make a difference to the policies ultimately adopted.

III SMART LEGAL DESIGN

We close this chapter with some targeted observations about what legal responses are needed to counteract comprehension asymmetries occurring in this worst-case quadrant. As a brief recap, recall that in the last chapter we argued that while comprehension asymmetries are often ignored, in cases when they are recognized, the conventional solution is to shore up the audience's processing capacity. This is accomplished either by providing the audience with reinforcement or capping the costs needed to understand a transaction. Yet, as also noted, these audience-focused reforms have generally not succeeded because they miss one critical piece of the puzzle: the fact that many speakers still benefit, on balance, from being incomprehensible. As long as the legal architecture is structured to encourage speakers to be incomprehensible, audience-centric reforms amount to little more than digging in the sand.

A successful reform must tackle misdirected speaker incentives head-on.[31] Speakers must lose – not gain – from failing to communicate effectively.

So how do we apply these general lessons to the more specific project of legal design?[32] The first and most direct path toward reform of individual legal programs places all the costs of reasonable misunderstandings on the speaker in ways that alter the speaker's incentives for incomprehensibility. In addition to ensuring that all relevant information is shared, the speaker would have to ensure that a reasonable audience could understand the key messages or pay for the costs of the resulting confusion. The speaker's success would hinge, in other words, on effective communication. If communication isn't clear, the speaker would take the hit – with fines and the possibility of being foreclosed from even conducting the activities at all. And, crucially, the size of that hit must exceed whatever benefit the speaker might otherwise derive from keeping the audience in the dark.

However, intrinsic to the nature of comprehension asymmetries is a Catch-22 type of problem: To prove that a communication is not reasonably comprehensible, the audience must invest considerable energies in mastering and making sense of it. Like information asymmetries, then, a default rule may be necessary that assumes that communications are presumptively incomprehensible unless the speaker has documented – before or after the communication – his or her effort to rigorously communicate the message. In this way, victims bear a much more manageable burden of establishing a communication breakdown. The speaker carries the first burden of establishing comprehensible communications that the victim-audience must rebut with evidence of their own.[33]

Once speakers' successes are judged by how well they communicate key information, they will begin to compete on that basis. Rather than a contest over which speaker is best at exploiting the audience's limitations, the incentives would be turned in the opposite direction. Speakers would derive strong, competitive benefits from communicating in a clear and accurate way with their audience.

In some complex markets this direct, incentive-based intervention may prove inadequate, however; speakers can still sidestep the cooperative-communication requirement by devising activities and transactions that are simply "too complex" to explain.[34] And this is true even when the audience is expert in the field. In these settings, a second supplemental reform would require the speaker to assemble and share a diverse set of accessible facts about his activities, as well as providing accessible and accurate narrative explanations of those facts. This diversified information portfolio approach, originally devised by Henry Hu for financial regulation, provides the target audience with sets of key facts they can use to evaluate the speaker's activities on their own.[35] Speakers would also bear the burden of establishing they have provided clear, accessible facts that a reasonable audience could readily synthesize to assess their activities or products.

A third, gentler approach would simply spotlight the incomprehensibility itself, underscoring the problematic nature of the speaker's communication. This reform approach creates speaker accountability for the comprehensibility of his or her message, without placing added sanctions or requirements on the speaker. The speaker can then determine how important comprehensibility is to the transaction or deliberation, but cooperative communication is no longer a requirement or effective prerequisite to communication.

Expert intermediaries that protect and educate the audience could be added as a supplement to each of these reform approaches. These intermediaries' processing capabilities must be at least equal, and ideally would exceed the processing capabilities of the speaker. By overpowering the speaker in his or her ability to extract the messages, expert intermediaries can reverse the speaker's incentives through shaming, legal liability, and other means. But since this last approach works only when the intermediaries stand in the shoes of the audience *and* enjoy a processing capacity and motivation on par with the speakers, relying on intermediaries alone is likely to be unstable.

Regardless of which path(s) are taken, the basic architecture for reform remains the same. Rather than attempt to artificially elevate the processing power of the audience, reformers must focus their energies on speakers' incentives, eliminating their existent incentives to remain incomprehensible.

IV CONCLUSION

This chapter has taken up the consequences of the legal system's neglect of comprehension asymmetries. We have considered what happens when the law ignores comprehension asymmetries and yet speakers remain predisposed to externalize these processing costs on to the disadvantaged audiences.

Now we turn to case studies to ground-truth these abstractions. Is it in fact the case that the architecture of some legal programs has neglected underlying comprehension asymmetries to their detriment? If so, is this mis-design consequential or simply a trivial feature? In settings in which both questions appear to be answered with a yes, we close the chapter with preliminary suggestions for specifically tailored reforms designed to address the underlying problems.

PART II

Application

4

Comprehension Asymmetries in Consumer Protection Law

Inhaling oven cleaner is not good for you, and the kids who used it to get high knew that they were taking risks. But they sprayed it into zip-lock bags and inhaled it anyway. For them, immediate gratification overshadowed the potential harms listed on the product's package. The consequences were sometimes severe; at least one teen died and dozens of others suffered from a variety of lifelong injuries caused by exposure to the cleaner.

The oven cleaner already carried a huge, red label warning that death could result from inhalation, but the manufacturer faced potential tort liability since inhalation is a "foreseeable misuse" of the product. Because manufacturers are in the best position to minimize recurring, preventable harms from their products, tort law in the US requires that manufacturers take responsibility for adjusting ingredients, warnings, or even purchase options when injuries are likely. This responsibility is particularly important when children are at risk.

The manufacturer was at its wit's end in figuring out how to stop the teens' dangerous activities. In desperation, it sought the help of a prominent tort defense lawyer. Should it make the warnings even larger, more prominent, or include more details?

No, the attorney replied. To reach these teens, the manufacturer must convince them that the risks outweigh the benefits. Current warnings directed to risk-averse housewives will not do. "What do kids worry about more than death or injury?" the attorney asked. "How they look, of course. So, we wrote the warning to say that sniffing the stuff could cause hair loss or facial disfigurement. It doesn't, but it scared the target audience and we haven't had a liability claim since then." "That's why," he added, "I'm paid $370 an hour."[1]

The moral of this story is that when a speaker — whether it be a manufacturer, a retailer, or even a government — has strong incentives to communicate its message to a target audience, it will find a way to do so. Motivated speakers will even go the extra mile and misrepresent facts when doing so improves their ability to get the key message across to a particularly vulnerable audience.

But as we shall soon see, while this happy ending for oven cleaner offers hope – a glimpse of the positive power of the law to save lives and improve welfare – that is not how the law works in most other areas of the consumer market. Tort liability for defective warnings, at least for oven cleaner, is unfortunately the exception rather than the rule.

Consider Verna Emery's case. Ms. Emery sought out and agreed to a $2,000 loan from American General Finance (at 36 percent interest over 30 months) that she secured with her TV, typewriter, and a few other personal assets.[2] After six months, the bank sent Ms. Emery a letter rewarding her steady payments with a second "easy" loan. The letter, signed by a branch manager, read:

> Dear Verna:
> I have extra spending money for you.
> Does your car need a tune-up? Want to take a trip? Or, do you just want to pay off some of your bills? We can lend you money for whatever you need or want.
> You're a good customer. To thank you for your business, I've set aside $750.00* in your name.
> Just bring the coupon below into my office and if you qualify, we could write your check on the spot. Or, call ahead and I'll have the check waiting for you.
> Make this month great with extra cash. Call me today – I have money to loan.
> FN* Subject to our normal credit policies.[3]

The bank structured the second loan as a refinancing of Ms. Emery's first loan. By proceeding in this way, the bank was able to wrap the second loan under the original terms, which – when all the math was done – allowed the bank to charge the equivalent of a 110 percent interest rate on the new cash ($200). In responding to this invitation for a second loan, then, Ms. Emery unwittingly committed to making additional payments in interest and fees that exceeded the $200 payment she received.

The judges presiding over Ms. Emery's case – a case that made five appearances up and down the federal court system – conceded that the bank had used sleazy techniques to lure Ms. Emery into an unprofitable deal. Seen from Ms. Emery's perspective, Judge Posner observed, "the letter is seen to be replete with falsehoods and half truths." "[T]he purpose of offering her more money is not to thank her for her business but to rip her off."[4]

Judge Posner also observed that Ms. Emery "belongs to a class of borrowers who are not competent interpreters of such forms *and that the defendant knows this and is out to take advantage of it.*"[5] Indeed, the terms of the loan were so opaque that both Judge Posner and counsel for the bank conceded that they were not able to figure out the amount of the extra charge imposed on Ms. Emery as a result of the refinancing.[6]

But ultimately, after her fourth visit to the federal courthouse, the judges concluded that there was nothing illegal about the bank's lending scheme. The bank had found a way to circumvent existing laws designed to require clear consumer disclosures. Because of its airtight contract and "creative" compliance with the Truth in Lending Act (TILA) and other consumer protection laws, the bank's activities were ultimately legal. "[A]lthough arguably manipulative and unethical, [the bank had] fully complied with the law."[7] As Judge Posner noted, "So much for the Truth in Lending Act as a protection for borrowers."[8] The Supreme Court denied Emery's petition for certiorari.

Verna Emery's experience underscores, yet again, the importance of speaker incentives. In contrast to the financial and reputational benefits that flow to a company from successfully persuading its consumers to refrain from inhaling oven cleaner, when a company stands to profit from luring consumers into deceptive transactions, it will find a way to do so. Both of our illustrative speakers seek to persuade consumers to behave in ways that ultimately advance the speakers' bottom line. The difference between the two scenarios is the role the law plays in setting up positive (versus perverse) incentives for this consumer education, communication, and persuasion.[9]

In this chapter, we explore comprehension asymmetries that arise in consumer markets. Our singular aim is to assess whether consumer law ultimately encourages or discourages cooperative communications between sellers and consumers in areas as diverse as home loans, cell phone plans, standard consumer contracts, and nutritional information on processed food. Although we focus in particular on consumer contracts, our compass also includes consumer products, at least insofar as these products and services are regulated with disclosure requirements that are intended to make consumer markets more competitive. The findings from this investigation are not reassuring. Rather than steadfastly encourage comprehensible communications in consumer transactions, existing legal requirements often ignore this seemingly vital feature. Indeed, in some cases the law even encourages sellers to be more incomprehensible, rather than less.

Our investigation of incomprehensibility in consumer protection law proceeds as follows. First, we consider whether and when comprehension asymmetries occur in unregulated consumer markets. We then consider how the law affects seller incentives for cooperative communication, focusing particular attention on contract law, legislated disclosure requirements, and First Amendment commercial speech jurisprudence. Finding that the law comes up short in insisting on cooperative communication in each of these legal areas, we close with some preliminary suggestions for reform. While more comprehensible contracts and disclosures will of course not solve all of the problems that afflict consumer markets, it is an important first step. Indeed, even with contracts of adhesion, consumers will at least know what they are signing up for and be able to discriminate among competitors as a result of this heightened understanding.

I THE UNREGULATED CONSUMER MARKET AND COMPREHENSION ASYMMETRIES

Resource and information imbalances between manufacturers and consumers in unregulated markets are well established, so we hit only the highlights of existing comprehension asymmetries between speaker and audience before proceeding with an analysis of the law. Keep in mind that in this exploration, our focus remains fixed on complicated consumer markets that are most likely to land in the problematic quadrant where a transaction has the potential to exceed the consumers' information-processing capacity. Markets that are *not* afflicted with these excessive processing costs – for example, shopping for produce or other relatively straightforward consumer purchases – are not explored here.

A *Manufacturers and Sellers as Speakers*

For their part, speakers – manufacturers and sellers – have a much better understanding of the quality and proper use of their products than the average consumer. Their superior processing capacity is due not only to the fact that they play a formative role in designing a product and how it will be marketed, but also because of the economies of scale operating within the market. Understanding the features and risks of a particular product or service is costly, but these costs are spread out over hundreds or more likely millions of individual transactions.

Because of their advantaged position, speakers also have incentives to withhold some of this information from their consumer audience when doing so increases profits. Concealing unflattering features of a product or exaggerating the product's virtues helps improve sales. Indeed, the law of fraud is built on curbing these problematic market incentives.

Our speakers not only have a superior understanding of the quality of their products and services, but they generally also enjoy superior abilities to exploit their target consumers' processing limitations as well. For example, they understand how much time and expertise consumers will likely devote to product comparisons. In addition, they often have valuable insights into how well-known biases affect how consumers process information.[10]

These informational advantages not only put sellers in the driver's seat relative to consumers, but may also give sellers who are willing to capitalize on their superior understanding a competitive edge. As Akerlof and Shiller observe, "unregulated free markets rarely reward ... those who restrain themselves from taking advantage of customers' psychological or information weaknesses." Instead, in these unregulated markets, civic-minded sellers "tend to be replaced by others with fewer moral qualms."[11]

B *The Consumer Audience*

The consumer audience, by contrast, is much more limited in its capacity to process information regarding the quality and comparative attributes of complicated products and services relative to the sellers. Rational consumers, by definition, can be expected to put only as much time into reading and comprehending product options and associated warnings as they expect to benefit from this investment of time and energy.[12] Some consumer inattention and limited processing is thus sensible, even when the costs of error fall on the consumer. Omri Ben-Shahar observes that in some consumer markets a "decision not to read/know/care is actually a smart decision. Spending effort to read and to process what's in the contract boilerplate would be one of the more striking examples of consumer irrationality and obsessive behavior."[13]

Heuristics further aggravate a consumer's challenges in processing complicated information. Consumers, particularly when faced with more information than they can process, experience a number of "decision-making biases, including overconfidence [and] overoptimism."[14] The empirically established tendency of consumers to ignore or underestimate future or deferred costs serves as one of many examples of how these heuristics can affect a consumer's processing of information.[15] And Tess Wilkinson-Ryan's research reveals that consumers may actually defer more to complicated legalese in complex transactions than plain language because the legal terms "appear morally and legally legitimate in a way that non-contractual policies do not."[16]

The comprehension asymmetries resulting between a speaker (the seller) and audience (the consumer) in unregulated consumer markets can thus be substantial. The purchases of a cell phone plan, credit card service, and home mortgage are particularly intricate and unwieldy transactions.[17] Consumers often must make a high investment in processing costs to understand their most basic features. Even for transactions that are seemingly straightforward (for example, the purchase of cereal or protein drinks), however, sellers can take advantage of comprehension asymmetries.

Not only can we expect some sellers to take advantage of the limited processing capacity of consumers, we can also expect inequities with regard to which consumers are the most likely to be exploited. As a general rule, the most sophisticated consumers and those with the greatest ability to invest in information processing are taken advantage of less frequently than less sophisticated, financially stretched consumers. It should not be surprising, therefore, that a "very large body of work" in economics and finance consistently reveals that "[t]he sophisticated/informed almost always do better than the naïve/uninformed" in consumer markets.[18]

C Anticipating Objections to Comprehension Asymmetries in the Marketplace

There are several potential objections to our contention that comprehension asymmetries disrupt the effective functioning of consumer markets, and we consider those arguments before proceeding with our investigation. Readers who are already convinced that the market does sometimes fail can skip this section, but others will understandably demand a more thorough discussion of these issues. We consider first whether the issues created by comprehension asymmetries in the marketplace are already addressed by existing market pressures. We then consider whether the issues created by comprehension asymmetries are actually worth addressing or whether they are simply an inevitability of the "rough and tumble" marketplace.

1　Features of the Market that May Already Correct for Comprehension Asymmetries

Three existing features of consumer markets may, at least theoretically, discourage sellers from exploiting the limited processing capacities of consumers. We discuss each of these market features in turn.

Variations in Consumer Processing Capacities. The first market corrective for comprehension asymmetries arises from the fact that in any given market, there will inevitably be variations in the information-processing capacities of market participants. This heterogenity will yield some particularly persistent, expert consumers who are also willing to invest hours in studying contracts and terms. And, ideally, through their hard work and dedication, at least a few of the exploitive practices by sellers might ultimately be caught and disciplined.[19] The work of a subset of persistent consumers (the "informed minority") thus could, in theory, help generate competitive pressure on sellers to establish comprehensible contracts and terms that also benefit less attentive consumers in that market.[20]

While heterogeneity among consumers may help to counteract some exploitive practices in a few consumer markets, the imbalance between the most capable consumer and the standard producer is still large enough to render many consumer markets "noncompetitive."[21] Indeed, recent empirical work suggests there are very few (and perhaps none) of these capable consumers in some markets. In a study by Yannis Bakos and coauthors, for example, only about one or two of every thousand internet consumers ever accessed the license agreement, and this handful of readers rarely read the entire agreement.[22]

Moreover, as we discuss later, one tactic some sellers use to avoid consumers that are willing to invest the time and energy needed to thoroughly examine products is to change their marketing practices in ways that exclude these consumers.[23] Rather than be held to account by attentive consumers for a complicated and ultimately onerous home loan, for example, a seller can target a subset of purchasers that are likely to lack the expertise and resources to investigate the basic features of the complicated transaction. As Oren Bar-Gill and Elizabeth Warren observe, in some "markets, informed consumers may get safer products, but there is no reason for that benefit to carry over to the uninformed consumers."[24]

Expert Intermediaries. In addition to buyers and sellers, most consumer markets also include some type of expert intermediary, such as consumer groups. These intermediaries reap greater benefits (financial, reputational, or other) from deciphering complex terms and conditions of products and services as compared with individual consumers. Even better, the intermediaries tend to have specialized expertise, which makes their engagement less costly. Because intermediaries reap higher benefits from processing information and can do so at a lower cost, this subgroup of consumers or consumer-proxies is able to interpret complicated consumer transactions in ways that increase accountability and lower costs for consumers more generally.

Although, as we discuss later, intermediaries such as consumer assistance groups can be extremely useful in translating the true terms of strategically convoluted transactions for consumers, these intermediaries face their own limitations in processing capacity that may fall short of what is needed in some complex consumer markets. If the sellers' incentives are too powerful and the asymmetries in processing capacity too great, even legitimate expert intermediaries may lack the expertise and resources needed to decipher complex transactions in ways that are useful to consumers.[25] Moreover, market forces by themselves are unlikely to be sufficient to ensure intermediaries will exist in all markets where they are needed.

Market Forces. Market pressures may drive firms within a field to standardize products and terms. Anna Gelpern and coauthors observe a standardization of boilerplate in the bond market, for example, that is explained on these grounds.[26] Interestingly, their study found that while the speakers themselves often did not understand the details of their own boilerplate, they felt that using the boilerplate was nonetheless essential to success in the marketplace.

While market forces may encourage standardization in some markets, this appears to be the exception rather than the rule. Instead, research reveals a number of significant consumer goods and services that are, for all practical purposes, non-comparable and perhaps deliberately so.[27] Additionally, even where products and terms have been standardized, if these terms are unintelligible, consumers will not have the information they need to make informed purchasing decisions.

2 Some Consumers Are Operating in the Wrong Market

A second objection to the assertion that comprehension asymmetries matter in unregulated markets challenges the framing of the problem; the true problem, according to this argument, lies not with the speaker but with consumers who are participating in markets in which they do not belong. When consumers' processing capacities are exceeded, they should exit the market. Incomprehensible contracts should signal to these disadvantaged consumers that they are proceeding at their own risk. If the consumers persist in participating in the market, some consumers will find they are not fit to survive – caveat emptor. Such is the nature of markets, where not everyone (particularly those ill-equipped to participate) can be winners.

There are two grounds for rejecting this survival-of-the-fittest consumer argument. The first is empirical. There is now considerable evidence that consumers' limitations are actively preyed upon by some producers in the consumer market.[28] Consequently, in many cases consumers may not even realize that they do not understand the terms of the deals they are agreeing to. In such cases it is hardly realistic to expect them to "voluntarily" leave the market. In *Phishing for Fools*, George Akerlof and Robert Shiller document numerous exploitive tactics used by sellers to "phish" the hapless consumer. The authors (both of whom are world-renowned economists) conclude that the free market simply does not lead to efficient outcomes in the many settings in which trickery and deception are part of the equation for competitive success.[29] In cases where consumers are actively preyed upon by sellers who enjoy considerable information-processing advantages, the playing field is thus badly lopsided at the starting line; the assumption of a level playing field, critical to the doctrine of caveat emptor, is absent.

The second basis for rejecting this survival-of-the-fittest consumer objection is conceptual. Lying beneath the "consumers should exit" argument is a chicken–egg problem. Is the market defined by those consumers that the seller targets or those the seller actually reaches? If a seller is earning profits from a consumer base that is unsophisticated and vulnerable to manipulation, does that create a responsibility for the seller or do we chalk it up to a market full of suckers who deserve whatever happens to them? If a median or reasonable consumer lacks the processing capacity to knowledgably participate in the market, it seems appropriate for the seller deriving profit from that consumer to bear at least some responsibility for correcting any reasonable consumer misunderstandings. Indeed, in some markets consumers may have no ability to realistically exit (e.g., in the purchase of student loans).

II THE ROLE OF LAW: STOP ONE – CONTRACTS

If the market cannot always be trusted to counteract significant comprehension asymmetries between consumers and producers, what role does the law play in encouraging cooperative communication between these two parties? Our legal study begins with the oldest body of law regulating the consumer market – contract law. (Tort law also regulates unsafe and fraudulent products, but it does not click in until a consumer is physically injured by a product; we thus consider tort law only as it interacts with contract law in addressing consumers' comprehension asymmetries).

Contract law is common law; it focuses on the particular, individualized setting of the transaction to enforce mutual agreements. While contract law no longer pretends to require a "meeting of the minds," contract law does insist on an objective manifestation of assent that has not been obtained by false assurances.[30]

In the abstract, contract law appears to epitomize a full-throttle commitment to requiring sellers to communicate effectively to buyers.[31] Contract law looks at the contracts that undergird consumer sales from the vantage point of how a typical person entering into that contract would understand the terms.[32] While long, complicated contracts sometimes proliferate in the consumer market, the courts attempt to search out and protect against the worst abuses. "We give words their 'ordinary meaning' viewing the subject of the contract 'as the mass of mankind' would view it."[33]

Additionally, consumer contracts must communicate the seller's promises to the buyer, with all omissions and ambiguities interpreted against the seller-drafter.[34] Consumer products also carry an implied warranty of merchantability or fitness, and, accordingly, material risks must be warned against by sellers to avoid expensive damage claims.[35]

There is a significant catch to all of these consumer protections emerging from contract law, however. Because consumers are entering into market transactions voluntarily, those challenging a contract or transaction bear the burden of proving that a contract is invalid. Our disadvantaged consumers, in other words, must take it upon themselves to first understand their legal rights and second to find legal assistance in order to prove to the court that a contract was drafted in ways that prevented effective assent.

From this legal structure we can see a Catch-22 emerging; the overwhelmed consumer is responsible for rooting out and enforcing the law against transactions that are too confusing for a reasonable person. Yet, as long as consumers are disadvantaged in processing information relative to the seller, their ability to protect themselves through this private litigation will be limited at best. Indeed, as we discuss later, consumers may even unwittingly sign away their right to challenge a contract in court because they have not adequately processed the legal implications of the contract terms.

Before delving further into the more specific features of contract law that exacerbate existing comprehension asymmetries, we pause to note that contract law is currently in flux. The consumer market today is quite different from the markets that preoccupied common law courts hundreds of years ago when the common law principles were emerging. Not surprisingly, courts applying the common law today are thus struggling to bring contract law up to date.[36] Despite the generalizations offered here, then, there is a great deal of uncertainty in predicting how stringently an individual contract will be assessed by a court.[37] Nevertheless, for our purposes it suffices to note that some courts are still behind the times and "fall back on archaic canons of interpretation."[38] Hence the overview of contract law we provide still fairly characterizes the law in many courtrooms.

So, with the qualification that we are shooting at somewhat of a moving target, we turn our attention to exploring how well contract law encourages speakers to communicate meaningfully with their target audience. We begin with our seller as Rule-Follower, followed by the Rule-Bender.

A *Rule-Followers*

Remember, our Rule-Follower unflinchingly follows the law's commands. But the law tends to focus the Rule-Follower's attention on sharing complete information, while providing much less encouragement to ensure that the contract is also reasonably comprehensible. There are several strands of contract law that, despite their protective orientation for consumers, tend to ignore the need for comprehensible contracts in the consumer market. Indeed, several of these doctrines unwittingly could lead Rule-Followers to actively inflate the processing costs for consumers in drafting contracts in ways that become difficult to distinguish from the incomprehensible contracts drafted by Rule-Benders.

1 Anticipatory Drafting: More is Better

Contract drafters understand that because a contract lays out all the terms of the agreement, the contract should be as complete as possible. If a contract drafter does not anticipate a contingency or fails to protect himself against a risk, then the resulting loss may well fall on his or her shoulders. If the consumer disagrees with the meaning of a term or condition, then the contract drafter again may take the financial hit for any misunderstanding.

As a result, contract drafters will invest considerable effort into putting their preferred meaning into writing in ways that are as thorough as possible.[39] Contingencies will be anticipated and guarded against. Conditions and expectations that affect the agreement will be stated with precision and itemized in detail. "The last thing [contracting parties] want is to unintentionally leave a situation [open-ended,] so that a court will later on be forced to puzzle through the best course of action ... To prevent this, the parties cover all their bases in great detail, so that, no matter what may come, they have a document to guide them."[40]

Even with respect to individual terms and conditions, a longstanding rule of contract interpretation, applied with particular force in the consumer contract area, is that ambiguities are interpreted against the drafter. This is known as the doctrine of "contra proferentem."[41] "[A] provision of a policy is ambiguous if reasonably intelligent people, viewing the contract as a whole, could disagree as to its meaning and more precise language could have eliminated ... the ambiguity."[42] The drafter is then held responsible for any resulting lack of clarity. And while some drafters may respond to contra proferentem by editing out text that could be misunderstood, others will provide still more detail to eliminate any possible ambiguity.

The Parol Evidence rule further reinforces the inclinations of drafters to ensure the contract covers all conceivable possibilities thoroughly and in detail.[43] The Parol Evidence rule precludes the court from enforcing promises made during the negotiations that do not make their way into the written contract.[44] The Plain Meaning rule can have a similar effect on drafting. The Plain Meaning rule bars courts from considering the evidence from negotiations leading up to the contract unless the contract terms are ambiguous; to be safe, the relevant details should be set out in the written contract.[45] The impetus of both rules again points the drafter toward pinning down every detail in writing and erring toward a "more is better" method for drafting a contract.

It is easy to see from these legal directives why the Rule-Follower might err on the side of drafting contracts with specific terms and conditions that anticipate every worst-case scenario. Uncertainties about the future lead to more anticipatory drafting.[46] In essence, "[b]ecause these rules harm parties who fail to put all terms in writing, they encourage parties to write more detailed and complex contracts."[47]

And, although tort law plays only a supporting role in the consumer market, it is worth noting that tort law creates a similar incentive. In theory, liability can attach every time a foreseeable significant risk is not warned against and that risk materializes.[48] As Kip Viscusi observes: "Firms may potentially incur tort liability penalties for underwarning. Yet there are no penalties levied for overwarning."[49]

Of course, not all contracts fall into this "more is better" rut. As Karen Eggleston, Eric Posner, and Richard Zeckhauser point out, there *are* simple contracts in some settings.[50] Yet the default incentives mapped by theorists tend to point both courts and drafters toward opting for more details, more contingencies, and more text, without parallel incentives for ensuring that this work be reasonably comprehensible to the target audience, whether they be businesses or consumers. Claire Hill and Christopher King, for example, offer a "stylized picture of US complex business contracts" as: "very long," with "a great deal of explanation, qualification, and limitation in the language," and filled with "a great deal of 'legalese.'"[51] The *Harvard Business Review* is less charitable. It asks: "What do you call a dense, overly lengthy contract that is loaded with legal jargon and virtually impossible for a nonlawyer to understand? The status quo."[52]

Not surprisingly, courts are not wholly oblivious to the perverse effects of these legally backed incentives on contract drafting. To counteract these risks in some specialty areas, courts have devised doctrinal refinements.[53] In insurance law, for example, some courts have developed a "reasonable expectation" doctrine to protect against too much consumer confusion from complicated contracts.[54] Under this test, unexpected text placed in fine print is unenforceable.[55] Somewhat similarly, in securities regulation, there is a "buried facts" doctrine that penalizes a needle-in-the-haystack approach to conveying important information. This doctrine warns contract drafters that important features of the agreement cannot be slipped into the last sentence of the third paragraph on page 12 out of 30.[56] And although neither of these doctrines demands that a contract actually be comprehensible to the average customer, they at least advance on this larger goal by honoring only those terms that the customer might reasonably expect and understand.[57]

Despite limited progress in select areas of contract law, however, the courts' cumulative opinions still signal that contract drafters are far better off ensuring all contingencies and risks are specified in detail and with precision. This is true even if it may cause the resulting contract to be long, convoluted, and considerably less comprehensible to the target consumer. As Eggleston, Posner, and Zeckhauser observe, "Lawyers may view adding many contingencies to the contract as their professional and ethical responsibility, whereas the cost of such detail is of little concern to them."[58] And, while some Rule-Followers might ultimately make a voluntary effort to spotlight the most serious risks and conditions in bold or even yellow highlight, they will also ensure that all relevant details, caveats, and conditions are anticipated and added to the body of the contract.

2 Duty to Read

A second, contractual doctrine – the "duty to read" principle – sets up a default rule that shifts most, if not all, of the processing costs associated with understanding a contract to the consumer-audience. As its name implies, "the duty to read" principle requires consumers to invest whatever effort is needed to understand what they are signing.[59] If the contract contains a great deal of information, consumers must pick through the terms to decide what is trash and what is treasure.[60] As one federal district court judge succinctly put it, "[A] party who signs a written contract is conclusively presumed to know its contents and assent to them."[61]

In order to prevent contract drafters from carrying this doctrine to the extreme, a minority of courts make it clear that the "duty to read presumption" will not excuse the seller from providing clear and understandable terms for the most important features of the contract.[62] Most courts also enforce an outer-limit "shock the conscience" test to invalidate contracts they find to be so deceitful they are "unconscionable."[63] (We discuss this doctrine next.)

Yet despite these qualifications, the duty-to-read doctrine still reminds drafters to err on the side of putting all conceivable risks, concerns, terms, and other conditions into writing, regardless of whether they are communicated in a way that is comprehensible to the consumer. The terms will bind the consumers, whether read (or readable) or not. Together with the prior, "more is better" incentives, the duty-to-read doctrine instructs drafters that when in doubt, throw it in.

3 The Legal Backstop of Unconscionability

The doctrine of unconscionability, as just discussed, would seem in the abstract to provide an important deterrent to sellers who are otherwise inclined to draft incomprehensible contracts. Yet, as currently devised, this test – which is generally only available to consumers as a defense against contract enforcement – imposes little more than a speedbump to discourage this behavior. [64] Before outlining the doctrine's limitations, we first provide a brief overview of how the test works.

The doctrine of unconscionability is used by courts to invalidate contracts that "shock the conscience" with respect to drafters' underhanded methods of confusing signators and depriving them of basic rights. This exploitation of consumers can occur even when the unfair terms are put into writing.[65] The legal test for determining whether a contract is unconscionable involves evaluating whether the contract is presented in a way that deprives the consumer of a meaningful choice (the process or procedural test) and whether the contract is one-sided or oppressive (the substance test).[66]

In the past, courts rarely held a contract to be unconscionable; the doctrine was considered locked in "arrested development."[67] In the last few decades, the number of contracts declared unconscionable has increased slightly.[68] One court, for example, was willing to invalidate a binding arbitration clause because the signators could not comprehend the terms, even after seeking help from the contracting party.[69] Yet despite a brief flurry of activity in applying the procedural prong of the unconscionability test over the last decade, commenters now observe a distinct "retrenchment" in the courts' use of the doctrine.[70]

But even if the courts do become more receptive to the doctrine, unconscionability still provides few incentives for Rule-Followers to draft contracts that are comprehensible. First and most obvious, the reach of the doctrine touches only the most overtly unfair contracts and typically operates as an affirmative defense.[71] These limitations thus leave the vast majority of convoluted, and excessively long contracts unaffected. Russell Hakes observes that as of 2011, "[t]he [unconscionability] doctrine is available, but its name, as well as concepts like 'oppression,' 'unfair surprise' and 'shocks the conscience' make it applicable only to deal with extreme provisions in contracts. The doctrine and its use still reflect strong deference to the provisions that appear in the contract."[72]

Second, in applying the unconscionability test, courts look only to the contract text and endeavor to determine whether the contract is reasonably accessible to a hypothetical reader.[73] In doing so, the courts generally neglect to consider the real world pressures faced by the target signator and assume instead that the signator will have the time and resources to read the contract front-to-back, for example in a library or coffee shop. Slawson underscores this important deficiency in the administration of the unconscionability test: "Courts often accept large or differently colored print as proof that the consumer received notice of a provision, without regard to whether the consumer was reasonably expected to read it in time to be warned by it."[74]

Finally, given the limited reach of the unconscionability doctrine, contract law still leaves the Rule-Follower with the overarching directives that, in drafting contracts, "more is better" and to "put all terms in writing." At most, to protect himself from an unconscionability claim, a Rule-Follower might underline or bold a few passages. But this modest effort will stop well short of legally requiring a Rule-Follower to ensure that the contract is reasonably comprehensible to the target consumer.

4 Summary

The net effect of contract law, then, may accomplish little more than direct the Rule-Follower to draft contracts that "yell even more loudly at the deaf man."[75] As long as the burden for information processing falls on the consumer, even well-meaning speakers will tend to shift processing costs to consumers and cut corners in investing in cooperative communication. The law does gesture toward the need for consumer comprehension in some submarkets, but most judicial interpretations of even these more aggressive doctrines stop short of requiring the speaker to get in the shoes of the average consumer.

B *Rule-Benders*

If contract law tends to lead Rule-Followers toward drafting contracts that err on the side of shifting excessive processing costs to the audience, imagine how Rule-Benders will react to this legal oversight. We recount some of the evidence in this section. The implications are bleak; it appears that firms are not only routinely exploiting the processing limitations of their consumer audiences, but they actively compete with one another to be the most devious in that regard. Moreover, the accounts of this behavior reveal that "[e]ven if consumers always catch up eventually, this cat-and-mouse game imposes welfare costs" in the interim.[76]

1 Strategies to Deliberately Raise Audience Processing Costs

Several recurring Rule-Bender strategies have been documented in the literature:

Databombing. Long contracts take more time for consumers to read than short contracts, and so length alone can allow speakers to obscure some undesirable features of the product or transaction from busy consumers. This simple strategy of databombing is deployed in a number of areas of consumer and even expert contracts. In *More than You Wanted to Know*, Ben-Shahar and Schneider provide measurements, word counts, and visual images of a variety of ridiculously long contracts.[77] They note, for example, how a number of contracts and service agreements are so long that they are routinely called "bed sheets."[78] They compare the length of one particular financial disclosure to the length of Romeo and Juliet. The authors even go so far as to print out 32 pages of an 8-point font iTunes contract and dangle it from the University of Chicago Law School atrium (and include a photograph in the book).

Fine Print Manipulations. In her book *Boilerplate*, Mary Jane Radin provides numerous examples of the lengthy and convoluted "boilerplate" that can be loaded into consumer contracts. This fine-print text is not just benign databombing; some of it can alter fundamental legal rights, such as the ability of the consumer to sue in court for negligently inflicted harm.[79]

The inflated processing costs that arise from this tactic are affected not just by the length but the density and complexity of the substance of the text itself. Ben-Shahar and Schneider, for example, document how some consumer contract provisions – even those found in mandated disclosures – can demand an unrealistically high literacy level (in some cases, only about 4 percent of the population) from those who sign them.[80] Judges from the bench and billionaire investors concur; despite being experts, even these sophisticated readers cannot understand some basic insurance policies directed at the average consumer.[81]

David Gilo and Ariel Porat identify several market benefits that flow to Rule-Benders who deliberately exploit consumers' comprehension limitations in this way.[82] They observe, for example, how gratuitously complicated contracts make comparison shopping more difficult for consumers, which in turn "support[s] an equilibrium in which competition is less fierce, and profits, accordingly, higher" for Rule-Benders who deploy this tactic.[83] Suppliers operating in these more complex markets can also get away with raising prices far above their marginal cost.[84] Unduly complicated contracts can even serve as an entry barrier to new firms that sell long-term goods, such as cell phone contracts. This barrier occurs because consumers cannot reliably compare offerings and are thus reluctant to leave their existing providers.[85]

Bait and Switch. Fine print contracts also provide ingenious Rule-Benders with a platform for manipulating consumers through bait-and-switch techniques, while still remaining safely inside the outer perimeter of the law.[86] In bait and switch, consumers are alerted to favorable features of the product with headlines and highlighted text, while the adverse features are buried in fine print. As a result, consumers are "phished" or hooked by a seductive attribute, while equally important caveats and exceptions are lost in convoluted paragraphs that follow.[87]

Bar-Gill discusses how sellers can strategically bundle multiple products into a single transaction, making the salient costs for some items low (e.g., the handset in a cell phone package), while nonsalient costs for other items (e.g., the costs of cellular service or features of that service, such as the data plan) are excessively high.[88] This bait-and-switch technique thus allows the seller to bury the bad news and headline the good news. Beyond the difficulties for busy consumers in trying to extract this underlying cost distribution is the even more daunting challenge of comparing competing packages across sellers, particularly when each package is unique. Bar-Gill suggests that as a result of this bundling technique, "[m]ore choice comes at the expense of *meaningful* choice."[89] Comparing home loans, for example, would require simultaneously comparing 10 to 15 price dimensions and then determining the impacts of these prices on the costs of the loan.[90]

Complicating the Transaction Itself. Contracts can be drafted in overly complex ways, but in some cases this complexification carries over to the structure of the transaction itself. Oren Bar-Gill traces how strategically increasing the "[c]omplexity [of the transaction] allows providers to hide the true cost of the contract."[91] A typical credit card arrangement can involve an average of nine fees and costs, for example.[92] Bar-Gill also provides detailed examples of how the resultant "[i]ncreased complexity . . . allows them to hide the true cost of the credit card in a multidimensional pricing maze,"[93] and draws quotes from industry itself admitting to this practice.[94]

And in the cell phone service arena, service plans are so complex and numerous that the marketplace offers consumers "more than 10 million different plans and add-on combinations."[95] Bar-Gill concludes that this level of complexity "has reached a point beyond what we should expect if it was simply a response to rational consumer demand."[96] Instead, some of the complexity evident on the market today "represent[s] a strategic response by sophisticated issuers to imperfectly rational card-holders [and other consumers]."[97] Indeed, to stay competitive, the service providers must exploit the complexity – and yet this very fact also leads to ever more tactics and techniques to earn profits by taking advantage of the customers' limited time and attention, particularly for complex and detailed conditions.

Targeting the Most Vulnerable Audience. In some areas – especially in credit cards and home loan financing – computing technology makes it possible for lenders to differentiate among borrowers and tailor their noncompetitive, over-priced loans to a subset of the audience based on that audience's uniquely severe processing limitations.[98] Producers know consumers' purchasing patterns from carefully collected sales and use data. They can thus create fine-print terms, craft contracts that exploit different vulnerable groups in different ways, and devise other tricks that prey on these vulnerabilities (e.g., subtle features of opt-outs and excess charges).[99] At the same time, they will highlight features that are most important to these same subsets of consumers (e.g., upfront cost).[100] And since markets are different, providers can create different packages that target the weaknesses of different audiences. Indeed, providers who do not play these specialized audience-targeting games can find themselves at a competitive disad-vantage in certain markets.

Although audience-targeting can be applied across the board, vulnerable seg-ments of the market are particularly easy marks for these exploitation strategies. Lauren Willis recounts how subprime home lenders developed targeted marketing strategies for vulnerable borrowers with the greatest processing limitations. These vulnerable consumers were located by "search[ing] courthouse records for home loan owners facing foreclosure or tax liens" and "buy[ing] lists of home loan owners with overdue balances on their credit cards or medical debt."[101] Once located, these consumers would be offered a loan with a variety of legitimate-sounding, but inflated and superfluous added fees, such as origination fees, single premium credit insurance, document preparation fees, underwriting analysis fees, tax escrow fees, and escrow fund analysis fees. In some vulnerable consumer markets, these fees became routine and could involve as much as 20 percent of the loan amount, set atop the already high interest.[102]

Indeed, while one might expect the financial documents for those with limited education to be drafted in ways that are *more* accessible to these signators with added processing limitations, Bar-Gill observes that the mortgages in the more vulnerable markets actually tend to be more complex and incomprehensible as compared to the mortgages offered in more expert markets.[103] Perhaps not surprisingly, some empirical evidence now reveals that this is not an accident. Lenders understood and presumably intended this manipulation of borrowers who were particularly disadvantaged in processing information regarding lending arrangements.[104]

Box 4.1 Comprehension Asymmetries in Consumer Contract Law

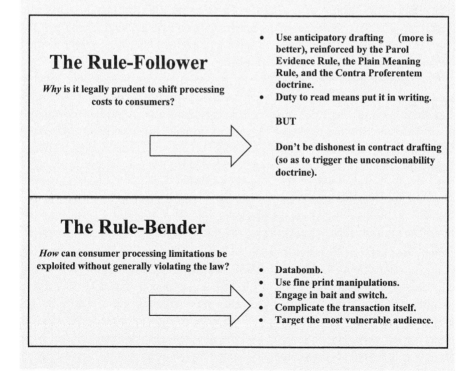

The Rule-Follower

Why is it legally prudent to shift processing costs to consumers?

- Use anticipatory drafting (more is better), reinforced by the Parol Evidence Rule, the Plain Meaning Rule, and the Contra Proferentem doctrine.
- Duty to read means put it in writing.

BUT

Don't be dishonest in contract drafting (so as to trigger the unconscionability doctrine).

The Rule-Bender

How can consumer processing limitations be exploited without generally violating the law?

- Databomb.
- Use fine print manipulations.
- Engage in bait and switch.
- Complicate the transaction itself.
- Target the most vulnerable audience.

2 What about Unconscionability?

But wait. The purpose of the unconscionability doctrine is to deter precisely these
types of exploitive strategies. Even if the unconscionability doctrine does not provide
the Rule-Follower with a strong directive to draft comprehensible contracts, it would
seem to at least discourage these more extreme "shock the conscience" drafting
tricks perpetrated by Rule-Benders.

But in some, and perhaps most cases, the unconscionability doctrine comes up
short in checking even these more egregious tactics. First and most central is the
design of the doctrine itself; the burden of proving an unconscionable contract falls
on the disadvantaged consumer. As one state appellate court summarized, "[A] party
raising a claim of unconscionability has the burden of showing some over-reaching
or imposition resulting from a bargaining disparity between the parties, or such
patent unfairness in the terms of the contract that no reasonable [person] not acting
under compulsion or out of necessity would accept them."[105] Thus, there is no
obligation for a drafter to show even preliminarily that he ensured that all significant
terms were comprehensible to the target audience. Instead, the burden falls on the
manipulated signator to prove that the terms of the unconscionability test have
been met.

In cases of significant comprehension asymmetries, this burden undoubtedly
serves as a practical barrier to enforcement. Our slighted audience member must
appreciate that she has been duped through sophisticated information tricks in ways
that are legally unconscionable and must then seek out a lawyer.

As a result of these legal impediments, private enforcement of unconscionable
contracts is likely to be significantly depressed. Yet even if a consumer perseveres
and identifies a problem that appears to fall within the reach of the unconscionability doctrine, the out-of-pocket expense of bringing an unconscionability case
seems likely to curb most private challengers. Claims of unconscionability are
notoriously expensive and complicated in ways that likely discourage some attorneys
from taking on these cases.[106] The unconscionability doctrine has been long criticized for its vagueness, for example, and some courts maintain that unconscionability is reserved for only the most clearly intentional and egregious transactions.[107]
Ironically, moreover, even whether a successful plaintiff can recover attorney fees is
complicated and can ultimately turn on the terms of the contract. In some states, for
example, courts honor "unilateral" clauses drafted by sellers that provide the contract drafter with reimbursement of his litigation expenses, but if the consumer
prevails in litigation, the consumer's expenses are not reimbursed.[108] If these cumulative impediments were not enough, the limited remedy for a successful claim is
likely the last straw. Under contract law, the very best award a consumer can hope
for is a full refund or replacement.[109] Individual consumers who are willing to
surmount these multiple litigation hurdles – only to void the agreement – would
thus seem to be few and far between.

Because of the low payouts for individual consumer contract cases, attorneys sometimes sweep hundreds of individual cases into a larger class action to make them economically viable.[110] Yet here again, Rule-Benders have devised a way around the class action threat using contract law. In this defensive move, Rule-Benders insert a provision in the contract that requires binding arbitration in lieu of judicial review, with a prohibition against class actions.[111] Such a clause not only forecloses the ability of an individual to obtain a precedent that helps other victims,[112] but it also forecloses the possibility of joining multiple claims through a class action.[113] The Supreme Court recently upheld the legality of these clauses in employment contracts.[114] Thus, it seems even more likely in the future that Rule-Benders will deploy these clauses to preclude both judicial review and class action enforcement.[115] Rule-Benders, in turn, often set the standards for the competitive market, causing Rule-Followers to adopt these clauses as well just to survive.[116]

Despite this formidable series of impediments to legally penalizing Rule-Benders for crafting unconscionable contracts, a few Rule-Benders might still be caught by determined consumers. But even here, reputational and economic harms can often be managed by a Rule-Bender using contract law. Unconscionability claims that threaten to harm a firm's reputation can be settled and sealed with nondisclosure contracts. Bonus payments encourage plaintiffs to sign these nondisclosure agreements, thus keeping particularly meritorious or damaging claims out of the public eye.[117]

Putting this legal analysis into economic terms, under contract law the Rule-Bender faces high payoffs and low risks to exploiting consumer limitations using incomprehensible contracts. The unconscionability doctrine can reach only a few deceptive contracts and thus its ability to deter these types of manipulative practices is weak, at best.

III THE ROLE OF LAW: STOP TWO – STATUTES

The ability of firms to exploit consumers' information-processing limitations has not been lost on policymakers. Legislators can intervene with a range of more finely calibrated tools if they perceive that sellers are drafting contracts or related communications that cannot be comprehended by the intended audience. Indeed, federal and state legislators, local governments, and regulators at all levels have attempted to do precisely that.

Among the approaches legislators have at their disposal are strict legal prohibitions that preclude sellers from taking "unreasonable advantage" of a consumer's limited processing capacity.[118] Agencies such as the new Consumer Financial Protection Bureau (CFPB), for example, are tasked with enforcing these types of prohibitions against major actors within the financial services industry, using a "cop on the beat" model.[119] Rule-Benders face potentially significant costs to exploiting consumers with incomprehensibility tactics as a result of these new laws and government enforcers.

Although these legislative prohibitions are headed in the right direction, their effectiveness has been limited for a number of reasons. First, the prohibitions are generally drafted narrowly, leaving many bad behaviors unaddressed. Second, enforcement of the prohibitions is expensive. Catching and penalizing violators requires government agencies to be equipped with ample investigation and litigation resources. Finally, the deterrence created by these prohibitions ultimately depends on whether firms perceive a risk that they will incur significant sanctions when they violate the laws. Given limited enforcement budgets and other constraints, firms may perceive little risk in violating some prohibitions.

To reach a larger swath of activities, legislators regularly deploy a second, much broader tool – disclosures. These disclosures aim to require speakers to use formats and terms that consumers can understand and that also allow for cross-comparisons of products or activities.[120] In the wake of the financial crisis of 2008, for example, Congress required the CFPB to develop model disclosures for home mortgage contracts that are "written in plain language comprehensible to consumers."[121] Accordingly, "[u]nder the new Consumer Financial Protection Bureau's auspices, newly simplified mortgage disclosures have been generated, tested in labs for readability and efficacy, and launched under the slogan 'Know before you owe.'"[122] Lenders must comply with these disclosure formats or face sanctions.

Alongside these legislative disclosures for the mortgage market are complementary disclosures requiring clearer terms and conditions in consumer lending. Beginning with the Truth in Lending Act of 1968, Congress required lenders to provide consumers with information on credit terms that Congress intended to be sufficient to allow for cross-comparisons of competitors then on the market.[123] Because of ambiguities in these requirements, which in turn led to creative compliance by companies, this Act was followed by several more legislative efforts to improve the quality of information provided to borrowers.[124] The CARD Act (Credit Card Accountability, Responsibility, and Disclosure Act of 2009) is the most recent law in this series: One set of requirements endeavour to enhance the understandability of information made available to consumers in the credit card market.[125]

Mortgages and credit cards are only two examples of the types of activities subject to various legislative requirements for disclosures. Called "targeted transparency" by Archon Fung et al., the number of legislatively mandated disclosures that seek to simplify the information provided to consumers has been on a steady rise over the last few decades. In *More than You Wanted to Know*, Ben-Shahar and Schneider tick off a number of legislative and regulatory disclosure proposals from the SEC, the Consumer Financial Protection Bureau, the Affordable Care Act, workplace safety, toxic releases in communities, and even nutrition content on food.[126] These disclosure requirements have as their primary aim providing information to consumers to facilitate market comparisons.[127]

However, despite these well-meaning efforts to put a stop to the ability of sellers to exploit limitations in consumers' abilities to process information, most of the legally mandated disclosures have been disappointing, if not outright failures. Ben-Shahar and Schneider argue that virtually all mandated disclosures, including requirements for informed consent, have failed.[128] Fung et al. similarly recount a rash of significant inadequacies in legally mandated disclosures, particularly for complex settings such as the mandated "material safety data sheets" that are intended to provide workers with information about hazards in the workplace.[129]

In her work, Lauren Willis puts her finger on the underlying problem running through these various disclosures: Sellers still lack incentives to ensure that the audience truly understands them. In her words, "No matter how well the bureau's ... disclosures perform in the lab, or even in the field trials, firms will run circles round these disclosures when the experiments end, misleading consumer and defying consumers' expectations ... Even without any intent to deceive, firms not only will but must leverage consumer confusion to compete with other firms that deceive customers."[130]

Willis's cautionary note also reminds us that precisely because of the critical role of speaker incentives, disclosure requirements do not always fail. Disclosures can be effective if the speakers are motivated to communicate meaningfully with their target audiences. Disclosures only fail when the speaker is highly motivated to find a way around them. These determined speakers can generally sidestep disclosure requirements using a variety of clever techniques that exploit their audience's limited processing capacities without violating the letter of the legal requirements.

However, while we will see that Rule-Benders present by far the largest challenge to disclosures, even the Rule-Followers can sometimes find that mandated templates impede rather than facilitate their ability to communicate meaningfully with their audience. We discuss these two actors next.

A *Rule-Followers*

Rule-Followers are poised to communicate effectively with their target audiences; thus, disclosures generally advance cooperative communication for this group of speakers. But in some settings, disclosures can impede even our well-meaning Rule-Followers from communicating key messages to their target audience. This occurs in large part because disclosures force speakers into a template that may not always fit the specific communicative situation. Instead, in some market transactions, truly cooperative and effective communication requires creativity, motivation, and tailored messages.

To take an example from the opening of this chapter, if oven cleaner manufacturers were subjected to a prescribed warning requirement and prohibited from giving other warnings (e.g., identifying the dangers of misuse), without an overarching incentive to minimize deaths and injuries, teens would likely still be dying today. Similarly, a doctor who is legally required to follow a checklist for patient informed consent might be distracted from connecting with and explaining the true risks and alternatives for an individual patient with particularized concerns.

Haeberle and Henderson argue that precisely this problem occurs in corporate financial disclosures. The required disclosures omit valuable information that otherwise should be conveyed, but because it is not required (and disclosing this information could increase legal liabilities), this information drops out of the picture. Ironically, too, as a result of the prescriptive script, there is no wiggle room for tailoring a disclosure to particular audiences, even if the speaker was otherwise inclined. As a result, the disclosure requirements can become "anti-disclosure laws" for some key messages.[131]

Some mandated disclosures can also operate perversely to focus Rule-Followers on ignoring the overarching goal of meaningful communication in an effort to achieve successful compliance. Out of necessity, disclosures focus on some audiences or messages at the expense of others,[132] and in some cases this laser-like focus can lead to communicative slippage. In a somewhat analogous setting, Daniel Ho finds that even when restaurants perform well on the variables used in the disclosure-based restaurant grading, the overall risk of foodborne illness in the food served is not necessarily reduced.[133]

Vigorous compliance by Rule-Followers cannot only eclipse more meaningful communications but can lead to behavior changes that undermine the reason for the disclosure in the first place. In environmental regulation, some industries change the way they operate so their total emissions fall just under the high threshold for reporting requirements, relieving them of any communication of hazardous emissions at all, even though their total emissions can still be high enough to pose potential health risks to neighboring committees.[134] In the use of Report Cards, hospitals can alter their patient-base to make compliance easier – for example by avoiding complicated patients. They simplify their reporting requirements while earning higher health care scores.[135]

B *Rule-Benders*

The greatest disappointments in the effectiveness of disclosures, however, arise from the strategic work-arounds crafted by Rule-Benders. As the old adage suggests, "Where there is a will, there is a way." Mandated disclosures do not change the will; they only (in best cases) eliminate one way, leaving others wide open.

Rule-Benders have pioneered a variety of techniques for complying with disclosure mandates while still deceiving or obscuring the key messages those disclosures are intended to convey.[136] A few of these tricks are highlighted in the pages that follow.

1 "Bury the Lede"

Perhaps the most straightforward way for Rule-Benders to avoid unwelcome disclosure requirements is to bury the disclosure in other, more complicated and largely unilluminating paperwork. As one example, Congress has required in two sequential statutes that lenders provide several mandated disclosures to consumers to ensure the consumers understand the basics of the transactions. Lenders cannot avoid providing these clear disclosure statements, but lenders have discovered that they can bury or crowd out the required information with many other forms and superfluous information. In these "bury the lede" strategies, some lenders require more than 50 forms to be signed in a single transaction, causing the true information to be lost on overwhelmed consumers. Willis observes that "[a]lthough some of these disclosures are required by state law, the excess 'disclosures' are part of sales tactics designed to 'overload, overwhelm, distract, and fatigue' borrowers."[137]

Debt collectors have also found ways to "overshadow" a disclosure by "burying it in long, meaningless boilerplate language."[138] Karen Schulz recounts how "[o]ne debt collector buried the disclosure on page eight of a sixteen-page letter. Another included the disclosure in small, light grey font at the end of an information-rich document."[139]

Other product manufacturers downplay the significance of mandated information by touting other features in large font with headline-grabbing messages. Nutritional labels require manufacturers to provide nutritional information and ingredients in the familiar chart on the back of the product package. But the regulations do not control the front package matter except to prohibit false statements. Clever manufacturers thus cover the front of their product boxes with eye-catching virtues – organic, GMO free, high in protein, high in vitamins, etc. – without revealing that about half of the daily recommended maximum intake of sugar is contained in a single serving. Some of the health-promoting Kashi Go-Lean cereals (see photo), for example, contain sugar levels roughly equivalent to other notoriously sweet cereals such as Captain Crunch and Fruit Loops.[140] But only by comparing the grams of sugars (13g) between the back panels of various cereals would consumers discover this bittersweet surprise. See Figure 4.1.

2 "Creative" Compliance

A related, even more devious technique some firms use to obscure mandated disclosures is to reframe them in a way that suggests a very different message than what the underlying disclosure was intended to communicate. Through this clever reframing technique, firms can evade requirements by meeting "the letter but not the spirit of the rules."[141] For example, restaurants in New York were forced to post their health inspection grades – A, B, or C – in store windows. At least one restaurant learned how to post its less-than-stellar "B" grade in a way that was cleverly deceptive.[142] See Figure 4.2. Another restaurant learned that the grade cards faded quickly in the sun; the solution to a poor rating was to "take your C letter grade home and hang it in direct sunlight, in about 7 days it will be very faded."[143]

Nutrition Facts
Serving Size 3/4 Cup (53g/1.9 oz.)
Servings Per Container   About 7

Amount Per Serving

Calories 190 Calories from Fat 30

	% Daily Value*
Total Fat 3g	5%
Saturated Fat 0g	0%
Trans Fat 0g	
Polyunsaturated Fat 1g	
Monounsaturated Fat 1.5g	
Cholesterol 0mg	0%
Sodium 100mg	4%
Potassium 330mg	9%
Total Carbohydrate 38g	13%
Dietary Fiber 8g	31%
Soluble Fiber 5g	
Insoluble Fiber 3g	
Sugars 13g	
Protein 9g	13%

FIGURE 4.1 Obscuring High Sugar Content with Health Claims
© Used with permission from Leslie Nutt Photography

Some credit card issuers adopt a similar strategy in response to the CARD Act, which restricts and/or requires heightened transparency on a limited list of fees.[144] Rather than lose profits by revealing true pricing structures, the credit card companies have created a whole new string of non-salient fees and back-end terms not covered by the law. Willis reports that banks are also attempting to shift consumers to other types of cards not covered by the statute, such as prepaid debit cards.[145]

Willis recounts ways that payday lenders managed to keep one step ahead of regulators through a "parade of sleights" that sidestepped the jurisdictional reach of the existing regulations.[146] For example, some lenders continued to recoup high profits for high-priced, small-dollar loans (payday loans), despite legislatively set caps on interest rates, by bundling the loans with other services such as insurance, check cashing, or credit-repairs, or by acting as loan managers that help borrowers acquire loans from other sources.[147] Payday lenders can also structure the loans so that they are just a bit larger than the regulated size, restructure the loans as installments, or engage in other techniques that help them sidestep legal requirements entirely.[148]

The Physician Payments Sunshine Act requires disclosures of payments to physicians by major pharmaceutical companies, but these firms have created ways to evade tracking through sloppy data entry. Fagotto and Fung recount a *ProPublica* study documenting how some "drug companies list several drugs associated with the same payment, making it impossible to break down the contribution for each drug.

FIGURE 4.2: Creative Display of a "B" Grade
© Used with permission from Zach Seward

Sometimes they misspell the names of drugs or use alternative names for their products. As a result, disclosed data may be unreliable."[149] Presumably, some of these errors can lead to fines, but between the low probability of being caught and the advantages of noncompliance, these types of errors likely accrue to the company's benefit.

Creative compliance was also at the heart of the Enron scandal. Enron strategically reported its earnings and expenses in misleading ways designed to attract investors, but that technically did not violate disclosure laws.[150] Congress ultimately responded to this practice by, among other things, amending the reporting requirements for corporate disclosures.[151] (We discuss the success of these efforts in the next chapter.)

While creative compliance is inevitable in any enforcement regime, creative compliance is particularly likely with disclosure requirements because of the rapidity with which motivated firms can devise work-arounds. Indeed, by the time a disclosure requirement takes legal effect, the affected industry may have already blazed a way around it. As Lauren Willis notes, "Regulators might improve disclosure and design rules, but firms often quickly outpace improvements and regulators can rarely stay caught up for long."[152]

3 Manipulating Underlying Processes

Some companies are even willing to invest resources in attempting to manipulate the implementation of the disclosure requirements themselves to avoid costly violations when they do step over the line. In his fascinating study of restaurant grading referenced earlier (a scheme, by the way, that was previously hailed as a disclosure success), Daniel Ho discovered a puzzling distribution of restaurants in New York that clump as low "A"s in an A, B, C rating system.[153] In attempting to make sense of this mystery, Ho identifies considerable variability in the substance of inspections (which involve subjective judgments), evidence of political pressure on inspectors, and evidence of financial bribing of inspectors (or inspector solicitations of bribes).[154] He also discovered that an appeal process provided restaurant owners with a second bite at the apple, as well as creating other benefits for the restaurants. For example, the simple process of filing the appeal allowed the restaurants to postpone posting a poor grade, which is a benefit in and of itself.[155]

In all of these cases, since the disclosure requirement does not place responsibility for meaningful communication on the speaker, reluctant companies – or our Rule-Benders – can and do find ways around these requirements. As Lauren Willis observes, to stop this cycle firms must have an incentive to "educate rather than obfuscate."[156]

IV A CONSTITUTIONAL RIGHT TO BE INCOMPREHENSIBLE

The analysis up to this point has traced how the law can fail to reverse a seller's underlying incentives to deceive or distort, but there is one final counterproductive legal contribution to this dismal state of affairs. The courts are creating a constitutional right for sellers to be incomprehensible. Through a relatively recent addition to First Amendment jurisprudence, the courts have held, in essence, that companies have a constitutional right to inundate their audiences with excessive, superfluous information unless the government can prove that this speech is false, deceptive, or untruthful.[157] Databombing, in other words, may be a constitutionally protected activity.

Rather than a default that expects sellers to be comprehensible in market transactions, this emerging case law flips the burden. Sellers can be as incomprehensible as they wish until the government can establish, with supporting evidence, the ways in which this speech is deceptive.

As a brief orientation, the courts' interpretation of the First Amendment as extending to corporations (rather than just individual citizens) is itself a relatively recent innovation that started in 1976. Over the last 40 years, the courts have taken very different positions on how to conceive of these corporate First Amendment rights in the area of commercial speech.[158] The original 1976 case extended the First Amendment to corporations and their commercial speech in order to protect the consumer audience – more specifically, to ensure that consumers had access to necessary information in the market.[159] As the Court stated in its watershed case, *Virginia Pharmacy*, one of the First Amendment guarantees is the right of citizens to "receive information and ideas and that freedom of speech necessarily protects the right to receive."[160] The purpose of extending the First Amendment to commercial speech, accordingly, was to ensure that consumers receive full information. It was thus the audience's perspective that informed whether a government restriction infringed on the First Amendment rights of corporations.[161]

In a series of more recent cases, the courts have altered this focus in two ways. First, the courts have moved from the more permissive, rational basis test used in *Virginia Pharmacy* to a more searching *Central Hudson* test to determine whether the government's restriction of a corporation's misleading claims is more extensive than necessary.[162] The government must now show a compelling justification in order to regulate commercial speech. This more intensive level of scrutiny, in turn, places a higher value on the seller's message as democratically valuable speech in its own right, regardless of whether the speech is political in nature. As the Court observed in *Liquormart*, the government's effort to regulate "truthful, nonmisleading commercial speech ... may sometimes prove far more intrusive than banning conduct."[163]

Second and even more important, Robert Post and Amanda Shanor observe that the courts' commercial speech jurisprudence today is shifting from a focus on advancing the consumer or listener's interests in full information on the open market to a focus on the effect of government restrictions on corporate speakers themselves as democratic actors.[164] Perhaps this move endeavors to merge commercial speech into traditional First Amendment protections. But whatever the underlying rationale, Post and Shanor argue that the courts' current speaker-orientation for administering commercial speech protections is badly mistaken. "The fundamental question [is] whether the state has impaired the public circulation of information. Unless courts keep this question clearly in mind, they are liable to become lost."[165] This evolving speaker-focus for First Amendment commercial speech protection also blinds the courts to the important question of whether the audience will in fact will be able to accurately understand the speaker's message. Without attention to this seemingly critical issue, the new case law not only misses but is poised to undermine the original goal the Court advanced in *Virginia Pharmacy*.[166]

In practice, then, this evolving First Amendment case law threatens to further tip the playing field in favor of the sellers. Now a seller's incomprehensibility strategies can be restricted by government regulators only when a public enforcement officer can prove that the seller's databombing, use of fine print, or drafting of obfuscating agreements is "deceptive" or otherwise untruthful. Yet the government's burden is in reality higher since courts tend to insist on case-by-case proof that a particular seller stepped over these outer limits with respect to its packaging and promotions.

Despite these problems, the Supreme Court appears unwavering in instituting this new, jurisprudential direction for commercial speech. A 2011 case, *Sorrell*, for example, *explicitly* adopts a more information is better presumption in holding the government lacked a substantial governmental interest in restricting information regarding physician prescription practices.[167] In the Court's words, "Information is not in itself harmful ... people will perceive their own best interests if only they are well enough informed, and the best means to that end is to open the channels of communication rather than to close them."[168]

V A MORE COMPREHENSIBLE FUTURE

Incomprehensible transactions will thrive in consumer markets as long as speakers can profit by exploiting their audiences without penalty or restrictions. But these misplaced incentives are precisely the kind of problem the law is well-situated to fix. Of course, improving the comprehensibility of consumer contracts and disclosures is only one step in the longer road toward improving inefficiencies and inequities in the consumer market. Contracts of adhesion, targeted advertising, and many other problems remain.[169] Yet, if comprehensibility is improved, at least consumers will have greater information about the choices available to them. Comprehensibility, in other words, is an important component of a functioning consumer market, even while it is not sufficient on its own to lead to a competitive market.

In this section we string together cutting-edge work proposing various reforms to contract and disclosure laws that place initial responsibility on the *speakers* for ensuring that the contract, disclosure, or transaction is comprehensible to reasonable members of their target audience. (Since these reform proposals are preliminary and the First Amendment jurisprudence is still evolving, we do not undertake an analysis of the intersection between the two in this discussion).

Before examining possible reforms, however, we pause briefly to reiterate that the problems we have surveyed in this chapter occur only in the very worst consumer markets or quadrants. In consumer markets where there are only one or a few items of interest that are not complicated to understand or compare, and/ or where perverse incentives for sellers to exploit consumers' limited processing capacity are not present, disclosures sometimes succeed.[170] Mandated nutritional labels on salad dressings appear to provide this kind of success story. Before the legal disclosure requirement, consumers could not reliably distinguish between salad dressing products, despite considerable variation in fat content. After mandated disclosures, the more trustworthy and readily comparable information on fat content led to strong competitive dynamics among salad dressing manufacturers. In response, higher fat dressings fell significantly in market shares.[171] Somewhat similarly, Fung et al. recount the success of mandated disclosures of rollover rates for vehicles required by the National Highway Traffic Safety Administration (NHTSA).[172] Once rollover rates between competitor vehicles could be compared, the pressure (in tort law as well as the reinforcing market) to produce vehicles with good records became much stronger. Car manufacturers understood that these easily accessible records could be used against them in litigation if a vehicle design compared unfavorably to its competitors.

Yet, as is also clear from the prior discussion, these success stories are not necessarily the norm. In other market settings, merely prescribing scripts on specific product qualities without changing the underlying incentives of speakers for mis-representing information does not correct problems of consumer confusion. This is particularly true when Rule-Benders are highly motivated to exploit consumers' limitations. As Willis observes in the debt collection area, "Requiring certain words to appear in debt collectors' letters to consumers is a very long way from achieving consumer comprehension of their debt collection rights."[73]

One important step to correct these persistent problems in the market is for the law to reverse speaker incentives powerfully and directly.[74] In consumer markets[75] this revised legal approach would require the speaker to take full responsibility for at least what a median audience member participating in a transaction would understand.[76] The reform places the burden on sellers for establishing that their transactions are reasonably comprehensible to average consumers and, when they are not, places the costs of the confusion back on the sellers.

Lauren Willis proposes a regulatory requirement – what she calls a "comprehension rule" – to serve exactly this function. Under Willis's comprehension rule, a firm must show a significant portion of its target customers can "pass a customer confusion audit."[77] If a producer's advertisement or contract is structured to showcase the good news and hide the bad in ways that reasonable purchasers might misunderstand, the comprehension rule will assign the resulting costs of misunderstanding on the speaker in the form of penalties.[78] A subset of FDA usage and dosing regulations, as well as forthcoming regulations in the European Union governing front-of-package nutrition claims, adopt an analogous type of performance-based standard.[79] Compliance with mandated disclosures thus requires a showing of an acceptable level of empirically demonstrated consumer comprehension.

This "performance-based" approach to disclosures replaces the prescriptive disclosure approach by instituting strong incentives for cooperative communication, rather than incentives for gaming the system at the consumers' expense.[80] Indeed, a vital feature of Willis's comprehension rule is the requirement that the speaker demonstrate comprehension levels of actual customers, thus reflecting not what firms disclose, but what real customers understand or what the firms successfully convey.[81] We cannot do justice to all of the nuances of Willis's thoughtful proposal in this short summary, but a few quick examples offer at least some flavor of how this comprehension rule would work in practice. Subject to oversight by the regulator, firms would be required to conduct a "customer confusion audit" of specific types of transactions to ensure that the firms' own customers are reasonably comprehending the most significant costs and benefits of the transaction.

- For example, to ensure consumers know when they will be charged overdraft fees and the amount of those fees, a consumer confusion audit would proceed as follows: "'Third parties [paid by a regulated bank] could test a bank's customers with questions such as 'Which, if any, of the following recent transactions overdrew your account?' followed by a list of recent transactions and their dates. If the customer indicated knowledge of a transaction that overdrew the account, the follow-up question could be 'How many dollars did your bank charge you in fees as a result of overdrawing your account on that date?'"[182]

- Various add-on products (e.g., credit life insurance) are sometimes wrapped into transactions in ways that do not alert consumers of their existence, much less inform them they have the option to decline these added expenses or accurately convey the limited benefit these products actually provide. A consumer confusion audit would elucidate whether consumers actually do understand their options in specific cases. In anticipation of this audit, firms would "draw their customers' attention to these add-on products at the time the transaction takes place and ... educate their customers about limits on the benefits add-ons provide. Alternatively, firms could redesign add-on products to conform to their customers' expectations."[183]

Willis's comprehension rule would be overseen by regulators, but a similar type of incentives-focused approach has also been proposed in the area of consumer contracts and would be enforced by courts in private litigation.[184] Ayres and Schwarz, for example, suggest that the validity of key features of consumer contracts should be conditioned on a form of ex ante "term substantiation" by the contract drafter. This substantiation would typically demand empirical evidence that the information is comprehensible to the median customer.[185] "[T]erms that [the target] consumers incorrectly believe are more favorable to them than they actually are" would become unenforceable.[186] Contract drafters could avoid this result primarily by employing rigorous survey methods in advance of the transaction to uncover "whether the median consumer has accurate beliefs about her contract rights and duties."[187] In this way, Ayres and Schwartz transform the consumer's *duty to read* into a seller's *"duty to learn."*[188] (Note: Consumers might still suffer from myopia or other biases in agreeing to a contract; the focus is only on an accurate consumer understanding of the terms of the contract in a given transactional setting.)

Ben-Shahar and Strahilevitz offer an alternative contract reform that similarly seeks to realign the speakers' incentives for cooperative communication with their audiences. Under the terms of their proposal, a court presiding over a challenge to a consumer contract would commission a survey that polls a large number of disinterested respondents on their interpretation of the contract.[189] The end result assesses the fairness of the contract by aligning its legal interpretation with "the meaning that the parties to the transaction assign to the text."[190] Speakers ideally will begin to anticipate this empirical test and devise transactions that are more understandable to avoid litigation losses. (Note, however, that this proposal appears to separate the contract from the sales pitch and other real-world features of the transaction, which may limit its effectiveness.)

Although both the Ayres and Schwartz and Ben-Shahar and Strahilevitz proposals assess incomprehensibility in consumer contracts at different points in time and with slightly different details, both proposals attempt to counteract the perverse incentives of the speakers to exploit consumers' limited processing abilities.[191] As Ayres and Schwartz suggest, without this type of counter-pressure, "firms have an incentive to, and likely do, degrade contract content" for optimistic consumers.[192] Their proposals thus complement Willis's "performance-based" "comprehension rule" that analyzes the consumer transaction or contract with respect to whether actual customers did understand it.[193] "Demonstrating sufficient consumer comprehension could be a precondition firms must meet before enforcing a term or sharing a fee, or firms could be sanctioned (or rewarded) for low (or high) demonstrated comprehension levels."[194]

Thumbnail Sketch of Consumer Law Reform

1   Institute a type of "comprehension rule" that places the burden on the seller/actor to establish that the disclosure or contract is reasonably comprehensible to the target audience.
2   Comprehensibility is assessed empirically using the target audience in realistic settings.
3   Deploy both public and private enforcement and encourage or subsidize market intermediaries to assist.

To be truly effective in altering speaker incentives, however, the comprehension requirement must be enforced rigorously by regulators and private parties and it must capture the entire consumer transaction, including the marketing. In regulation, a confusion audit could be deployed in some settings as a condition of entry into the market. After the fact, contract law provides a natural tool for private enforcement, and with a lighter burden that effectively creates a presumption against the speaker, this private enforcement will likely be more vigorous.

Still, in some market sectors it seems likely that plaintiffs bringing the cases will be few in number and the ultimate sanctions may not be high enough to create a deterrent to reverse perverse speaker incentives for incomprehensibility. Public enforcement will thus serve a critical supplement to encourage more cooperative communication in consumer transactions.

Public enforcement, like private enforcement, must focus on ways to incentivize sellers to be comprehensible in their transactions.[195] The FTC already utilizes, at least in part, an audience-based comprehensibility test to evaluate deceptive advertising on privacy.[196] But in some cases, the FTC apparently refers to industry-best practices or similar proxies to assess this audience-based perspective in determining whether transactions are "unfair" or "deceptive."[197] Ultimately, empirically based tests of the target audiences may be necessary to determine whether a speaker's communication is accessible and clear in a given market setting.

The CFPB has the authority to provide an even stronger public enforcement presence in policing consumer practices that are "unfair, deceptive, or abusive."[198] As Willis discusses, the CFPB is thus particularly well positioned to craft and enforce a comprehension rule grounded in empirical testing. The CFPB could use this comprehension rule to locate and sanction violations of the federal standards.[199] Perhaps the CFPB could even focus public enforcement initiatives on areas of consumer contract where private enforcement is particularly limited (e.g., by arbitration clauses).

Ideally, market intermediaries could be subsidized or otherwise created to place still more pressure on firms to ensure their communications are comprehensible to target audiences. Intermediaries who are directly affected include insurance companies and certain investors; these groups are impacted by an incomprehensible transaction because they might be forced to pay for some of the downstream harm that results from miscommunications.[200] Other intermediaries include those whose primary purpose is to enhance consumer protection, such as consumer watchdog groups and businesses that provide niche translation services to select consumers.[201]

The literature offers a range of interesting proposals for supplementing the work of these intermediaries to discourage speaker incomprehensibility.[202] Radin offers an ingenious proposal to develop computer program intermediaries that can interpret and summarize contracts and identify problematic clauses quickly for consumers.[203] Ethan Leib and Zev Eigen propose an "independent academic process" that would serve as an intermediary to provide an "interpretation of the key surprising or potentially 'unfair' terms of the contract" during the sign-up process.[204] However, because intermediaries may be corrupted and often lack adequate resources, their role in addressing these issues is likely limited in most consumer protection settings.

Before closing, we remind readers once again that our primary focus in these reforms is on realigning speakers' incentives with cooperative communication. For these proposals to ultimately become operational, however, a number of important details still need to be worked out. These details include how to: calibrate the comprehension rule so that important subsets of consumers are not ignored; identify the most significant issues in a transaction that must be comprehended; empirically assess audience comprehension; and specify remedies that motivate speakers to be comprehensible.

Because of this focus, we also pass over more prescriptive, albeit promising, reform proposals. Radin, for example, suggests that clauses for mandatory arbitration and exculpatory agreements should be prohibited in consumer contracts as a matter of course.[205] Bar-Gill emphasizes the need for summary information to provide consumers with a reliable way to compare actors on the market.[206] Ultimately, these additional requirements may prove necessary as well. But given the regressive state of the law as it currently stands, our first round of reform is aimed solely at encouraging sellers to engage in comprehensible transactions with their target audiences.

Ultimately, and however it is accomplished, we join the chorus of other scholars who conclude that there is more to be lost than gained from experimentation with legal reform of contract and consumer protection laws. As Willis notes, only after we make efforts to improve consumer comprehension that can we know "when and where informed consumer decisionmaking is worth its price."[207]

5A

Comprehension Asymmetries in Financial Regulation

A few years after the global financial crisis of 2007, JP Morgan experienced an unexpected, multi-billion-dollar trading loss. When JP Morgan's CEO, Jamie Dimon, called in his internal analysts on April 30, 2012 to show him "everything!" he reported that – after seeing the details – he "couldn't breathe."[1] The analysts had not been intentionally withholding their unrealistically optimistic assumptions about risky ventures. But, in the complex models they provided, the underlying choices were effectively opaque to everyone but the analysts themselves.[2] And even the analysts had a difficult time processing all of the data in a coherent way.

Enron's financial collapse in 2001 is legendary not only because of the wide-ranging fiscal ramifications, but also because some of those closest to the action apparently didn't see it coming. The Powers Report, commissioned in Enron's aftermath, concluded that the Board of Directors of Enron "failed to understand the economic rationale, the consequences, and the risks of their company's ... deals – and the directors sat in meetings where those deals were discussed in detail."[3] In *Conspiracy of Fools*, the investigative journalist Kurt Eichenwald "convincingly argues that ... Enron's chief financial officer didn't understand the full economic implications of the deals, either, and he was the one who put them together."[4]

Our previous analysis has emphasized the need for speakers to have incentives to communicate information clearly with their audience. As these examples illustrate, however, speakers must also have the inclination and wherewithal to first extract the key risks and other relevant facts regarding their own situation. JP Morgan and Enron did not communicate the risks they were facing in part because they did not have a sufficient understanding of the risks themselves.

In settings in which speakers are best positioned to understand the facts, a successful legal approach therefore includes strong incentives for the speaker not only to communicate the facts effectively but to understand the underlying reality itself. Such an understanding is particularly vital in complex markets where the audience is unlikely to be able to gain this information on its own.

The imperative that regulatory actors (or speakers) actually *understand* the risks of their activity, then, adds a critical step to our conceptual model that was only implicit before. Legal requirements are insufficient when they focus only on ensuring that information is shared (like the rote transfer of files and paper from regulated parties to other actors), without ensuring that this information is first digested or understood. Instead, regulatory programs that depend on speakers for an accurate portrayal of the potentially adverse impacts of their activities must also place strong incentives on those speakers to understand the risks themselves. Regulatory requirements must ensure *comprehension* as well as *comprehensiveness*.

So, do our regulatory programs work as intended, providing speakers with incentives both to understand and communicate these risks rigorously and clearly? In this and the two chapters that follow, we explore this question, beginning with financial regulation and then moving to two other criticized regulatory programs – patents and chemical regulation. Our legal coordinates in these three interrelated chapters shift from the consumer market to technical regulatory programs. Accordingly, the target audience shifts from lay consumers to experts, such as government regulators and sophisticated market actors.

Despite the fact that the audiences in these three chapters are generally quite knowledgeable and expert (we bracket less sophisticated audiences to simplify the analysis), our speakers (the regulated parties) nonetheless can still enjoy significant comprehension advantages over their expert audience.

This first chapter in the trio explores how well our legal design overcomes deep-seated comprehension asymmetries in pockets of financial regulation. Specifically, we zero in on one single feature of financial regulation – the disclosure requirements that are imposed on financial actors. Since mandated disclosures are intended to enhance expert audiences' understanding of the risks of financial arrangements, identifying limitations in the ability of disclosures to deliver on this goal is an important step in ensuring the rigor of the larger financial regulatory system.

Our study of comprehension asymmetries in financial disclosure regulation unfolds in three parts. In the first part, we lay out the basics of financial regulation and situate the Security Exchange Commission's (SEC's) disclosures within that system. We also identify the background incentives of our audiences and speakers to be comprehensible. The chapter then turns to an examination of whether and how well legally mandated disclosure requirements provide added, legally directed incentives for speakers to assess and understand the risks of their activities and communicate those risks to expert audiences. The chapter closes with a preliminary sketch of reforms that may help to rectify deficiencies in the design of disclosures. And, while the abbreviated analysis here cannot begin to do justice to the many nuances of this complicated area, the financial regulatory literature is sufficiently accessible to allow non-specialists like us to translate the major findings as they pertain to comprehension asymmetries.

The first step in exploring how the law impacts the incentives of financial actors is to understand the basics of the regulatory program itself. We begin with a general overview of the history and use of regulatory disclosures in complex capital markets. We then consider the primary background incentives of our lead players – regulated financial actors (the speakers) and regulators and other sophisticated market participants (the audience). We ask whether these players are poised to process complicated information regarding financial risks or instead whether perverse incentives and comprehension asymmetries impair effective communication in some settings.

After this orientation, we explore how the law does (or doesn't) ensure that financial actors both understand and communicate the risks of their activities.

A *Financial Regulation and the Role of Disclosures*

The US regulation of capital markets, ushered in by the Securities Act of 1933, is premised on two simple but related beliefs: 1) that corporations and investors operating in an open market are in a superior position to distinguish good investments from bad,[5] and 2) that markets work best when they operate with minimal interference from regulators. However, because Congress also acknowledged that "[m]arket forces alone are insufficient to cause all material information (in a transaction) to be disclosed,"[6] laws were put in place to ensure that the information disseminated by sellers is complete and robust. These laws created the very early version of the regulatory disclosures that predominate in financial regulation today.

The core purpose of mandating disclosures is to require regulated firms to identify the most significant sources of risk associated with their transactions so that investors and others can act accordingly. Disclosure requirements, by their nature, are thus *not* intended to proscribe "good" financial practices or penalize "bad" ones. Instead, disclosure requirements simply ensure that everyone participating in complex capital markets has access to the needed, critical information to operate on a level playing field. Once access to key information is provided, so it is assumed, markets will function efficiently and the government's job is done.[7]

Disclosures are not the only form of regulatory controls within the larger multi-faceted financial regulatory system, however. Commercial banks are subjected to significant restrictions and requirements that constrain their operations. Investment banks and hybrids are also subjected to various forms of supplemental regulatory oversight.[8] And, on the flip side, not all firms are required to provide disclosures, even though these gaps in coverage may create problems in ensuring a well-informed market.[9] In our focus exclusively on existing regulatory disclosure requirements, then, we do not mean to imply that these other features are not also important to a holistic understanding of financial regulation. We focus on disclosures in part to keep the analysis simpler and in part because even though disclosures are only one component of financial regulation, they are an important component that sheds light on comprehension asymmetries.

Since their creation, mandated financial disclosures have served as a cornerstone in financial regulation. Even during deregulatory activity in the 1990s, disclosure requirements were kept intact for most regulated parties because they were perceived as necessary supplements to a well-functioning capital market.[10] Not surprisingly, in the aftermath of the panic following Enron and again after the financial collapse of 2007, mandated disclosure requirements were reinforced and continued as the dominant form of government oversight for most of the financial industry.[11] Today, "companies are required to disclose more information than ever, and the Securities and Exchange Commission (SEC) continues to adopt new disclosure requirements."[12]

To ensure this disclosed information is as accurate as possible, disclosure requirements have been revised over the years to address various shortcomings. To stave off the ability of firms to paint too rosy a picture of their financial situation, disclosures now must be written specifically through management's eyes.[13] To counteract the jargon-filled, sometimes unintelligible text of technical disclosures, regulated parties are now also required to write them in "plain English."[14] Congress even requires visual representations of information in some cases (e.g., graphs, charts, and tables) to make the information accessible.[15]

In disclosures, regulated parties are required to document their financial operations and associated risks in numerous forms and other informational representations. The forms require explanations and accompanying data that must be submitted annually regarding the financial position of the firm, including: profits, losses, and liabilities; changes in equity and cash flow; significant events and transactions; and other information. These standardized analyses are designed not only to inform other market participants of the firms' financial status, but to allow for cross-comparisons with other firms.

Such a regulatory approach works extremely well when a regulated party has strong incentives to master and communicate key messages clearly. Motivated financial actors will rigorously assess the impact of their market activities and communicate this information, with various limitations and other empirical caveats, to market participants and regulators in ways that can be reasonably understood.

The regulatory program also works well in cases where the audience is well-equipped to understand and verify the regulated parties' self-assessments. Even if the speaker is not enthusiastic about clear communication or rigorous analyses, when the audience has the motivation, resources, and experience to sniff out gaps or even deception, the audience will learn of these risks and discipline the speaker through the market.

B *Speakers and Audiences*

But do the background incentives and capabilities of our major players lead to this type of cooperative communication in all complex capital markets? We take inventory of the major incentives of these speakers and audiences here to assess whether cooperative communication is always likely to happen on its own.

1 Speakers: The Regulated Entities

In the abstract, one might expect the speakers – large financial entities – to be highly motivated to understand their own financial prospects and to communicate their activities and risks to other market actors. After all, these firms benefit from an efficient and well-functioning market, right?

Well, in theory, yes. But it turns out that some financial entities may find it profitable to forgo a rigorous self-assessment. Among the most important reasons is simple economics: Rigorous self-analysis is both costly and difficult. Indeed, proper self-assessment can require a veritable army of expert staff. Beyond the direct costs of the staffing itself, coordinating an expert team entails considerable resources and manpower. Staff analysts can be so dispersed organizationally that it becomes difficult to synthesize their analyses into an overall risk assessment.[16] As a result, even when the CEO of a large firm is eager to understand relevant risks and problems, he or she may face a series of impediments in making sense of the staff assessments. These limitations in understanding by the CEO can be as basic as even knowing what types of issues to explore or which questions to ask.[17]

At the same time, particularly from the market perspective, there are not always rewards for regulated financial actors to engage in this sort of rigorous analysis. Instead, the net incentives may lead *against* thorough self-assessment. These incentives can include high payoffs, time delays, and bailouts.

> **High Payoff from Risky Deals.** Some gambles produce such high payoffs of "striking it rich" that financial actors are willing to proceed without a complete understanding of risks.[18] The managers who make risky deals, moreover, tend to be protected from legal claims that they failed to adequately monitor the risk. The underlying logic of this limited liability in corporate law is to free managers up to be entrepreneurial and innovative.[19] But even if managers are caught and sanctioned, the worst that could happen is that "he may, at most, lose his job and suffer reputational losses. On the other hand, a successful gamble could mean lifetime wealth."[20]
>
> **Time Delay.** Financial actors will also sometimes discount risks that materialize into the future because of the gap between the risk-taking behavior and the legal and financial consequences that might result. "[M]any of the material risk exposures on certain derivatives occur years after the execution of the transaction."[21] A number of intervening factors

can also enter the picture to blur the lines of causality and blame. Moreover, given the churning in financial industry employment, these risks may materialize long after the relevant CEOs, investors, and traders have collected their profits and moved on.[22]

Bailouts. For the largest financial institutions, the government may also step in to soften the blow when losses are large. As a result, moral hazard problems also exist for financial actors in identifying some catastrophic, low probability risks because of this possibility of a government bailout.[23]

As a result of these features, the background incentives for financial entities to carefully analyze and communicate the risks of their activities can sometimes be insufficient. A profit-seeking financial actor, when presented with a lucrative deal, may opt for high payoffs and dismiss the attending uncertainties or insufficiently processed risk information. Indeed, some financial institutions might even have strong incentives *not* to understand some risks associated with products and services. As Hu suggests, "Banks even have affirmative incentives to avoid investing in the development of such information. More complete information on the 'soft spots' may trigger stricter regulation."[24]

In general, then, we can imagine a set of circumstances in which the net cost–benefit analysis leads some financial actors away from investing resources in fully understanding or communicating hyper-complicated transactions. As history has shown, ignorance of long-term risks for the sake of short-term gains can sometimes be the strategy of choice for financial actors.

2 Audience: The Expert Regulators and Market Participants

The audience for our analysis here consists of regulators and other sophisticated market participants who receive and analyze the financial entities' disclosures. However, both sets of parties face limitations that can impair their ability to process complex financial information on their own.

Regulators' ability to rigorously process the complex information provided by financial entities is limited by several important factors. These include expertise, time and resources, and capture:

Expertise. Government agencies are at a disadvantage in recruiting top financial experts because "[g]overnmental pay scales cannot compete with Wall Street for talent."[25] Steven Schwarcz argues that this more than "two-to-one income disparity" between the experts of the financial industry and financial regulators leads to a "significant difference in employee intellect and abilities," which might even include the regulators' good judgment.[26]

Time and Resources. Regulators also face limits on the time and resources available to process relevant information communicated by financial institutions. Financial regulatory agencies appear to be underfinanced compared to their private counterparts,[27] with multiple responsibilities and fragmentation that limit and distract from their ability to process individual filings completely.[28]

Capture. Regulators' limitations are not completely resource-based. Some financial industry regulators may also be prone to traditional forms of regulatory capture (when regulators become unduly influenced by the industry they regulate), particularly with the lure of future, more lucrative employment.[29] Indeed, the risk of this type of capture may be greater in the financial sector than other regulatory fields because financial regulation tends to disproportionately attract individuals with materialistic interests.[30] The high pay scale of the private sector, coupled with the penchant of private firms to hire government insiders, makes the revolving door phenomenon potentially even more prevalent.[31] James Kwak has suggested that there may even be a type of "cultural capture" that arises from regulators' repeated intensive interactions with financial entities.[32] These non-material influences may reduce, in the aggregate, the skepticism regulators apply to financial actors' self-assessments as compared to assessments prepared by entities lacking these repeat interactions.

Investors and other market experts – the other primary audience considered here – do not share the regulators' difficulties in competing for talent. Nor do they necessarily lack resources to process information in the abstract. Their willingness to invest substantial resources in processing risk information may be limited, however, by a rational cost–benefit calculation. As Judge notes, "A potential investor will not expend greater resources collecting and processing information about a security than the excess returns that investor expects to receive from that investment."[33]

It is well-known that attempting to analyze the risks of a transaction can be quite expensive for even the most sophisticated market participants. To gain a reliable understanding of particularly complex transactions, market participants may need to invest considerable time and resources. For example, "[o]ne stock analyst took the unusual step of hiring a squad of bankers, accountants, and foreign-currency analysts to help him analyze the currency activities of Dell Computer."[34] The step was unusual precisely because the analyst believed the high costs of the investigation were justified by the benefits of doing such a thorough assessment. Schwarcz similarly observes, "An understanding of the levels of complexity [associated with financial actors' transactions] sometimes challenges experts at even the most sophisticated financial firms."[35] "Investors find that the disclosures as to the complex risks financial services firms are exposed to are, in the words of KPMG, 'very hard' to evaluate."[36]

Market actors may also be hampered by many of the same self-interested incentives that affect financial entities. Both the opportunity for high payoffs in the short-term and the extended time frame for sanctions over the long-term reduce investors' incentives to gain a rigorous understanding of all of the technical nuances of a transaction, including its long-term stability.

In sum, and in terms of our model, the audience consists of *both* regulators and expert financial participants, but both are often at a disadvantage in processing information relative to the speaker-financial actor. Even when speakers and market participants are on a level playing field in terms of expertise and motivation, however, if the speaker does not invest the effort to make sense of his own risks, the audience faces an uphill task compensating for this deficiency. As long as the privileged speaker remains willfully ignorant about assessing the risks of his activities, all parties to the communication may also be deprived of this critical information because they are even less equipped to make the investment. These asymmetries will not always occur, but their occurrence is likely enough that in financial markets we can expect some comprehension asymmetries to significantly impede effective communication.

II DOES THE REGULATORY SYSTEM COUNTERACT COMPREHENSION ASYMMETRIES?

Given this backdrop, the primary objective for regulatory disclosures is clear. If financial entities are sometimes disinclined to make sense of and clearly communicate the risks of their activity, it is vital that the design of regulatory requirements – like disclosures – change these incentives. Without this intervention, the financial market will continue to operate, to some extent, in the dark.

So how does our regulatory program fare right now when it comes to forcing this comprehensibility in financial disclosures? Not as well as it could.

As we explain subsequently, one of the reasons – and this is just one of many reasons – is that the important step of requiring regulated parties to make sense of their financial risks and explain those facts and figures to even the most sophisticated audiences has been inadequate.

The existing, prescriptive disclosures in financial regulation (following much of the same patterns emerging in consumer markets discussed in the last chapter) fall short of changing speaker incentives. What is worse, the disclosure requirements can inadvertently exacerbate the incomprehensibility problems as a result of the emphasis on *complete* information without corresponding attention to the *comprehensibility* of information.

We begin our analysis by exploring how the existing disclosure requirements fall short of encouraging Rule-Followers, who are well-meaning, legally compliant actors, to rigorously assess and communicate the risks of their financial structures and transactions. The analysis is then followed by an examination of how these same legal requirements might be exploited by the more strategic Rule-Benders who game the system in order to advance their own self-interest.

A *Rule-Followers*

Rule-Followers are inclined to understand and communicate the risks of their activities to expert audiences, but if legal and market pressures serve on balance to discourage this kind of investment, Rule-Followers will forgo self-assessments and/or clear communications. There are several ways that financial regulatory requirements may cause Rule-Followers to skimp on providing comprehensible self-assessments of their financial risks to expert audiences.

1 "More Information Is Better"

Like a lighthouse beacon, the law in financial regulation sends out a clear, unambiguous signal to Rule-Followers: Disclose everything of possible relevance, even if it seems like too much. "Securities regulation is motivated, in large part, by the assumption that more information is better than less."[37] Withholding potentially relevant information is a practice subject to multiple legal and market correctives; by contrast, providing the audience with excessive information quells concerns about a financial actor's compliance with regulatory requirements. These correctives include:

Avoidance of Fraud Claims. Fraud in the law encompasses not only blatantly false statements, but also statements that mislead investors with partial information. Consequently, providing excessive information can help ward off fraud claims. During his time at the SEC, former Commissioner Paredes observed, "Anecdotally, lawyers have suggested to me that companies often disclose information not to better inform investors, but to reduce the risk of liability for omitting a material fact or disclosing a 'half truth.'"[38] This has led to a "shift": Financial actors no longer ask, "Why disclose?" but rather: "Why not disclose?"[39]

Compliance with Legal Requirements. Sharing more information than is necessary – including literally too much information – also helps insulate financial actors from being charged with violations of regulatory disclosure requirements. A firm that leaves one item of information out of its disclosure could theoretically be sued for noncompliance with the law. Moreover, as we shall see, the risk of inadvertently revealing unflattering information is counterbalanced by the possibility that no one will have the time or energy to put the pieces together.

Market Positioning. In complex markets, excessive transparency sometimes helps serve as a crude proxy for a firm's trustworthiness and stability. Buyers may be comforted by the fact that abundant information is available, even if that information is difficult to comprehend as a practical matter. Volunteering additional information thus helps signal that a company is operating on the up-and-up. "[T]he market is much quicker to punish a company if questions are raised about the company's transparency and whether it has something to hide."[40]

A particularly good example of this incentive is provided by General Electric's effort to "ride the transparency wave." After enduring criticism for its secretive policies, the CEO and chairman, Jeffrey Immelt, adopted a new approach of voluntarily disclosing dozens of new business segments within GE. He even made a public announcement about this approach. "I want people to think about GE as we think of GE – as a transparent company. If the annual report or quarterly report has to be the size of the New York City phone book, that's life."[41]

This strategy is hardly a panacea; some investors will be put off by too much unprocessed information.[42] Overall, however, when in doubt, regulatory and market incentives tend to work together to encourage firms to share, rather than withhold potentially relevant information, even when it is unprocessed and ultimately may create more noise and distraction than assistance to the audience.

Disclosures Can Be Huge. At the same time that legal pressures tend to orient Rule-Followers to a default rule that "more is better," we see that the resulting disclosures can sometimes be quite large. Hu offers a few snapshots of the girth of individual disclosures, each of which lack "obesity limits":[43]

> The Form 10-K for 2012 for the Bank of America Corporation is 288 pages; Citigroup Inc.'s, 299 pages; The Goldman Sachs Group, Inc.'s, 246 pages; and JP Morgan Chase & Co.'s, 352 pages – not counting exhibits and information incorporated by reference from proxy statements. The English-language 2012 annual report of Credit Suisse Group AG is 400 pages, excluding the Appendix. This, despite the liberal use of microscopic font.[44]

Large disclosures can also be dense – brimming over with technical details that may sometimes distract and burden attentive audiences. Selecting from 2 of the 50-plus requirements in "Regulation S-K," Paredes summarizes some of the information required in these disclosures. "Item 303" (known as the Management's Discussion and Analysis of Financial Condition and Results of Operations or MD&A), for example, requires companies to report "liquidity capital resources, results of operations, and any other information the registrant believes is necessary to understand its financial condition and results of its operations over the previous three years."[45] Item 402 requires detailed disclosures regarding executive compensation, including non-cash rewards and deferred income. Companies must also disclose their general compensation policies, adding still more pages of complex and intricate data that the audience may (or may not) need.[46] And again, that is only two of the 50 requirements.

And, although size alone does not make disclosures incomprehensible, excessive length does contribute to the audiences' processing costs. Size thus provides a partial indication of the energies an expert audience must dedicate to make sense of a disclosure.

2 Disclosed Information Need Not Always Be Comprehensible

At the same time that Rule-Followers are encouraged to err on the side of sharing too much information, there are very few enforceable legal requirements that this information also be comprehensible. Instead, regulated parties are required to share details and technical models without necessarily mastering this information for themselves, much less making that mastery accessible to other regulators and investors.

Rather than placing the burden squarely on the speakers to make sense of and communicate their financial situation and risks, then, the law often allows this processing effort to fall on the audience's shoulders. As Paredes notes, for all the prescriptive itemization of information and formats for disclosures, "[r]elatively little attention is paid to how the information used – namely how investors and securities market professional search and process information and make decisions." Yet "if users do not process [the resulting, mandated] information effectively, it is not clear what good mandating disclosures does."[47]

Targeted studies in fact find that these financial disclosures regularly fail to present relevant information in "an easily accessible or usable way."[48] The Chartered Financial Analyst (CFA) Institution, for example, identified certain qualitative financial disclosures as "uninformative" and had low confidence in their reliability.[49]

Expert audience members – investors and traders in particular – concede they are sometimes unable to make sense of disclosures. The hedge fund investor Paul Singer complains that "even with 110 investment professionals, he 'cannot ... understand the financial condition of any bank [or other] major financial institution' and that '[investment professionals] have no idea what that derivatives section means.'"[50] Dwight Churchill, a vice president at Fidelity Investments, conceded at a round table five years before the financial crash that the structure of the law requires "analysts to sift through a huge amount of information." The mandated disclosures, like the MD&A, which is a section of the SEC's 10-K form, don't "help them a whole lot, and so they end up having to sort back through to figure out exactly what's going on. It's putting too much of a burden on them. And, given the economics and the number of companies these different analysts are following, it's very difficult for them to draw the correct picture of an organization."[51]

The usability of disclosures is not wholly ignored in regulatory design, however; over the last 20 years a number of improvements have been made. In 1998, SEC promulgated a rule requiring "plain English" for prospectus filings and other communications with shareholders in the hopes of making disclosures more usable. One study reports that in the wake of this requirement, firms did improve on SEC's plain English measures, such as using a shorter "average sentence length, average word length, [and less] passive voice, legalese, personal pronouns, and negative/superfluous phrases." Whether the disclosures themselves were "more effective or more accessible" in communicating key information was outside the scope (and measures) of the study, however.[52]

The Dodd Frank Act of 2010 also makes a number of added efforts to discourage incomprehensible disclosures. For example, Section 919 requires that disclosures to retail investors contain "clear and concise information" about the financial status of the firm. Another requirement on credit ratings directs the Commission to ensure that the disclosures "are clear and informative for investors having a wide range of sophistication who use or might use credit ratings."[53] Proxies to solicit shareholder approval of golden parachutes, as one example, must be placed in a "clear and simple" form.[54] And other sections (including some discussed in Chapter 4), contain multiple mandates to ensure that disclosures to consumers are particularly "clear," "conspicuous," and "comprehensible," and even "prominent" in a variety of different financial transactions.[55]

Each of these additional requirements for disclosures move in the right direction, but they stop short of targeting the speaker's incentives directly. Compliant firms can go through the motions and assemble the requisite information, but they can sometimes do this without ensuring that they understand the disclosed information themselves. As Steven Schwarcz observes, disasters like "Enron prove[] . . . that in an age of increasing financial complexity the 'disclosure paradigm' – the idea that the more a company tells us about its business, the better off we are – has become an anachronism."[56]

3 Disclosures Can Sometimes Raise Processing Costs for Both Speakers and Audiences

By prescribing a rigid (and incomplete) format for the disclosures, rather than encouraging cooperative communication, legal requirements may even get in the way of facilitating audience understanding in some settings. There are at least three features of the current disclosure requirements that could sometimes have this unintended effect.

Translating market and contract complexities into disclosures involves multiple steps, each of which can actually impede understanding and introduce errors.[57] Financial institutions regularly translate financial contracts into mathematical models and then use these models to draft written prospectuses. However, some steps in this translation process not only increase the likelihood of errors, but increase the complexity of the information that is reported.[58]

Disclosures impose still another translation step on top of this already precarious operation. Even the most well-meaning and compliant firm will encounter sometimes insuperable obstacles in capturing their complex legal and quantitative arrangements in plain English disclosures. Hu observes, for example, that "[d]rafting the disclosure in plain English increases the possibility of inconsistency" between the complex, underlying transaction and how that transaction is described in the disclosure.[59] An American Bar Association committee similarly takes note of the fact that the complex transactions "described in the disclosure documents have occasionally differed from, and conflicted with, [these same transactions set forth] in contractual documents."[60]

To make matters worse, the legal formats required for some disclosures, in and of themselves, can compound confusion and "make it difficult, if not impossible, for the investor to actually map" the simplified descriptions in the disclosure against reality.[61] Indeed, in the course of complying with the numerous items on the disclosure checklists, Rule-Followers may even become distracted and divert resources to compliance, rather than mastering what this information actually means to their own financial stability. As a result, misunderstandings and errors about the underlying realities can become further amplified.

And yet, if the financial institution stops short of comprehending and/or communicating the critical information clearly, it is the investors and regulators who bear the costs of processing this information.[62] As long as the letter of their legal obligations has been satisfied, regulated parties need not invest in lightening the processing burdens that their disclosures might create for the marketplace unless it is in their market interest to do so.

Disclosures are malleable in ways that can increase the processing costs of the target audience. Exacerbating these challenges in translation are numerous opportunities for quasi-invisible discretionary judgments to be incorporated into the financial institutions' disclosure of information. Some disclosure requirements entrust reporting parties with the power to determine how best to fulfill their particular legal obligations in describing their operations. Yet, the expert audience can receive a disclosure without knowing what role (if any) the financial organization's discretion played in key parts of the underlying analyses.

Hu in fact identifies the legal tolerance of "soft information" in some disclosure requirements as a significant source of "disclosure malleability." This soft information, which consists of "opinions, predictions, analyses, and other more subjective evaluations," is "heavily driven by managerial judgments and more resistant to objective verification."[63] Assessing the reliability of this information is costly for the audiences and, in some instances, may not be possible.[64]

Hu also identifies considerable sources of disclosure malleability in other areas of the financial system. One particularly good example comes from the discretion tolerated by the SEC's Value-at-Risk methods in their "Market Risk Rule."[65] As currently structured, this rule gives regulated parties considerable latitude in the design of models, including discretion in specifying assumptions and developing algorithms. Regulated parties are even allowed to select the confidence intervals and time horizons they use for reporting, for example. Moreover, regulated parties are not required to present important information like projections of losses during economic turmoil or worst-case projections. At the same time, there are no mechanisms to require an evaluation of a model's reliability, including information on how the model has historically performed.[66] (Note that national and international standards for regulating banks are more stringent, and, for banks, many of these sources of discretion are not allowed.[67]) In other words, while financial organizations *are* required to provide certain information under rules like "Market Risk," they're also given potential control over *how* or *whether* that information will be interpreted or understood.

SEC disclosures attempt to counteract some of this discretion by at least explicitly requiring not only that the disclosures be understandable, but conveyed through the eyes of management.[68] Yet with respect to a rigorous self-assessment, this added specification still neglects the underlying possibility that management itself may be disinclined to master their own financial condition. Offering detailed financial information on a financial entity through its "management's eyes" thus simply transfers the out-of-focus picture to others.

Disclosure requirements can sometimes become outdated, which can also lead to increased processing costs for the audience. Given the speed with which financial markets change, it is extremely difficult to prescribe disclosure formats that ensure all relevant financial information will be included. Indeed, prescriptive disclosures in complex and dynamic settings are difficult, if not impossible, to design before the fact. In effect, then, regulatory disclosure requirements can become at least partly obsolete quickly due to the fast-moving pace of financial markets.

B *Rule-Benders*

Rule-Benders will deliberatively exploit these same structural flaws in disclosure requirements to advance their own self-interest. Several techniques for this Rule-Bending behavior emerge from the literature.

The most straightforward strategy for thwarting communication with expert audiences is willful ignorance. Rule-Benders will be not only careless, but will intentionally avoid analyzing the risks of their activities when they perceive that learning more might yield bad news.[69] Rather than simply following the path of least resistance and cutting corners on self-assessments, then, Rule-Benders strategically avoid rigorous self-analyses. From their standpoint, ignorance is bliss, or at least better than a costly self-assessment.

More aggressive Rule-Benders do not stop at deliberate ignorance but will actively increase the complexity of their operations in order to insulate themselves from accountability. Rule-Benders can do this in several ways. First, firms can deliberately complicate their disclosures and public statements. By shifting additional processing costs to the audience, they can overwhelm the audience in ways that lead to incomplete communications and misunderstandings. Enron apparently adopted this tactic (among others). Jonathon Macey observes that

> Enron was vanishingly close ... to having complied with the accounting rules [governing disclosures] ... The truth wasn't hidden. But you'd have to look at their financial statements, and you would have to say to yourself, What's that about? It's almost as if they were saying, "We're doing some really sleazy stuff in footnote 42, and if you want to know more about it ask us." And that's the thing. Nobody did.[70]

Second, Rule-Benders can deliberately complexify the transactions themselves. Kapoor argues that "Wall Street has a very strong incentive to make things as complex as possible. Complexity is used as a tool to fool regulators and to avoid tax. You set up new subsidiaries, you make new products that haven't been addressed by regulations. Regulators are very hard-pressed to get any information."[71] Judge similarly traces how firms create new "nodes" or "financial innovations" outside of heavily regulated areas to accomplish the same "complex arrangement" end without triggering the same securitization oversight. She writes that "efforts to reduce the cost of regulatory compliance . . . are among the key drivers of financial innovation."[72]

When these complexifying tactics are deployed, it is up to expert audiences to learn about and analyze the risks of new innovative financial structures.[73] But because of the high processing costs needed to do this work, the audience may be unable to make sense of them and some of the new structures may even fall outside the jurisdictional reach of the regulatory programs. Hu details a number of the ways that sophisticated market audiences have been stymied by these complicated operations, observing that "the growing complexity of transaction structures has 'seemingly outpaced discipline in drafting.'"[74] On the regulatory side, Robert Weber observes that "[t]o the extent regulators rely on industry itself to provide the information they require . . . they risk complexity capture,"[75] where complex structures and nomenclature can be used to keep regulators at arm's length.

The resulting financial transactions may be so complex that even those creating them do not understand the risks. Judge describes, for example, how innovation in mortgage securitization "provided transaction sponsors with an almost endless array of spigots they could use in constructing the waterfall which determines when cash from the underlying home loans is paid out to each of the tranches of securities issued."[76] Once these new arrangements were set up, they could not be simplified. "As a result, a home loan, which started as a bilateral arrangement between two parties, becomes embedded in a complex web of arrangements that may grant tens or even hundreds of investors an economic stake in that loan."[77] Judge further observes that "each investor has only a very small stake in the performance of any particular loan underlying its investment and the investor would face a massive informational burden if it actually sought to understand all of the loans underlying its investment."[78]

Hendrik Hakenes and Isabel Schnabel have even developed a mathematical model to explain how large banks can ward off less sophisticated regulators by developing especially complex arrangements and arguments – a practice akin to "capture by sophistication." According to their model, "[i]f reputational concerns [or presumably resource limitations] prevent the type-L regulator from admitting that he does not understand the argument, he will [protect his reputation by simply] rubber-stamp[ing] even weak banks."[79] Hakenes and Schnabel apply the model to a diverse number of regulatory settings, such as the development of risk-based models to be used by regulators in bank capital regulation.[80] As the authors note, their model introduces the potential importance of asymmetries in sophistication into the literature and shows the ways those asymmetries can be exploited by regulated parties who add "complexity into games of persuasion."[81]

As a practical matter, the public ramifications of these Rule-Bending strategies could be significant. Some analysts hypothesize that the collapse of the financial market in 2007 may have been partly due to strategic and even intentional efforts by Rule-Bending financial actors to exploit complexity as a way of evading regulatory sight lines. For example, financial actors took the liberty of classifying unconventional instruments, such as credit default swaps, as "stock" rather than "insurance contracts," which reduces the extent and nature of their regulatory obligations.[82] Judge notes how, by making it more costly for banks and regulated financial institutions to extend and hold loans, regulations inadvertently "increase[d] the potential economic gains from financial innovations that enable financing activities traditionally performed by banks to move into markets or other less regulated domains."[83] Complex transactions reduce regulatory controls while making the stability of the financial landscape more precarious.

Box 5.1 Comprehension Asymmetries in Financial Regulation

The Rule-Follower

Why is it legally prudent to shift processing costs to regulators and other experts?

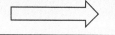

- More information is better to avoid charges of fraud and noncompliance with disclosure requirements.
- Disclosures require multi-step translations, but each step can introduce complications and errors.

AND

Disclosed information need not communicate the information in a meaningful way (beyond plain English requirements).

The Rule-Bender

How can the audience's processing costs be increased still further without violating the law?

- Adopt willful ignorance about financial risks.
- Obfuscate disclosures.
- Complexify transactions.

C *Summary*

Information asymmetries have rightly been an important focus of financial regulation, but this focus has come at the expense of equally vital attention to comprehension asymmetries. Robert Weber argues that, in financial markets marked by great complexity, this complexity, "along with widening information asymmetries between regulators and regulated firms, has removed regulators from their privileged perch as 'expert' superintendents as contemplated by the New Deal theorists."[84] In this setting, even sophisticated "[m]arket participants . . . cannot see for themselves all the pertinent aspects of the objective reality that the corporation relied on in generating" their disclosures.[85] In effect, because of gaps in regulatory design, in some settings no one – neither the financial institutions nor the organizations meant to regulate or invest in them – has a clear grasp of the risks of their activities.

III RECOMMENDATIONS FOR NEXT STEPS

In contrast to the more straightforward comprehension asymmetries that arise in the consumer market, the speakers in complex capital markets themselves sometimes lack sufficient incentives to understand the risks of their transactions. As a result, a reformed approach must encourage the speaker to understand its financial reality, as well as to communicate that understanding to audiences in a way they can reasonably process.

Three steps are suggested to accomplish this reformed approach. The first – and by far most difficult step – encourages the development of rigorous self-assessments by the speaker. The second step provides the audience with some assurance that these speaker assessments are in fact rigorous and reliable. The third and final step holds the speaker accountable for meeting these obligations, including communicating this information in a meaningful way to the target audience.

In these reforms, as noted earlier, our target audience consists of expert regulators and market intermediaries, like investors.[86] This expert audience is poised to invest a great deal of energy in processing information, but at base the communication must be such that the target audience, after investing in reasonable processing costs, can understand. As such the new proposals focus less on what the audience should know and more on motivating the speaker to process and then communicate key information to other experts.

A *Step One: Enhance Speaker Incentives to Understand Reality*

1 General Concept

Step one in a reformed approach creates strong net incentives for the speakers to understand the risks of their activities, as well as to communicate those risks to the expert audience. This step is by far the most challenging, but perhaps because of this, it has generated the greatest attention from top financial regulatory scholars. In the pages that follow, we draw in particular from Henry Hu's widely acclaimed work on financial regulatory reform.[87] Hu first carefully details the limitations of existing disclosures – what Hu calls "intermediary depictions" – to provide the target audience with all the information they need to make informed decisions. To produce these disclosures, the speaker-firm "stands between objective reality and the investor. The corporation observes and analyzes the objective reality, crafts a depiction of the pertinent aspects, and transmits its depiction to investors."[88] As a result, regulators and "[m]arket participants cannot ... see for themselves all of the pertinent aspects of the objective reality that the business entity relied on in generating the depiction. The business entity's depiction will have to suffice, apart from whatever information that market participants may have from other sources."[89]

The resulting disclosures thus sometimes and perhaps often fall short of providing the target audience with the information it needs to understand financial risks and structures. Hu argues that "the path forward [for reform instead] lies in an eclectic, comprehensive conception of 'information,'" and he develops a new conceptual framework for information to support this reform.[90] This new framework consists of not only these intermediary depictions, but two other vital types of information: "pure" information (such as raw data) and "moderately pure information" (which includes models of the pure data and other representations).[91] Hu shows how all three modes of information should be included as part of a firm's information portfolio to provide a more comprehensive understanding of financial risks.[92] See Figure 5.1.

The genius of Hu's reform thus lies in the ways that it would supplement existing mandated disclosures with additional types of information that should encourage more rigorous self-assessments through the use of new "depiction tools."[93] The speaker becomes more motivated to understand its risks because it must share more revealing, less subjective information with its expert audience. Expert audiences, which include not only regulators but investors, can use the additional information to check the speaker's disclosures. Moreover, none of the additional types of

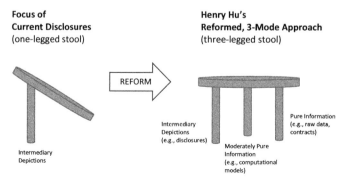

FIGURE 5.1 An Oversimplified Model of Hu's Conceptual Framework for Information

information replace the financial entities' own statements of their financial status. Instead, they add to and increase accountability for the existing information.[94] We thus believe that Hu's proposal should be required in place of the existing disclosure system.

While it may initially seem that multiple types of information as to an entity's financial status are much *less* comprehensible than a single disclosure, the added processing demands on the expert audience should be more than offset by the increased accuracy.[95] Importantly, in Hu's reformed approach, the needed ingredients for assessing risks are provided to the expert audience in a relatively standardized and easily digested way, thus allowing for more rigorous cross-comparisons among firms. Since the expert audience will have some capacity for synthesizing information, improvements in the rigor, analytical transparency, and standardization of information presentations make this expert synthesis job easier and less error-prone.[96]

2 Specifics

Because the reformed incentives on the speaker to understand reality must be strong and focused, the core requirements for these additional types of information need to be carefully specified.[97]

Under Hu's framework, "pure information," which includes such items as actual contracts and raw market data, would be added to the firms' information portfolio requirement.[98] Thanks in part to advances in computer- and web-related technologies, the corporation would transmit pertinent aspects of objective reality as "pure information" that could then be downloaded and analyzed by market participants. The resulting, accessible data thus allows highly engaged audiences to conduct their own analyses.[99] Turning over this key data in and of itself will not necessarily eliminate comprehension asymmetries – and as we have seen, in some settings it could make them worse. But this pure information is one important leg of the stool that complements information from other, very different sources.

Hu's conceptual framework also involves the inclusion of a third, new type of mandated information – "moderately pure information" – which is a hybrid between pure and the descriptive information contained in disclosures.[100] An example of such an approach offered by Hu involves a firm running its assets through computational models that have been designed by regulators to generate useful information about the firm.[101] All entities would use the same model(s), with underlying assumptions that are "fully observable" by market participants.[102] The regulators' standardization of models also removes some significant sources of judgment and provides an additional means of comparing the risks across entities.[103]

However, this particular type of model-based information is ultimately contingent on the quality of the model(s) specified by regulators, which could be compromised by administrative and regulatory pressures.[104] To ensure rigorous models, regulators ideally could be instructed to follow a "precautionary" approach advocated by Lawrence Baxter. Assumptions built into each model would be calibrated to adopt reasonable, worst case assumptions about complex forms, uncertainties, and ambiguities.[105]

As another example of the moderately pure information, Hu proposes that regulated parties could be encouraged or perhaps required to develop and use their own computational models to describe market risks and structures. To control for variability and elucidate some biases in these firm-based models, a standardized input, consisting of "a single set of hypothetical assets industry-wide," would be run to enable cross-comparisons among firms.[106] Ultimately, as a result of this requirement, some entities may converge in their modeling "since having an 'outlier' model may attract market participant skepticism. On the other hand, rewards could sometimes cut in the opposite direction; outlier models may signal to some market participants that the financial entity is ahead of the curve on modeling."[107] This type of use of moderately pure information is in fact already being field-tested; preliminary implementation of an analogous approach by international bank regulators suggests "clear evidence that differences in modeling choices can be very important drivers of variability" in the assessment of bank portfolios and risks.[108]

We would supplement Hu's proposed solutions with a requirement that firms be required to provide a summary of the most important findings and risks of their activities that emerge from this more diverse information portfolio. All requirements currently imposed on disclosures – e.g., plain English, visuals, formats, etc. – would be lifted for this particular narrative depiction. The regulated entity would have full discretion to decide how to prepare and communicate its summary. The requirement would thus take the shape of a kind of performance-based, comprehensibility rule similar to the one proposed in Chapter 4. The sole obligation of the summary would be to assess and explain the most significant information and risks to the expert audience in a way that these regulators and investors can reasonably understand.

B *Step Two: Encourage the Reliability of the Information in This Diversified Information Portfolio*

Step two focuses on providing audiences with additional information that they can use to assess the reliability of all three types of mandated information. Even rigorous, standardized requirements for producing "moderately pure information," for example, may offer opportunities for bias. To provide added assurance of the reliability of this additional information, we propose two additional requirements that could be implemented singularly or in tandem.

First, firms could be required to provide an accessible explanation of the *methods* by which all of the information was produced. We call this a "pedigree" statement. The pedigree would include background (e.g., conflicts of interest) about the authors of the models, assessments, and collectors of the data (authorship); the procedures the authors used to develop the models or information, including the extent of diverse scrutiny from disinterested experts; and an accounting of the challenges encountered in developing and running the models and conducting the analyses.

Pedigree statements would be modeled on scientific conventions. Scientific journals require statements of authorship, disclosures of conflict of interest, disinterested peer review, and sometimes even the underlying data and algorithms used in quantitative models. Since there is irreducible discretion in this technical information that cannot be eliminated altogether, requiring information about the process used to create the information forces speakers to explain to an audience "how" they generate the information.

Thumbnail Sketch of Financial Regulatory Reform

1 Require a diversified information portfolio from financial entities to produce a clearer analysis of financial risks from multiple vantage points.
2 Require each type of information and summary to be accompanied by a pedigree statement that details how the information was analyzed and communicated.
3 Provide public and private enforcement to ensure the diverse information in a firm's portfolio is both rigorous and reasonably comprehensible.

A pedigree statement in financial regulation would thus accompany all three types of information produced by a firm, providing the audience with basic procedural information about how the data was collected and the models were run. Particularly for the development of the entity's own model(s) as "moderately pure information," this pedigree requirement creates further incentives for regulated firms to produce more robust models. Additionally, even the comprehensibility of the pedigree statements themselves should be judged from the audience's perspective: Would a reasonable expert audience be confused or misled by the pedigree? Sanctions for noncompliance should be significant enough to cause regulated financial actors to comply. Perhaps a market niche could even develop for highly certified and trusted analysts to conduct the modeling and data collection work for some of the new types of information required of financial entities.

Pedigree statements could also be standardized to allow for cross comparisons between firms. International requirements already impose some analogous process-type requirements on banks to assess the reliability of their assessments, like back-testing of the models as well as a description of the "approaches it used for validating and evaluating the accuracy of internal models and modeling processes."[109] Thus there is already a type of pedigree requirement in place for some mandated self-assessments.

The second requirement that might improve the reliability of some of this information is a mandatory audit or similar expert oversight process to assess its comprehensibility. Specifically, the speaker's narrative statements and some of its depictions and other moderately pure information would be submitted to (or audited by) a publicly established group of skeptic-contrarians who would provide a qualitative assessment of the rigor and accessibility of the information for the target expert audience. Brett McDonnell and Dan Schwarcz, for example, have proposed the use of "contrarians" in complex regulatory systems to provide a type of focused peer review function.[110] One can even imagine certified boards of contrarians instituted to review the rigor and accessibility of certain depictions or models on a regular (e.g., five year) basis.

C *Step Three: Hold Speakers Responsible for Comprehensible Information*

The third and final step holds speakers in violation of the law when this mandated information is misleading or incomprehensible to a reasonable, expert audience. Fines and perhaps even injunctive relief may be necessary to impose costs sufficient on speakers to ensure their information is rigorous for their intended use. Much like the "comprehension rule" proposed by Willis in the last chapter, then, the speaker must communicate the key messages clearly and in a way that expert audiences can understand, or else face costly penalties. Of course these new requirements must also be clear and predictable to guard against overly risk averse behaviors by firms.

Private parties could be enlisted for enforcement, perhaps lured with additional bounties, but for this private enforcement the burden to bring a case should be high. For example, the private enforcer could be required to establish that a financial entities' information portfolio is "wholly inadequate" to enable a reasonable expert audience to understand the relevant information. If the accuracy of some of this information is also in question, the private enforcer could be required to establish that the suspect information is "in significant conflict with the available evidence or is unsupported by evidence." While this high burden means that only the most egregious violations would be caught, it still creates a deterrent effect that should discourage financial actors from loading their portfolio with excessively biased or unreliable information.

IV CONCLUSION

In settings with significant comprehension asymmetries between speakers and audience,[111] it is imperative that the law supply incentives for financial entities to first understand and then communicate the risks of their transactions. Indeed, if the law fails to do this, we are almost certainly poised for trouble.

The reforms described here should help create stronger speaker incentives for both understanding and communicating the risks of financial structures and transactions. These adjustments will not reverse speakers' incentives to shirk on clear communication in all cases. The proposed reforms instead simply raise costs to a speaker associated with proceeding with incomprehensible transactions.

Ideally, once Hu's requirements for a diverse informational portfolio are in place, market forces will begin to reward firms that provide the clearest, most comprehensible assessments and penalize those speakers whose financial situation is more difficult to evaluate.

The net effect of these new information requirements may even create a type of ceiling on the complexity of the transactions themselves. When descriptions or models cannot be put in terms that are understandable to experts, the transaction or structure may be naturally discouraged or could even be prohibited. A "complexity cap" would then emerge organically from a system that rewards rigorous, accessible representations of financial risk.

5B

Comprehension Asymmetries in the Law of Patents

A patent is a government-bestowed entitlement that encourages innovation by providing an inventor the equivalent of a time-limited property right on an invention. With a patent in hand, the inventor can lay exclusive claim to the invention – an effective monopoly in the market – and earn millions and sometimes billions of dollars over the patent's finite life-span. But even when there is little market demand for an invention, the inventor can still protect that property right against "infringement" by other inventors. Indeed, for some inventors, the primary monetary benefit of a patent stems from this right to extract fees from individuals and companies who appear to infringe on their claim.[1]

Given their value, we would expect a restrictive process for granting patents that requires inventors – who have the best information and the most to gain from this public entitlement – to carry the burden of persuading government patent examiners to award a patent. For example, we would expect that an inventor would be required to demonstrate how his or her discovery is an advance over previous inventions, with any doubts and errors counting against the inventor. The inventor would also be required to specify the claim in crystal-clear terms, delineating the precise nature of the invention in relation to the "prior art."

As we shall soon see, however, the design of the patent process almost (although not always) turns these incentives for justifying a patent upside-down. At many steps in the patent process, it is the audience – the Patent and Trademark Office (PTO) patent examiner and others – who bears the burden of making sense of the precise nature of an invention as well as determining the value of that invention to society. The inventor, by contrast, enjoys a legal presumption in favor of a patent.

As a result of this legal design, a rational inventor can shift the costs of understanding her invention to the patent examiner; a particularly crafty inventor will actively exploit this flaw in the process. Comprehension asymmetries once again rear their ugly heads as a fundamental feature of this communication structure that is not only ignored but aggravated in the basic architecture of the patent process.

If examiners bear the primary burden of processing the value and nature of a complicated invention and yet face limitations in the time, resources, and expertise available to do so, we would predict these patent examiners to dole out some "bad" or invalid patents. And this prediction is borne out in practice. As Adam Jaffe and Josh Lerner observe, "Given this challenging environment, it is not surprising that the patent examination process generates some degree of error, including errors that result in a large number of invalid patents being issued."[2] A number of analysts are in fact busy documenting the extent of this problem.[3] Mark Lemley and Bhaven Sampat, for example, report an unexpectedly high rate of patent grants – more than 70 percent of applications are ultimately approved,[4] while Jaffe and Lerner report that patents issued in the US are of declining quality relative to patents issued globally.[5] Moreover, because examiners lack the time and resources to clearly specify patent boundaries, the reach of patent claims is sometimes so unclear that the only way to resolve disputes is in court. In *Patent Failure*, Michael Meurer and James Bessen note that, for at least some patent claims, "[t]here is . . . no reliable way of determining patent boundaries short of litigation."[6]

If unworthy and poorly specified inventions receive patent protection, and yet the claim is honored against future innovators, we can also expect some unfortunate economic consequences. Again, evidence bears out this prediction, revealing that the approval of patents that are not worthy of patent protection exerts a substantial drag on the economy and may chill innovation because inventors fear infringement suits. Not only are the costs of this patent infringement litigation high, with a median of $5 million for major lawsuits, but the existence of unworthy patents "may also lead small companies to drop products rather than defend their legality."[7] As Melissa Wasserman and Michael Frakes conclude, "There is general agreement that the US Patent and Trademark Office (Patent Office or Agency) is issuing too many invalid patents that are unnecessarily reducing consumer welfare, stunting productive research, and discouraging innovation."[8]

Perhaps just as concerning, these patent problems may be intensifying over time. Today, even with steady increases in staff, "[t]he continual acceleration of patenting rates strains both public and private actors' capacities to perform all the various activities necessary for a patent system to function effectively."[9] Jaffe and Lerner warn that "the PTO has become so overtaxed, and its incentives have become so skewed toward granting patents, that the tests for novelty and non-obviousness that are supposed to ensure that the patent monopoly is granted only to true inventors have become largely non-operative."[10] Indeed, there is a real risk that as applicants learn about this permissive granting process, they may become inclined to submit still more bad applications.[11] The resulting patent system imposes excessive demands, not only on the PTO, but "also generates strains on the information-processing, decision-making, and financial capacities of private firms, individuals, and courts."[12]

As the applications pour in faster than they can be reviewed, analysts ask, "How can we process such a large and increasing number of claims in a way that cost-effectively advances social goals?"[13] Over the last ten years, a good portion of the patent literature has not surprisingly been focused on answering this question, and an emerging consensus points to the design of the patent system itself as largely to blame for the current deluge.

This chapter begins with a discussion of how the patent system works and the role of speakers and audiences within the system. We then discuss how the patent system addresses comprehension asymmetries that arise from its general structure. We consider first how applicants who are Rule-Followers and naturally inclined toward cooperative communication might behave under the existing system. We then consider how the crafty Rule-Benders might be able to strategically exploit the system's design. The chapter then closes with some general suggestions for reform.

I BLUEPRINT: HOW THE BASIC SYSTEM WORKS

At each step of the patent system, the legal treatment of comprehension asymmetries is the same; the comprehension asymmetries are almost always ignored. As long as all underlying and sometimes unprocessed information regarding the viability of a patent claim is disclosed, the patent applicant (our speaker) enjoys a "presumption" in favor of a valid patent claim.

The basic structure of the system proceeds in three steps. At Step 1, the inventor files an application with the patent office to lay claim to his or her intellectual property that, if approved, will protect the invention against other inventors and competitors. The application must include a detailed description of the claim(s) as well as a disclosure of known "prior art" that intersects with the invention.[14] On the other hand, the inventor need not understand himself exactly how the invention works; all that is required is that the inventor accurately describe what the invention is.[15]

At Step 2, patent examiners at the PTO review the application. But, as we will discuss in greater detail, the review process is structured so that most of the processing costs needed to evaluate the nature and novelty of the invention are borne by the examiner-audience. In theory, the examiner can reject an application if the specification of the invention is unclear or excessively ambiguous.[16] But in practice, this type of rejection appears under-utilized.[17] Instead, the examiner is expected to work with the applicant to craft a more comprehensible and precise description of the invention. If this collaborative effort is not successful, the process encourages the examiner, when in doubt, to approve rather than deny an application.[18]

Thus, in cases in which an examiner lacks the resources or experience to understand a claim completely or assess its novelty, the examiner will generally save time (and possibly earn credits for high productivity in the PTO) by granting rather than rejecting the claim. As Jonathan Masur concludes based on his study of the causes for "patent inflation," "Like most administrative agencies, the PTO wishes to avoid appeals and especially reversals. In order for the Agency to accomplish this, it need only err on the side of granting excessive numbers of patents – even invalid patents – for which there is no appeal."[19] This default in favor of inventors was so strong that, in the past, the PTO used to refer to applicants as "customers."[20]

At Step 3, after claim issuance, the inventor can sue others who infringe on her patent. In these private enforcement cases, the inventor's patent enjoys a "presumption of validity." If the defendant-infringer claims the patent is invalid, he or she must support that argument with "clear and convincing" evidence that the PTO erred.[21] Thus, even if the PTO mistakenly granted a patent, the inventor enjoys a presumption in her favor in subsequent litigation.[22]

If we insert an incomprehensible patent application at the beginning of this three-step process, we see that at each step, the costs of processing what the invention is, as well as its novelty and creative value, are externalized to the PTO and others, such as courts and other inventors. This regulatory design thus signals to a speaker-inventor that the processing costs needed to understand his invention are generally not his responsibility.

II COMPREHENSION ASYMMETRIES

While the overarching structure appears problematic, it is possible that more specific doctrines and rules will counteract the tendency of inventors to shift processing costs to their audiences. Before considering the doctrinal nuances, we first explore the respective capabilities of our audience (the patent examiner) and speaker (the inventor) to understand the nature and novelty of an invention.

A *Audience*

The patent examiner is our primary audience for purposes of this analysis.[23] There are important secondary audiences – competitors and even the judicial system – but the examiner is the first stop and primary gatekeeper over the language used in an approved patent.

1 Patent Examiner

Under patent law, as just discussed, it is the examiner and not the applicant who must determine whether an invention is deserving of a patent. This entails a careful review of all prior patents, all relevant literature, commercial sales, and other diverse information to determine whether the invention makes a significant contribution to the field.

To do this work, the examiner must master the nature of the invention itself – the claim(s) – and then conduct research on how the claim(s) fit with prior inventions. Yet while an examiner is at least as able to conduct comprehensive research on past inventions as the inventor, an examiner's resources and expertise in understanding the nature of the basic invention are likely to be relatively more limited for several reasons:

- *Resources.* To avoid an enormous backlog, examiners are required to complete their review of each application within about 18–19 hours over a three- to five-year period.[24] To avoid adverse performance evaluations, examiners who have complex applications that take longer than the allotted time may simply work overtime without pay, particularly at the end of a performance cycle, to stay on track.
- *Expertise.* A shortfall in resources might be offset by superior expertise, but here again the PTO struggles to keep up with the inventor in understanding the merits of specific claims. Some of this expertise gap is a result of the inventor's (speaker's) greater experience with the actual invention in question. But even with respect to more general experience in the relevant technical field, the PTO examiner can sometimes be at a disadvantage relative to the speaker because of the high turnover in examiners at the PTO as a result of the "sweat shop" culture.[25] In 2008, for example, the GAO reported that one examiner left the PTO for every two new hires the agency made,[26] and some of that attrition involved more experienced examiners.[27] See Figure 5.2.

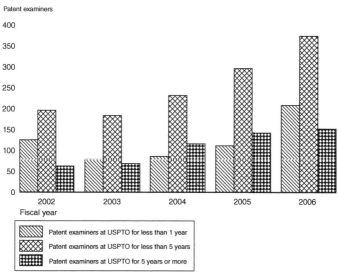

Source: USPTO

Note: In each fiscal year, the number of patent examiners at USPTO for less than 5 years is inclusive of those at USPTO for less than 1 year.

FIGURE 5.2 Patent Examiner Attrition by Years of Experience
GAO, Testimony: "US Patent and Trademark Office Hiring Efforts Are Not Sufficient to Reduce the Patent Application Backlog" 9 (2008)

At the same time that PTO examiners face limitations in the time available to process complicated patent applications, the benefits to an examiner of going the extra mile and working overtime to master convoluted applications are reduced as a result of how the process is designed. As noted, in general the patenting process encourages examiners to grant patents when in doubt. Examiners who resist this inclination and dedicate additional effort to dig deeper may find themselves penalized or at least unappreciated. This occurs for several reasons:

- *A patent rejection carries more paperwork and litigation risks than an approval.* If a patent is granted, considerably less explanation is required from the examiner, and the decision is generally (not always) free of litigation or third-party interventions. However, if a patent application is rejected, the examiner must provide specific reasons for why the patent claim is denied, and the PTO examiner's explanations will be put under the microscope if the unhappy applicant decides to appeal the rejection.[28] As Wasserman observes, "The longstanding PTO policy requiring examiners to articulate the reasons for rejecting patent claims but not for allowing patent claims means that examiners often have to work harder to reject rather than to allow a patent application."[29] Jaffe and Lerner similarly observe that the current system causes examiners to "go easy" on applicants since rejected patents require considerably more time than patent approvals.[30]

- *Continuing Applications.* In most patent areas, applicants whose applications are rejected can file an unlimited stream of repeat claims at the cost of a few hundred dollars each (called Requests for Continued Examination or RCEs).[31] Examiners may sometimes receive multiple rounds of these repeat applications. In fact, more than one-fourth of the application filings are continuing applications.[32] The repeat claims may even be perceived by management as evidence that the examiner isn't doing her job properly. One way for the examiner to stem the flow of these unwelcome repeat applications, as well as to appease management, is thus to grant the application earlier in the process.

- *Fees.* Financial incentives also tip the PTO as an institution toward erring on the side of granting applications.[33] The PTO receives fees from the individual applicants that rise with patent approvals; on the other hand, when a patent is denied and the applicant appeals, the costs of defense come out of the PTO's budget for each stage of the proceeding, from internal review to defending the decision in court.[34] While concerns about these litigation expenses probably do not affect the individual examiner's incentives, they would seem to have an impact on the Office's policies for applicant processing.

The general incentive scheme just outlined is not uniform, of course. Most important, there does appear to be strong counter-pressure from management – both culturally and evidenced in performance reviews – to reward examiners for being tough. If an examiner is quick to approve an application or rarely demands additional clarifications or information, suspicions will be raised that the examiner is not doing his job. On the other hand, these pressures may not be enough to force the examiner to master the important but obscured details of an application. Thus, while the examiner may be rewarded for a tough review, with iterative requests for clarification within a single examination process, these incentives tend to flip at the final decision step. At that final step, the examiner's incentives are impacted by the costs and benefits just discussed regarding granting a patent versus rejecting it. Indeed, while management does expect critical review by examiners, at the same time management is eager for finality and resolutions that do not raise the ire of politically influential constituencies.

In sum, the design of the process explains why the PTO examiners, in general, may err on the side of approving bad claims rather than the reverse.[35] Masur observes that "[p]atent law thus offers applicants a nearly unique opportunity to capitalize on institutional asymmetries to the detriment of outside actors."[36] It's faster and cheaper just to approve an application during the final hours of the review period.

2 Other Audiences

Other audiences are also engaged in the patent process, although not as directly or immediately as the patent examiner. They include competitor inventors and the judicial system (judges and juries). Both sets of audiences also face limitations in processing abilities relative to the speaker.

A COMPETITORS

In the current patent system, competitor inventors can sometimes engage in the review process by offering critical comments on a patent application.[37] These competitors generally have a high level of expertise. Some competitors are also motivated to participate since they may be producing the same or similar invention and do not want to end up as defendants in subsequent infringement litigation.

Yet engagement by competitors in reviewing patent applications is generally limited because the benefits of flyspecking an unapproved application do not justify the financial investment.[38] As a result, all but the most directly affected third-party competitors are likely to opt out of participating in a patent review, even when a competitor has some access to and stake in the proceedings.

B JUDGES AND JURIES

Judges and juries are brought into patent disputes either when an applicant believes a rejection was arbitrary or when a patent holder believes another inventor has infringed on his invention. In both cases, the courts are usually obliged to interpret the claim. In contrast to the examiners and competitors, however, this particular audience is limited in expertise. Even specialist judges find that some complicated claims outstrip their expertise and resources. And, in the case of judges at least, even if they are able to overcome this disadvantage in theory, doing so means diverting precious time and energy away from other important cases in practice.

While judicial processes have been adjusted to account for some asymmetries in expertise, particularly in claim construction, these efforts are still imperfect.[39] As a result, judges and juries will be particularly flummoxed by those claims that even the more expert PTO examiners cannot understand or process within a reasonable period of time.

B *Speaker*

The inventor and her attorney – our speaker here – will generally understand the basic nature of the field in which the discovery was made, what the invention is and does, its limitations, and even to some extent how the invention stacks up against prior inventions. In most cases, then, the inventor-speaker's processing costs – compared to the examiner – will tend to be lower.

Yet, as discussed, an inventor-speaker's motivation to dedicate resources to translate this superior understanding of the invention into a crystal-clear claim is another matter. Effective communication of the key features of a complicated invention can be costly, even when the communication is intended for another expert. The mere task of converting highly technical information into clear text can entail multiple steps and sources of error. Even effective translation of a patent that was obtained in a foreign country into English for the US patent process can entail significant expense.

The costs of making a case for novelty run still higher for the inventor. Identifying the specific attributes of an invention and conducting some reconnaissance research to verify that the invention is novel and has creative value can be a protracted research endeavor. As a result, the inventor himself may not fully appreciate what makes his invention different from predecessors.

Set against these costs to the inventor-speaker are the low benefits that can sometimes flow from cooperative communication. For their part, the inventors who hope to patent undeserving inventions are likely to find it to their advantage to keep the examiner in the dark as much as possible; clearly communicating the merits of the invention is likely to lead to a rejection. But even for the strongest inventions, inventors can sometimes recoup benefits (while saving costs) by drafting fuzzy descriptions that shift processing costs to examiners. For example, if an inventor describes a claim in an ambiguous way that can be interpreted broadly, the open-ended nature of the description could lead to a more expansive legal claim. Tun-Jen Chiang and Lawrence Solum observe that "patentees have an inbuilt incentive to be disingenuous: to portray the claim narrowly to the PTO examiner (to persuade the examiner to issue the patent) while portraying the same claim broadly to competitors (to deter competition)."[40] And Oskar Livak similarly notes that "[c]laim drafting has become a relatively unconstrained game of requesting valuable intellectual real estate rather than an exercise in concisely delineating the substantive invention."[41]

As a result of this general cost–benefit in drafting clear claims, the inventor is likely to cut corners, both in understanding and explaining his invention. A patent application does not require the applicant to master the nature of his invention or its novelty.[42] And the inventor need not even ensure that the claim itself is readily comprehensible.[43] Most of the costs associated with making sense of the filing are instead shifted to the PTO.

But this is just the very basic incentive system – from a high altitude. As one zooms in on the legal details, one would hope that the patent process has been designed to incorporate a number of nudges that encourage applicants to communicate the terms of their claims clearly. It is to that more intricate design we now turn.

III THE DESIGN OF THE PATENT SYSTEM AND COMPREHENSION ASYMMETRIES

A variety of more detailed rules and procedures built into the patent process appear at first blush to be well-calibrated to counteract comprehension asymmetries occurring between inventors and examiners. For example, patent law explicitly requires that the "specification" (which is the entire patent application) be clearly stated to provide the examiner with an accessible understanding of the nature of the invention. Section 112(a) states:

> The specification shall contain a written description of the invention, and of the manner and process of making and using it, in such full, clear, concise, and exact terms as to enable any person skilled in the art to which it pertains . . . to make and use the same . . .[44]

The PTO's own rules underscore this accessibility requirement. If the specification is not drafted clearly, this singular deficiency can ultimately provide the basis for a final patent rejection.[45]

The rules also require inventors to summarize their claims in a single sentence[46] and to fit their application into a rigid format. Both requirements appear designed to improve the understandability of the claims and larger specification to the PTO.[47]

But in practice, all of these comprehensibility-focused requirements are implemented in ways that stop well short of encouraging cooperative communication by the inventor. Although examiners can reject claims when the application fails to meet the clarity-based requirements of Section 112(a), they seldom do so in practice.[48] Indeed, that basis for rejection may even be discouraged; an excellent invention, so the thinking goes, should not be rejected just because drafting is sloppy or the translation poorly done. As the United States Court of Customs and Patent Appeals stated: "[W]e are of the opinion that the PTO has the initial burden of presenting evidence or reasons why persons skilled in the art would not recognize in the disclosure a description of the invention defined by the claims."[49] As a result, an examiner typically uses "nonfinal rejections" (iterative requests for clarifications issued in the course of the review process) to prod applicants to formulate clearer descriptions, without formally rejecting the application.[50] However, once the examiner nears the end of the review process, if the specification is still fuzzy, the examiner faces net incentives to approve it.[51]

The use of templates and one-sentence limits to encourage more comprehensible claims are even more ineffectual. In some applications, these single sentences can go on for pages and be difficult to follow.[52] Moreover, and as we've seen before, templates and forms can be useful to structure communications, but in cases of significant comprehension asymmetries, they can fall well short of ensuring that the speaker is rewarded for comprehensible communications.

Still more problematic, the cumulative impact of other doctrines and rules embedded in the patent process may have the effect of encouraging inventors to shift processing costs onto their audiences. Rule-Followers will draft less clear specifications unintentionally in their well-meaning effort to stay on the right side of the law, while Rule-Benders will do so strategically to gain an advantage in the process. We discuss both structural problems in turn.

A Rule-Followers

Rule-Followers' sole objective is to follow the letter of the law, both in stating each claim and defending it in litigation. Yet despite the fact that Rule-Followers are naturally inclined to craft clear applications and claims, several perverse incentives arise from the patent process that can undermine these good intentions and lead the Rule-Follower to produce less comprehensible applications.

1 Inequitable Conduct

In a patent application, the patent applicant has the "duty to disclose ... all information known to that [applicant] ... to be material to patentability ... [including] prior art."[53] Applicants who do not disclose relevant information may be vulnerable to the dreaded charge of "inequitable conduct," known as the "atomic bomb" of claims because of the numerous adverse consequences (ranging from invalidity of multiple patents to spawning antitrust and unfair competition litigation to the award of attorneys' fees) that arise from a successful claim against an inventor.[54] Given the patent applicant's legal duty to disclose prior art of which she is aware,[55] providing a long list of citations of inventions to the examiner underscores the Rule-Follower's diligence and lowers the risk that the applicant can be accused of withholding information.

Inequitable conduct arose originally as a judge-made defense to claims of infringement in the 1930s.[56] The underlying idea was that if the applicant misled the PTO into mistakenly granting an application – most commonly due to withholding information or other forms of deceit – the patent would be unenforceable.[57] Over time, the courts vacillated on the level of conduct that would lead to a successful inequitable conduct charge, with lower and lower standards evolving to keep the patent bar vigilant. As a result, and particularly during the last few decades, some courts have held that even carelessness by an attorney during the patent prosecution process can be sufficient for a finding of "inequitable conduct" in disclosing material information.[58] This low bar has been blamed for spawning a "plague" of "inequitable conduct" claims. One study reported that 80 percent of patent litigation involved the claim.[59] Even if a high percentage of these claims might not ultimately be successful, the fact that the claim can be threatened so broadly creates strong incentives by the Rule-Follower for over-compliance with disclosure requirements.

To play it safe, then, a Rule-Follower will over-comply by inundating the PTO with more citations to potential prior art than the PTO may be able to process. As the Federal Circuit observed in *Therasense*, "With inequitable conduct casting the shadow of a hangman's noose, it is unsurprising that patent prosecutors regularly ... 'disclose too much prior art for the PTO to meaningfully consider, and do not explain its significance, all out of fear that to do otherwise risks a claim of inequitable conduct.'"[60]

And there is some evidence of this "tidal wave of disclosure" occurring in practice.[61] For example, one patent involved the "submission of nine hundred references without any indication which ones were most relevant" and another entailed the "submission of eighteen pages of cited references, including five pages listing references to claims, office actions, declarations, amendments, interview summaries, and other communications in related applications."[62] Empirical research also suggests that these extensive lists of prior art are not limited to a few applications. A study by Christopher Cotropia and coauthors finds that, for the top 10 percent of the patents with the most extensive prior art lists, the citation list exceeds 200 citations in a single patent application.[63] Examiners themselves acknowledge the problem, complaining about how "applications [can sometimes] arrive with box loads of supporting references [i.e., the list of prior art]."[64]

Even more problematic, Rule-Follower applicants may find it legally safer to provide the PTO with raw, unprocessed lists of possible prior art rather than take the extra step of analyzing and summarizing that information for the agency. This reluctance to prepare comprehensible summaries of prior art for the PTO arises from a rational fear that the resulting summary will be perceived as incomplete or biased, thus leading to an inequitable conduct charge based on providing a misleading summary. The ABA in fact observes how, because of the inequitable conduct doctrine, "applicants have a disincentive to say anything of substance about the materials they disclose. Concern that even a well-intended effort to advance the examination, e.g., by pointing to the more pertinent references in the record, could later be characterized as misleading or purposely incomplete keeps applicants quiet."[65] Perversely, the doctrine thus "punishes applicants who attempt to provide useful information and explanation about their patent applications."[66] Cooperative communication becomes a liability in a system focused unilaterally on "complete information" rather than meaningful communication.

As citation lists continued to expand (sixfold over the last 40 years),[67] the Federal Circuit took note of the problem and raised the requirements for "inequitable conduct" in their en banc resolution of *Therasense* decided in 2013.[68] In the wake of their opinion, allegations of "inequitable conduct" must now be bolstered with evidence of the applicant's specific intent to deceive, as well as evidence that this bad conduct materially influenced the PTO's decision to award a patent.[69]

Nevertheless, and even with this judicial retreat from a broader "inequitable conduct" charge, it is still in the interest of the patent bar to err on the side of providing too many prior art citations rather than too little. Without requirements for comprehensibility, the net incentives created by the law – even with more limited sanctions – still favor over-compliance.

2 Judicial Review

In theory, the courts deciding infringement cases interpret the terms and breadth of a patent claim by looking to what a "person well-versed in the art" would understand from the approved claim.[70] Yet in practice, the courts interpret claims in ways that sometimes depart from this expert perspective. From the standpoint of the Rule-Follower, the courts create several new impediments to cooperative communication since claims must be drafted to be comprehensible to courts, as well as to the examiners.

A GENERAL UNPREDICTABILITY

At a general level, courts make the entire process of claim-drafting more unpredictable, which can lead to some hedge-betting in claim-drafting. Burk and Lemley observe, "Claim construction is sufficiently uncertain that many parties don't settle a case until after the court has construed the claims, because there is no baseline for agreement on what the patent might possibly cover."[71]

Rule-Followers, accordingly, will attempt to anticipate the full range of possible judicial interpretations. Rather than simply drafting a claim that is comprehensible to the expert examiner, the claim will be drafted in a way that attempts – however crudely – to also stave off major risks of a judge misinterpreting the claim.

These drafting challenges are amplified still further by the fact that multiple courts may be involved in a patent dispute, each of which utilizes different approaches to claim interpretations. "The Federal Circuit reworks patent claims that have already been construed by district court judges, and the patent system increasingly revolves around the definition of terminology rather than the substance of what the patentee invented and how significant that invention really is."[72]

B AMBIGUOUS AUDIENCE

A second, related problem for the Rule-Follower arising from judicial review is the "ambiguity of the audience".[73] It simply isn't clear from whose expert perspective the claim should be read; is it an ordinary person with expertise, or the inventor, or a patent lawyer? Yet the choice of the audience makes a difference in drafting some claims. Burk and Lemley conclude that: "It should not be surprising that we will have difficulty in defining terms clearly if we don't know whose understanding of the claims matters [to the courts]."[74]

For more complicated claims, the Rule-Follower might try to draft his claim in a way that is understandable to two (or more) different audiences. Communicating with these dual audiences, however, can lead to contortions in drafting as the Rule-Follower becomes focused on drafting claims that survive interpretation by multiple audiences, each of whom may use different interpretative tools. Indeed, because of the nontrivial risk of subsequent malpractice claims for drafting errors by patent attorneys, Rule-Followers may be even more obsessive about drafting claims that are resilient to numerous, sometimes even conflicting interpretations.[75]

C THE ANTI-REDUNDANCY CANON

In interpreting patent claims, the federal courts have also created various interpretive rules that can lead to anticipatory drafting practices that further complicate how claims are explained.[76] One example, called the anti-redundancy principle, holds that each term in an application has distinct meaning. Since redundancy is one means of communicating the most important features of a message, the application of this doctrine in some patent settings can perversely serve to undermine more comprehensible claims.

John Golden discusses the problem this canon can produce for clear claim-drafting.[77] If every term is distinct, then "some claims [will be] deliberately drafted to be narrower than other claims (i.e., to generate no more than partial redundancy)" to ensure no feature of the claim is left out. Each distinct claim will also use "different language not as much to distinguish them but instead to try to increase the chances that at least one claim, whether redundant with other claims or not, will have a desired level of coverage."[78] Golden cites parallel advice from David Pressman's "Patent it Yourself": After writing a first set of claims, a patent drafter should "consider writing another set of claims" for the same invention because, even though such claims "will not always give your invention broader coverage," they "will provide alternative weapons" in infringement litigation.[79]

B Rule-Benders

Rule-Benders exploit the mis-design of the patent system to advance their own, narrow self-interest. To the extent that the structure of the law is designed in ways that provide Rule-Benders with leverage to shift processing costs to the PTO, they will take full advantage of that opportunity. We assume for the most part that these Rule-Benders are drawn from a smaller subset of applicants who seek patents for weak inventions and who thus benefit from utilizing strategies that increase the odds their patent will be granted.

1 Claim-Drafting Strategies to Increase the PTO's Processing Costs

For some applications – particularly those inventions that are of lower quality – inventors can deliberately obscure weaknesses in their applications in the hopes that the busy examiner will not discover them. Rule-Benders will also strive for a broader claim than their invention deserves, but they will again draft the claim in ways that require considerable effort by the examiner to discover these sleights of hand.

The tactics for increasing the examiner's processing costs run the gamut. A few familiar techniques include:

Bag of Parts. One particularly well-known claim-drafting strategy is the "bag of parts" trick. In this maneuver, applicants increase the burden on examiners by intentionally crafting the application in a way that obscures the basic nature of the invention. As one reformed patent attorney admitted: "I was originally taught to write patent applications by obfuscating the invention. Specifications were required to include all of the information that was claimed, and the way I was taught was to include all kinds of details of the invention without any overview or 'big picture' context ... There was never any structure to the parts, or even a paragraph that described the context of the invention."[80] By leaving it to the examiner to piece together how the parts interconnect and what the claim consists of, there is a chance that the review time will end before the examiner has figured out the puzzle (with a default favoring patent approval).

A Rule-Bender can replicate this "bag of parts" trick by providing drawings and textual descriptions that do not link together in clear or accessible ways. An examiner may get bogged down in endeavoring to understand these diverging descriptions. Discrepancies between drawings and text in fact can even lead claims to be read more expansively in infringement litigation, particularly when the text is broader than the drawing.

Still another maneuver in this same "bag of parts" trick is the utilization of unconventional "fancy" words to cover the same features of an invention that could be described with more straightforward terms (e.g., in one technical field, "fly-eye lens" versus "integrator" versus "lenslet array" can all mean the same thing). To catch this deception, the examiner must first invest resources in understanding what the fancy term actually means as a practical matter. The examiner must then figure out that the fancy term is effectively a synonym for other, more commonplace descriptive terms. And finally, the examiner must broaden his Boolean search of the prior art database accordingly to ensure he is not missing a number of inventions that were patented using more straightforward terminology. If the examiner does not do this homework, the inventor's use of fancy words can obscure the fact that an invention is not novel and instead duplicates prior art.

Deliberate Ambiguity. Along these same lines, patent drafters can strategically deploy deliberate ambiguities to avoid providing too much specification of the core features of the invention. Polk Wagner notes that "a patentee will almost certainly seek substantial vagueness, thus gaining flexibility to effectively alter the scope and description of the patent according to changing circumstances."[81] Burk and Lemley elaborate: "The applicant has the power to define the patent claims, but many applicants don't specify what they mean by ambiguous technical language, either because they don't think about the issue or because they intend to exploit the ambiguity in obtaining or enforcing the patent."[82]

The authors of the book *The Patent Writer: How to Write Successful Patent Applications* provide a straightforward illustration. "One way to help avoid having a patent with narrow protection is to include a number of claims of varying scope to ensure proper protection of the patentable subject matter."[83] They illustrate the technique with a hypothetical illuminated hammer invention. If the hammer is made of wood, they advise that there is no need to put "wood" in the application; the applicant might want to later stake the claim to illuminated hammers made out of other materials. And, while we might judge this a relatively benign and even legitimate tactic for describing hammers, these overly general descriptions and tactical ambiguities can become a deliberate drafting strategy to create expansive and more open-ended claims when inventions are complicated.

While the effects of ambiguity on the success of an application vary within the life cycle of a single application, the net effect of ambiguity – particularly at the examiner's final make-or-break decision regarding whether to accept or reject – tends to cut in favor of an ambiguous application. At this crucial point in the process, the examiner may be more vulnerable to being tricked or "bamboozled" because he is out of time.[84] The resultant ambiguity, in turn, can then be used by the inventor to assert more expansive claims post-grant in an effort to scare away competitors.[85]

Prior Art. As discussed earlier, the Rule-Follower is already inclined to inundate the examiner with lists of prior art to avoid inequitable conduct charges, but a Rule-Bender will turn this well-meaning compliance strategy into a deliberate effort at databombing. In the existing patent process, examiners are formally required under the law to review all the cited references,[86] but "[a]lthough technically required to review each document cited in an Information Disclosure Statement ("IDS"), examiners cannot realistically do so when literally hundreds are cited at a time."[87] By burying the "needle" – the citation to prior art that comes closest to the invention – in this larger list of unhelpful citations, the applicant wears down the examiner while preserving a paper record of compliance with disclosure requirements.[88] Excessive IDSs also provide added insulation from infringement claims since the courts presume that the PTO has reviewed and essentially blessed the long list of prior art citations as not overlapping with the new claim. This long citation list thus helps make the patent more "bulletproof" in subsequent litigation.[89]

Added Evidence and Terms. Rule-Bender applicants can also exaggerate the apparent technical and/or legal complexity of an application in an effort to raise the examiner's processing costs to the point where the examiner might capitulate and grant the claim. Applicants can also file affidavits by experts in support of their patents and inundate the PTO with this supplemental evidence. Since there are no limits to these filings, there is no downside to loading in these added processing costs.

In fact, a growing body of empirical evidence reveals that these tactics work. One of the most significant indicators of whether a patent will be granted is the time the examiner has available to review the patent. Based on their study of the rate of patent grants correlated with the level (and time) afforded the examiner, Frakes and Wasserman find that "the less time given to an examiner to review an application, the less active she is in searching for prior art, the less likely she is to make time-intensive rejections, and the more likely she is to grant the patent."[90] Specifically, "As examination time is cut roughly in half, our findings suggest that grant rates rise by as much as 10 to 19 percentage points, or by roughly 15% to 28%."[91]

2 Manipulations of Continuing Applications

As noted earlier, inventors can file multiple, repeat applications, and in some areas of patent activity, repeat applications can theoretically go on forever.[92] When the first application is rejected, the applicant can simply file a second, almost identical application with the same examiner and try again.[93] These repeat applications (called RCEs) are quite inexpensive for the applicant. Even without the explicit threat of a continuing application, the examiner is well aware that a rejection of a patent may boomerang into a second duplicate claim for which they are likely to have still fewer resources available for review.[94]

A Rule-Bending inventor can blatantly abuse this re-file opportunity by holding the examiner's feet to the fire on the original claim. For example, a Rule-Bender could strategically inundate the examiner with massive (unhelpful) amendments and arguments at the very final stages of the review process or staunchly resist providing helpful explanations in response to an examiner's questioning. Both the examiner and the inventor know that if the examiner calls his bluff and rejects the application, the examiner is likely to see the exact same application filed again a few months later.[95] But on this second round, the examiner will have even less allotted time and fewer professional rewards to conduct the review.[96]

Empirical research shows that this deliberate, repeat filing strategy pays off with higher grant rates, at least in some patent areas. Frakes and Wasserman conclude from their empirical study that the patent areas that suffer the highest over-granting problems are also those areas with the highest repeat-filing rates; they link these problems directly to the perverse incentives placed on examiners for granting applications earlier as a result of the repeat filing problem.[97] Several expert patent attorneys similarly observe that the "ability of the PTO to rid itself of a determined applicant" through this process "may explain, at least in part, the high Allowance Percentages and Grant Rates."[98] While even Rule-Followers may utilize this repeat system, the Rule-Bender will actively exploit it by resubmitting applications without significantly improving them or endeavoring to limit the number of repeat filings.

Yet, to date, reforms of the continuing application and RCE process may inadvertently backfire by placing further constraints on the examiner's capacity to process these RCEs. One recent reform, for example, imposes additional limits on the time that examiners may dedicate to reviewing repeat applications.[99] As an internal matter, management also appears to frown on those examiners who dedicate a significant portion of their review time to RCEs at the expense of newly assigned cases.[100] Less time for the examiners, however, means more opportunities for Rule-Benders to exploit their comprehension asymmetries.

3 Gaming Judicial Review

Rule-Benders will also take full advantage of drafting overbroad claims in ways that they believe will inure to their benefit later, during infringement litigation. As Burk and Lemley note, "If the patent lawsuit were focused on the central features of what the patentee invented, overclaiming wouldn't work. But if the focus is on the words of the patent claims, then patent drafters can deliberately introduce ambiguity and patent litigators can exploit both deliberate and accidental ambiguities."[101] For example, applicants can expand their claims by loading in added details to individual claims that extend beyond the summary. Since "the anti-redundancy canon" treats all words as distinct, this method of claim interpretation offers one way to expand claims through strategic ambiguity.[102]

Box 5.2 Comprehension Asymmetries in Patent Law

The Inventor as Rule-Follower

- Discloses too much rather than too little to avoid inequitable conduct.
- Drafts claims to survive review by multiple audiences, including courts who sometimes utilize idiosyncratic interpretive tools.

Why is it legally prudent to shift processing costs to patent examiners?

AND

Uncertainties in assessing claims generally cut in favor of granting a patent.

The Inventor as Rule-Bender

- Uses claim-drafting strategies like "bag of parts" and "deliberate ambiguity" to increase the examiner's processing costs.
- Manipulates continuing applications.
- Games judicial review by crafting confusing claim descriptions that might be read more expansively.

How can the examiner's processing limitations be exceeded to increase the chance of a valuable patent grant?

4 Summary

The cumulative rules in the patent process not only allow "inventors . . . to file even dubious patent applications,"[103] but to do so in ways that exploit the vulnerability of the examiner to excessive information-processing costs. In fact, some evidence reveals that "the marginally issued patents [awarded by particularly time-strapped examiners] are of weaker-than-average quality."[104]

To the extent that applicants are not only allowed but actively rewarded for gaming the patent system through obfuscation and other tactics, however, it creates perverse incentives within the patent system. The more strategically applicants use information games, the more likely it is that their unworthy patent will make it through the system.

Perhaps equally important, to the extent that the design of the patent system becomes oblivious to these high costs to the PTO of processing information, applicants will be treated inequitably. Strategic actors who play aggressive information games do better.

IV REFORM

The architecture for the patent process is unstable in part because it sets up perverse incentives for the inventor "to draft patent applications that effectively obscure the true scope of the invention and its relationship to the prior art."[105] As Polk Wagner argues "only by understanding [and reforming] the mechanisms of patent quality – the incentive structure that not only discourage 'good' patent behavior but also encourages 'bad' patent behavior – will we make any real process in improving the situation."[106]

In this section we suggest preliminary reforms to counteract these perverse incentives. Our reforms involve a two-step claim description process. As will become evident soon, none of these suggestions is particularly radical; indeed, several are based on processes already well established in European patent practice. Yet together they could help shift the incentives of the inventor toward more cooperative communication of the underlying attributes of his invention.

A *Step 1: Robust Representations of the Invention*

The first step for reform lifts lessons from financial regulation and applies them to patent decision-making. In an ideally designed system, inventors must have strong incentives not only to communicate the nature of their inventions but also to isolate the inventors' distinctive contribution. The rules thus need to place the burden on applicants (rather than the examiner) to master why their invention deserves patent protection. Hu's concept of a diversified information portfolio can be used to adjust the legal requirements in the patent process to ensure that the inventor is motivated to provide a more accessible and accurate public portrait of what an invention offers society.

The patent process already requires two distinct but complementary representations of the invention from the applicant that help delineate the claims. As we already know, the applicant must provide a textual description of the claimed invention. The applicant is also required to provide drawings of the invention. These dual representations provide overlapping portrayals of the invention.

We propose to supplement these two representations with a third "inventive statement" requirement. Under our reform, the inventor would be required also to describe how the invention contributes in an original and creative way to the field. More specifically and modeled on European patent processes, the inventor would be required to provide an accessible (e.g., dinner-party-styled) description of the problem with the prior art and explain how the invention solves that problem, making the invention "inventive" and useful.[107] "Bag of parts" tricks, ambiguities, and indefinite and unclear features of the application will be less effective when the inventor must communicate clearly her invention's core contribution.

An inventive statement will also provide the examiner with a clearer base from which to assess the invention's novelty and non-obviousness. Rather than starting from scratch – based on piecing together text and the drawing – this added statement provides the examiner with a third depiction both of what the invention is and why it is valuable. The examiner's assessment of the merits of an invention (which would otherwise stay the same) will thus be better informed by these three distinct but overlapping descriptions.

Yet, while the inventive statement will inform an examiner's assessment of novelty, the statement itself will not determine patentability. Given the examiners' access to databases and familiarity with prior inventions, the PTO is still best situated to assess the novelty of the invention. But the inventive statement informs this assessment. In this statement the inventor is forced to extract and explain the core genius at the heart of his own discovery – or, more simply, what it is in the invention that is new.

B *Step 2: A Comprehensible Claim Statement*

After providing a more robust description of the claim and its contribution, the second step of our reform is to ensure that the inventor is highly motivated to make the information in the application reasonably comprehensible to the examiner. Clear and frank communications of the claim must be rewarded with swifter and more assured rates of approval. Conversely, incomprehensible claims must be sanctioned, and if the invention remains obscure, ultimately rejected.[108]

1 Sanctions to Encourage Greater Comprehensibility

The most direct path toward realigning speaker incentives with producing comprehensible applications is to create stronger enforcement of existing Section 112(a) requirements that require comprehensible applications. In the current legal system, examiners are already able to provide "nonfinal rejections" that include an itemization of features of the patent claim that are unclear or involve excessive ambiguity under 112(a) and (b). This iterative dialog between the examiner and applicant works to improve the description of the claims, as well as an assessment of the invention's novelty and non-obviousness (creative value). But because of the limited resources of the examiner, if the nature of the claim is still unclear at the end of the process, these unworthy patent applications may get passed through the system and ultimately approved.

The proposal here provides more teeth to 112(a). To that end, we offer three alternative approaches that vary in the aggressiveness of the reform.

Strong Sanctions. A strong sanction approach requires inventors to provide an accessible, clear description of the claim (along with the invention's contribution to innovation, as described previously) at the start of the application process. Until this clear statement is provided and formally approved under 112(a), no patent is issued. The strong sanction thus reverses the soft presumption that an application is clear; now the application is presumed to be *unclear* until the examiner formally approves it.

To underscore the imperative of a clear claim, a distinct 112(a) step could be added to the longer patent process. Under this approach, the examiner must provide a formal assessment of the application purely with respect to the clarity of the claim and inventive statement.[109] Rather than the current approach, which allows examiners to *reject* claims for lack of clarity under Section 112(a), our proposal would invert the structure and require the examiner to issue a formal *approval* of the application with regard to clarity.

In cases where the claim is not sufficiently explained or detailed, the examiner would follow the existing process and issue nonfinal rejections, but in contrast to the existing process, nonfinal rejections issued under 112(a) would carry added costs to the inventor. At the time of the nonfinal rejection, the patent process clock would be stopped until the examiner approves – as a final matter – the clarity of the specification. Thus, between the time of the first nonfinal rejection and the final approval (or rejection) of clarity under this 112(a) step, the examiner would face no time pressure to clear the application. At the same time, the examiner's time for further review of the reparations would be compensated on an hourly rate by the applicant. Applicants could challenge "arbitrary" delays or charges by the PTO through an administrative appeal process, but the deference would lean heavily in favor of the PTO.

To ensure that examiners do not abuse this new authority to hold up applications and recoup expenses, an outer limit of a year or two would be set on the "stop the clock" 112(a) proceedings. Examiners might also be required to respond to applicant's efforts to repair the application within a set time (perhaps three months). Ultimately, some managerial approval or even an abbreviated, expedited appeal process might also become necessary to discourage examiners from taking advantage of this new authority. As just one possibility, the PTO might establish a special board of review for 112(a) rejections (perhaps with separate boards for each technology center). These special boards could review each 112(a) nonfinal rejection, providing individual examiners with support and ideally some legal backing for issuing these new decisions, while also penalizing examiners (or even terminating them) if they abuse the tolling provision.

A potentially reinforcing incentive could involve altering the rules for filing RCEs for claim rejections based on a lack of clarity under 112(a).[110] Applicants with final rejections for a lack of clarity might be allowed only one repeat filing for their application. While final rejections based on clarity might still be rare, if such a rejection led to a near "death penalty" for an invention, inventors might have stronger incentives to write the claim clearly at the outset.

As a statutory matter, this particular reform – although the most radical of the three alternatives – still may not require significant legal amendments. Requirements for clarity are already written into the statute. Thus, this proposal would involve at most a minor statutory or perhaps even regulatory adjustment that allows inventors to add new material to an application after filing, if and only if that new material responds to section 112(a) concerns raised by the examiner.

Less Draconian Sanctions. A less dramatic, but possibly still effective, sanction would submit applications to third-party review for all nonfinal rejections based on clarity and indefiniteness (112a and b). These nonfinal rejections could be posted on the PTO's website to solicit third-party comment. An electronic notification process could be designed to alert competitors in the general field of the comment opportunity.

Third parties would have a set period (e.g., 60 days) to file comments on the description and application that the examiner could consider. Third-party review would be limited, however, only to the claims that are of concern. To keep this third-party review in check, the participants may also need to be constrained by page and other filing limits.

This approach draws from the use of third-party review in the America Invents Act, but attempts to focus third parties on sharpening the drafting of the claim statement itself.[111] If this type of adjustment were made to existing process, it might be necessary to make allowances for the likely delays associated with receiving and processing comments. More resources will also be needed for the examiner to process some applications.

It is unclear at this point whether this kind of third-party review will ultimately be informative or instead be used to delay or harass inventors and examiners. Yet, for now, we raise this as yet another option to consider in devising ways to elicit cooperative communication from inventor-speakers.

A Gentle Slap. The lightest sanction could simply create adverse publicity for inventors and their attorneys who fail to provide clear, definite claims and inventive statements in their initial applications. The PTO could post the details of all nonfinal rejections under 112(a) in a way that shames applicants who fail to provide clear statements at the start. The PTO could also tally these results by formulating quantitative scores for legal firms and individual attorneys as part of its registration practice. The larger marketplace might then (hopefully) single out inventors and attorneys for poor or strategic draftsmanship. Recordkeeping could also be developed to track the extent of comprehensibility problems with repeat applications, perhaps categorizing them by inventor or attorney names. The examiner might even be able to estimate, for example, the amount of time and energy dedicated to making sense of an application and how those costs were shouldered by other applicants and the process at large.

Summary. However it is accomplished, the key objective is to place primary responsibility on the inventor to describe his invention clearly and accessibly. When the inventor fails in this responsibility, the resulting costs of the incomprehensibility should fall on the inventor rather than on the examiner and third parties.

2 Rewards to Encourage Comprehensibility

A supplement or alternative to sanctioning unclear claims (or bad behavior) is to create stronger rewards for clear claims (or good behavior). Applicants who invest considerable effort in providing the PTO with exemplary descriptions of their invention should sail through the process more quickly. Note, however, that these rewards will be generally ineffective in changing the Rule-Bender's behavior, since inventors with bad patents who strategically take advantage of the mis-designed system will still proceed unimpeded. Nonetheless, a strong signal for clear patents seems capable of producing negative stigma and feedback for intentionally obfuscated patents.

Our reform proposal would reward only "imminently comprehensible" claims by creating a two-track patent system – one track for excellently crafted applications and a second track for the rest of the applications. The inventor would choose which track best fits his application. The reform is modeled after Lichtman's and Lemley's *Gold-plated Patents*. In their proposal, inventors are rewarded with a particularly strong patent claim by undergoing a much more intensive review process; the applicant thus earns "a significant presumption in favor of patent validity" if they invest in a more costly patent process.[112]

In the imminently comprehensible track proposed here, a patent is granted more swiftly and inexpensively (contra the Lichtman and Lemley proposal) when the application is drafted in a way that is very clear and comprehensible for examiners and more general audiences.[113] Criteria for these "imminently comprehensible" specifications would be developed by the PTO in advance. The rewards for taking advantage of this alternative track are thus tied primarily to a reduced speed and cost associated with obtaining a patent, rather than the durability of the claim itself. To ensure the speed of the review, this imminently comprehensible version of the gold-plated track could be staffed by a subset of experienced examiners. (Page and claim limits for each application may also become necessary to enable an expedited review, but we leave that and other details for others.)

Only inventors who are confident of their applications would select this track, however. If the examiner concludes that an application has been inappropriately slotted into the fast-track because of ambiguities or a lack of clarity that run afoul of 112(a) (as discussed), there would be a significant monetary sanction associated with the mistake, along with added processing time. The application, for example, would be rerouted to the normal, non-gold-plated process and the new examiner's clock would start at the beginning, initiating a fresh review all over again. However it is accomplished, it is important to design this system so that the applicant is significantly worse off for having tried but failed the gold-plated track. Indeed, a signal could be attached to these applicants indicating that they failed in this particular process.

Borrowing more directly from the gold-plated patent idea, additional rewards could be bestowed on those applicants who take advantage of this imminently comprehensible fast-track and succeed. Imminently comprehensible patents could enjoy the added advantage of being afforded extra deference by courts for an approved claim in a *Markman* hearing. The judge would take note of the fact that the claim is particularly clear, and considerable deference would be provided to the examiner's record in this regard. Polk Wagner has suggested a parallel approach in his work; "[i]deally, the courts could largely defer to an administrative opinion on claim scope," thus "fix[ing] the meaning of a patent claim at as early a stage as possible" before the issue reaches litigation.[114]

Imminently comprehensible patents might also enjoy privileged status during an examiner's prior art search of other competing patents. Any ambiguities that arise when a claim appears to encroach on an imminently comprehensible patent would require added explanation from the second inventor. Indeed, perhaps the gold-plated patent holder would be consulted directly for comments on claims that appear close to his patent, providing yet another bonus.

C *Reinforcement from Competitors*

Competitors could be enlisted to serve as intermediaries to help improve and identify incomprehensibility in applications. As one possibility, all applications could be subject to a formal comment period immediately after filing. The application and a concise summary would be posted, along with a portal and deadline for submitting comments on the application. (This stands in contrast to the current process for protesting a patent under existing law).[115] Instituting this formal, early review could provide the examiner with a more focused application as a result of deploying a mini-adversarial process at the start of the proceeding. If creating this new step in the application process actually does lead to greater third-party engagement with applications, inventors, in theory, will anticipate competitors' arguments in drafting their application and be more inclined toward cooperative communication as a result of this added scrutiny.

A third-party review step earlier in the process would need to be closely monitored, however. The use of third-party review late in the proceedings, under the America Invents Act, has had mixed success. At least one set of industry participants has expressed the concern that greater intervening rights to third parties may cause them to "be incentivized to present absurd positions of claim scope" and "abuse the reexamination process by initiating multiple reexamination proceedings in an attempt to create argument-based intervening rights."[116] Raymond Mercado's empirical study in fact reveals that at least one-quarter of the opposition proceedings mounted by third parties in the post-reform era were abusive and involved some form of misconduct on behalf of the challenging parties.[117] Participants observed, for example, that third parties "often use the unlimited page limit in the Request to [cause] an impracticable number of rejections/unadopted rejections to be present in the re-exam, which prevents the focusing of issues." Another participant noted that the third parties' "strategy seemed to be to inundate the examiner with so many rejections and combinations of prior art that the examiner would never have time to adequately respond to each and every point."[118]

The PTO itself confirms that these third-party proceedings add burdens to already overstretched staff. They note, for example, that third-party requests averaged 246 pages each and that "the very large size of the requests has created a burden on the Office that hinders the efficiency and timeliness of processing the requests."[119]

As a result, third-party filings would need to be strictly limited in number, page limits, and other features to focus on the specifics and not make the review process even more unwieldy. These limits may need to be extreme to protect the examiner: for example, a two-page limit for each commenter. Inventors would also need to be provided an opportunity to reply to questions and comments, again with strict limits for the unified response (e.g., a 10-page response). To deter abuse of process, the examiner could be afforded discretion to fine frivolous or otherwise unhelpful comments and responses, and the fines would in turn compensate him for overtime work. If fines are levied, these transgressions ideally would also be publicized on a website that identifies by name – e.g., the attorney, firm, or other author – those associated with the transgression. Fines could even escalate over time. A particular attorney who files frivolous comments will find the second or third offense is tenfold more costly than the first offense.

Although it may be excessive and unnecessary, for patents that generate less attention there could be prizes for the best student comments and even academic awards to universities that engage students in this type of scrutiny. As long as there are experts scrutinizing the claim-drafting process, there will be fewer benefits to hiding in the weeds.

However it is accomplished, the underlying gist of the proposal is to develop an early iterative process that serves to narrow, rather than broaden, the issues for concern in the patent review. If, however, the examiner is inundated with comments and responses in ways that further complicate the review, despite financial penalties levied on abusers, this particular reform should be abandoned.

Thumbnail Sketch of Patent Law Reform

1. Require applicant to provide an inventive statement that details the invention's contribution to the field.
2. Impose sanctions (e.g., limiting continuing applications) for specifications and claims that are not comprehensible to a reasonable examiner.
3. Create rewards (e.g., a "gold-plated" track) for applications that are "imminently comprehensible."
4. Enlist competitors to participate in the review of applications.
5. Encourage courts to defer to an examiner's characterization of the claim.

D Mix and Match

Although we present the adjustments individually, they could be paired in different combinations to further increase the inventor's incentives for cooperative communication. For example, if third-party commenters raise significant problems with the clarity of an application, that application could automatically enter a probationary review under 112(a) that stops the clock on the examination while clarity issues are addressed. Conversely, if the commenters appear to be abusing the process and the claimant convinces the examiner of this fact, the application could actually be (in rare cases) moved by the examiner into the gold-plated system to create added consequences – beyond fines and reputational harm – to competitors who seek to abuse the system.

As another combination of reforms, if third-party review becomes institutionalized early in the process, it could create an added inducement for the gold-plated system; inventors would be relieved of third-party review if they choose the gold-plated system. And conversely, if a gold-plated application is not up to snuff, third-party review could then serve as an added cost to being slotted back into the "normal" process. The applicants will find themselves back at the beginning of the application process; yet in this case, competitors and other third-party reviewers would be alerted to the fact that the applicant did not meet the gold-plated standards, making the application even more vulnerable to critical scrutiny by peers.

E *Judicial Review*

The courts must interpret claims in ways that reward clarity and sanction ambiguities and indefiniteness. This requires both fine-tuning and focusing the interpretive tests that the courts currently use.

The first and most important doctrinal adjustment is already in play and would simply direct courts to interpret all ambiguities and uncertainties in claim construction against the inventor.[120] As Burk and Lemley suggest, for example, in interpreting claims, the courts should "start with the patentee's invention itself, construing patent claims narrowly and in light of the actual invention when the claim terms are ambiguous."[121] As a result, unclear claims will not be read broadly, but will be consistently read as narrowly as possible. Inventors will not enjoy a windfall in infringement cases for drafting open-ended claims.

Several other doctrinal reforms could further sharpen the courts' role in encouraging clearer claims. Golden suggests fine-tuning the "anti-redundancy canon" in order to encourage more cohesive claims and valuable summary statements.[122] His proposal is fully consistent with producing interpretive rules that encourage and reward comprehensible claims.

Courts may even be able to create deference tests that look to the PTO examiner's characterization of the claim rather than consulting a dictionary or utilizing other judge-devised interpretive tools. (We leave the specifics to experts in patent litigation and federal courts, however, and offer it here only as another reform option to explore). In infringement cases, for example, a defendant could raise arguments from the PTO's record that informs the scope and nature of the claim. To make this effective, examiners would likely need to be required to place into the record all concerns about claim construction and even to qualify approvals based on their own understanding of the claim. In return, the inventor would understand that these identified weaknesses will limit the strength of his approved claim in any subsequent infringement litigation. If an inventor is eager for a strong claim, he or she will devise a patent application that examiners find clear and accessible.

V CONCLUSION

The patent process is designed in a way that aggravates comprehension asymmetries and resulting miscommunications. Inventors will focus their energies on sharing all information, but will sometimes not take the added step of mastering the nature of their invention or communicating its key attributes in a clear and accessible way. Reforms of the patent process do not require a radical overhaul of the existing process. However, any reform that is developed must pay heed to producing strong incentives for cooperative communication. Inventors should thrive only when they provide clear and accessible descriptions of their invention in ways that examiners and others can reasonably understand.

5C

Comprehension Asymmetries in Chemical Regulation

Ignorance about chemical risks has been a signature feature of US chemical regulation for nearly half a century.[1] In 1984, almost one decade into the chemical regulation program, the National Academies of Science conducted a study that found there was *no* information available to assess health or environmental toxicity for more than 80 percent of the nearly 50,000 chemicals sold in commerce.[2] More recent replications of the study for high-production chemicals report that the vast majority of chemicals are so lacking in toxicity data that a basic risk assessment is not possible.[3] And even for the chemicals that have been rigorously studied, the reliability of existing tests leaves much room for improvement.[4]

But even when there is some testing available, this information is rarely analyzed to evaluate the long-term safety of the chemical. Although the toxicity data on a few "headline" chemicals eventually do undergo rigorous evaluation,[5] the information available on the long-term safety of the majority of chemicals and related products remains unassessed.[6] Even the most rudimentary analysis of these chemicals' long-term hazards is rarely conducted. Instead, the data, studies, and reports pile up in file cabinets and sometimes on websites, with little effort devoted to analyzing their implications.

This limited testing and assessment helps explain the nearly complete ignorance surrounding some widely used, reactive chemicals.[7] When the chemical MCHM (4-methylcyclohexane methanol) spilled into the Elk River in West Virginia in 2014, for example, public health and environmental scientists were stunned to learn that, after 50 years of use, there was *no* long-term toxicity data available on the chemical.[8] Scientists were forced to make informed guesses about what the 7,500 gallon spill of this reactive chemical in a public waterway might do to drinking water supplies, public health, and the environment.[9] The same ignorance helps explain the lack of procedures in place to prevent and mitigate disasters such as Bhopal, which involved mass deadly exposure to toxic chemicals.[10] Even at the most mundane level, consumers notice that, while they are able to buy plastic water bottles labeled

"BPA-free," they have no information about whether the substitute plastic is any safer.[11] They also take note of the belated discoveries of unexpected hazards in familiar consumer products, such as the discovery of cancer-causing asbestos fibers in a 120-year-old product, Johnson & Johnson's baby powder.[12]

The limited assessment of chemical hazards also helps explain why agencies have taken so little regulatory action to restrict the use of dangerous products. The Consumer Product Safety Commission (CPSC), for example, has imposed few binding regulatory restrictions on consumer products based on long-term risks, in large part because the agency lacks the resources to conduct the assessments and tests needed to justify regulatory action.[13] OSHA has set protective standards for only a small fraction of the toxic chemicals present in the workplace, including chemicals that are known to be causing worker fatalities.[14] The EPA has subjected only a tiny subset (200) of the 70,000 chemicals in commerce to mandatory testing over the last 40 years, despite the alarming lack of information about them.[15] And the EPA has banned still fewer chemicals – five chemicals to be precise – as unreasonably hazardous during that same time frame.[16]

As a result, many chemical products fall between the cracks – causing harm, but for no good reason. Consider the case of a highly toxic asphalt sealant. This particular sealant is substantially more toxic than its competitors, but it is neither more effective nor lower in cost than alternative sealants.[17] There is no good reason, in other words, why such a highly toxic sealant should be allowed on the market. Yet the existence of this unreasonably hazardous product was not discovered by expert regulators nor volunteered by the sealant manufacturers. Instead, the toxic sealant was discovered by accident by wildlife biologists who were trying to pinpoint the cause of a sudden sharp decline in the population of an endangered salamander in Austin, Texas.[18] In testing the water of the spring-fed pools, biologists identified a sudden influx of a dangerous toxin (PAHs) that corresponded with the timing of the salamanders' decline. The spike in PAH concentrations was methodically traced to a newly paved apartment parking lot upslope from the salamander's habitat. The owner of the parking lot had unknowingly used an asphalt sealant that was many times higher in PAHs than competitor products. While the City of Austin and a few local governments now ban this unreasonably toxic sealant, CPSC and the EPA never took regulatory action.[19]

How can it be that, after so many years of regulation, we still know so little about the long-term risks of most chemicals and have made so little progress in regulating them? As with financial and patent processes, one of the root causes appears to lie in the design of a regulatory system that fails to counteract existing comprehension asymmetries between manufacturers and regulators. Specifically, the chemical manufacturers (speakers) face no responsibility for learning of or communicating the long-term risks of the chemicals they produce. Instead, this burden is placed on time- and resource-strapped regulators and consumers (audience). Making matters worse, manufacturers face substantial tort liabilities that can sometimes lead to bankruptcy if the hazards associated with their products are brought to light. But, by contrast, manufacturers receive few market or regulatory benefits if these chemicals are found to be safe. As a result, manufacturers will generally (although not always) resist learning about the long-term risks of their chemical products, particularly those already on the market. Some manufacturers will go even farther and actively obstruct efforts by regulators and consumers to learn of the long-term risks of their products.

Our exploration of the comprehension asymmetries embedded in the design of chemical regulation is divided into three parts. In the first part, we discuss how background pressures from tort law and the market provide almost no incentives for manufacturers to assess the long-term risks of their chemicals. In the second part, we consider how the existing legal design not only fails to counteract, but actively exacerbates these existing comprehension asymmetries. Manufacturers are legally allowed and sometimes tacitly encouraged to shift excessive processing costs to the regulator-audience. In some cases, they may even benefit from inundating regulators with more unprocessed information than they can reasonably manage. We then offer preliminary suggestions for reform.

I BACKGROUND

In this section, we meet the main participants in chemical regulation and consider whether they are already predisposed to learn of and communicate the risks of their chemicals to regulators and other expert audiences. We begin with a brief orientation to chemical regulation to situate our participants within the larger legal landscape.

A *Orientation to Chemical Regulation*

Chemicals come in contact with consumers on a daily basis, but not all reactive chemicals present risks worthy of a regulator's attention. In general, "the dose makes the poison." As a result, existing regulatory approaches generally do not prohibit toxic chemicals altogether, but instead seek to minimize risks to public health and the environment by regulating exposure.

To implement this overall approach to protecting health and the environment, Congress created a number of statutory fiefdoms, each governing different chemical uses (e.g., chemicals in pesticides, chemicals in commerce, chemicals in air, chemicals in drinking water, chemicals on land). Each fiefdom – or regulatory program – defines acceptable risks for toxic chemicals differently and restricts them according to the extent of public harm they are capable of causing. For example, because of the higher exposure risks (e.g., ingestion), pesticide residues in food are regulated at more stringent levels than hazardous pesticides dumped on land.

In setting these standards or restrictions, the burden rests with the agency to assemble the evidence and make the case of an unreasonable risk. Fundamental to the agency's burden is assessing the risk of individual chemicals using whatever research and data is available. Manufacturers, by contrast, are relieved of all legal responsibility for assessing these risks, despite their key role in producing and profiting from a chemical. However, although chemical manufacturers are relieved of conducting assessments, they are sometimes required to turn over certain relevant information to regulators and, in rarer cases, to conduct specific tests.

There are three information-sharing requirements in chemical regulation that will help structure our analysis in this chapter.

New Chemicals versus Old Chemicals. A consistent theme running throughout the regulatory programs governing toxic substances is that manufacturers of *new* chemicals must share relevant information relating to potential risks with regulators before the chemical can be marketed.[20] Thus, for new chemicals, the regulator obtains at least some baseline information from the manufacturers from which to assess chemical risks. Although the burden for doing this assessment still rests with the regulator, there is at least a requirement of information disclosure required for the manufacturer of a new chemical.[21]

The manufacturers of *existing* chemicals, by contrast, are not required to provide basic, underlying information to regulators about the safety of their products.[22] Instead, existing chemicals and chemical products (with the important exception of pesticides) are generally presumed safe, and it is up to the regulator to determine otherwise. Even when the manufacturer enjoys exclusive control over information that may be relevant to the regulators' assessment, statutes require regulators to collect this information.[23] Thus, in contrast to financial and patent regulation, in chemical regulation the manufacturers of existing chemicals are relieved of providing "known" information on chemical risks to regulators except for limited adverse effects.

Regulators can demand only specific, additional tests. In most (but not all) chemical-based regulatory programs, the regulator is given limited authority to require additional specific tests to be performed to assess the hazards of a product. In using these authorities, however, the regulator must identify the tests that are needed and make the case that additional testing is warranted.[24] Manufacturers can and do challenge these testing orders. Indeed, up until 2017, a chemical manufacturer could successfully defend against a testing order by arguing that when nothing was known about a chemical, the regulator could not support its burden of proof that testing was needed because there was no evidence that the chemical was hazardous – a classic Catch-22.[25]

Adverse Effects. Manufacturers of both new and existing chemicals are required to share information about significant risks of chemicals that come to their attention after the chemical is marketed.[26] While manufacturers enjoy some discretion in determining what information triggers this notification requirement, the gist of the requirement is that when manufacturers become privy to new, post-market information that may be relevant to assessing a chemical's risks, they must provide that information to the regulator and allow the regulator to update and revise his assessment.

B *The Speaker and Audience*

We can already see the potential for comprehension asymmetries within this basic structure of chemical regulation. There is essentially no burden on manufacturers to understand and communicate the risks of their chemicals. Regulators are instead expected to do this important work.

But perhaps market and other legal pressures, like the tort system, already provide sufficient incentives for manufacturers to ensure this assessment work is occurring? Or perhaps the regulator is more able to conduct these chemical assessments? We investigate these possibilities next.

1 Manufacturers as Speakers

Chemical manufacturers are the "speakers" in our model. They are well positioned to assess the risks of their chemical products, but their incentive to do so is low.

Manufacturers (speakers) are in the best position to assess risk. Even for the most thinly financed start-up company, as the creators of a chemical the manufacturer enjoys an advantaged position in assessing the long-term risks of its products.[27] This occurs in large part because the manufacturer is privy to the chemical formula, and this formula alone offers important clues about a chemical's reactivity, known as the "structure–activity relationship."[28] Indeed, this information is so vital that manufacturers enjoy a legally protected right to classify their chemical formulas as "trade secrets."[29]

Manufacturers also acquire firsthand information about chemical risks from their own research, development, and sales activities.[30] In the course of producing a chemical, for example, manufacturers can learn about various dangers, acute harms, and exposure risks that are associated with working with the chemical.[31] Even consumer complaints of injuries caused by the chemical that arise after marketing can provide manufacturers with anecdotal but useful clues regarding chemical risks.[32]

Manufacturers also have the unique ability to adjust the composition of a chemical product iteratively, as the product is developed. If a chemical formulation is assessed and appears excessively toxic, for example, the manufacturer sometimes can alter that formulation to make it less hazardous, before the product goes into development.[33] Since over 70 percent of the investment in producing a chemical is dedicated to the *final* stages, after the product is designed, this early approach to testing is vastly more efficient.[34]

In addition to being well positioned to assess risk from a technical perspective, manufacturers are well positioned to assume the costs of testing. By including testing costs in the product price, manufacturers spread the cost of testing across the consumers who benefit from the expenditure. Moreover, at least for widely used products – those for which testing is generally the most important from a public health perspective – the increase in price associated with testing will be relatively small because these costs will be spread over a large base of sales.[35]

Manufacturers have few incentives to do assessments. Although manufacturers are well positioned to assess the long-term risks of the chemicals they produce, they face few incentives from either market competition or tort law to conduct these assessments. Only when they are fairly confident the results will be favorable are they likely to perceive some, albeit modest, rewards for making the investment. There are several reasons manufacturers are likely to choose ignorance in these situations.

First, the costs of conducting assessments can be high.[36] A chemical assessment typically involves identifying all relevant information, weighting its reliability, synthesizing it, and soliciting expert peer review to scrutinize the conclusions. In some cases, additional toxicity testing must also be completed before the assessment is done.

Second, an assessment of long-term risks will probably *not* improve sales, no matter what that investigation reveals.[37] Long-term risks of a chemical are a negative market feature, and so learning about these risks does not improve a firm's competitive position. But even favorable toxicity findings will generally not be rewarded with higher sales without a way to certify the reliability of a manufacturer's self-assessment.[38] This "good news" is thus at risk of being dismissed as biased or self-serving by consumers.

Third, consumers tend to overreact to any evidence of risk, however minimal. Cancer is dreaded. Evidence of some long-term toxicity, even if the information is inconclusive, can quickly lead to negative repercussions in the market.[39] Given the media firestorm resulting from the discovery of trace amounts of benzene in Perrier water and Alar-tainted apples, for example, it is not surprising that manufacturers are gun-shy about learning about potential risks associated with their products (even if these risks are small).[40]

Finally, the tort system aggravates manufacturers' incentives for ignorance, at least for existing products. If a manufacturer's chemical causes unreasonable harm to users, consumers, or even bystanders, then the manufacturer can be required to pay damages in suits brought by these victims. In these cases, however, it is the plaintiffs who bear the burden of proof for establishing a causal connection between the product and their harm.[41] Until the evidence supports this connection, the manufacturer is spared liability. Even if the manufacturer negligently or even reck-lessly refuses to conduct research, tort law requires plaintiffs to provide compelling evidence that a chemical in fact caused harm in order to proceed with a claim.[42]

By contrast, once evidence of long-term harms is available, the manufacturer is on the run and becomes vulnerable to tort claims. The on-off switch that determines successful litigation is thus heavily influenced, if not controlled, by the manufactur-ers' own testing and assessment program. In some cases – such as asbestos, tobacco, and a few other extremely hazardous products – excessive harms were discovered by third-party research, but these are exceptional cases and not the rule.[43]

It is important to note, however, that tort law's effect on manufacturers' incentives for assessing risks can sometimes cut the other way and encourage rigorous in-house assessments. The threat of tort liability can be controlled for new chemicals by ensuring that dangerous chemicals are not produced in the first place. If a chemical is found to be dangerous early during product development, that product can be abandoned before exposures and potential tort liability occur. Also, as already noted, it can sometimes be relatively easy to adjust the chemical composition of a product during research and development. At this early stage in product development, then, there may be more upside than downside for a manufacturer to invest in rigorously assessing a chemical's long-term risks.[44]

For existing chemicals, however, tort law generally has the opposite effect. Not only has the manufacturer sunk considerable monies into production, marketing, and distribution of existing chemical products, but because consumers have already been exposed, unexpected evidence of long-term risks have the potential to trigger costly lawsuits. If a manufacturer is unsure of what a long-term risk assessment will show for chemicals already sold on the market, the manufacturer will rationally either opt for ignorance or may even conduct biased assessments and impede others from learning adverse information about its products.[45]

In most chemical markets, then, investing in chemical assessments – at least for existing chemicals – may put the manufacturer at both a competitive and a legal disadvantage. As Mary Lyndon has observed, the chemicals market creates a "market for lemons," where the least-studied chemicals generally fare the best.[46]

2 The Agencies as Audience

The expert regulator is the primary audience in our analysis. As compared with the speaker, the regulator encounters several disadvantages in assessing long-term chemical risks.

Regulators lack the resources needed to conduct assessments and improve assess-ment methodologies. The most important limitation by far that regulators face in assessing chemical risks is a shortage of resources available to do the work. In the chemicals regulation program alone, as noted, there are more than 70,000 chemicals in commerce.[47] The limited staffing of the EPA's chemical regulation program creates a ratio of more than 200 chemicals to every 1 staffer, including support staff.[48] This personnel shortage explains, at least in part, the EPA's notorious backlog in assessing chemicals.[49] The EPA's pace in setting health-based standards for chemicals in a related program ("Integrated Risk Information System (IRIS)"), for example, is so slow that the General Accounting Office identified the program as at risk of becoming obsolete.[50] Agencies also lack the staff needed to improve the rigor and breadth of available methods for testing the neurological, reproductive, developmental, and other long-term risks associated with exposure to a chemical.[51]

Regulators lack the knowledge about specific chemicals needed to make effective use of their expertise when assessing chemical risks. At a general level, regulators do enjoy important advantages in expertise in assessing chemicals relative to manufacturers. Regulatory agencies are staffed with teams of specialized scientists whose training covers a wide swath of relevant disciplines needed to evaluate risks.[52] Regulators are also less prone to biases in reviewing risk information since their career structure tends to reward rigorous research; this may not be the case for some manufacturers given the liability risks just discussed.[53] These regulatory experts also enjoy the ability to search and collect scientific research in ways individual manufactures cannot – for example, by demanding information from individual manufacturers through information collection powers.[54]

Typically, the expertise of regulators (the audience) would reduce their information-processing costs and in so doing reduce comprehension asymmetries, but this generalized expertise is offset by regulators' lack of particularized expertise about individual chemicals. Unlike manufacturers, regulators do not enjoy firsthand knowledge of how individual chemicals are prepared, how they react or even how they are used, or their exposure pathways. Indeed, if this information is classified as a trade secret or withheld from the agency,[55] the agency's expertise may become effectively irrelevant.

3 Other Audiences

Regulators are not the only entities with an interest in assessing chemical risks. On the contrary, investors, downstream purchasers in production chains, and competitors are also audiences of manufacturers. Yet, for these audiences, comprehension asymmetries with respect to the chemical manufacturer will tend to be even greater than for regulators. While some of these entities will certainly be motivated to process information on chemical risks to make better investments, improve purchasing decisions, or improve the competitive positioning of products (assuming for the sake of this discussion this information is communicated by manufacturers), the costs of making such assessments will typically exceed their expected value for these audiences. Moreover, unless all manufacturers provide the information needed to make risk assessments, the value of conducting such assessments might be dramatically reduced. To make a sound purchasing decision, for example, the risks of all (or at least most) competitor products would need to be evaluated.[56] Knowing only the long-term risks of one product generally does not provide enough information to be of use in making market decisions.

Needless to say, comprehension asymmetries for less sophisticated consumers (including victims of exposure to hazardous chemicals) will be even greater than for other types of audiences. Indeed, one of the primary justifications for regulatory programs is to address asymmetries in understanding between consumers and manufacturers.

II CHEMICAL REGULATION AND COMPREHENSION ASYMMETRIES

In light of these comprehension asymmetries, does regulation serve to close the gap between the manufacturers' superior capacity for understanding and explaining the long-term risks of their chemicals and the regulators' disadvantages in doing this work? We first trace how the legal rules might affect our Rule-Following manufacturers' incentives for understanding and communicating chemical risks. We then track this same legal program's impact on Rule-Benders.

A *Rule-Followers*

While manufacturers who are Rule-Followers would seem eager to provide the regulator with a rigorous understanding of the long-term risks associated with the chemicals they produce, existing legal requirements may discourage even the most "green" manufacturers from investing in this effort, particularly for chemicals already on the market.

1 Dutifully Provide Known Information to Regulators but do not Volunteer to do More

The primary obligation of the Rule-Follower under the existing law is to turn over all "known" safety information to regulators, both before a new chemical reaches the market[57] and after marketing if there are discernible adverse effects.[58] However, regulatory requirements do not require, nor even encourage, regulated parties to assess the risks of their products. The manufacturers' sole obligation instead is to provide raw, unprocessed information regarding potential risks to the agency.[59] It is then up to the agency to process and make sense of this hodge-podge of information, reports, data, and studies. Indeed, since the manufacturer's sole legal responsibility is to transfer certain "known" information to the agency (for example, information on adverse effects), a Rule-Follower will be inclined to err on the side of including information that could ultimately turn out to be irrelevant or unhelpful, just to stay on the right side of the law.[60]

To make matters worse, because any self-assessment a Rule-Follower does conduct could trigger the adverse effect notification requirement, the law may inadvertently penalize some Rule-Followers who take the initiative and do a self-assessment
of their chemicals on their own. More specifically, if an initial in-house assessment
suggests some possibility of a significant risk – no matter how preliminary – that
information must be turned over to the EPA within 30 days after it is created. The
information must also be made public.[61] Months later, after the Rule-Follower's in-
house assessment is completed, the Rule-Follower may ultimately learn that there
was no cause for concern. But by now, the regulatory wheels are in motion.
A subsequent final report by the Rule-Follower that backpedals on the first may
be viewed as suspect and self-serving.

Moreover, if the law does not require manufacturers to provide accessible
summaries of the long-term risks of their products, and there are no market or
regulatory benefits to producing them, then it is hard for the Rule-Follower
to justify the expense. Perhaps even more important, if corporate management is
not sure what the chemical evaluation will reveal, then doing this analysis could
lead to costly repercussions that are outside the company's control, such as
additional regulatory restrictions, tort liability, or the loss of market shares from
adverse publicity. These cumulative dangers may even place the Rule-Follower's
management at risk of a claim of violating its fiduciary duty to shareholders
if it proceeds with uncertain self-assessments that can jeopardize the firm's
financial stability.

2 Avoid Waiving Trade Secret Protections

Rule-Followers may unwittingly complicate the regulator's processing burden by
being overly risk-averse in classifying the information they submit as trade secret.
This trade secret classification imposes costly barriers to public access; indeed, even
within the agency, a regulator must be officially "cleared" before being allowed to
view the information.[62]

The Rule-Follower will be inclined to err on the side of overclassification of
information as trade secret because if he does not assert the privilege when he first
submits information to the regulator, the trade secret protection will be deemed
waived forever.[63] Busy Rule-Followers may not have the time or resources to
carefully review each and every scrap of information they submit to regulators to
determine whether it involves some in-house intellectual property. And, if the law
does not require the Rule-Follower to justify a trade secret claim, even conscientious
Rule-Followers will cut corners and assume – when in doubt that information
involves some potentially valuable in-house secret.[64] However, even when a justification is required by law, a Rule-Follower will err on the side of assuming there is a
valid claim since the costs are substantial if he underestimates the intellectual
property value of the information.

3 Provide Comprehensive Comments on Agency Assessments

Rule-Followers will be eager to educate the agency as it conducts a full-blown assessment of their chemicals, and this enthusiasm could lead to further costs for the regulator. In these communications, the Rule-Follower will not attempt to confuse or overwhelm the agency; however, the Rule-Follower will be motivated to ensure the agency's assessment is true to the research and does not jump the gun in making dire assessments when there are rampant uncertainties.

Under existing law, the agency is required to solicit feedback on its analysis from all affected parties, and there is no limit to the volume, length, or number of comments that an affected party can submit. In commenting on the agency's assessment of its chemicals, then, the ever-diligent Rule-Following manufacturer will take every opportunity to offer feedback. Rule-Followers will go the extra mile in order to be thorough and also to avoid waiving arguments down the road.[65] The possibility that – for some comments – the regulator's own processing effort may be greater than the value of the comments is at best a secondary concern.[66]

4 Summary

Ultimately, then, the Rule-Follower may find that voluntarily conducting self-assessments on the risks of existing chemicals increases both his costs and his legal vulnerabilities. A studious Rule-Follower will follow the straight and narrow path – comply with the law by providing all potentially relevant information to the agency without any analysis – and let the chips fall where they may.

B *Rule-Benders*

As long as Rule-Bending manufacturers are relieved of the responsibility of providing an accurate assessment of the long-term risks of their chemicals, they will not only find it beneficial to proceed in ignorance, but will actively obstruct regulators' efforts to assess these risks if there is a chance the assessments will be unfavorable. Several Rule-Bending tactics emerge from the literature as particularly successful.

1 Bury the Regulator in Information, Whether Useful or Not

The first and simplest line of attack for Rule-Bending manufacturers is to overwhelm regulators with information, particularly information of uncertain quality and relevance. Doing so requires still more processing by the overwhelmed regulators. This databombing can even cause regulators to abandon a project altogether.

Manufacturers' compliance with the adverse effects notification requirements (discussed earlier) offers a straightforward example of how this tactic plays out. To avoid self-incrimination by reporting an adverse effect, some manufacturers send benign or even irrelevant information on the chemical to the agency as an FYI ("for your information") submission.[67] The FYI submission allows the manufacturers not only to obscure potentially serious risks, but to overwhelm the agency at the same time.[68] There is some evidence this databombing tactic works; the EPA regulators do not always (or perhaps often) have the resources needed to rigorously analyze the incoming information submitted under these adverse effects requirements.[69]

Beyond pure databombing, the manufacturer can also raise regulators' processing costs by submitting information of dubious reliability.[70] Biased research may lend a patina of credibility to a manufacturer's claims that its chemical is safe, but the regulator will need to invest considerable effort in evaluating the reliability of this information. As a result, the regulator's effort to complete a chemical assessment might be slowed by the added work associated with assessing the reliability of this manufacturer-supplied information. In some cases, the regulator might even capitulate and treat the incoming sponsored research as presumptively trustworthy in order to save scarce resources.

The design of the regulatory process adds yet one more insult in exacerbating preexisting comprehension asymmetries: It fails to impose sanctions on Rule-Benders who deliberately engage in this kind of mischief. Short of fraud (which requires evidence of intentional wrongdoing), the agency has few ways to penalize Rule-Benders that strategically submit low quality and misleading studies. The agency does not even request basic information that provides some indication of research reliability, such as the existence of nondisclosure contracts in sponsoring research. From the Rule-Bender's vantage point, then, there is everything to gain and almost nothing to lose from submitting biased research.

To produce this ends-oriented research, manufacturers have devised multiple ways to design and conduct a study to increase the odds of reaching a favorable result.[71] As one of many examples of how this scientific manipulation is accomplished, consider a company eager to convince a regulator that its factory process is not hazardous to workers. To produce this desired finding, the Rule-Bender can design an epidemiological study that carefully selects "exposed" and "control" populations near the factory in ways likely to conflate the two.[72] "Exposed" workers might include all employees of the company, even those who work blocks away in the law and accounting offices. "Control" or unexposed persons might include subcontractors or other employees working under short-term contracts who receive the highest exposures on the assembly line, yet are not on the companies' full-time payroll. By conflating "control" and "exposed," the study is likely to produce a "no effect" result.[73] Scientists conducting sponsored epidemiological research have in fact developed a veritable toolkit of these ends-oriented tricks in designing studies to ensure favorable outcomes for their sponsors.[74]

The Rule-Bender's motivation to provide biased research can be so substantial that the Rule-Bender will even hire an entire cadre of scientists and reserve – through contract – the right to control their research.[75] In a 2005 survey of 3,200 US scientists, 15 percent admitted that they had changed the design, methodology, or results of a study under pressure from a funding source.[76] Yet, even without direct contractual control, one can imagine how, if a sponsor of research is affected by the outcome of that research, the sponsor may carefully select only sympathetic researchers and specify the questions that a study is designed to answer in ways that benefit the manufacturer.

Dozens of books and articles published in the last few decades document many other subtle ways that research has been produced in ends-oriented ways by sponsors with a stake in the outcome.[77] And, although these biases certainly do not infect every sponsored study, in the aggregate, there is persuasive evidence that a sponsor's interest does affect the findings of the sponsored research. In a series of meta-studies that examine financial conflicts of interest statements in relation to research outcomes, researchers have identified a strong, statistically significant "funding effect." A comprehensive review article summarizing 1,140 biomedical research studies, for example, concluded that "industry-sponsored studies were significantly more likely to reach conclusions that were favorable to the sponsor than were nonindustry studies."[78]

EPA's effort to determine whether to reregister the controversial herbicide Atrazine provides an example of how these Rule-Bending techniques can be combined. In assessing the risks of Atrazine, the EPA was faced with analyzing over 6,000 studies that were pertinent to the inquiry, 80 percent of which were not published and over half of which were produced by scientists with financial ties to manufacturers of the herbicide.[79] Under the law, however, the manufacturer was not required to ensure the reliability of the more than 3,000 studies it sponsored. Instead, the EPA was required to use its own staff and resources to do this work, reviewing the thousands of studies "with a fine tooth comb."[80] And, since the manufacturer had ample opportunity to comment on the agency's work, the EPA was required to process the manufacturer's voluminous feedback as well.[81] Ultimately, the EPA decided to approve the herbicide for re-registration, despite the existence of "several prominent studies by independent academic scientists in well-respected scientific journals showing negative reproductive effects of atrazine in animals and humans."[82] At the time of EPA's decision, Atrazine had been banned in the European Union (despite the fact that the manufacturer is a Swiss company).[83]

2 Impede Access to Relevant Information

Rule-Benders not only err on the side of classifying information as trade secret in order to protect their intellectual property, but they will deliberatively take advantage of this loosely defined privilege to keep information out of pubic view. Once chemical-related information is classified as a trade secret, the information must be stored in a secured separate location or database. Agency staff who erroneously allow the trade secret information to be released face the possibility of spending up to one year in prison.[84]

Under the current law, there are no sanctions imposed on Rule-Benders for asserting trade secret claims later determined to be unjustified or even frivolous.[85] In some regulatory programs, the manufacturer is not even required to explain the basis for its claims. [86] Instead, it is up to the regulator to evaluate whether a trade secret claim is warranted, and only after the regulator has initiated proceedings to disclose the information is the manufacturer required to justify its claim.[87] Since the burden of judging the legitimacy of these claims rests on regulators, manufacturers benefit from claiming trade secret protections but face no costs for making claims that are unjustified.

Mounting evidence reveals that Rule-Benders have been overclaiming trade secrets for decades. Trade secret classifications in chemical regulation are widespread – as of May 2016, nearly two-thirds of the 22,450 chemicals added to the TSCA list since 1979 involved trade secret claims on the identity of the chemical[88] – and a potentially sizable portion of these claims appear to be unwarranted. An audit of industry's trade secret claims reported extensive evidence of overclaiming.[89] Some manufacturers even stamped news articles and information in corporate reports as being "trade secret" protected. Yet these clearly erroneous classifications had not (yet) been reviewed or rejected by busy regulators.[90] A 2001 study in fact found that when manufacturers are required to provide justification for their claims, they are 10 to 1,500 times less likely to classify information as trade-secret protected.[91]

3 Submit Machine Gun Comments

Rule-Benders also invest effort in bogging down the agency's assessment by submitting comments that are both voluminous and lead to scientific dead ends that nevertheless require considerable effort to puzzle through. Since the regulator is required by law to solicit comments and consider all of them, the law effectively invites Rule-Benders to raise the regulator's processing costs still further through unhelpful comments.[92]

The first line of attack is to databomb the agency. Rather than provide succinct, significant feedback, the Rule-Bender will file convoluted and sometimes trivial comments that have the "machine gun" effect that James Landis observed nearly 50 years ago.[93] A subset of overstretched, technical regulatory staff will find themselves combing through dozens or hundreds of issues and challenges mounted by Rule-Benders whose primary goal is not to illuminate and improve the agency's decision but rather to simply wear the agency down. Rule-Benders' propensity to launch these critiques may well explain why so many agency chemical assessments can take decades to complete.[94]

In mounting these ends-oriented critiques, Rule-Benders do not stop at raising scientifically valid criticisms but also raise invalid claims whose primary goal is to obfuscate and "gum up the works." One common type of obfuscating comment, called "deconstruction," takes issue with features of an individual research study in ways that reputable scientists would find trivial and sometimes dishonest, but that sound legitimate to non-scientists. Specifically, in deconstructing a study, the Rule-Bender challenges basic, consensual conventions that have been hard-baked into the experimental methods and are necessary to make experimentation possible. Examples of these conventions include testing chemicals on the most vulnerable strain of mice or counting all tumors instead of those known to be malignant.[95] These types of conventions cannot be empirically validated (after all, the conventions are used because we don't know which options to use at these junctures). The clever Rule-Bender will opportunistically ignore that fact and insist that these consensual features be verified as a scientific matter before a study can be trusted. Defending against these faux attacks increases agency processing costs and exacerbates existing comprehension asymmetries.[96]

Rule-Benders can also take the datasets used by the agency and "dredge" them using statistical techniques. This data-dredging extracts more favorable (purely ends-oriented) findings simply by running the data through every conceivable statistical program until a more welcome result emerges. Data-dredging is the antithesis of good science since it starts with a favored result and uses statistical tests to get there.[97] Even though these findings are analytically unsound, the Rule-Bender will often provide explanations for these statistical analyses that sound legitimate. Regulators must devote scarce resources toward scrutinizing these analyses to evaluate their reliability.

Each of these moves not only succeeds in weighing the regulator down, but in delaying the assessment and regulatory process. Indeed, as Stuart Shapiro observes, regulated parties have become quite skilled at alleging faults in the regulators' assessments that serve to "delay decisions that might impose significant costs upon them."[98]

4 Reframe the Regulator's Task

Despite the fact that the existing legal framework allows Rule-Benders to exploit their processing advantages at the regulators' expense, Rule-Bending manufacturers are not averse to working to adjust this framework so that it is even more beneficial to them. In some cases, this is accomplished by lobbying Congress or the White House to increase the analytic requirements with which the agency must comply. Several such maneuvers have been documented in the chemical regulation literature.

First, the Rule-Bender can portray the regulatory project as requiring a "corpuscular" study of each piece of information that informs the larger risk assessment of a single chemical.[99] As McGarity explains, this corpuscular approach endeavors to denigrate or even exclude particularly unwanted research from consideration by full throttle attacks on individual studies.[100] The tactic not only dramatically increases processing costs (because every study used in an assessment must be reviewed), but also shifts the agency's regulatory focus. Rather than conducting a general comparative assessment focusing on whether a chemical is safer and more effective than its competitors, the agency is required to investigate every conceivable risk, exposure, and use of each chemical. Moreover, it must do this enormous analysis for every shred of evidence that is relevant to a chemical's assessment, regardless of the benefits (and agency expense).

Second, and working in tandem with this corpuscular approach, is a parallel mis-framing of the scope of the project as exclusively a scientific exercise. Any gaps in scientific information must doom regulation under this framing approach since the regulator lacks the evidence to indict a chemical. As the Fifth Circuit opined, for an agency "to make precise estimates, precise data are required."[101] Depicting risk assessment as scientific in nature not only makes it difficult for the regulator to summon the evidence needed to meet this unrealistic demand, but allows Rule-Benders to argue that the regulator is scientifically incompetent in processing the information.[102] A Rule-Bender using this tack will attempt to throw doubt on the regulator's assessment by carefully selecting other plausible alternatives at each policy juncture and arguing that the regulator's choices are unscientific.[103] One industry think tank even launched a formal legal challenge, arguing that the National Oceanic and Atmospheric Administration's heavily peer-reviewed cli-mate-change models should be withdrawn and eliminated because some of the inferences were at odds with alternative plausible, but untested, scientific hypotheses.[104]

Third, the Rule-Bender will endeavor to alter the process itself by adding mul-tiple, new "attachment points" to the agency's analytical requirements, each of which can then be used as a basis for litigation.[105] At present, when conducting an assessment, the agency must follow a maze of intricate sub-requirements and instructions, each of which "shall" be followed if the agency's decision is to be upheld in subsequent litigation. Each added requirement increases the processing burden on the agency and creates additional opportunities for the agency's decision to be overturned or delayed through litigation.

The case of *Corrosion Proof vs. EPA* offers an illustration of how these mis-framing techniques can be combined to block regulatory oversight.[106] In *Corro-sion Proof*, asbestos manufacturers challenged the EPA's effort to regulate asbestos in the late 1980s, several decades after the long-term hazards of asbestos had been accepted by the scientific community.[107] Despite a 45,000 page record, 22 days of public hearings, 13,000 pages of comments from over 250 parties, and a rule that was 10 years in the making, the Fifth Circuit held that the agency failed to make a compelling case for the ban of asbestos and sent the rule back to the agency.[108] The asbestos manufacturers, the court suggested, had been victim-ized – their products were prematurely subjected to the "death penalty."[109] To justify a ban of asbestos under the law, the court said, the agency would instead need to:

(1) Quantify future deaths and injuries caused by asbestos
(2) Assess available substitutes for asbestos and conduct a cost-benefit analysis on each of their net risks relative to asbestos

(3) Prove that other alternative methods of regulation for asbestos, like warnings or restricted uses, were insufficient to control asbestos' significant long-term risks

Since there are dozens of major uses of asbestos, moreover, the court implied that the agency would need to conduct multiple technical assessments for each use. In this enormous assessment project, the manufacturers bore no responsibility other than to critique the agency's work. As a result of the court's decision, the EPA abandoned its effort to regulate asbestos (and Congress ultimately stepped in).[110]

Box 5.3 Comprehension Asymmetries in Chemical Regulation

The Rule-Follower Manufacturer

Why is it legally prudent to shift processing costs to regulators?

- Dutifully provides all known information, even if it isn't relevant.
- Avoids waiving useful trade secret claims, even though the regulator may ultimately determine some are not valid.
- Provides copious comments on regulators' assessments, even if some are not ultimately helpful.

AND

Remembers that any uncertainties in risk assessments cut in favor of assuming the chemical is safe since the regulator has the burden of proof.

The Rule-Bender Manufacturer

How can the regulators' processing burdens be increased still further without violating the law?

- Databombs with irrelevant and poor quality information that requires considerable effort to evaluate.
- Classifies information as trade secret if it is advantageous to hide it from public view.
- Inundates the regulator with convoluted, machine-gun comments and feedback.
- Reframes the regulators' project as requiring decisive scientific evidence and a corpuscular study of every piece of information.

5 Summary

Rule-Benders will not only endeavor to ensure agency regulators bear sole responsibility for processing long-term risk information, but also work to ensure that this burden is as high as possible to limit the potential for bad news and heightened regulatory restrictions. By infusing the assessment with analytical requirements and sowing the process with technical confusion, the Rule-Bender can slow or halt the agency's work, as well as the ability of onlookers to make sense of it.

This Rule-Bender strategy in fact enjoys a striking similarity to a famous tactic used during a naval battle in the War of 1812. In facing off against the British fleet in Lake Erie, Admiral Perry enjoyed a temporary advantage at a late point in the battle. From this slight advantage, he commanded the US fleets to move in close and bombard the British ships with rapid fire cannons, guns, and every form of missile, without a break.[111] Even though the smoke was so thick that the sailors could not see where they were shooting, they kept firing until the British surrendered. Like Admiral Perry, a motivated Rule-Bender can overwhelm the regulator with processing costs until it surrenders, either by halting the project or capitulating to some of the manufacturer's demands.

III EXISTING REFORM: THE LAUTENBERG ACT

It is not surprising that most chemical manufacturers – whether Rule-Followers or Rule-Benders – take advantage of the fact that they are not required by law to either assess or communicate the latent risks of existing chemicals. It is not in their interest to invest in assessments that may ultimately reveal unexpected dangers that could cost them dearly on the market and in tort litigation.

Precisely because of the well-known deficiencies in existing chemical regulation, Congress passed major amendments to the EPA's chemical regulatory mandate in 2017, known as the Lautenberg Act. The amendments provide the agency with some new powers to regulate chemicals – including broader authority to require testing and a lower, health-protective standard for conducting an assessment of chemical risks.[112] The amended statute also allows the agency to require regulated parties to pay for up to 25 percent of the costs of chemical assessments.[113]

But under the amended 2017 statute, the EPA not only retains full responsibility for processing chemical risks, as before, but the agency is faced with dozens of new analytical requirements and demands.[114] Rather than address the core problem – the fact that manufacturers are in the best position to assess product risks but are legally relieved of this responsibility – the new amendments to TSCA rub only more salt in the wound. Existing comprehension asymmetries are left unaddressed, while new assessment requirements increase the regulator's already high processing burden.

Assessment of Existing Chemicals. In the 2017 amendments, the EPA still bears full responsibility for assessing chemical risks, although the endpoint for the assessment is now more health-protective, leading in theory to greater environmental and health protection.[115] Unfortunately, in practice, for the agency to get from point A (assessing a chemical) to point B (issuing restrictions if a chemical is unreasonably risky), the agency must surmount a veritable obstacle course of new, mandated analytical steps and requirements. These requirements arguably increase the burden on the agency severalfold as compared to the prior statutory requirements.

First, and as a preliminary matter, the EPA must master and categorize by riskiness the entire universe of chemicals sold in commerce. The 2017 amendments require the EPA to identify all chemicals sold on the market[116] in order to prioritize these chemicals based on risk.[117] The EPA must then select the chemicals that pose the greatest risk. (This work must be completed under judicially enforceable deadlines with notice and comment.)[118]

Once the EPA begins the job of actually processing the relevant risk information on particularly hazardous chemicals, it must follow a series of analytical steps, each of which is statutorily prescribed and subject to notice and comment. First the agency must conduct a scoping report that provides a preliminary assessment of what the assessment should include.[119] Then the agency must conduct a risk evaluation.[120] Only then can the agency propose regulatory restrictions if evidence suggests restrictions are necessary to protect health and the environment.[121]

But that is not all. Nested within each of these analytical steps are statutorily required sub-requirements. For example, in conducting the risk evaluation, the EPA must satisfy a number of enumerated requirements,[122] which include describing "whether aggregate or sentinel exposures to a chemical substance under the conditions of use were considered, and the basis for that consideration,"[123] and taking into account "where relevant, the likely duration, intensity, frequency, and number of exposures under the conditions of use of the chemical substance."[124]

New Chemical Assessments. The EPA also bears full responsibility for assessing the risks of new chemicals; only under the new 2017 amendments, the EPA's assessment is now mandatory rather than discretionary. Within 90 days after a manufacturer provides the EPA with all "known" information about a new chemical or new use, the EPA must make an official determination as to whether that new chemical "presents an unreasonable risk of injury to health or the environment, without consideration of costs or other nonrisk factors, including an unreasonable risk to a potentially exposed or susceptible subpopulation identified as relevant by the Administrator under the conditions of use."[125]

Meta-Scientific Standards. When conducting assessments for both new and existing chemicals, the EPA is required to comply with congressionally devised "scientific standards." To take one example from five legislative requirements, in each of its analyses, the EPA must "consider" – subject to judicial review – "the degree of clarity and completeness with which the data, assumptions, methods, quality assurance, and analyses employed to generate the information are documented."[126] The EPA is also required to share all of the information and the studies it relies on, identify the information that justifies its decisions, and provide nontechnical summaries for each risk evaluation.[127]

No Manufacturer Burden for Assessment. While the EPA is busy with all of these new steps and demands, what new demands are placed on the manufacturers? None. As before, manufacturers must share only the information they are aware of – and that only for new chemicals. Manufacturers must also respond to the agency's testing demands for targeted chemicals, but that response could consist of litigating the agency's order, rather than complying with the order and producing the requested toxicity data.[128] Moreover, under the 2017 amendments, manufacturers are afforded not just one but at least four opportunities to offer comments on the agency's proposed restrictions of a single chemical. And, given the multiplicity of new sub-requirements that bind these regulatory assessments, manufacturers enjoy dozens of new attachment points for challenging the agency's findings. Even for trade-secret classifications made by manufacturers, the burden of reviewing and sometimes even learning of justifications for trade secrets rests with the regulator.[129]

Certainly, the fact that the EPA can collect 25 percent of its assessment costs from industry will be useful in defraying some of these expenses, but those funds seem likely to make only a small dent in the budget the agency will need to carry out this substantially increased workload. (And, when the agency's budget is slashed – as is the case under the Trump Administration – the ability of the agency to make progress in regulating chemicals is further compromised.)[130]

IV LASTING REFORM

To make lasting progress in chemical regulation, the law must force manufacturers to bear full responsibility for assessing and communicating the long-term risks of their chemical products. Rather than sinking the agency in never-ending processing costs, manufacturers' incentives must be redirected toward mastering (or at least reasonably understanding) the long-term risks of their chemicals and communicating that understanding to others.

To get from here to there, three separate steps are needed for reform. These steps parallel the proposals we advanced in both financial and patent reform. The first reform step involves ensuring that all manufacturers obtain a rigorous understanding of the toxicity of their chemicals based on the available evidence. The second step requires that the manufacturer provide rigorous indicia of the reliability of their understanding. The third step requires manufacturers to communicate meaningfully that understanding to expert regulators and other expert audiences. We take each step in turn.

A *Understanding Toxicity*

A reformed regulatory regime must require manufacturers to master and assess the available research regarding the toxicity of their own chemicals as a condition to marketing. To check some of the most obvious sources of bias, manufacturers should be required to provide specific, overlapping representations of the long-term risks of their products. This requirement should generally follow the proposal sketched by Henry Hu for financial regulation.[131] This diversified informational portfolio underlying the risks of a chemical will force manufacturers to "see" reality a bit more clearly (even if they do not want to), while at the same time provide other experts with vital information to evaluate the manufacturers' assessments. Note that we do not propose added testing since our single aim here is to ensure that existing information is processed in a comprehensible and rigorous way. Nevertheless, it seems likely that by encouraging manufacturers to conduct self-assessments, manufacturers may also voluntarily conduct added, specific testing to resolve key uncertainties and may even develop much-needed, improved testing methods to rigorously evaluate long-term hazards.

We suggest four separate types of representations of latent chemical risks to provide a more well-rounded informational portfolio. Three of these informational representations would be mandatory.

Mandatory Representation #1. Manufacturers are well positioned to conduct literature searches on the toxicological properties of their chemicals and should be held legally accountable for doing so. The first mandated representation thus requires manufacturers (not the government) to collect and share the universe of available research and data on the toxicity of each of their chemical(s), including unpublished, in-house information.[132] At least for new chemicals, this is already partly required by law,[133] although our reformed requirement does not stop at "known" information but requires an affirmative and comprehensive search of all of the scientific literature.

The effort needed to make this public repository of information usable to the agency and others must be borne by the manufacturers. Manufacturers, and not agencies, would be required to enter all of this information in the agency's standardized website. If extraneous information is included, the manufacturer would be fined; carelessly shifting processing costs to the audience is no longer allowed. Somewhat similarly, manufacturers that attempt to claim information as confidential business information would be required to justify these claims first.

Mandatory Representation #2. To provide regulators with an accessible synthesis of this scientific information, a second, mandatory representation would require the chemical manufacturers to run the existing toxicity information collected from Representation #1 into several stock regulatory models. This second informational requirement will involve added expenses associated with stripping out and weighting the raw data and other studies that serve as the inputs. (Note that considerable discretion and sources of error can arise in this process that cannot be controlled simply by imposing prescriptive protocols and methodological requirements. We consider ways to counteract this discretion later.)[134]

The EPA would develop these computational models, which would utilize different types of assumptions and present differing exposure scenarios to gain purchase on a range of possible risk outcomes.[135] The models would also be designed in a way that affords as little discretion to the manufacturers as possible. Once all data is entered into the system, the manufacturers would then run the models to produce a variety of standardized findings that not only inform understanding of the long-term risks of each individual chemical but allow for cross-comparison with competitor chemicals as well.

To ensure that the models do not reward under-testing or biased research, the models would utilize defaults that adopt worst-case assumptions about missing information or information of poor quality. If there is no research on the carcinogenicity of a given chemical, for example, the model(s) would identify the most carcinogenic chemical within that larger chemical family (drawing from a body of work on chemical structure-activity) to assess carcinogenicity risks. With regard to weighting research, a standardized format would be developed that provides weights for each inputted study based on objective process features that affect the reliability of research (e.g., whether a study was peer reviewed, prepared under a nondisclosure contract with the manufacturer, followed standardized protocols, etc.).

In instances in which there are hundreds or even thousands of studies available on a chemical, competitors could be allowed to pool resources to strip out this model-ready information.[136] Cost-sharing could proceed much in the same way that underlying testing is currently shared in US pesticide licensing.[137] The regulator could even do the extraction work and be reimbursed by manufacturers according to their pro-rata share of the national market (or some other allocation scheme).

Voluntary Representation #3. The inevitable contestation over the agency's construction of the Representation #2 models is mitigated by a third, voluntary representation that invites manufacturers to develop their own models for assessing the toxicity of their chemical(s). To ensure these models can be readily cross-compared by expert regulators and others, however, the models would be standardized by requiring manufacturers who develop them to run pre-set datasets through them.[138] This benchmarking step helps the audience evaluate and compare the veracity of different manufacturers' model(s), at least at a crude level.

Substantial discrepancies between competitors' models, for example, might spotlight assumptions and other algorithms that need to be investigated further or explained by a manufacturer.

Mandatory Representation #4. A final, mandatory representation would be a narrative statement by the manufacturer that summarizes in an accessible yet rigorous way the gist of the preceding information. The narrative statement would not only illuminate the chemical's absolute risks, but would compare the chemical's risks to the top competitors (e.g., three chemicals with the largest market shares for that same use category) as well as at least one non-chemical alternative for each major use.[139] If the chemical's primary use is as a cleaning agent, for example, the chemical would be compared against other top competitor chemicals, any other competitors the company wishes to identify, and at least one non-toxic substitute, such as cleaning vinegar, sold on the market.[140] (If the manufacturer takes the position there is no non-chemical substitute, this will need to be explained clearly and accessibly, with ample documentation.)

The comparative risk statement is particularly important since it places responsibility on the manufacturer to justify the public value of its chemical. If a relative-risk comparison reveals that a manufacturer's product is more toxic than competitors' through one type of exposure (e.g., ingestion), for example, the manufacturer will presumably explain in this narrative statement why its product is superior nonetheless and adds value to the market (e.g., less risk of exposure, lower doses, other risk factors are more favorable, etc.). Similarly, if a manufacturer markets a chemical for a new use, an assessment will also be required for this new use since both the competitors and the exposure routes might be different.

To produce the comparative risk statement, the manufacturer would use their competitors' representations #1–3.[141] Such a comparative step, conveniently, will engage the scrutiny of high stakes competitors in the work that each is doing, thus providing even more motivation (ideally) for manufacturers to produce bulletproof assessments. For example, in comparing its chemical against others, A manufacturer may discover sleights of hand, unsupported assumptions, or data-collation errors in a competitor's submission.

Although the narrative statement is vital, precisely how it is designed will benefit from trial and error. Some manufacturers may provide superb, accessible narrative statements, and others may provide garbled or even deceptive summaries of the evidence. The audience for the summaries (primarily the expert regulator and other expert market actors) may ultimately find that other, more specific summaries are more helpful (e.g., simply a summary of the relative risk of the chemical as compared to chemical and non-chemical substitutes).

Costs of the Representation Requirements. On the agency side, the additional costs of this reform proposal would arise primary in developing the models and data-inputting methods for Representation #2. Some, but considerably less, regulatory effort would be needed to establish the public-sharing forum for manufacturers' data and studies, as well as for posting results. However, beyond these directives for how the representations must be produced and shared, there would be no regulatory oversight other than enforcing the representation requirements. Like financial regulation, the idea is that once other experts can access comprehensible information regarding risk, market competition will re-enter and help to improve the quality of assessments and products themselves.[142]

On the manufacturer side, producing this new information will involve added expense, although likely less expense than the costs of conducting additional, new toxicity tests. For example, by comparison to reforms like REACH, the proposal advanced here should generally be less onerous, particularly for some under-tested chemicals with little data to input into the models.

For those chemicals for which the existing research is substantial and data entry accordingly onerous, the agency could alleviate the manufacturers' burden by organizing cost-sharing among affected manufacturers. Some heavily studied chemicals could even be exempted entirely if they have already been subjected to multiple rounds of peer review by Science Advisory Boards or the National Academies.[143] Even for the scantly tested chemicals, some exceptions may be needed when there is a *de minimis* risk of harm from a chemical, either because of small market share or low exposure or both. Exemptions would be set up to place a heavy burden of explanation on manufacturers for the waivers.

Ultimately, however, at least for those chemicals that might be sold in high quantities or that might be toxic to health or the environment (or both), placing responsibility in the first instance on manufacturers to produce a rigorous assessment of the health and environmental risks posed by their chemicals in relation to competitors is both equitable and efficient. In response, firms will begin to take toxicity into account more rigorously, innovating around this new responsibility.[144]

B *Reliable Representations*

A second vital step to reform will require the resulting representations to be reliable and trustworthy. We propose three overlapping mechanisms to encourage the rigor of the manufacturers' risk assessments.

Strong Enforcement Mechanisms for Missing and False or Misleading Representations. Enforcement authorities should be added to existing statutory requirements to provide both the EPA and private parties with the ability to sanction a manufacturer's representations, syntheses, or narrative statement if they are "patently misleading," "grossly unreliable," or "effectively incomprehensible" to expert audiences. Since manufacturers will be reviewing the analyses produced by competitors, presumably in some detail as part of their own mandated narrative statement on relative risk, they too are well-placed to contribute to this enforcement work.

Pedigree. Second, as with financial regulation, manufacturers should be required to produce a "pedigree" statement that explains how each representation was prepared, by whom, under what contractual circumstances (e.g., a nondisclosure contract), and whether the modeling and other representations were submitted to vigorous independent peer review. This pedigree statement would accompany each representation, including the narrative statement. The EPA could develop a standardized template for preparing the pedigree statement.

Expert Audits of Representations. Finally, and again paralleling the recommendations for financial reform, a panel of "contrarians" or "skeptics" would be assembled to spot check manufacturers' representations.[145] It is not realistic to institute this review for each and every representation, but a nontrivial chance of an audit could still serve to enhance a manufacturer's incentives for meaningful compliance with the regulatory requirements. Of course, significant sanctions will need to be levied against subpar representations to deter others from doing them.

Manufacturers might hire certified contrarian boards to conduct their own peer review to protect against these enforcement risks. This self-instituted peer review could also be used as a type of quality endorsement, lending legitimacy to the reliability of a manufacturer's own assessments for the agency, competitors, and other private participants.

C *Comprehensible Representations*

Third, and following the notion of a "comprehension rule" advanced in Chapter 4 for consumer markets, the speaker-manufacturer would be held responsible for providing reasonably comprehensible and reliable representations, including the summary statement. Enforcement of this responsibility must be sufficient to alter manufacturer behavior, but must not go too far the other way to lead to frivolous litigation and over-deterrence.

To walk this tightrope, we propose two separate arms of enforcement. The first would equip private parties – both consumers and expert audiences like regulators and competitors – with the ability to bring enforcement actions against manufacturers for paperwork violations. If the audience can prove that one or more representations are "patently unreliable" or "wholly inadequate" to enable a reasonable expert audience to understand the risks, the manufacturer will be liable for fines and could be enjoined from selling the chemical until the problem is corrected. The fines, moreover, would act like bounties to encourage this policing work by private parties, but the burden on enforcers would be high enough to ensure that only the very worst abuses are taken to court.

Second, to keep manufacturers vigilant, a more threatening cause of action could be available for victims by providing full reimbursement for any harm that can be traced to an inadequate representation. The violation could also be treated – through legislation – as equating to "egregious conduct," thus making punitive damage awards more likely. On the regulatory side, this type of violation – at least if it is reckless – could also provide grounds for criminal sanctions.

Thumbnail Sketch of Chemical Regulatory Reform

1 Require a diverse information portfolio from chemical manufacturers to produce a clearer analysis of long-term risks based on the available scientific information, including multiple modeling vantage points.
2 Require chemical manufacturers to synthesize these multiple representations of information and provide a comprehensible summary of long-term risks.
3 Require that each representation and summary be accompanied by a pedigree statement that details how the information was collected and analyzed.
4 Provide both public and private enforcement to ensure representations are both rigorous and reasonably comprehensible.

However it is accomplished, the simple regulatory demand that manufacturers provide clear and rigorous assessments of the risks of their chemical products does not seem like a radical requirement. One could in fact argue the opposite – that it is radical as a matter of simple economics (considering economies of scale, negative externalities, and long-term inefficiencies) *not* to impose this basic processing responsibility on manufacturers. And, while this assessment approach is partly embedded in the European requirements for testing that is embodied in REACH,[146] the proposal here takes a different tack by de-emphasizing the need for new, standardized testing and instead focuses on requiring manufacturers to process and explain the information that already exists (or doesn't exist) on long-term hazards.[147]

D *Add In Political Reality*

Thus far we have put to one side the reality of politics. Some chemical manufacturers and perhaps the majority will not prosper in this reformed world and may work tirelessly to oppose the reform from being passed and implemented.[148] Since manufacturers enjoy significant political advantages given their resources and stakes, their opposition to this reform could succeed in blocking it, particularly if the problems cannot be made salient to the general public.

In theory, much of the proposed reforms could occur without legislative amendment of the existing statute; the only vital amendment would involve providing mechanisms for public and private enforcement of the representation requirements. Yet in practice, the EPA may find significant risks to taking this much initiative in regulatory reform, even in a political climate that is hospitable to providing greater health and environmental protection.

In the real world, then, the proposal just described could be whittled down to a bare-bones approach that may be more politically viable. We propose two possibilities for this scaled down approach that are not mutually exclusive.

Whittled Down Version #1. Rather than mandating the representation requirements, this scaled-down version would make the requisite representations purely voluntary. The agency would set up the websites, the requirements, and the models as proposed. However, whether a manufacturer chooses to take advantage of this self-assessment for a chemical would be wholly at its discretion. The one catch is that to get positive credit, a manufacturer would need to do all of the representations and could not pick and choose those that were least expensive or most likely to be favorable.

It is possible that manufacturers of low-risk chemicals will participate if they are eager to advertise the advantages of their products.[149] To further bolster the credibility of their self-assessments, the EPA could even assemble a rigorous, independent peer review for all voluntary representations. This review would provide still more legitimacy for those manufacturers who do invest the effort.

If enough manufacturers availed themselves of the voluntary program, the market might react as well. Chemicals that are supported by rigorous self-assessments and comparative risk statements would be valued more highly if the results show comparatively lower risks of these chemicals versus the alternatives. These manufacturers would have a means – not available currently – to signal the superiority of their chemical products relative to others. And, as an added bonus, a manufacturer's voluntary compliance with the requirements could provide public relations benefits as well, positioning it as a "civic-minded" company that is going the distance to produce publicly beneficial products. The regulatory reform would thus provide both the forum and a means to verify self-interested promotions that are reliable and deserved. The voluntary system would provide a way of officially encouraging hero-manufacturers to emerge and be rewarded in the market.

Whittled Down Version #2. A second, scaled down version of the proposal could require only one representation – the narrative in Representation #4. Along with this statement, manufacturers would also be required to share the "pedigree" of how this representation was prepared (e.g., peer review, independent analysis, etc.). Under existing law, the EPA can arguably already require this type of statement and accompanying pedigree.[150] A simple rulemaking – one that is open-ended and nonspecific on the nature of the statement and pedigree to avoid deadlock – could start the ball rolling. The weak version, then, would not involve the need for legislation or even a complicated rulemaking.

Under this weak version, dramatic manufacturer noncompliance (either by not providing the information or providing misleading or obfuscating information) must still be harshly sanctioned. Ideally, legislation could be passed that creates a citizen suit provision for competitors to discipline false or misleading statements by their peers. Alternatively, the agency could enjoy added funding to conduct contrarian audits that increase the risk of manufacturers being caught when submitting distorting information. Sanctions could even take the form of adverse publicity on the agency's website or other forms of blacklisting for procurement contracts if monetary sanctions prove too difficult to levy.

The core idea, again, is that the chemical manufacturers must bear the processing costs for assessing the toxicity of their chemical products. While this weaker proposal for a single, narrative statement will be less effective, it is nevertheless an improvement over the status quo.

V CONCLUSION

Manufacturers should be forced to internalize the processing costs associated with assessing long-term risks. By producing more robust representations of the hazards of chemical products that can be cross-compared between products, a reformed approach promises to jump-start the market and create a "race to the top." Manufacturers will be rewarded for developing chemical products that rank – through these existing representations – most favorably.

The insight from the proposed reform, however, lies not in the specifics but in the general argument; for chemical regulation to work effectively, the processing costs associated with understanding chemical risks must be borne in the first instance by manufacturers. Under the current legal structure, the agency is not only responsible for conducting these chemical assessments, but faces a "machine gun" spray of added processing costs that result from the law's perverse incentives on manufacturers to bog down and confuse the agency's work. Until the incentives for understanding the risks of chemicals are borne by the manufacturers, we will be stuck in a rut of perpetual ignorance.

6

Comprehension Asymmetries in Administrative Process

The legitimacy of the administrative state is advanced in part by accountability processes that provide opportunities for vigorous participation and oversight by affected parties.[1] Yet, much like the other legal and regulatory programs explored in this book, the basic design of this legal program neglects a vital variable – namely that these deliberations must involve cooperative communication.

Administrative law is certainly not inattentive to impediments to participation. For over 50 years, scholars and reformers have been not just preoccupied but obsessed with rooting out information asymmetries that block vigorous participation. This focus on combatting information asymmetries is completely understandable. By the 1960s, it became clear that the promised engagement by all affected parties was being eclipsed by a "capture" of agency staff by well-funded regulated parties. Information asymmetries – the backroom deals between regulated parties and regulators – became a systematic worry that undermined the promise of meaningful participation in government decisions.

To open this administrative process up to the "sunlight," legal visionaries pressed for a system of rules that would give the public greater access to administrative decision-making.[2] Their battle against smoke-filled rooms populated only by well-heeled insiders bore fruit. An explosion of laws followed to address information asymmetries that include: requiring open records,[3] rigorous processes for advisory groups,[4] access to congressional deliberations,[5] and demands that agencies go the extra mile to include all interested participants earlier in the development of a rule proposal.[6] During this same time, the courts also stepped up their oversight of the agencies. Most notably, they expanded standing rules to enable public-interest representatives to challenge agencies in court when agency rules diverge significantly from promises made by Congress.[7]

Yet through this flurry of legal reforms, the comprehensibility of the public deliberations has been neglected. Even worse, what administrative architects failed to anticipate was that from this new commitment to "sunlight,"[8] a large, dense cloud of detailed and technical information would emerge. Indeed, in some cases, this information is so incomprehensible that the transparency promised by operating in the "sunlight" is completely obscured.

Today, in fact, the existence of incomprehensible rules in some facets of administrative law is an unfortunate, albeit accepted reality. Prominent law scholars reference the "mounds of regulations, all densely packed with bizarre terms and opaque acronyms"[9] that "escape understanding."[10] Cynthia Farina, Mary Newhart, and Cheryl Blake observe that from the perspective of affected citizens, an agency's rule and accompanying analysis "is about as accessible as if the documents were written in hieroglyphics."[11] The net result is an administrative process that – despite its promises otherwise – has become increasingly inhospitable to meaningful engagement by stakeholders in general and citizen groups in particular.[12]

However, despite a widely shared concern about the complexity of unwieldy administrative processes, some and perhaps most administrative lawyers view the glut of information as the inevitable result of the information age that must be begrudgingly accepted. Mainstream thinkers observe that while bureaucratic processes are "untidy," they nevertheless represent "an open, visible system that the electorate can get to know and can, over time, cause to respond to at least the deeper currents of public philosophy."[13] In addition to pressure from court challenges, "executive branch interpretation is kept within acceptable bounds by political pressure, public accountability, and a properly modest approach to the exercise of these broad powers by the President."[14] Indeed, some posit that agencies may in fact "be the only institution[] capable of fulfilling the civic republican ideal of deliberative decision-making."[15]

We argue these views are too complacent, and that incomprehensible regulation is neither inconsequential nor inevitable. Participation and deliberation work only when there is a legal design that ensures that agency actions will be reasonably understandable to the target audience. If comprehension asymmetries are not rectified, administrative deliberations can break down in ways that privilege well-funded groups over those without these advantages. The incomprehensibility of US regulation is also not inevitable. Rather, it is in part attributable to a poorly constructed legal design. An essential structural element – the insistence on cooperative communication – is missing from the basic structure of administrative process.

In this chapter, we trace this missing element – comprehensibility – in administrative process and explore how its neglect over the decades has reduced the legitimacy of regulatory work and made it less effective.

Because the chapter covers a lot of ground, it has been broken into three major parts. The first part provides a focused orientation to administrative law as it relates to our study of comprehension asymmetries. We begin this part by offering a few samples of what incomprehensibility looks like in various agency rules. We then explore the background incentives of our alternating speakers in the course of developing a single agency rule.

In the second part we consider the legal structure of administrative law with respect to the incentives it creates for cooperative communication between participants. This examination reveals not only a legal obliviousness to processing costs in institutional design, but a number of ways that legal requirements tacitly encourage incomprehensibility from advantaged speakers.

In the third part we consider whether there are tangible problems that flow from this mis-design and whether anything can be done to correct these problems. We first notice how this flawed design has been replicated in other programs and itemize some of the adverse consequences that result. The chapter then closes on a hopeful note by proposing preliminary reform recommendations.

While instituting strong incentives for comprehensibility into administrative law will not solve all impediments to diverse and vigorous participation, such as collective action and representation problems, it is nevertheless a vital ingredient to the design of a successful deliberative process.

I ORIENTATION AND SETTING THE STAGE

The democratic legitimacy of agencies is premised in part on both their expertise and their accountability to those whom their decisions affect.[16] This procedural commitment to meaningful transparency and deliberation equates in our model to cooperative communication. The more visible the options, framing, assumptions, and methods embedded within the agency's regulatory decision, the more accountable the agency's decision will be.[17] In an ideal setting, stakeholders would also be actively solicited by the agencies to ensure their most important concerns are taken into account. Called "interest group pluralism," the agency's legitimacy rests at least in part on this vigorous oversight by parties affected by its decisions.[18]

Although the notion of reason-giving and accountability to affected parties is now considered central to administrative law, the actual design of administrative process lacks assurances for cooperative communication between the agency and participants.[19] Instead, some administrative doctrines not only tolerate but tacitly reward incomprehensibility from the participants. This first section provides a crash course on administrative law, followed by several concrete illustrations of what incomprehensible rules can look like in the administrative state. We then offer a brief account of the background incentives for cooperative communication that agencies and stakeholders encounter in the regulatory decision-making process.

A *Administrative Process* 101

One of the primary roles for administrative agencies is to act as the nation's experts – carefully settling Congress's broad legislative directives into fine-tuned rules. But the nation's problems cannot be solved solely by technical tools or analytical formulas.[20] Judgment, discretion, and even trial and error are an inevitable part of devising rules for the regulatory state. In order to hold these expert agencies accountable, Congress passed a process statute in 1946 – called the Administrative Procedure Act (APA) – that provides enhanced accountability mechanisms for constraining the exercise of agency discretion.[21]

Foremost among Congress's goals in the APA was to encourage the agency to provide reasons for its decisions, which in turn would enable affected groups – at that time regulated industry – to hold the agency accountable when the agency drifted too far from the facts, the statutory mandate, or both. Specifically, the APA provides any interested party with a right to participate in an agency rulemaking.[22] If the agency ignores a commenter who has identified flaws in the agency's interpretation of its statute, material errors in its fact-finding, or logical inconsistencies in its reasoning, or if the agency violates procedural requirements, then that commenter can challenge the agency's rule in court.[23] The resultant threat of litigation helps ensure that the comment process is taken seriously by the agency and is not simply a paper tiger. Moreover, by enlisting affected parties to engage with agency rules, Congress endeavored to use this participatory process to keep the agencies in check, with the courts serving as legal referee.

The APA thus establishes our current design for the administrative state, grounding it in part in an accountability process run by the affected parties themselves. Rather than rely solely on civil servants to locate "objectively correct solution[s] to the country's problems,"[24] the agency's legitimacy is ensured in large part by this vigorous oversight by those affected by its decisions through the resultant interest group pluralism.[25] The Attorney General's Report in 1946, for example, stressed the importance of this pluralistic oversight to the success of the administrative state: "Participation by these groups [economic and community-based] in the rule-making process is essential in order to permit administrative agencies to inform themselves and to afford adequate safeguards to private interests."[26]

Reinforcing the critical role of affected parties in administrative process are important institutional checks from the political branches.[27] Both Congress and the president enjoy multiple opportunities to influence and in some cases overrule an agency when it strays too far from what a political branch views as appropriate. Through direct means (for example, when Congress amends the agency's statutory authorization), or more indirect means (for example, pressuring or cajoling administrators), these two branches can exert a strong arm over agency decisions.

Thus, while the average citizen need not be able to comprehend agency rules for the APA's accountability system to work, broad, vigorous, and diverse participation by the significant affected groups is central. This engagement provides the support beams that hold up the otherwise fragile Fourth Branch and ensure that agency decisions are responsive to the concerns of the broader public.

B *Incomprehensibility in Administrative Practice*

Given this legal structure for administrative process, the prospect of incomprehensible rules seems unlikely; the entire purpose of much of the process is to engage

affected groups in cooperative communication. And yet, as noted in the introduction, top administrative scholars express dismay at the incomprehensibility of some
agency rules, and they are not alone in noticing the problem. Over the last several
decades, both Congress and the president have openly criticized agencies for being
incomprehensible.[28] In order to make headway toward more comprehensible rules,
both Congress and the president have tried to curb this behavior. As one, limited
gesture, multiple laws and Executive Orders now insist that agencies write rules in
"plain English" and in ways that can be understood by participants (and presumably
elected officials).[29]

Yet despite these efforts to make agency decisions more understandable, some
rules remain effectively incomprehensible to the vast majority of expert participants,
and the situation may be growing worse. A recent study by Cynthia Farina and
coauthors found, for example, that executive summaries written in response to a new
presidential initiative for greater clarity "are now being written at a grade level not
even close to the suggested seventh to ninth grade level."[30] Ironically, the authors
also found that these summaries tended to be even more complicated than the text
of the rule they were summarizing.

More generally, commentators note that agency rules in the aggregate are
getting longer, are growing more unwieldy, and the records and issues are multiply-
ing over time.[31] To gain more purchase on these incomprehensibility problems
in pockets of administrative law, we take several close-up views of the rules
themselves.

1 Horse's Mouth

An agency's own explanations for its decision provide some of the best examples of
incomprehensibility in rulemakings. An incomprehensible explanation is one where
the processing costs for the target audience exceed the time and effort that audience
is able to spend on the effort. So if readers must read and reread the agency's
explanation multiple times to understand not only what the agency did but how well
the agency's analysis and evidence supports its decisions, then the rule is likely
incomprehensible to at least a subset of participants. Indeed, after making an
unreasonably significant investment of time, readers might still be confused. Added
expert reinforcement may ultimately be needed, or alternatively the readers may
simply choose to give up altogether.

Consider the example that follows, drawn from a relatively typical technical
EPA rule. While the purpose of the selected text is to "explain" the agency's decision
on one particular, controverted issue, the text offers little in the way of communicating the relevant facts or agency choices. There is no orientation to the relevant
industry operations, no effort to identify for readers plausible alternatives or choices,
no explanation of the assumptions underlying the agency's technical findings, and

little to no evidence to support the agency's conclusions in keeping with the authorizing mandate.

Experts from within industry, particularly those intimately involved in negotiating and drafting the agency's rule, might be able to make sense of this agency explanation in a reasonable amount of time. But other affected expert stakeholders (not to mention non-experts) will likely require significant time just to understand this one paragraph. One can see why elite lawyers working for the top environmental public interest groups report that they typically must set aside at least 40 hours to review and comment on a single, typical EPA rule.[32] Processing costs can be very high.

The problems, moreover, arise not just because the information is inherently complex, but because the agency's analysis and reasoning isn't clearly explained. Not all agency rules, including science-intensive standards, are incomprehensible. In some rulemakings, the agency does provide a clear, albeit lengthy, explanation of its analysis that includes: highlighting the policy questions at issue; explaining the methods and choices made in the technical analysis; identifying important uncertainties; and justifying the ultimate policy judgments selected in a final rule.[33] In other words, sometimes the agencies can and do cooperatively communicate their process and reasoning to onlookers, even when the information is technical and complex. Agencies just don't do this all (or perhaps even most) of the time.

Box 6.1 Excerpt from a Preamble Explaining an EPA Decision

In this excerpt, the EPA is explaining how it responded to significant comments on its emission standard restricting hazardous air pollutants from Acrylic and Modacrylic Fiber Production industries:

ii. *Can the pollution prevention control techniques being used by several of the plants with suspension spinning operations be used for the solution process in existing facilities?* Although the air emission and source characteristics for all other emission point types (i.e., tanks, equipment components, wastewater treatment units) are similar throughout the source category, the solution and suspension processes associated with the spinning operations differ from each other in the processing steps and the acrylonitrile concentrations in the process materials and associated emissions. Solution polymerization spin dope for fiber production contains, by product and process design, a significantly higher concentration of residual AN monomer than does suspension polymerization. The public comments [filed by industry] argued that the application of the pollution prevention techniques being used for suspension processes (e.g., steam stripping of excess monomer, scavenger solvents) to existing solution processes is not viable because of the physical nature of the solution polymerization process. Specifically, application of high efficiency residual AN polymer steam stripping (incorporated to reduce downstream emissions) is technically feasible to incorporate into the suspension process and is not feasible for a solution polymerization process because the latter does not produce a solid polymer product that can be introduced to direct steam contact without contamination. At solution polymerization facilities, other pollution prevention or source reduction measures which formed the initial technical basis for determining the 100 ppmw action level for all spinning lines may not be capable of achieving the higher AN removal rates of the higher residual monomer concentration present in solution polymerization fiber spinning operations. We agree with the public comments that incorporating the pollution prevention techniques to an existing solution process spinning line is not viable.

From: EPA, National Emission Standards for Hazardous Air Pollutants: Generic Maximum Achievable Control Technology (Generic MACT), Part II, 64 Fed Reg. 34918 (1999)

2 Super-Sized Rules

Agency rules are rarely short; the one paragraph explanation excerpted above must be multiplied at least a hundred times to reach the length of a typical EPA rule and accompanying explanation.[34] But this is just an average rule. At the extreme, agency rules and explanations can run more than a hundred pages of 10-point font, 3-column text per *Federal Register* page.

And, along with these mammoth-sized rules are similarly voluminous records and public filings from affected groups. Inquisitive readers are often directed to these background documents for further information. A rule's comprehensibility is thus informed not only by the published text but by this accompanying record.

Accounts of select rulemaking projects spotlight their breathtaking size and complexity. Kimberly Krawiec's study of the public deliberations on implementation of the Volcker rule, which regulates proprietary trading of financial institutions, underscores the enormity of some rulemaking projects.[35] The Financial Stability Oversight Council requested public input on possible approaches to drafting a proposed Volcker rule and received more than 8,000 comments.[36] While the vast majority were simply form letters, the remaining 150 comments were quite lengthy and detailed, with an average word count ranging between 2,500 and 5,000 words and the longest comment reaching 19,000 words.[37] The agencies drafting the proposed rule met with affected parties more than 400 times over a 14-month period before the rule proposal was even published.[38]

In the environmental arena, Cary Coglianese describes similar rulemakings at EPA. A single hazardous waste rule, for example, involved 481 commenters, required 800 hours from one contractor in one week alone just to begin to assemble and process the comments, and another 1,600 hours in EPA staff time to process the comments right before the final rule was promulgated.[39] James Q. Wilson, in his classic book, *Bureaucracy*, describes a huge record compiled for an OSHA standard that took the agency four years to process and that included 105,000 pages of testimony "in addition to uncounted pages of documents."[40] And, this super-sized rule problem appears only to be getting worse, not better.[41]

In the course of reviewing challenges to agency rules, judges similarly complain about the problematic size and inaccessibility of the agencies' rulemakings. In *Florida Peach Growers*, the Fifth Circuit lamented that the agency's record was "some 238 documents occupying approximately two and one half feet of shelf space" that contains a mix of technical information.[42] And in another case, *Aqua Slide*, the Fifth Circuit judges observed, again with some consternation, the "jumble of letters, advertisements, comments, drafts, reports and publications . . . run[ning] for almost 2,000 pages . . . [with] no index."[43] Even back in the 1970s, judges scolded the EPA for incomprehensible rules. In upholding an EPA decision supported by a record that spanned more than 10,000 pages, Judge McGowen observed that:

> [T]he record presented to us on appeal or petition for review is a sump in which the parties have deposited a sundry mass of materials that have neither passed through the filter of rules of evidence nor undergone the refining fire of adversarial presentation . . . The lack of discipline in such a record, coupled with its sheer mass . . . makes the record of informal rulemaking a less than fertile ground for judicial review.[44]

Of course, a rulemaking's large size, standing alone, does not equate to an incomprehensible rule. Enormous agency rules can still be comprehensible if they are written with coherent organization, a clear summary, lucid explanations, and helpful background information for the target audience. Similarly, stakeholder input, even while voluminous, could reinforce the agency's lucid text by providing concise comments that offer relevant and persuasive information on key issues in contention. The processing costs for huge rules, in theory, can be "reasonable" when all participants are determined to get their key messages across in a way that their target audience can understand. This is what cooperative communication is all about.

However, if the text of a draft rule is generally garbled and inaccessible, then the excessive length of the rule and voluminous comments by stakeholders serve only to aggravate the incomprehensibility of a rule. Each unintelligible page of a rule or comment burdens the relevant audience with still more work. And, when readers of a 100-page rule cannot get past the first few pages of explanation in a reasonable amount of time, they may surrender without giving the other 98 pages a chance.

3 All Together

When size and unintelligible text combine into a single rule, the resulting rulemaking product can become incomprehensible to almost everyone. Experience with a technical EPA rule offers a practical example of the resulting deliberative lapses.

FIGURE 6.1 A "Tank Farm"
© Used with permission from Timrobertsaerial@Dreamstime LLC

In this illustrative rulemaking, the EPA was directed to set emission standards for air toxins that reflect the best available pollution-control technology within the industry. In this particular case study, chemical plants were the target industry of the emission standards rulemaking. Among the various sources of air toxics within these industrial plants are large tanks or vats of chemical-laden products. These "tank farms" can volatilize large amounts of dangerous toxic substances. As a result, one of several needed emission-control requirements is that each tank be sealed with an airtight lid. See Figure 6.1.

In promulgating an industry standard for emissions controls, including a leaking lid requirement, the EPA methodically collected and analyzed information, considered input from all affected groups, and promulgated a proposed and ultimately final rule. EPA's final rule, for all intents and purposes, appeared comprehensive and rigorous.

Yet, over time, neighborhoods located next to some large chemical plants continued to report very high levels of emissions, particularly nearer the tank farms. Inspectors conducting periodic air samples just outside the fence line of these tank farms sometimes grew ill and had to wear full breathing apparatuses to finish up their work. The levels of carcinogens and other toxic gases in the air were well over an order of magnitude above the levels considered safe by health professionals.[45] Yet, in these instances, there was little evidence that the companies were violating regulatory standards.

This air pollution mystery triggered a full-blown, detective-style investigation of the rules themselves, which in turn identified at least one possible explanation for these high levels of air toxins.[46] While the EPA had required sealed lids to be installed on all chemical tanks in tank farms, the agency was considerably more lax in its requirements to ensure the seals on the tank lids were working. Specifically, to ensure that sealed lids were operating effectively, the EPA could have drawn from several available technological options to develop monitoring and maintenance requirements. The operator of the plant, for example, could have been required to install continuous emissions monitors at the rim of the tanks. Or the operator could have been required to conduct regular (e.g., monthly) inspections of each tank with a sniffer, like natural gas companies use to detect gas leaks. (In fact, this technique was used for other types of leak detections at the plants in EPA's final rule).[47] These approaches would have provided some objective assurance that tank lids are adequately sealed, while utilizing available, affordable technologies to address the "leaky lid" risk.

However, in the final rule, the EPA instead simply required unspecified "visual inspections" by a company employee to ensure the seal was intact, even though this kind of open-ended visual examination cannot be verified and seems vulnerable to human error.[48] To make matters worse, with regard to the frequency of this self-monitoring, the EPA could have required weekly or even monthly examinations given the seemingly low expense of the visual self-inspection. The EPA instead set the inspection interval at one year. And, rather than require immediate repair if tanks are discovered leaking, the company is given another 45 days to correct the problem, with two additional, self-administered (by the company) 30-day extensions.[49] To complete the picture, the companies' documentation of their compliance with self-inspection requirements are stored on-site rather than with the state or federal agency.[50]

How could this permissive requirement survive the fierce adversarial pressures of rulemaking? The size of the overarching rulemaking project provides a clue. The *proposed* rule, which included three other subparts, was over 187 pages long. After publication of the proposed rule, 22 industries and industry associations – nearly all of them household names – and a smattering of public-interest advocates engaged first in formal notice and comment and then presented their concerns at a public hearing. In addition to carefully considering all written comments, the agency met with affected parties multiple times.[51] EPA's final rule in fact identified more than 100 significant issues in contention.[52]

Emerging from this bloated decision process was a final rule and preamble that spanned over 223 pages and over 195,000 words in the *Federal Register*. And even though the agency pushed the process through in 3-1/2 years from start to finish to meet its statutory deadline, because of a vocal constituency of unhappy interest groups, the EPA reopened public comment on one of the key issues in the rulemaking within 18 days after publishing the final rule. It then received another 60 formal communications. Before it could issue a revised rule, one of the companies petitioned for reconsideration of the entire rulemaking. The EPA ultimately issued a proposed clarification to the original rule two years later, received another 20 comments on its proposed clarification, and issued a final revised rule at the end of 1996. [53] Indeed, the subsequent history of the rule reveals at least two more reopenings of the rule since that time.[54]

Yet, for all of this activity, there is barely a mention of the leaking lid problem or the justification for EPA's visual requirement in the agency's discussions. Only a few cryptic sentences in the preamble of the final rule explain this seemingly important decision: "For some emission points, such as storage vessels and some wastewater operations, continuous parameter monitoring is not feasible in certain circumstances due to the design of the control device or other operational and system design characteristics of the emission points or control technologies."[55] For more curious readers, the EPA later explains that: "More information on inspections and non-continuous monitoring is provided in chapter 6 of BID volume 2B for wastewater operations and chapter 3 of BID volume 2A for storage vessels."[56] If persistent participants made the effort, they would find – after obtaining these documents through the Freedom of Information Act (a process that can take months) – only another dead end.

Several more weeks could be invested into this wild goose chase to uncover what really happened in the mysterious case of the leaking lids rule. But based on the evidence assembled thus far – reinforced by EPA's own silence on the matter – it appears that in the process of negotiating the hundreds of requirements and navigating the frenzy of contestations, this particular item got lost in the shuffle.

But, returning to the communities living at the fence line, the lesson from this rulemaking story is much more personal. Sporadic, voluntary inspections by state health officials currently provide the only measure of how well the 220-page rule is actually working on the ground, and the news thus far is not good. But even more discouraging are these inspectors' impediments to identifying the major contributing causes of elevated toxic air levels. Government inspectors that are prepared to sink limited resources into actively "sniffing" the dozens or perhaps hundreds of tanks for leaks from within a facility, as well as searching for other contributing causes of excessive emissions within a large chemical plant, must first obtain a warrant and set aside the time and resources to conduct a facility-wide inspection. But, even if an inspector perseveres and discovers that some tanks are leaking in significant ways, that fact alone would not amount to evidence of a violation since the inspectors would also need to prove that the company's earlier, visual inspections were not done properly. Like a house of cards, the assurance of air quality in these communities depends on unverifiable visual self-inspections that were put into place through the tumultuous and error-prone rulemaking process just described. The burden for understanding why their air is unsafe is placed on the poor communities located at the fence line. By contrast, the facilities with superior processing capacity – expertise, resources, and access to facility-specific information – are relieved of responsibility for measuring the toxicity of their own emissions.

4 Predicted by Theorists

Theorists have long been watching these same inflated processing costs in administrative fora from their distant perch, predicting the types of harms that excessive processing costs can do to deliberative processes. William Gormley's classic model of administrative practice, for example, selects as one of the two key variables a decision's "complexity" to predict the settings in which the needed, rigorous participatory processes will break down. Because of the drain they impose on participants, these "complex" rules are particularly susceptible to dominance by the most well-funded groups, leaving other affected parties in the dust (what Gormley calls "fit for the boardroom").[57] James Q. Wilson's classic four-quadrant model is less explicit about rule complexity, but he nevertheless recognizes that in rules where some affected groups lack resources to participate, only the most intensely affected and well-financed (usually regulated parties) will be able to afford to participate in the agency's deliberative proceedings.[58]

And yet, while this prescient work underscores the potential for excessive processing costs to undermine rather than advance administrative legitimacy, these theorists still miss the underlying problem. It is not *just* that agency rules are unduly complicated for their own sake or that interested parties can strategically bombard the agencies with information in order to overwhelm them for the fun of it. On the contrary, the real culprit lies in the design of administrative law itself. The legal structure of the process is generally oblivious to the need to place full responsibility on the privileged speakers to communicate meaningfully. And, when these speakers take advantage of the mis-designed process by deliberately overwhelming their target audience, the legitimacy breaks down. Reasons may be given, but they cannot be understood, much less checked by vigorous deliberations.

C *Alternating Speakers and Audience*

It is fair to wonder whether something is amiss in a process that generates rules that are so convoluted and massive that critical provisions escape scrutiny by the relevant participants. This result seems doubly problematic given the emphasis on stakeholder and political oversight and deliberation as an important means of ensuring the accountability of agency rulemakings.

Our now familiar speaker–audience model helps lay the final backdrop for the analysis that follows, but before beginning our discussion, it is important to highlight two important differences in the communicative landscape for administrative process as compared with the other legal programs we survey in this book. These differences, as we shall soon see, help to explain some of the worst examples of incomprehensible agency rules.

The first unique communicative feature of administrative process is that the roles of speaker and audience alternate in a formal way between the agency and its stakeholders. Rather than one-way communication from a fixed speaker to a fixed audience (as we traced in the previous chapters), administrative process establishes a formal dialog between the parties. Although in practice the true dialog can be even more fluid, Figure 6.2 isolates at least two formal points where the *agency* serves as

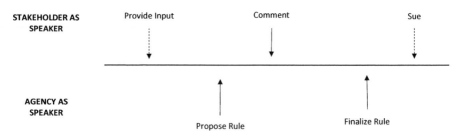

FIGURE 6.2 The Alternating Roles of Stakeholder and Agency as Speaker during the Course of a Rulemaking

speaker – the point at which a rule is proposed and the point at which the rule is finalized, after comments. We also see at least one important point in the process where *stakeholders* serve as speakers – when they lodge comments on an agency proposal. (Note, though, that in some rulemaking settings, stakeholders also serve as speakers during an initial conversation between the agency and stakeholders, which can then inform the framing of the rulemaking project).

Second, the stakeholder community (both as audience and speaker) involves substantial variation in processing capacity among participants that is far greater than the heterogeneity we have encountered in other settings. Recall that in administrative process, the intended audience for agency rules is – in theory – the public at large. In practice, however, we appreciate that few members of the public will be actively engaged in the effort. (This inactivity is attributable to the free-rider problem, a lack of resources and/or expertise to engage, a failure to understand the implications of the issues, and any number of other reasons.)[59] Instead, agency rules will tend to spark interest primarily from a smaller constellation of stakeholder organizations, including those who represent the diffuse public.[60]

Yet even given a narrower set of organized stakeholders, there will be substantial variation in processing capacity. On one side of this stakeholder continuum are well-financed industrial actors who enjoy privileged access to information that is critical to regulatory decisions. These stakeholders are typically willing to make sizable investments to process information relating to rules that affect their interests – particularly rules that have the potential to restrict or impose costs on their operations through emissions controls, disclosure requirements, or even prohibitions.

On the other side are thinly financed organizations that represent diffuse members of the public and/or poor communities. Because their work is poorly funded, the ability of these stakeholders to process information relevant to regulations is low, and often many times lower than well-financed industrial stakeholders.[61]

Since the processing capacity of these disadvantaged groups, even in cases where they have organized as a nonprofit or other funded collective, can sometimes approach zero for individual rules, we assume that the minimally equipped stakeholder participating in a regulatory process will at least be represented by an attorney with law school training in the relevant specialized law. We also assume that this attorney is able to devote at least 10 hours to the task of translating and commenting on an agency rule.

Some readers might balk at assuming such a high level of expertise for the most thinly financed stakeholders, but we do this to err on the side of understating our argument. If this minimally funded target audience lacks sufficient processing capacity to participate, one can only imagine the implications for groups that do not have the resources to hire a lawyer for 10 hours to assist them in participating in an agency rulemaking.[62]

In these alternating speaker–audience roles, are the participants generally predisposed to communicate cooperatively, at least before factoring in the incentives created by administrative process? We consider these issues first from the perspective of agencies and then evaluate them from the perspective of the stakeholders.

1 The Agency

In the abstract, the agency staff developing a rule would seem generally inclined to communicate meaningfully with stakeholders when soliciting advice on a proposed or final rule. They are eager to produce a rule that is vetted in ways that could help reduce the risk of unwanted interventions from the courts and political branches down the road. Yet in practice, the incentives for cooperative communication by the agency-as-speaker may be absent in a subset of rules.

Speaker. As speaker, the agency enjoys some superior processing capabilities when it comes to crafting a proposal or rule (or other policy). Most obviously, the agency's superior processing ability stems from the agency's control over the framing of the rulemaking project, its decision about which information is relevant, and its synthesis of the evidence into a rule proposal. Even if the agency has not mastered the content of its own rule, as the author of the text the agency nevertheless enjoys an inside perspective on the nature of the choices and forces at play. If the agency does not explain its analysis and design clearly, participants not involved in the agency discussions can have a difficult time making sense of what the rule does and how it works.[63] As a result, comprehension asymmetries can arise between the agency and a subset of the stakeholder audience.[64]

Given its advantaged position, is the agency motivated in the abstract to make its decisions comprehensible to participants? The answer to this question will vary considerably, as we discuss later. But there are at least two circumstances in which the agency may not face strong background incentives for cooperative communication in its role as speaker.

First, and particularly when a rule is complicated and technical, that rule can become difficult and costly to explain. Since agency resources are notoriously in short supply, the agency faces a zero-sum game; should it allocate its scarce energies to drafting clearer explanations for a broader swath of affected groups or instead dedicate those energies to other pursuits, like more rigorous analyses or research?[65] Unless the agency perceives high benefits to cooperative communication, it may place secondary import on ensuring that a complicated rule can reasonably be understood by the average, affected stakeholder.

Second, when key decisions in the agency's rule create both winners and losers in the affected stakeholder communities, the agency's incentives for cooperative communication may also decline. The more understandable the rule is, the more likely the losing group of stakeholders will find something in it they do not like and will be eager to challenge it. If incomprehensibility can help insulate the rule from these complaints, then the agency may find it is *not* ultimately in its interest to invest in reaching out or explaining its decisions and choices clearly. From the agency's perspective, the less the political world understands about its work, the faster it can get the rule finalized and move on to the next assignment.[66]

Audience. When the agency moves over to become the audience, however, the agency may sometimes find itself on the losing end of comprehension asymmetries. This is particularly likely when certain key issues lie partly outside the agency's expertise, making it dependent on privileged stakeholders to become informed. The agency may also find itself struggling to process comments when stakeholders are numerous and participate vigorously.

Thus, even while the agency in the abstract could be highly motivated to understand and process all stakeholder comments,[67] in practice the agency may occasionally lack the capacity to do this processing work.[68] And when the agency's resources do fall short, it will find itself disadvantaged relative to at least some of the more privileged stakeholders.

2 The Stakeholders

In a typical rulemaking process, stakeholders operate as "speakers" during the formal comment period. They also sometimes educate the agency about key issues early in the rulemaking, before the proposed rule is published. See Figure 6.2.

Speaker. Some stakeholders enjoy specialized expertise in the key technical issues that often lie at the heart of a rulemaking, and when this happens, comprehension asymmetries are likely to arise between these speakers and the agency as audience. For example, understanding how pollution-control equipment works inside a particular factory involves know-how that only the firms installing and using this equipment may fully understand. An agency rule-writer, who must master how this equipment works when developing a rule, is thus dependent on these regulated parties to provide this specialized information in a reasonably accessible way.[69]

While in theory we might expect these stakeholders to convey information accessibly to the agency, in practice we see circumstances when these assumptions may not hold true. Engaging in cooperative communications, particularly for technical rules, can be expensive for stakeholders as well as regulators.[70] These communication expenses become higher still in those rules in which the agency itself has been less than clear about the nature of the issues to be addressed. Here the costs of cooperative communication to the stakeholders involve not only conveying key points they wish to make, but processing what the agency has provided so they can be sure they understand the larger context and issues. The more jumbled the agency's project, the more it will cost stakeholders to craft reasonably understandable comments.

In a subset of rules, privileged stakeholders may be not only agnostic, but inclined against cooperative communication because they perceive some strategic benefits from shifting excess processing costs to others. By forcing their audiences to search for evidentiary support, invest in added technical expertise, or guess at the ramifications of technical positions, privileged stakeholders can keep their stakeholder opponents and agency staff underinformed and overwhelmed. The higher the processing costs for the agency and opposing stakeholders, the more ineffective these groups will be in participating.

Audience. When stakeholders shift to the role of audience, it is the stakeholders with the fewest resources who now find themselves at the *losing* (rather than winning) end of comprehension asymmetries. It is well-known that thinly financed stakeholders encounter impediments to participation when the rules become increasingly complicated and difficult to process.[71] If the agency is not inclined to craft rules that are accessible and clear, this deficiency will impact the ability of thinly financed groups to remain engaged.[72] Some stakeholders with particularly limited processing capacity may not even know whether they are affected by a rule in the first place when a rule is drafted in convoluted ways.[73] By contrast, comprehension asymmetries are less likely to affect well-financed stakeholders who are able to commit the needed resources to decipher the meaning and implications of complicated rule proposals.

3 Summary

Putting these alternating speaker–audience roles together, we see that both the variation among stakeholders and the incentives of the participants for cooperative communication are important features in rulemaking deliberations. When the incentives of both speaker and audience encourage meaningful communication, the process should work beautifully.

Conversely, if both the agency-as-speaker and the stakeholders-as-speaker benefit from incomprehensible communications, the result can be disastrous. Poorly drafted rules may alienate all but the most advantaged and determined participants, while the privileged stakeholders in turn ramp up processing costs still further by providing comments on incoherent rules. Herculean effort will be needed by the agencies to untangle, evaluate, and assess the merits of dozens or even hundreds of issues and disagreements.[74]

Rules are particularly vulnerable to severe comprehension asymmetries when key issues are technical and complex (hence costly to communicate) and the affected stakeholders vary in their capacities to process information (e.g., have different levels of expertise and resources). In situations where these "worst case" rules arise, the alternating speaker roles of agency and stakeholders can devolve into a type of nuclear arms race, only this one involves a competition to produce incomprehensible messages. The alternating speakers take turns overwhelming their target audience with incomprehensible messages in a perverse effort to gain control over the end product or, alternatively, bring the rulemaking process to a screeching halt. See Figure 6.3.

Upward spiraling processing costs also exacerbate already existing imbalances among stakeholders. Stakeholders with the greatest processing capacities can effectively control the conversation in ways that not only disadvantage the agency-

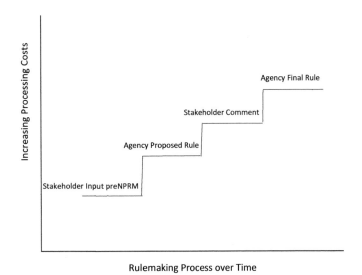

FIGURE 6.3 The Escalation of Processing Costs in a Rulemaking over Time

as-audience, but effectively preclude thinly financed stakeholder-adversaries from participating in the process.

Legal designs to counteract these incentives are thus critical. As long as cooperative communication is not required in the rulemaking process, the incomprehensibility of at least a subset of rules will almost certainly grow worse, rather than better.

II COMPREHENSION ASYMMETRIES IN ADMINISTRATIVE PROCESS

Given these background incentives, just how successful is the structure of administrative law at encouraging effective communication between the agency and affected parties?

Our investigation begins on a glum note. As a structural matter, administrative process, however inadvertently, tends to place the information-processing burden on the audience at each step in the deliberative process. It is up to the commenters (audience) to process and make sense of a rule. And it is up to the agency (audience) to process and make sense of the comments. As a result, when a participant's turn as speaker comes up, his primary goal is to convey all of the relevant, detailed information to the audience. Whether the information is also comprehensible is generally irrelevant as a legal matter. And therein lies the crux of the problems we are about to explore.

In this section we first scour administrative process for overriding requirements that rules (or comments) be reasonably comprehensible to their intended audience. Finding none, we then search for more indirect incentives for our alternating speakers to be reasonably comprehensible to one another.

We focus initially on the Rule-Followers. If the system is not devised to encourage meaningful communication from speakers who operate as Rule-Followers, then it should take little imagination to conceive of ways that Rule-Benders might exploit the structural flaws in administrative process. We then close Part II by surveying the ways Rule-Benders can and do exploit this oversight in the architecture of administrative process.

A *Rule-Followers*

Rule-Followers will endeavor to communicate key concepts effectively to the target audience unless the structure of the process leads them to cut corners in this cooperative communication. In surveying the ways that administrative process sets up the proper incentives for cooperative communication, we begin with settings in which the agency serves as speaker, and then turn to stakeholders as speakers. In both cases, we consider only these groups' behavior when they operate in good faith as Rule-Followers.

1 The Agencies

Theoretically, we might expect administrative process to impose direct requirements on agencies to draft comprehensible rule proposals since agency
accountability turns in large part on mechanisms of pluralistic engagement
and deliberation. In this section, we explore how these incentives operate in
practice.

A NO DIRECT REQUIREMENTS FOR COMPREHENSIBILITY

The courts have interpreted the Administrative Procedure Act to force agencies to
give reasons for their decisions, and those reasons must provide "persuasive
responses to cogent objections by outside parties."[75] As noted, the APA not only
demands that agencies solicit comments on their proposal but that they "consider"
those comments in crafting the final rule.[76] Both requirements are enforced by the
courts.

But note that this legal structure stops well short of requiring an agency to actually
solicit and engage stakeholders. The agency must hold out its proposals for notice
and comment and is forced to take into account the comments it receives. But how
comprehensible those decisions actually are lies beyond the reach of the APA's
requirements. Administrative deliberations are thus based on a passive or market-
based model of public participation – an "if you [agency] build it, they [commenter]
will come" approach.[77]

As a result, one key structural element is missing from the design of administrative
law: The agency is not required to ensure that affected groups are engaged, able to
engage, or even alerted to the rulemaking.[78] If only well-financed interest groups
can afford to participate because the rules are very difficult to understand, so be it.
Indeed, under the current design of administrative process, the agency is not even
required to track whether the most adversely affected groups weigh in. If large sets of
affected groups are silent and offer no input on significant rules that affect their
interests, this seemingly devastating fact is irrelevant to the legality of the final rule.
Even the Rule-Following agency will be inclined to forge ahead since it is relieved
of the burden of soliciting broader views on its proposal.

From this design, we can see how the mandated *means* of ensuring participation
in administrative process – procedural requirements for notice and comment and
judicial review – have become decoupled from the overarching *end goal* of meaningful participation as an important means to ensure agency accountability.[79] This
disconnect occurs because the measures for engaging participation are legally
enforceable, but are severed from the equivalent demand that the agency proposal
be reasonably comprehensible to the participants.[80] As a result, "the current rulemaking process, despite its formal promises of transparency and broad participation
rights, routinely and systematically disadvantages consumers, small business owners,

local and tribal governmental entities, nongovernmental organizations, and similar kinds of stakeholders, as well as members of the general public."[81]

Interestingly, this missing foundational feature may have actually been anticipated in the original 1946 design of administrative process. In the text of the APA, Congress did require that agencies provide a "concise general statement" of their proposals and rules.[82] But over the last 60 years of litigation, this well-meaning directive has been lost in the shuffle. Indeed, and as detailed subsequently, rather than embrace this demand for accessibility, the courts have unwittingly made the requirement effectively irrelevant in their insistence on comprehensive records and elaborately supported rules. As Richard Pierce notes, "The courts have replaced the statutory adjectives, 'concise' and 'general' with the judicial adjectives 'detailed' and 'encyclopedic.'"[83]

B ADMINISTRATIVE PROCESS MAKES MATTERS WORSE

But administrative law is not simply passive in tolerating incomprehensible rules. It actively exacerbates incentives for agencies to load in processing costs in ways that can impair both the balance and rigor of the resulting deliberations with stakeholders.

(i) The Courts' Role

Over the last 60 years, a series of judicially supplied directives emerging from the courts' cumulative review of challenges to agency rules emphasizes the necessity of thorough and complete information in agency explanations, sometimes at the expense of comprehensible information. A diligent Rule-Follower agency may draft rules that are less comprehensible simply to stay on the safe side of the courts' requirements.

Hard Look and Substantial Evidence. The courts' hard look doctrine, which is used to review some agency rules, is notorious for exerting pressure on agencies to become obsessively detailed in their final rules, sometimes at the expense of maintaining a grasp of the big picture and communicating that big picture to stakeholders.[84] In "hard look" review, the court closely scrutinizes the agency's rule to ensure that it has adequately considered *all* comments and supported *all* contested assumptions.[85] As the D.C. Circuit reminded the agencies: "What we are entitled to at all events is a careful identification by the Secretary, when his proposed standards are challenged, of the reasons why he chooses to follow one course rather than another."[86] This test emerged in the early 1970s as a way to increase oversight of what was then viewed as unbridled discretion by agencies and the corresponding risk of capture by regulated parties.

Despite its apparent good intentions, when a rulemaking has dozens or even hundreds of moving parts, agencies will dedicate their limited energies toward ensuring that the contested details are pinned down first. For substantial rules, the "reviewing court, assisted by able counsel for petitioners, almost always can identify one or more issues the agency addressed poorly in its statement of basis, and purpose."[87] Agencies thus work hard to avoid getting caught in this "gotcha game" – missing a fine point that can later hang them up in litigation. Cooperative communication of the agency's reasoning and the coherence of the larger rulemaking project will take a back seat as the agency is redirected by the hard look doctrine toward ensuring that no criticism is left unaddressed.

The most responsible course of action for the agency when faced with these judicial demands, then, is an unwavering attention to detail in developing the final rule.[88] Every comment that raises a credible-sounding issue, even a peripheral one, should receive a complete and detailed response. In preparing its rule for challenge, the agency will also work hard to support, or at least give the appearance of supporting, every challenged assumption with information from the technical and scientific literature. Moreover, because the agency is not required to be concise in its use of this technical information, and there is no requirement that this information be even moderately accessible to all target audiences, there are no downsides for the agency to include reams of technical verbiage designed to fend off litigation. Indeed, the rational course of action for Rule-Following agency-leaders is to engage in information overload – to defend itself from possible legal attack by anticipating every potential legal problem in its explanation of the final rule.

And this prediction maps against what scholars observe about a number of agency rulemakings. Richard Pierce, a long-time critic of judicial review, argues that this form of judicial scrutiny has forced agencies to engage in excessive data analysis and explanation, filling hundreds of pages of the *Federal Register* that courts ultimately "may, or may not, consider an adequate response to the 10,000–1,000,000 pages of comments" received.[89] In her study of the effects of judicial review on EPA, Rosemary O'Leary similarly concludes that "the proliferation of court decisions has forced what one EPA staff member called 'non-user-friendly' regulations. According to EPA technical staff, the Office of General Counsel often rewrites regulations, notices, and proposals in anticipation that a lawsuit is imminent. Lawyers have the last word in most EPA actions."[90] And, in an article on *Vermont Yankee*, Richard Stewart also takes note of the informational consequences of hard look review: "In response to these [hard look] rulings, agency lawyers sought to bolster the agency's position by elaborate documentation, while respondents and interveners submitted contrary documentation which they themselves developed or obtained from agency files through Freedom of Information Act litigation. These various documents provided an elaborate record for judicial review."[91]

Today, hard look tends to be the exception in judicial review rather than the rule; a number of courts now grant the agency considerable deference.[92] Yet the chance that the agency will get unlucky and draw a hard look panel remains a distinct risk, and it is nearly impossible for an agency to know in advance what the panel's predilection will be.[93] Jerry Mashaw observes that because of this significant unpredictability in the applicable standard of review, the courts essentially function "as robed roulette wheels."[94] And it is this chance that the judicial roulette wheel will settle on a hard look standard that leads agencies to assume the worst.[95] Shep Melnick observes from his study of agency rulemakings: "Since agencies do not like losing big court cases, they reacted defensively [to the courts' requirements], accumulating more and more information, responding to all comments, and covering their bets. The rulemaking record grew enormously, far beyond any judge's ability to review it."[96] And "[t]hus began a vicious cycle: the more effort agencies put into rulemaking, the more they feared losing, and the more defensive rulemaking became."[97]

Logical Outgrowth Test. A second problematic doctrine from the standpoint of encouraging comprehensible agency proposals is the "logical outgrowth test." This judicially created test encourages agencies to develop a proposed rule that is as complete as possible.[98] Under the test, any material changes made to final rules that are not presaged in the agency's proposal require a new proposed rulemaking, with its own separate notice and comment period. In theory, the purpose of the test is to make participation more meaningful by ensuring that the agency's final rule grows out of its proposal.

But in practice, the logical outgrowth test may have the opposite impact on the comprehensibility of a rule proposal and resulting deliberation. In order to develop a rule proposal that anticipates all major changes that might happen as a result of notice and comment, the Rule-Following agency is best advised to negotiate its proposed rule with the most litigious stakeholders in advance. Indeed, there is evidence that some agencies do exactly that. Empirical research of EPA rulemakings reveals considerable agency-regulated industry dialogs occurring prior to the publication of the proposed rule.[99] In one set of EPA rules, regulated industry communicated with the EPA on average 84 times before the proposed rule was published.[100] In some cases, the agency also shared its draft-proposed rule with the industry for their comments, before making the proposal public. As one agency staff remarked in a related program, "We help them; they help us."[101]

Negotiation-styled discussions with one set of expert stakeholders could improve the comprehensibility of a rule, but this approach could also cut in the opposite direction. The many choices, evidence, and compromises reached by the Rule-Follower during these pre-proposed rule negotiations may be difficult to translate and explain in the agency's perambulatory discussion. Negotiated terms could make a rule even more intricate and labyrinthine. At the same time, even well-meaning Rule-Followers may not be eager to advertise these compromises to the larger stakeholder-constituency. In some cases, then, the logical outgrowth test may inadvertently cause some rule proposals to become still more inaccessible to the outsider-groups not privy to the negotiations, despite the rule's purpose in protecting stakeholders' right to participate.[102]

Counter-Incentives for Explanation. There is at least one important judicial directive that can move Rule-Followers in the opposite direction and encourage them to invest greater effort in cooperative communication. This is the "reasoned explanation" requirement established by the courts when reviewing challenges that allege agency rules are "arbitrary and capricious" under the APA.[103] In these opinions, the courts consistently insist that agencies show their work and provide a "reasoned explanation" for their decisions. This doctrinal demand would seem to hit the bull's-eye with respect to encouraging cooperative communication from the agencies, and in some cases there is strong evidence that the doctrine accomplishes exactly this goal.[104]

There are a number of reasons, however, why the "reasoned explanation" requirement is no panacea when it comes to encouraging cooperative communication across all rulemakings. First, and most significant, the demand for reasoned explanation pertains only to agency choices made in a final rule. If the agency's proposed rule and accompanying discussion are impenetrable, this defect does not appear to be actionable unless commenters create a record of that fact in their comments and litigate the problem. The proposed rule stage, which is the most important in engaging stakeholders, is thus left largely untouched by the reasoned explanation test.

Second and somewhat relatedly, the reasoned explanation requirement is applied narrowly. Litigants locate one or more agency choices in a final rule that – based on the comments – appears "arbitrary" and is insufficiently explained. Challengers regularly take issue, for example, with an agency's choice of assumptions or algorithms used in a regulatory model or the agency's decision to include or exclude evidence in its analysis.[105] Yet these grounds for challenging "arbitrary" agency action are – again by necessity – only slices of the larger rule. As a result, the reasoned explanation tends to focus on specific issues, and the effort devoted to addressing these issues may come at the expense of ensuring the larger rule project is reasonably understandable to the target audience.

Third and finally, the courts generally insist only that these reasoned explanations be present *somewhere* in the rule and preamble (or in the record); this is clearly not the same as requiring the agency's explanations to be reasonably comprehensible to stakeholder participants. Indeed, some courts go to great lengths to extract and translate the agency's sometimes garbled text in search of an explanation they can review. The courts' laments, noted earlier, attest to the effort and energy they are willing to invest in scouring the "sump" of documents and disarray of justifications and evidence to re-create the agency's sometimes convoluted reasoning. Rarely (and perhaps never) has a court struck down a rule because locating and understanding the agency's proffered explanation required an unreasonable investment of effort from the court (and by extension an expert stakeholder).[106]

(ii) Additional Institutional Checks

In addition to judicial review, institutional checks by Congress and the president also place pressure on the agencies that, in theory, could produce incentives for cooperative communication.[107] In practice, however, these political pressures are more likely to lead Rule-Following agencies to produce rules that are less comprehensible.[108]

Thomas McGarity sums up the scholarship on this "political" side of administrative law. He observes that administrative lawyers now must also trace the influences produced by "interactions between high-level agency personnel and desk officers in OIRA, between high-level agency officials and their counterparts in other regulatory agencies, and between high-level agency officials and the staffs of the agency's authorizing and appropriations committees in Congress."[109]

What are these sources of formal political influence? On the White House side, the president enjoys several direct mechanisms to influence agency decisions. Through increasingly strong means of presidential control – now including a clearance process for all significant agency proposals and final rules before they are published – the White House can influence and even control agency decisions that catch its interest or are brought to its attention by stakeholders.[110] In the course of this review, the White House sometimes advances "its own extra-statutory policy preferences over another agency's statutory goals" and can succeed in changing the text of the agency rules and accompanying analyses and explanations.[111] At least some of these changes, moreover, occur over the objection of the agency.[112] As a result, the White House can exert a substantial impact on the agency's work by altering or delaying rulemakings,[113] forcing agencies to withdraw rules altogether,[114] and causing agency rules to be reversed in the courts.[115]

Congress, for its part, directly participates in the development of agency rules by offering comments, vetoing rules under the Congressional Review Act, or amending the agency's statutory authority. Much of Congress's influence is indirect, however. Congressional members exert influence indirectly by staging embarrassing oversight hearings, threatening wayward agencies with budget cuts, or preparing reports and instigating GAO studies that can lead to unflattering media coverage.[116]

We can quickly see that these interventions from the political branches will not be welcome to an agency eager to get its work done. As a result, the Rule-Following agency may sometimes be relatively unenthusiastic about cooperatively communicating with these political overseers.[117]

In *Agency Self-Insulation under Presidential Review*, Jennifer Nou explores the various reasons why agencies may want to avoid presidential oversight and explores a range of techniques used by agencies to insulate themselves from this intervention.[118] Nou notes, for example, that "the more an agency invests in ... research, the more costly it becomes for the President to contest the agency's decision."[119]

Agencies can also insulate themselves from unwanted review by using "jargon" and obfuscating assumptions in ways that make it more difficult for non-experts, like the president, to understand the underlying analysis.[120]

Congress's intervention is similarly unwelcome to a conscientious agency endeavoring to get the job done. Former Securities and Exchange Commission (SEC) Chairman Arthur Levitt observes that the congressional oversight of rules is "a 'kind of a blood sport' in which the regulated industries attempt 'to make the particular agency' promulgating an unwelcome regulation 'look stupid or inept or venal.'"[121] And Congress may even use these various political tools to enhance its own image. As Shep Melnick observes, the agency is "every elected official's favorite whipping boy."[122]

It is no wonder that agencies determined to bring their rulemakings to completion sometimes view these political overseers as hostile.[123] Indeed, to the extent these political interventions are justified as democracy-enhancing,[124] the political pressures could ironically have the opposite effect on both the coherence and the comprehensibility of a subset of particularly technical and controversial agency rulemakings. And, as Dan Farber and Anne O'Connell document, these interventions from the political branches have become increasingly prevalent over the last few decades, altering how administrative decisions are made.[125]

These are simplistic caricatures of the interactions between agencies and the political branches, to be sure; yet much of the literature documents how these political branches interfere with, rather than enable, the agency's work. Incomprehensibility may provide the Rule-Following agency with an escape from at least some of this political scrutiny by raising the costs to the overseers in their ability to second-guess the agency's rulemakings.

2 The Stakeholders

While incentives for meaningful communication may be lacking on the agency side for some rules, what about the agency's conversational partner – the stakeholders? Perhaps the stakeholders will draw out the crux of the agency's analysis and facilitate clear, accessible rulemakings as a result of their succinct, penetrating comments that cut to the heart of a rulemaking. As we shall soon see, however, Rule-Following stakeholders often forgo this valuable investment in cooperative communication to satisfy the overriding goal of providing complete information.

Create a Record. To preserve their ability to challenge rules in court, the first and most important goal for Rule-Following stakeholders in administrative practice is to ensure that they submit detailed comments on every conceivable issue of concern. If an issue is not raised with specificity, it is deemed waived in any subsequent legal challenge stakeholders may wish to bring.[126] Like a contract, then, it is vital for stakeholders to get all conceivable information into the record during the comment period.

Attorneys working for industry in fact underscore that the most important task for their clients is to "build the best record" that they can. "Written comments are the single most effective technique" for doing so. They thus instruct their stakeholder-clients to "[m]ake sure that you submit to the Agency *all* relevant information supporting your concerns in the rulemaking. This is the best way to convince the Agency to respond favorably to your concerns."[127]

No Limit to the Size, Detail, or Number of Comments. Conveniently, in terms of preparing this record, there are no limits to the information that can be submitted. Since the agency must consider all of it, the urgency of cooperative communication again drops away; once the comments are made, they can be enforced in litigation. As one trade association representative conceded in preparing comments on EPA's hazardous waste rules:

> EPA started its proposals and our comments took up a space on my bookshelf this thick [respondent holds hands about 1–1/2 feet apart]. So to me the fact that we whittled it down to 100 pages [to meet the appellate court's page limit] is pretty remarkable. There were a lot more issues that we conceded later were not – you know we were just whining – we didn't have a good recommendation for an alternative approach for EPA to take. So a lot of issues fell off over the years.[128]

Comments Are Critical. The courts require that only comments filed during the official "notice and comment" period serve as the basis for challenges to the rule in court,[129] and thus Rule-Followers will be overly diligent (or perhaps obsessive) in ensuring that every conceivable concern is detailed in these all-important comments.[130] This judicially (and sometimes legislatively) imposed limitation on challengers originates from the well-meaning notion that parties must exhaust their administrative remedies before seeking judicial redress.[131] But by insisting that all information must be received during this time-limited comment window without also ensuring that the information must also be reasonably comprehensible, the speakers' incentives are pointed more toward data-dumping than toward cooperative communication.

In his case study of an OSHA rulemaking, Patrick Schmidt traces the way that stakeholders respond to these legal incentives by carefully lacing the record with multiple grounds for suit and then using those issues to hold the agency hostage under the threat of litigation.[132] On the other hand, when participants fail to lodge comments and preserve their right to judicial review, the agency is legally permitted to completely ignore their concerns.[133]

Comments Must Be Specific. The courts have made it clear that more general comments from affected parties – even if lodged in writing and on time – are usually not material enough to have any legal bearing on the agencies; instead comments must be specific.[134] To preserve issues for litigation, Rule-Following stakeholders are thus best-advised to provide comments that are detailed and well-documented.[135]

This seemingly reasonable requirement for specificity again may encourage some Rule-Following parties to provide too much documentation, too many technicalities, and too much detail, all of which exacerbates the agency's costs to process comments.

Agency bears the burden of processing all comments, with the costs of all misunderstandings falling on the agency. Finally, the courts have made it clear that the processing burden for making sense of stakeholder comments rests on the agency's shoulders.[136] The agency ignores these comments at its peril.[137] Yet with no limits on the extent or nature of the information the Rule-Following stakeholders can file, and with no legal responsibility for ensuring that those comments are reasonably comprehensible, the best course for stakeholders is clear: load up the comments to preserve every conceivable argument and issue for subsequent litigation.

B Rule-Benders

Our agencies and stakeholders are not always so innocent. In some settings, both of these groups behave as Rule-Benders when they take over the role of speaker. Agencies may deliberately manipulate the process to advance a particular goal held by the president or self-interested staff. Stakeholders may exploit the permissive design of the administrative process by overwhelming resource-strapped agencies with processing costs in order to gain control over both the substance and the pace of the rulemaking exercise. We consider both sets of Rule-Benders in turn.

1 The Agencies

Although there is not much evidence in the literature of Rule-Bending agencies deliberately exploiting rulemaking participants' processing limitations in order to advance some predetermined end, there are some circumstances in which we can imagine this occurring. Two sets of circumstances seem particularly likely.

First, when the president or political appointee has a policy goal that is both important and may not be effectuated if all participants are vigorously engaged, agencies may be directed to "get the policy through." Agency staff will see the easiest way to do this is to make the rule unintelligible to those who might oppose it. As Stuart Shapiro observes, "Agencies have reacted to … th[is] legal climate in which they operate by producing analyses that are often inscrutable to anyone besides those with a great deal of expertise and resources."[138]

Some of former EPA Administrator Pruitt's rules, promulgated under President Trump, illustrate this Rule-Bending strategy. Pruitt was candid about his deregulatory agenda, yet at least some of the rules and decisions that implement his deregulatory plan are misleading.[139] For example, Administrator Pruitt developed a rule that purported to "strengthen science" and "data transparency," but in reality, the rule was designed to allow the political administrator to control the evidence allowed into the technical analysis, under the façade of good science.[140] Many onlookers, even those well versed in this legal area, had a difficult time understanding the inner workings of the proposed rule, although most were convinced that it was loaded with trickery.

Second, when the agency staff itself is "captured," it might endeavor to actively sidestep meaningful stakeholder deliberation and operate as a Rule-Bender. Perhaps key agency staff hope for lucrative private sector jobs soon after the project is done and thus endeavor to draft a rule that appeals to future employers. Or the agency rule drafters are rotating through the government temporarily (usually in a political position) with the specific intent of stacking the deck in favor of their home organization. As long as the legal process tolerates incomprehensible rules, the best way to control the regulatory outcome is to make the rule effectively unintelligible to those who might otherwise object.

However they come to be Rule-Benders, Rule-Bending agencies could draft proposed rules that are incomprehensible using a variety of familiar techniques such as:

- Proposing rules that are likely to accomplish very different ends than the agency publicly proclaims, like promoting "good science," when in truth the rules are crafted to reduce regulatory burdens on select constituencies.[141]
- Providing explanations that do not identify the key choices, much less reasonable alternative choices, underlying an agency's decision; instead readers must extract these choices on their own and re-create plausible alternatives not taken nor analyzed.[142]
- Citing lengthy documents as support for key features without listing page numbers, without making the documents publicly accessible, or sometimes even mis-citing the documents.[143]
- Itemizing significant changes to a proposed rule in an exhaustive, non-prioritized manner that can have the effect of confusing readers.[144]
- Providing technical explanations using terminology and jargon that only those with specialized expertise can understand.[145]
- Providing a preamble that does not offer readers an accessible summary of the key choices of the rule or the implications of those choices, but rather dives into the details in dozens or even hundreds of pages.[146]

As long as the agency is not required by law to provide understandable summaries, roadmaps, and explanations, then the Rule-Bender agency can deliberately craft incomprehensible rules in order to obscure the errors and biases of their

ends-oriented decisions. Stakeholders must invest considerable effort to connect
the dots to identify the agency's underlying logic and prepare useful comments.

Incomprehensible rules won't affect all stakeholders similarly. Interest groups flush
with resources, time, and stakes are more likely to overcome these processing-cost
barriers than stakeholders who are short on resources. When the likely opposition
comes from these thinly financed sectors, however, Rule-Bending agencies will
likely find the benefits of incomprehensibility strategies irresistible. It is quite easy to
draft a rulemaking proposal in a way that makes it nearly impossible for thinly
financed stakeholders to identify the contestable choices and participate meaningfully
in the decisions.

2 The Stakeholders

When stakeholders enjoy privileges in resources or expertise on issues integral to an
agency rule, the stakeholders can also operate as Rule-Benders and use their
privileged position to its advantage. The tactics used by Rule-Bending stakeholders
to exploit comprehension asymmetries are almost as old as the Administrative
Procedure Act itself. Academics writing in the 1950s observed how information
games were already becoming a permanent fixture in regulatory processes, leaving
in their wake dramatically imbalanced representation and oversight. James Landis,
for example, observed in 1960 that regulated industry can have a "daily machine-gun
like impact" on the agency that leads to an industry bias.[147] And Jaffe suggested as
early as 1954 that, by virtue of their continuing presence, regulated parties "capture"
agencies through the constant torrent of information.[148]

In these settings, because the structure of administrative practice puts all
processing costs on the agency, the agency will find itself on the run. With the
burden on the agency "to consider" all the information submitted to it – regardless
of the volume or needless complexity – Rule-Bending commenters are in the
driver's seat. The agency is at their mercy. As O'Leary observes, stakeholders able
to raise "[m]atters suitable for litigation are the 'squeaky wheels that get the grease,'
while other important environmental problems fall by the wayside."[149]

The literature is replete with anecdotes and other evidence of stakeholder strategies devised to throw sand in the gears of a rulemaking and gain control of the
exercise by raising the agency's processing costs. Owen and Braeutigam underscored
four decades ago how stakeholders' "ability to control the flow of information to the
regulatory agency is a crucial element in affecting decisions."[150] Based on this
power, stakeholders can make available "carefully selected facts," withhold others,
and if delay is useful, "flood the agency with more information than it can
absorb."[151] When the agency seeks a particularly damaging piece of information
that can't be legally withheld, the stakeholder's "best tactic is to bury it in a
mountain of irrelevant material" or provide it, but simultaneously "deny its reliability and commence a study to acquire more reliable data."[152]

Box 6.2 Comprehension Asymmetries in Administrative Law

The Rule-Follower (both Agencies and Stakeholders)

- "Create a record"; when in doubt, include too much information.
- Ensure that comments and responses are specific and detailed.
- Dodge political interference to the extent possible.

AND

Why is it legally prudent to shift processing costs to the audience?

There is no requirement that communications must be comprehensible, so why invest the effort?

The Rule-Bender (both Agencies and Stakeholders)

How can the audience be overpowered with excessive processing costs?

- Databomb and sink key issues in mounds of paper.
- Provide explanations and comments that are not prioritized or accessibly explained.
- Use technical terms that only a few understand.
- Delve into details that are not significant and only serve to distract and confuse the main issues.

Advice by legal counsel to industry betrays similar strategies to wear the agency down during the rulemaking process by exploiting the law's indifference to comprehensible comments. One corporate counsel summarized their methods: "We will try to build a record that's persuasive . . . to sort of overwhelm the agency and create for them the impression that the world out there wants them to do something else."[153]

C *Summary*

When the legal default rules embedded in administrative law are stacked end-to-end, the message to the designated speaker in an administrative proceeding is clear – get all the potential issues and details into the document and don't worry about whether it is comprehensible. The processing burdens will fall on the corresponding audience. And, as the role of speaker alternates between stakeholders and agencies, the resulting process can produce a gradual upward spiral of complexity. Each speaker takes turns dumping more raw, undigested information into the deliberations, and the relevant audience capable of processing the mess grows smaller and less representative of the range of participants affected.

III DOES INCOMPREHENSIBILITY IN ADMINISTRATIVE PROCESS REALLY MATTER AND CAN IT BE FIXED?

But even if these comprehension asymmetries arise with some frequency in administrative process, does it really matter if agency rules are sometimes incomprehensible? And, even more to the point, if adverse consequences can be identified, is this a problem that can be rectified?

A *Repeating the Flawed Design in Other Regulatory Processes*

At the very least, we might tell ourselves, this problematic design for administrative process remains an isolated feature of our legal landscape that is limited to notice and comment rulemakings. Unfortunately, however, the same structure is repeated in other settings, each of which attempts to enhance the quality of public deliberations. And, while these programs sometimes do deliver on this deliberative-enhancing objective, they are structured in ways that make it just as likely that they will lead to the opposite result.

The earliest reincarnation of this type of participatory process was copied into the National Environmental Policy Act (NEPA), which requires agencies to conduct environmental impact assessments on major federal actions.[154] By the 1970s, it became clear that government actions were creating significant environmental harm. To address this problem, Congress passed a law that requires the federal government to assess the environmental impacts of its proposed actions, as well as to assess what might happen under other alternative courses of action – including no action – before building a dam, filling a wetland, building a prison, etc. Under the law, the agency proposing a significant action is required to do the analysis of its potentially harmful environmental impacts and solicit public comment.

It is no secret that agencies are often not enthusiastic about doing these assessments. NEPA requirements serve only to slow down agency progress, add paperwork burdens, and create new attachment points for litigation. And yet, if the agencies do not take the impact assessments seriously – at least in following the procedural requirements set out by law – the agencies will find themselves drawn into litigation and may be forced to start the analysis all over again.

While lawyers have found numerous ways to comply honestly with NEPA requirements, foremost in their creative compliance tools is to produce analyses so obscure and unwieldy that only a few stakeholders can follow them.[155] The Council on Environmental Quality identified precisely this perverse strategy in its assessment of the agencies' compliance with NEPA in 1997. Rather than providing a candid assessment of the project, the agencies sometimes turned the environmental impact statement (EIS) into a "litigation-proof" document that did not adequately raise or consider alternatives or engage in the underlying facts in a rigorous way.[156] Stuart Shapiro similarly observes that, while not always the case, "EISs [tend to be] excessively detailed and this detail conveys the false impression of precision, while obscuring the ability of outsiders to evaluate the accuracy of the analysis."[157]

The same structural problem is replicated in mandated rationality assessments of agency rulemakings. Rationality requirements direct agencies to prepare full cost–benefit analyses on significant rules, assess impacts on small businesses, and conduct various other related assessments of the likely impact of their rules.[158] These requirements, however, are once again afflicted with this same blind spot of lacking a strong incentive for the agency to make the analyses comprehensible.[159] While the summary tables do provide quick, "at a glance" ledgers of monetary costs and benefits, for example, the underlying methods and analyses tend to be highly discretionary and malleable. As a result, the true decisions can be buried in gratuitously complicated discussions. Case studies of the Regulatory Impact Assessment (RIA) process regularly find, in fact, that the agency's mandated cost-benefit analyses are: very lengthy (reaching into the hundreds or thousands of pages), highly technical, and so laden with assumptions that the summary tables provide an unreliable overview of the contents of the larger document.[160]

Stakeholders and other participants must invest considerable expertise and resources examining these regulatory analyses to truly understand them. But even more concerning is the possibility that a motivated agency might game the process through our now familiar "incomprehensible" loophole. For example, an agency could use its cost–benefit analysis strategically to make its preferred choices look good (e.g., headlining them in the summary tables) while leaving the all-important qualifications, reasonable alternatives, and contestable judgments in the fine print.[161] Empirical studies of agency practice with rationality requirements have in fact observed this exact behavior; the agencies sometimes produce rationality analyses in ends-oriented ways that support the agencies' preferred alternatives, but the limitations of the analyses can be difficult for a reasonable audience to discern.[162]

Ironically, then, rationality requirements – laid atop the notice and comment process – may serve only to further aggravate, rather than correct, the problem of incomprehensible rules. And this unfortunate outcome occurs despite the sole purpose of rationality requirements as facilitating greater agency legitimacy and richer deliberations.[163]

Targeted transparency initiatives, including online, searchable databases, sometimes suffer from the same incomprehensible fate. The agency is required to heighten transparency, but in some settings the agency's own incentives lead them in the opposite direction. As Jennifer Shkabatur concludes in her analysis of these policies: "The current architecture of online transparency allows agencies to retain control over regulatory data and thus withhold information that is essential for public accountability purposes. It also prioritizes quantity over quality of disclosures, and reinforces traditional barriers of access to information. Hence, although public accountability is the *raison d'être* of online transparency policies, these policies often fail to improve accountability."[164]

B *Adverse Consequences of Incomprehensibility*

In earlier chapters, we saw how comprehension asymmetries can undercut legal goals and lead to noncompetitive markets. Consumers can be unfairly duped by sellers. Financial markets can operate without rigorous analyses of financial risks. Inventors can be rewarded with patents on discoveries that do not deserve this legal entitlement. And chemicals can flood the market even though there is no way to make informed judgments about their comparative safety. But when deliberative procedures, such as rulemaking processes, encourage participants to be incomprehensible, the nature of the harms is more abstract. Yet the resulting problem can be just as serious.

1 Lopsided Deliberations

If a rule is difficult to understand and evaluate for some stakeholders, the first groups to exit the process will be those with the greatest organizational and resource limitations. Groups falling into this category run the gamut, but generally include small businesses, poor communities, and public interest groups that advocate on behalf of dispersed members of the public.

Over the last decade, a handful of empirical studies document that – even assuming diffuse publics are represented by a funded organization with attorneys (as we assume here) – their interests are still not represented consistently in rules that affect their interests. Indeed, in each of these studies, only about half the rules that affect the public involve at least one established, public nonprofit commenter. For the other half of the rules, there is only industry and occasionally a state or local government.[165] Moreover, in the rules in which a public interest representative does file a comment, the public-interest group is almost always outnumbered – at least twofold and in some studies tenfold – with respect to the number of comments it files relative to those filed by industry.[166]

Even if the nonprofits could keep up with industry in the regulatory arena, however, it is not clear that their positions will always capture the most significant public concerns. Some citizen members of nonprofits may not be alerted to or even able to learn about their organization's positions.[167] In other cases, a nonprofit may not know what the "mean" views of their membership are, and will be forced to guess in the course of their thinly financed representation efforts.[168] Incomprehensible rules add only further stress to these representational challenges since the diffuse public has no idea what the issues are, and the nonprofit representatives themselves must struggle to keep up, leaving even fewer resources for outreach and education.[169]

Once the high processing costs are factored into the evaluation of administrative processes, it becomes clear that the design of the processes may not be equitable after all. Well-financed participants can gain double advantages in the system, first by inundating agencies and second by endeavoring to complicate rules in ways that alienate their thinly financed opponents.[170] Moreover, without vigorous engagement by all significant affected groups, the accountability apparatus for administrative process breaks down. US administrative process devolves into a pay-to-play system, rather than a vigorous and open opportunity for all affected by a rule to participate.

2 Information Management rather than Problem Solving

Processing incoming information can become so central to the agency's daily work that it could even surpass the energies dedicated to the agency's mission of producing creative, effective public-benefitting regulations. Administrative requirements that direct agencies to "consider" excessive undigested information have the effect of diverting the agency's limited attention away from producing coherent regulatory policies. Instead, agencies find themselves preoccupied with information management.[171]

James Q. Wilson writes that "government management tends to be driven by the *constraints* on the organization, not the *tasks* of the organization."[172] The possibility that the agency may spend more time with the *constraint* of organizing, processing, and responding to information than actually synthesizing it into coherent regulatory policy seems more than a hypothetical worry. The mounds of highly technical information streaming in put a strain on the agency's ability to make coherent decisions.

As the agency's focus shifts away from imaginative problem solving to information management, repeat participants gain still more leverage in controlling the regulatory agenda. This is exacerbated by the fact that under the current structure of notice and comment, "private parties can be relied upon to tell the agency what it is doing wrong [in specific rulemakings], but not how it might improve."[173] Incremental decision-making, muddling-through, and satificing in response to this input begins to replace comprehensive problem solving.[174]

And, as noted, the pressure can be badly lopsided, leading to skewed policies. Squeaky wheels now drive the formulation and solutions to the regulatory problem at hand, narrowing the conception and analysis, as well as limiting the range of best policy responses.[175] The agency's legally based preoccupation with these squeaky wheels may be badly out of line with the public interest and the original goal of the statute.[176] As a result, a "system predicated on building consensus and refracting interests may prove painfully incapable of policymaking that transcends particularistic demands."[177]

3 Problem Grows Worse

For some rulemakings, the problem of incomprehensibility will not be self-correcting. One of the fundamental characteristics of incomprehensibility, at least in theory, is that the information excesses and accompanying imbalances in participation will worsen over time and resist easy fixes. Peter Schuck writes eloquently about a related phenomenon, which he calls legal complexity, and observes how at some point the issues, volume, specialized knowledge, and other features may simply take on a shape of their own, resisting mastery by any of the parties.[178] As the processing costs rise in an agency rulemaking, the opportunities for overriding these details and simplifying the decision become less and less likely.

Some EPA rules and regulatory programs appear destined to be on a path toward potentially hopeless complexity. In an article now more than two decades old, Eric Orts writes about the problem of juridification, when laws and requirements proliferate and become increasingly complex until the entire regulatory structure "breaks down under its own weight."[179] Others have echoed these concerns. McGarity, in his classic article on ossification, noticed an upward trajectory in the complexity and technical detail in *Federal Register* preambles.[180]

Given this evidence, is it even possible to put the brakes on a system that is likely to grow only more informationally overloaded and complex over time? It is to that question we now turn.

C *Reform*

We begin with good news. Not all huge, sprawling rules lead to incoherent decisions or convoluted processes. In his important book on the virtues of the US regulatory process, Steve Croley identifies a number of examples of high profile, public-protecting rules that generated diverse engagement from a range of experts and resulted in seemingly stable regulatory outcomes.[181] Some of these rules were also mammoth in size, technicality, and detail, yet Croley concludes that they exemplify the best of agency decision processes.

Among the reasons that some agency rules might be reasonably comprehensible is that individual agency leaders override the default legal incentives and develop supremely accessible proposals despite the temptation to do otherwise. Even if the political or legal system does not reward them, these officials follow their own internal compass and ensure vigorous and balanced deliberations on some agency decisions.

Other rules may be comprehensible not because of the serendipity of agency leaders, but because the pressures on agencies come from the full range of affected groups. In this circumstance, the agency may find it more expedient to craft comprehensible rules at the outset to limit the nature and types of issues under contention and keep matters under its control. The EPA's effort to set costly national ambient air quality standards provides a good example. The standards are closely watched by the entire continuum of affected parties, as well as by the president and Congress. After decades of unwieldy rules and supporting technical analyses that led to serious delays and extended litigation, the agency found it more cost-effective and beneficial to promulgate comprehensible rules and analyses. The EPA now invests considerable resources in providing multiple explanatory documents and supporting materials that are hailed as models of comprehensibility in science-policy circles.[182]

Finally, in some regulatory settings, there are no incentives for incomprehensibility. Instead, all participants – stakeholders and agency alike – are oriented to communicate cooperatively to solve a problem or puzzle. Meting out federal grants for academic research, identifying priorities for in-house agency research, and identifying best practices for research are but a few examples of these more cooperative deliberations. Agency survival here lies not in justifying a particular, challenged technical choice to a court, but in defending a "fair" process to a skeptical, diverse, and highly engaged set of participants. Indeed, in some cases, the agency decision is not even subjected to judicial review, and thus many of the perverse judicial incentives do not arise.

However, while some rules do not suffer from the incomprehensibility incentives discussed here, there is ample evidence that other rules *are* subject to these process problems. We focus in the remainder of this discussion only on this subset of rules that are in jeopardy of being incomprehensible.

Reform in this setting requires fundamental adjustments to administrative procedures so that agencies enjoy more benefits than costs to producing decisions and proposals that are accessible to the target audience. Likewise, commenters must succeed *only* when their comments are reasonably accessible to the agency and opposing stakeholders. To that end we offer several suggestions to move administrative processes in the right direction. Perverse incentives for incomprehensibility from speakers must be eliminated. Rewards should be instituted for comprehensible rules and comments. And finally, the agency should be rewarded or otherwise forced to ensure vigorous deliberation by the full range of affected groups.

1 Eliminate Perverse Incentives for Incomprehensibility

A few legal provisions perversely encourage incomprehensibility from speakers, so the first order of business is to adjust these doctrines in ways that curtail or at least limit these perverse incentives.

A EXHAUSTION OF REMEDIES

The "exhaustion of remedies" doctrine, created by the courts, tacitly rewards agencies for incomprehensible rules by limiting the risks of litigation to those stakeholders who can adequately make sense of a rule during notice and comment and ultimately file comments. While this well-meaning requirement was intended to preclude stakeholders from sandbagging an agency, it can have the perverse effect of rewarding an agency for alienating commenters. If affected parties cannot make sense of the agency proposal and hence sit out the comment process, they lose the opportunity to sue later.

Going forward, the doctrine should be revised so that agencies that do not show and explain their work should be more vulnerable to litigation, rather than less.[183] Accordingly, the exhaustion of remedies defense should not apply if an affected party establishes that the agency's rule was so incomprehensible that it precluded a timely comment. The challenger would bear the burden of establishing that unwarranted processing costs were needed for a reasonable commenter to decipher the proposed rule.

The commenter's burden in challenging a rule (without commenting first) will need to be heavy and the standards for incomprehensible rules clear to prevent abuse of process. As a preliminary recommendation, we suggest that the commenter be required to show that average commenters could not understand or review the agency's most significant assumptions, decision processes, and policy choices embedded in the rule proposal if they dedicated reasonable time (e.g., 10 or more hours of attorney time) to the effort. For technical rules, all commenters need not understand the intricacies of the agency's technical analysis; however, they should be able to understand the significant choices and processes the agency used to reach those findings and to judge the veracity of the process itself (e.g., if it lacked peer review; if political appointees were allowed to engage in the analysis alongside technical staff). In cases when litigants can establish that the agency's rule was simply too impenetrable to reasonably decipher or that the approach to the decision process itself was "arbitrary," then the litigants can move forward with their appeal.

B INCOMPREHENSIBLE, ALBEIT SPECIFIC COMMENTS

As noted, agencies are not alone in encountering perverse incentives to shift processing costs to their target audience; commenters may sometimes perceive benefits to inundating and overwhelming the agency with information, both to create a record and in some cases to tactically weigh the agency down.

Accordingly, a similar adjustment should be made to the requirements imposed on commenters. Rather than require *only* that comments be made "with precision" or in detail, courts should demand that stakeholder's comments are *also* reasonably comprehensible. This will discourage commenters from some of the data-dumping tactics that currently are used to shift processing costs to the agency.[184]

Under this reform, if the agency alleges that individual issues raised in a stakeholder's comments cannot be "reasonably processed by a diligent, but busy agency," then the commenter has the burden of rebutting this allegation. Commenters who databomb the agency with dozens of pages of unorganized, detailed comments or who make numerous allegations in their comments that are not supported with accessible evidence will find their comments at risk of being waived as a result of their lack of effort in making them understandable. Communication becomes a central goal in crafting comments and is no longer sidelined in the effort to create complete records and identify all conceivable issues.

This added demand placed on commenters also helps offset the tendency of an agency to cause the rule to grow more and more unwieldy as it scours each and every detail from the comments and attempts to address each one on its own terms. In the wake of this reform, the agency's responsibilities stop at considering only those comments that are shared in ways that are reasonably comprehensible.

Implementing this reform could be slippery unless the terms for what constitutes an "incomprehensible comment" are set out clearly. Without a predictable test, agencies will still err on the side of investing effort into extracting the signal from the noise, losing energy, and dissipating focus in their effort to consider all comments. To that end, agencies could be encouraged to provide guidelines for commenters that set up some basic requirements for those who wish to preserve their ability to litigate, such as (1) providing a clear summary of the comments that captures the main points (which then forms the basis for any subsequent litigation); (2) prioritizing concerns; (3) providing reliable, accessible evidence for any material factual assertions; (4) providing specific citations for any legal assertions; and (5) styling the comments so that an agency lawyer (or other rulemaking participant) could reasonably understand the technical issues. Definitions or explanations of key terms would also need to be provided. Ideally, this brief set of principles for comprehensibility would go through notice and comment rulemaking and inform the standards that courts apply to determine whether comments are comprehensible in a given rulemaking.

The courts may still encounter difficulty in determining whether a comment was comprehensible. However, these new determinations would seem less open-ended than assessing whether comments have been raised with sufficient specificity to enable a subsequent appeal.[185] Agency preparation of guidelines to narrow and focus the comprehensibility test, moreover, should be an improvement over the current ad hoc approach in which the courts must make judgments on a case-by-case basis.

2 Reward More Comprehensible Rules with Greater Judicial Deference

Agencies should also face stronger incentives for promulgating proposed and final rules that are reasonably comprehensible. While one approach to force this more comprehensible type of rulemaking is to sanction the agencies for promulgating incomprehensible rules, this is a problematic approach for a whole host of reasons. Among them, there are public tradeoffs to comprehensibility and balancing these priorities is best left to the agency. For example, the cost of crafting clear explanations could become so high for a technical rule that demanding this type of comprehensibility could discourage the agency from finalizing the rule. A comprehensibility mandate could also divert the agency from producing a rigorous analysis of an underlying problem. A comprehensibility requirement could even be subject to abuse; stakeholders might use it strategically to slow down the agencies' work by deploying it as another litigation attachment point. And courts adjudicating an agency's compliance with a comprehensibility mandate would enjoy still more discretion to determine when an agency choice passes muster, thus shifting power to the judiciary and away from the agency.

As a result, we propose a carrot, rather than a stick, to motivate agencies to engage in cooperative communication with participants and political officials. By leaving the choice to the agency's discretion, agency rules will become more understandable only when that goal can be accomplished without sacrificing other important features of the rulemaking project, such as ensuring that a rule emerges at all. Since the inducement takes the form of an optional reward, moreover, it cannot be used to bludgeon or exert outside control on the agency's choices. The reward improves the agency's position as a litigation matter but does not operate in reverse to create legal liabilities for the agency.

The carrot proposed here would provide greater judicial deference to an agency that produces a comprehensible rulemaking. Specifically, if the agency explains (and justifies) both its decision processes and its primary choices in a way that can be reasonably understood by the diverse constellation of affected (expert) participants, the court would afford the agency's rule extra deference (e.g., a "clearly erroneous" standard) in an arbitrary and capricious challenge.[186] Courts, in other words, must back off a full-bore hard look review when both the technical and deliberative processes appear rigorous.[187] Agencies may still make mistakes, operate in ways that appear "captured," or otherwise select unwise choices in contested rules, but if the agency proves that these mistakes are visible and that the political process is or could be engaged, the courts' role is no longer necessary unless statutory or constitutional issues are raised.

The proposal consists of an affirmative defense that is available to the agency when it can establish that its rulemaking emerged from a first-rate deliberative process. In specifics, the proposal draws from Louis Virelli's "deconstruction" of the hard look standard by elevating what Virelli terms "first-order" features of hard look review (procedural scrutiny of the decision process) over "second-order" features (scrutiny of substantive rationality).[188] In his work, Virelli documents the multifaceted nature of hard look review in the case law and shows how, in hard look review, the courts scrutinize two very different aspects of an agency's decision processes. Some challenges involve only "first-order" – or procedural – issues that include "record building, reason giving, input quality, and research scope."[189] Other cases include "second-order grounds" – substantive concerns regarding the "relevant factors and rational connection" of the agency's reasoning.[190]

This reformed approach thus spares the agency any second order review if it can establish through this affirmative defense that its particular decision process unambiguously satisfies all the demands of "first-order" review. In other words, if the agency can explain the ways that its rulemaking involved robust and accessible deliberations (on both science and policy) and also show that it presented reasons originating in these analyses and deliberations, the court must defer regardless of any second-order arguments raised by challengers. The agency can thus control its judicial review destiny simply by adjusting the extent it turns the rulemaking into a rich, deliberative experience with cooperative communication. Judicial review becomes reoriented toward what Jacob Gersen and Adrian Vermeule identify as a "reasonable agency action" rather than "rational agency action."[191]

At base, this proposal for greater deference is rooted in the premise that "greater accountability to the political branches is an animating theme of judicial deference to agencies" and that the courts' scrutiny should be calibrated to a showing of this accountability.[192] As Mashaw observes, "because agencies are more responsive to political will, courts should be reluctant to intervene too severely in administrative decision making beyond protecting agencies' accountability and transparency."[193] Indeed, greater judicial attention to the rigor of the agency's deliberations may be part of the "missing discourse[] of justice and authenticity in administrative law."[194] Moreover, judicial oversight of the agency's processes and explanations is "far more likely to be within the institutional competence of the judiciary" as opposed to review of the agency's "ultimate policy determination and its choices regarding which underlying factors are relevant to that decision."[195]

Once a rulemaking is conducted with a meaningful and rigorous decision process, the fact that specific choices are contestable is not reviewable except insofar as the choices lack any connection to the decision process (e.g., the record supports a range of decisions and yet the agency adopts one that is not supported in the record at all). Which choices and even the detail of the justifications are not subject to scrutiny provided the agency's reasons comport with the rigorous deliberations that preceded it.

Rather than expend time and energy focused on details and anticipating "gotcha" games, then, the agency will presumably find the greatest rewards flow from candor about open questions and choices, from engaging all parties meaningfully, and developing rigorous processes for both the scientific and the political deliberations.[196] The agency's goal will turn to "public communication of agency reasons," which in turn should "enable nonjudicial oversight of agencies, promote democratic transparency, and give agencies ex ante incentives to formulate rational policies, in light of the looming prospect that they will be obliged to explain the policies to third parties."[197]

While the details need refining, we offer at least an initial illustration of how this approach might work. In a complicated, technical rule, a successful use of this new defense could include the following showings that supplement the agency's documentation of its rich and diverse participatory processes:

- The agency documents the rigor of its technical analysis. For example, an agency could show how the analysis was conducted by staff scientists who were fire-walled from the political process.[198] The technical staff would also produce a report synthesizing the scientific literature and its implications for the agency's rule, including a rigorous exposition of uncertainties explained in an accessible way. This report would also be peer reviewed by prominent outside scientists in ways that comport with scientific practices.[199]

- The agency identifies its interpretation of the statute, the primary questions remaining from the technical analysis, and other open questions about the rule and explains how it addressed these issues. The primary policy choices are explained in a clear and accessible manner.[200] The agency also links its policy choices to the record.[201]

- In the proposed rule, the agency details how the agency arrives at its decisions, including the details of conducting both the technical analysis and policy outreach. Participants who lack the resources to scour the technical decisions can react instead to the process the agency has developed to ensure it produces a rigorous rule.[202]

- The agency could even obtain the help of a publicist or translator-editor who not only assists in ensuring the explanations are clear and thorough, but provides some substantiation of the comprehensiveness and comprehensibility of the agency's decision process and explanations. The agency could also conduct outreach and affirmatively solicit the views of all significant, affected parties rather than rely on a passive political and public deliberative process.

These are simply possibilities, however; there should not be rigid legal criteria that distract from the ultimate goal of cooperative communication. Instead, the agency must assume the burden of convincing the court that its communication with affected participants was meaningful and rigorous and that its rule is logically linked to that deliberative process. Indeed, because the agency can increase judicial deference by crafting meaningful deliberative processes, it may pull out the stops in creating and showcasing these rigorous deliberations. This evidence of cooperative communication with stakeholders thus moves the gatekeeping role of the courts to the outer perimeter of arbitrary and capricious review. Such a test also helps curb some manipulation by participants, particularly in rules where the agency signals it is revving up to seek out this particular added deference reward. Aware that high-stakes groups are standing at the ready to sue the moment the rule is finalized, the agency may go the added distance to make its rule eminently comprehensible and accessible. It may also nurture a rich deliberative process since this rigorous participation will then become the agency's shield that protects it (to some extent) from the potential lopsided litigation that awaits it down the road.

Proving up this affirmative defense should also provide added insulation to agencies with respect to the political process. Rich, documented deliberations position the agency as both expert and engaged in public administration. Executive vetoes of a deliberative agency decision process will now face the possibility of public backlash. White House offices will have a more difficult time adjusting rules in secret when the choices and decisions are out in the open and accessible to affected groups throughout the longer rulemaking process. Members of Congress will similarly find it difficult to second-guess agency rules that emerged from a certifiably rigorous deliberative process. Indeed, providing the agency with the incentives and opportunity to select out and defend their "good process" rules may cast greater suspicion on the rules for which the agency does not raise this affirmative defense, leading to still greater incentives for cooperative communication across the board.

Agencies will not always be able to credibly raise this defense. For example, if the agency selects a science-based standard well outside the range of the technical and public deliberations embodied in its record and decision processes, the agency would lose the defense since the process did not lead logically to the agency's ultimate choices.[203] Alternatively, if petitioners can show that the agency's "rigorous" process is in fact a sham – perhaps the agency never explains its decision process to stakeholders or its final choices have little to do with the technical analysis and stakeholder input that preceded it – then petitioners will be successful in overcoming the defense. Subterranean interventions by the White House will also limit the availability of the defense if the significant policy choices in a final rule are disconnected from the deliberative record.

Some readers may wonder whether an even more radical approach might be justified. Perhaps arbitrary and capricious review should be eliminated altogether, limiting the courts' role to policing process requirements (e.g., ensuring agencies follow the basic steps of the APA for rulemakings).[204] Without this litigation attachment point, so the argument goes, agencies and commenters alike would no longer find it in their legal interest to "create a record" or delve into extraneous details and obsessive support for minute points. Instead, both sets of participants would opt for more cooperative communication.[205] Public administration values would come to the fore, with collaborative and expert deliberations and problem solving.[206]

We believe that such an approach risks going too far; recall that it is not just the courts that encourage incomprehensible rules but also the political process. Removing the courts' oversight altogether could allow the perverse contributions of the political branches to go unchecked. Cooperative communication is in fact unlikely in settings in which the agency is deliberately trying to ram through an ends-oriented proposal (as Rule-Bender), when the agency staff is captured (as Rule-Bender), or even when the agency is more interested in dodging political oversight than engaging the full range of participants (as Rule-Follower). Without some judicial oversight, these abuses will go unchecked. As long as the incentives for incomprehensibility come from different sources, eliminating one of the perverse incentives could actually leave us with fewer tools to police the other sources of incomprehensibility.

3 Improve Comprehensibility by Encouraging More Balanced and Vigorous Rulemaking Deliberations

An indirect way to encourage more comprehensible rules is to push the rulemaking processes more solidly in the adversarial quadrant, where the agency must consider comments from all affected interests. This more balanced oversight then puts pressure on agencies to communicate their rules and reasoning. In other words, once a diverse audience is engaged, the communication problems are more likely to take care of themselves.

Thumbnail Sketch of Administrative Law Reform

1 Adjust existing doctrines that tacitly reward speakers for incomprehensibility (e.g., exhaustion of remedies; all comments must be considered).
2 Reward comprehensible rules with greater judicial deference.
3 Document and encourage vigorous and balanced rule deliberations through sanctions, rewards, and subsidies, including the use of proxy representatives.

This effort to ensure more diverse engagement by all participants could be accomplished either by creating costs on the agency when all affected interests are *not* represented or by instituting proxy advocates whose job it is to ensure that the agency receives litigation-backed comments from the perspective of all affected groups, including those with few resources. Moreover, if there are stealth interventions into the rule – outside of the transparent record by, for example, the White House – this more intense adversarial oversight should catch and discipline them.[207] We discuss each alternative in turn, although they could be implemented simultaneously.

A SANCTIONING IMBALANCED DELIBERATIONS

Imbalanced deliberations indicate a breakdown in administrative legitimacy, particularly with respect to ensuring accountability for agency expert and policy judgments. Yet, under the current legal requirements, when only one set of interests is engaged in a rulemaking, there are no adverse consequences that flow to the agency or that impact the legality of the final rule. There is not even basic tracking of the rigor of the rulemaking deliberations.

An amended approach would haul these imbalanced rules out into the light and subject them to some stigma in political and possibly judicial processes. One way to document the extent of balanced deliberations in a rule is to require each agency rule to be "audited" for its participatory qualities – perhaps following roughly on the concept of a "democracy audit."[208] Alternatively, agencies could be required to summarize by name and general affiliation (e.g., regulated industry, public interest, member of the public, academic) each of the commenters engaged during the rulemaking process. This inventory would be available to outsiders in an accessible way, thus creating some potential pressure on agencies to produce rules that are subjected to balanced deliberations. The inventories would also provide the court with valuable information. Either by Congressional amendment or through the course of judicial review, courts could even factor this deliberative record into their analysis informally or formally. When the agency's rule has been subjected to extensive deliberations by all affected groups, the agency could enjoy more deference than when the reverse is true, thus overlapping with the proposal just described.[209]

Additionally, some agencies already establish a "response period" for commenters to address each other; a variation of this approach could be a "response period" during which contrary perspectives are actively solicited by the agency to address specific, key comments. A modest fund within the agency could be used to subsidize this targeted review in cases where voluntary reviewers cannot be located. Prizes could even be meted out for rigorous "responses" to key comments (identified by the agency in advance).

The benefits – both in terms of political credibility and potentially more deferential judicial review – that flow from ensuring rigorous and balanced deliberations on rules could, in turn, help motivate the agency to actively solicit skepticism and diverse views. And by realigning the agency's incentives to ensure rigorous, diverse engagement on rule proposals, the agency may find that the surest way to engage all affected parties is to produce accessible rules in the first place. But even when this doesn't occur, the aftermath of rigorous deliberations are likely to expose some of the most convoluted, but important, features of a rule as a result of these adversarial pressures.

B SUBSIDIZING DIVERSE ENGAGEMENT

An alternate way to ensure rigorous deliberations is to require that all affected groups be adequately represented as a matter of law. This could be accomplished by subsidizing thinly financed, under-represented groups to participate,[210] by establishing one or more proxy representatives to serve on behalf of under-represented interests,[211] or other even more novel ways, for example by empaneling stakeholder advisory groups or "citizen juries" or developing more robust negotiated rulemaking processes.[212]

At a general level, if there are glaring gaps in the deliberative record – for example, no public interest representation – the agencies would be required to finance more diverse scrutiny from these absent groups. The agency could, for example, add a second 60-day period to its notice and comment process specifically to solicit missing viewpoints.[213] In cases where the agency is not able to locate commenters to represent affected groups, the agency could offer subsidies or other types of grants to ensure this type of participation. In all cases, however, whether certain sets of under-represented parties are in fact *adequately* represented by these public interest groups will become difficult for the agency to determine. Simple additional requirements may be necessary – e.g., the certification in advance of participating groups as adequate proxy representatives for certain diffuse interests or communities. This solution is hardly complete, but it is at least a step in the right direction.[214]

Alternatively, an office of advocacy within the agency could be established to identify and fill these participation gaps proactively. An ombud could be established specifically to advocate for under- or un-represented interests in each agency rule, for example.[215] In fact, for small businesses, Congress has done just that.[216] Although implementation of the small business protections has been controversial,[217] the existence of this advocacy program signals at least some legislative awareness of the very real impediments that under-funded groups face in participating in regulatory decisions.

The ombud could be expected to reach out to clearly affected, but non-participating, groups to solicit their views and then to advocate on their behalf within the constraints and legal contours of each individual rulemaking. The ombud would file detailed comments to protect the interests of these groups. Agencies could be charged for this ombud service only when it is needed; for rules subjected to vigorous and balanced engagement, the ombud (and the expense of this advocate) would not be necessary.

By creating more diverse oversight, the consequences of incomprehensible rules would be mitigated in part. But it is hoped that the ombud's engagement would accomplish still more by forcing the agency to anticipate gaps in deliberation and develop rules that are more accessible and complete at the start of a rule, making this remedial assistance by ombuds unnecessary.

The downside to this institutionalization of an ombud arises from the political vulnerabilities of the position. The ombud could be pressured or the funding removed if the proxy representative was "too effective" in ways that gored the ox of the most powerful constituencies.[218] How and whether this political manipulation occurs, moreover, is difficult to monitor from the outside, leading to the possibility that an agency's proxy representatives become a target for capture and manipulation.

Instead of an internal ombud position, funds could instead be made available for the *external* creation of this very same proxy representative to be managed by the public sector. The service would be privatized using either donor or government funds, or both. A proxy could be established by universities or coalitions of law and public policy schools, for example. The concept simply requires assembling a dedicated team of analysts to pore over agency rules and scrutinize them from the perspective of affected groups that are poorly represented in the individual rulemaking processes. These groups would file comments that put concerns in writing and serve as placeholders for future litigation brought by established nonprofits or others. Indeed, even if a proxy representative were institutionalized within the agency, a private equivalent would still provide valuable redundancy checks to provide still more representational balance in complicated rulemakings.

IV CONCLUSION

Since the heart of administrative process depends on a two-way conversation for its legitimacy, it is vital that both sides of the conversation understand each other. In theory, this would be accomplished by a process that creates a conversation where all participants – agencies, stakeholders, and other political institutions – are motivated to engage and communicate meaningfully.

In practice, however, administrative processes generally fail to direct these alternating speakers' incentives toward cooperative communication. This is because the legal structure places the processing costs (and resultant errors) on the audiences. As these processing costs grow higher, the audiences become increasingly unable to make sense of the information. At the same time, the speakers' own incentives remain fixed on shifting excess processing costs to their audience. To the extent that rigorous deliberative processes are vital in administrative law to ensure agency legitimacy, reform of this broken institutional process is imperative.

7

Comprehension Asymmetries in Legislative Process

Congress surprised its critics in 2016 when it passed the long-awaited Lautenberg Chemical Reauthorization Act by a landslide.[1] The 300-page bill updated and modified an existing statutory program that had been in place for nearly 40 years – a program that by all accounts was dysfunctional.[2] Given longstanding partisan gridlock, Congress's success in passing this major legislation was hailed a major victory. Only 12 Representatives and 2 Senators voted against the bill in the Republican-dominated Congress.[3] Senator Vitter, the Republican co-sponsor of the bill, boasted after its passage: "This is an historic day on which we've come together to pass significant chemical safety legislation." Despite compromises, Vitter observed, the resulting measure is "a comprehensive, effective, thoughtful, bipartisan bill."[4] Nearly every stakeholder participating in the process similarly credited the final passage as a step in the right direction. By all accounts, this was a major (and rare) congressional step forward.

But behind the congratulations and backslapping lay a hidden secret: No one, including perhaps the sponsors and party leaders themselves, quite knew what this bipartisan bill actually contained. In fact, rather than the clear, clean progress Senator Vitter prophesied, the actual bill was a voluminous, complicated piece of legislation that is vastly more convoluted than the social problem it purports to address.[5]

In particular, the final Chemical Reauthorization Act adds hundreds of new pages to the US Code and will likely add at least that much girth to the appellate opinions as well. Definitions of certain key requirements are not only ambiguous but sometimes even contradictory – forcing the EPA to essentially build its own bill behind the bill.[6] The steps and requirements mandated by the Act are labyrinthine and will likely tie the authorizing agency, the EPA, up for years.[7] What's more, even if the EPA can make sense of some of the provisions, those interpretations will be challenged through the dozens of attachment points loaded into the law that allow aggrieved stakeholders to block progress.[8] In other words, this legislative "triumph" was, in large part, a pyrrhic victory.

But how could this be? How could a bill pass through both houses of Congress and the Oval Office without anyone calling out its clear incoherence? In this chapter, we explore the phenomenon of incomprehensible legislation. Consistent with our model, we consider only a small slice of legislative activity – major legislation in which the party leaders enjoy considerable comprehension advantages relative to their audience (identified here as other voting members of Congress) and are more eager to get something through than to dedicate effort (or take risks) associated with ensuring that the bill is comprehensible to their colleagues. These leaders best understand a bill's policy vision and its drafting history, even while they might encounter challenges in understanding the bill text themselves. Indeed, in this slice of congressional activity, the primary motivation of our bill-drafters is to get a major law passed that is acceptable to their own political party and as many constituents as possible. The fact that the final bill may be convoluted or might even be incomprehensible is not a fatal flaw. In fact, as strange as it may sound, in a subset of legislative processes it is sometimes easier to pass laws when nobody understands what's in them.

For a subset of important and potentially deadlocked legislation, then, incomprehensibility may provide a magic bullet. Powerful congressional leaders – "speakers" – may find few impediments and perhaps even some benefits to putting together bills that are, or quickly become (in satisficing constituencies and other members), so opaque or convoluted that they are almost impenetrable. Voting members might be encouraged to toe the party line, a bargain they're willing to make if they can't figure out the general contents of the bill in the first place. Some constituents may also be pacified by certain provisions that appeal to their interests; when the bill is otherwise incoherent, these groups may rationally forgo investing added effort to understand the entirety of the bill since they have their "goodie" buried on page 320.

In the first part of this chapter, we examine evidence for the existence of at least some body of blind-lawmaking or "incomprehensible" legislation governing particularly important issues. We also consider whether there are comprehension asymmetries between speakers and their audiences in this subset of cases. This analysis then sets up our investigation of legislative process. There are multiple causes of incomprehensible legislation, but – consistent with this book – we explore how our design of institutional processes may be a potentially important contributor. In a third section, we examine some of the consequences of a legislative system that sometimes tolerates and sometimes rewards incomprehensibility. And, finally, as the chapter closes, we put forth some preliminary suggestions for counteracting those processes and rules that may be egging this phenomenon along.

Since congressional processes are highly complex and poorly understood, we necessarily make a number of simplifying assumptions in the analysis that follows. Yet there are enough independent sightings of comprehension asymmetries in the literature on legislative process to indicate that this area is worthy of further exploration. While our simplifying models and assumptions may ultimately not be the best way to approach this topic, the primary aim is to start a conversation about the issue.

I THE PROBLEM OF INCOMPREHENSIBLE LAWS

The precise categorization of a law as "incomprehensible" is necessarily fuzzy, but the fact that some major laws fall into this incomprehensible category is beyond question. Remember that what makes something "incomprehensible" in our model is determined by what the target audience can reasonably understand with the available support, time, and resources. So, applied to this setting, an incomprehensible law is one in which the majority of rank and file members of Congress cannot gain a reasonable understanding of the major features of a bill that they are asked to vote on. Incomprehensibility is always contextual and depends on the processing capabilities of the intended audience at the time of the conversation.

Concerns about a subset of "incomprehensible" laws emerging from Congress have been fodder for comedians for decades. A cartoon, sketched back in 1947 by George Lichty, sets the stage. See Figure 7.1.

But, humor aside, what is the hard evidence that legislation is being passed by members of Congress who could not make sense of the most important basic features of the bill at the time of voting?

A Specific Accounts of Incomprehensible Laws

The most systematic research, which draws from original interviews, case studies, and quantitative analyses of passed legislation, comes from James Curry's award-winning book, *Legislating in the Dark*. Curry uses these sources to identify dozens of laws that – for our purposes – are "incomprehensible." (The most determined rank-and-file member has little chance of making sense of the content of these laws, even at the most general level.) As Speaker of the House, Boehner conceded in the course of deliberations over an appropriations bill, "Here we are with 1,100 pages – 1,100 pages not one member of this body has read. Not one. There may be some staffer over in the Appropriations Committee that read all of this last night – I don't know how you could read 1,100 pages between midnight and now. Not one member has read this."[9]

Legal scholars reinforce Curry's findings with additional examples of statutes that are so flawed that it appears few members reviewed or understood the laws at the time of passage. The Bankruptcy Abuse Prevention and Consumer Protection Act of 2005, for example, was widely hailed as a legislative mess despite the fact that it was ultimately passed by large margins in both the House and Senate.[10] As Jean Braucher observed, "[t]he sheer complexity of the [resulting legislative] changes made the law hard to understand and its effects difficult to predict."[11] For instance, the final bill included redundant notices to debtors that strongly suggested the

"I admit this new bill is too complicated to understand. We'll just
have to pass it to find out how it works. . . ."

FIGURE 7.1 Poking Fun at Congress's Incomprehensible Lawmaking
George Lichty, "Grin and Bear It," *Los Angeles Times,* Mar. 12, 1947 Used with permission from Grin and
Bear it©1947 King Features Syndicate, Inc.

drafters of the legislation were not following out or fine-tuning their new legislative
requirements.[12] The statute was also visibly in disarray. "[T]ypos, sloppy choices of
words, hanging paragraphs, and inconsistences [fill the pages]. Worse, there are
largely pointless but burdensome new requirements, overlapping layers of screening,
mounds of new paperwork, and structural incoherence."[13] Bankruptcy scholars
seem to be unanimous in concluding that "the bill's poor drafting will require
judges to exercise their judgment simply in trying to determine what it means."[14] All
accounts place responsibility for the incoherence with the industry that drafted the
bill, yet sponsors and voting members passed these defects into national legislation.

Still worse in terms of legislative incomprehensibility are the so-called omnibus bills, which amalgamate dozens, or even hundreds, of *different* laws into one single bill. In "Uneasy Riders," Brannon Denning and Brooks Smith provide a particularly vivid account of the size of one omnibus bill and the members' reactions to it. In this particular case, the final legislation combined 8 spending bills together, selecting out from 13 that Congress had been unable to pass. The bill was a "3,825 page, sixteen inch tall, forty pound" law, which was changed and modified right up to the final vote.[15] In fact, "a final draft of the behemoth was not available until the middle of the day the House was to vote, and that final version 'include[d] hand-written notes in the margin, e-mail printouts inserted into the bill, and mis-numbered or unnumbered pages.'"[16] As Senator Byrd exclaimed, "Only God knows what's in the monstrosity."[17]

Denning and Smith, however, conclude that "[o]n the whole ... individual members of Congress tended to care not so much what others managed to insert, as long as their own pet causes made it in ... Thus most members held their noses and voted for it, even as they complained that Congress did too much, too quickly, and without fair warning."[18] In other words, rather than crafting a coherent bill, oriented toward changing a concrete feature of the American legislative landscape, lawmakers threw together "whatever worked," focusing on achieving individual political aims over the construction of a sensible and comprehensible law.

More general accounts of the processes surrounding key legislation underscore the limited effort dedicated to ensuring the legislation is reasonably comprehensible to fellow members. Rank and file members of the ruling Republican party in the 115th Congress – a party that enjoys trifecta control of all political branches – complain about the party leaders "jam[ming]" legislation through[19] and "coming up with a proposal behind closed doors" only to "spring it on skeptical members."[20] The rushed passage of the 400-plus page tax bill on November 16, 2017, provides a case in point. [21] As John Cassidy writes, "In the days of yore, whenever a major legislative proposal was put forward, each chamber would spend a good deal of time discussing and dissecting it. Hearings would be scheduled; experts would be summoned." "But ... [in the case of the 2017 tax bill, powerful sponsors] ... introduced their tax bill, which is more than four hundred pages long, [only two weeks before the final vote]. The chairman of the Senate Finance Committee ... released his version, which is equally long and complicated, [two days before the vote] ... This pace is more akin to downhill skiing than to traditional legislating."[22]

Perhaps the strongest evidence of incomprehensible laws, however, comes from those who are closest to the text – the federal judiciary. D.C. Circuit Judge Harry Edwards lamented that the judicial system is "choking, not on statutes in general, but on ambiguous and internally inconsistent statutes."[23] This legislative incoherence in turn prompts "'disagreement among different judges and panels" with resulting "inconsistency and unpredictability."[24] Writing more than 50 years ago, Judge Friendly observed this same "incoherent legislative" problem with laws that were "defective" in offering useful guidance.[25] Some of these were laws "in which the legislature has succeeded in literally saying something it probably did not mean."[26]

Even judges who are explicitly committed to extracting meaning only from the "plain text" of a statute occasionally acknowledge the problem of incoherence. For example, while Justice Scalia was on the D.C. Circuit, he remarked that the "Little Tucker Act claims were 'so imprecisely drawn' that '[i]ts language could reasonably be read ... [in] six quite different ways."[27]

Justice Ginsberg dedicated several articles to documenting the "foggy statute problem" in which "Congress has given us guidance that is defective in one way or another."[28] She provides "a brief, illustrative catalogue" of laws that are defective in ways that were fully preventable. One set of laws, for example, used wording that "made Congress's will unknowable" because the text admitted two contrasting interpretations.[29] As Justice Ginsburg notes, "Detecting the will of the legislature ... time and time again perplexes even the most restrained judicial mind. Imprecision and ambiguity mar too many federal statutes."[30]

B *Explanations for Incomprehensible Lawmaking*

So, if everyone is aware that a subset of legislation passed by Congress is incomprehensible, how is it that these laws continue to be passed? A search through the academic literature and judicial opinions provides several overlapping hypotheses that begin to answer this question.

Curry's targeted study, *Legislating in the Dark*, offers the most complete account both of the incomprehensibility problem and its likely causes. Indeed, our work here draws heavily from Curry's study. His central finding is that "meaningful and pervasive inequalities exist among members of Congress regarding the information they possess during the legislative process," and "these inequalities affect the balance of power and influence in the House."[31] "[T]hose holding formal leadership positions – party leaders and committee chairs – have extensive information about the legislation being considered and political dynamics surrounding the legislation." Rank-and-file members of Congress, by contrast, "have limited resources and find it very difficult to become informed about most of the legislation being considered at any time."[32] He identified "both party leaders and committee chairs" as using "tactics that aggravate the informational inequalities, making their rank and file even more dependent on them for information."[33]

In their pathbreaking two-part study, Abbe Gluck and Lisa Bressman place some of these behaviors into larger legal context and underscore the "glaring omission in the theoretical debates about statutory interpretation ... [namely,] there has been little discussion of Congress's obligations [to pass laws capable of reasonable interpretation]."[34] Their own investigation into congressional practices exposes the ways that Congress's "deep internal structural fragmentation" presents impediments to Congress's ability to pass laws that are consistently coherent and comprehensible.[35]

Judges similarly chalk up Congress's deficiencies to both resource limits and fragmentation in legislative processes. Justice Ginsburg, for example, concludes that "Congress ... bears considerable responsibility for both federal court creativity, and federal case generation. The will of the national legislature is too often expressed in commands that are unclear, imprecise, or gap-ridden."[36] Among the underlying problems, according to the judges, is the lack of adequate deliberation on some laws. Judge Friendly, for example, noted that members have a finite time [to legislate], which makes it difficult if not impossible for them to seriously engage in legislative details for more complicated legislation.[37]

The analysis that follows is thus not blazing new trails. Instead, we simply weave this existing work together through a slightly different conceptual model – that of comprehension asymmetries.

C *Limitation of the Analysis*

Before proceeding, it is important to spotlight one difficult issue we explicitly bracket in the analysis that follows – the question of *when* an individual law is in fact incomprehensible to rank-and-file members on one or more given issues. Reasonable observers might disagree, for example, about whether the Affordable Care Act (commonly referred to as "Obamacare")[38] and the Dodd Frank Act[39] are examples of incomprehensible laws. Some might argue that these particular bills should *not* be classified as incomprehensible. Despite the fact that each of the 2010 statutes dealt with complicated issues, they were subject to considerable deliberations. On the other hand, it is also true that both bills contain some exceedingly complex, but important, provisions that may not have been adequately explained to rank-and-file members.[40]

Fortunately, we do not need to wade into this taxonomic swamp. Our singular focus here is on the incentives major actors have to communicate cooperatively in legislative decision-making. Whether or the extent to which a particular law is incomprehensible goes beyond the scope of this project. We thus consider only the *why* question, without attempting to develop a detailed inventory of which laws are incomprehensible and which laws are not.

II COMPREHENSION ASYMMETRIES BETWEEN SPEAKER AND AUDIENCE

Our attention now turns to the question of whether there are institutional design issues that allow, or in fact encourage, incomprehensible laws to be passed. Our first pass at this question would seem to suggest that institutional design is not to blame. A basic civics course reminds us that the intense pressures on members of Congress for demonstrating high levels of productivity in policymaking serve to discipline lapses in legislative professionalism. Congressmen who sponsor and/or vote in favor of convoluted legislation are supposed to be stigmatized for endorsing bills that nobody can understand. Moreover, and particularly in the current partisan climate, bills that are incoherent seem ripe for attack. Indeed, as the vignettes in the previous section reveal, members do publicize the convoluted nature of bills when mounting their opposition to them. It seems likely that the powerful constituents who lobby for legislation would not be happy with incoherent laws either. These imprecise bills are risky and raise the possibility that some promises may not be kept during the inevitable implementation battles that follow.

Yet, as we have also seen, the cumulative penalties for incomprehensible laws do not always outweigh the benefits. Throughout the rest of this chapter, we focus on several structural incentives built into our institutional design that help explain the occasional entrance of an incomprehensible law onto the legislative scene. While these institutional processes, standing alone, are certainly not the sole cause of this problem, without question they contribute to it.

We begin this section by exploring at a high altitude the background incentives of our legislative speakers and audiences with respect to cooperative communication. The designated speaker within our model is the powerful chair or party leader (*not* the Speaker of the House) who serves as the promoter of a bill. On the audience side, while there are a number of potential target audiences, we consider in our analysis only the rank-and-file members of Congress. There are of course many audiences for legislation – agencies, regulated parties, lobbyists, courts, and some-times the general public. However, while each audience is important (and suscep-tible to comprehension asymmetries), we focus on voting members as the most important, given their obviously pivotal role in voting on the legislation.

In our orientation below, we consider whether the speaker does enjoy an advan-tage in processing the meaning of complicated legislative and related information as compared to the rank-and-file member. We also consider whether the speaker is motivated to ensure that the rank-and-file member understands the nature and nuances of his proposed law. If there are comprehension asymmetries between speaker and audience and the speaker is not inclined to communicate cooperatively, then Congress's legislative processes will need to be designed to correct this problem.

A *Rank-and-File Members as Audience*

In an essay entitled "Due Process of Lawmaking," published nearly 50 years ago, Hans Linde laid out the ideal world of legislative deliberations from the standpoint of the rank-and-file audience of congressmen. In this ideal world "there is no place for a vote on final passage by members who have never read even a summary of the bill, let alone a committee report or a resume of the factual document."[41]

"A member who never attends the committee meetings [would] at least examine the record of evidence before casting a vote, or be told about it, and [would] certainly never vote by proxy."[42] He imagined that "[t]hese kinds of demands are implicit in due process, if lawmakers are really bound to a rule that laws must be made as rational means toward some agreed purpose."[43]

However, Linde was quick to note how congressional reality fell far short of this due process ideal. In contrast to this romanticized account, in 1976 "[a] bill need not be explained by its sponsor on the introduction – it may, indeed be introduced ... with the sponsor's candid admission that he does not understand it."[44] Additionally, "[a] bill need not declare any purpose nor recite any legislative findings. It may be enacted by members whose minds are wholly closed to reasoned argument because of prior commitment to one point of view, ignorance and misinformation, lack of interest and lack of time, or simply because of absence of any opportunity for inquiry and debate."[45]

How could the legislative process tolerate uninformed voting? A close analysis of the rank-and-file voting member's available resources (our audience) supplies at least a partial answer. As our more specific itemization of the evidence reveals in the pages that follow, for rank-and-file members, the costs of understanding complex bills are exceedingly high. At the same time, most members are badly strapped for the resources required for effective deliberation. In other words: Congressmen are limited in their capacities to process all the information being thrown at them and aren't provided any real incentive structure for making sure they digest all he relevant information in a bill.

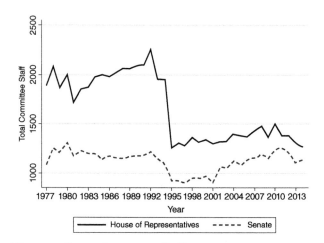

FIGURE 7.2 House vs. Senate Committee Staff, 1977–2014
Russell W. Mills and Jennifer L. Selin, "Don't Sweat the Details! Enhancing Congressional Committee Expertise Through the Use of Detailees," 42 *Legislative Studies Quarterly* 611, 615 (2017) © Used with permission from John Wiley & Sons

Costs of Processing. Consider first the resource limitations of rank-and-file members with respect to conducting this important legislative work. Although the number of staff provided to individual members has increased slightly over the last 20 years, most of this added staff is channeled to district offices to serve the home community and is not assigned to making sense of the bills coming down the pike. At the same time, congressional staff allocated to assist with committee work is dropping. See Figure 7.2.[46]

To make matters worse, a 2017 study reports that "[p]ay for committee positions such as staff directors and counsels have fallen by as much as 20%, leading to high turnover."[47] Combined "[f]actors such as long hours, relatively low pay, and decreasing benefits have resulted in an exodus of committee staff from Capitol Hill," leading to "an overall loss of legislative capacity and expertise, as senior committee staffers who possess greater policy expertise and institutional memory are more likely to leave."[48]

The support system for rank-and-file member deliberation, in other words, has decreased over time. At the same time, the size and complexity of the bills that members must review are increasing.[49] Although the bills ultimately enacted are dropping in number, the size of the bills is sometimes nearly threefold higher today as compared to the 1960s.[50] See Figure 7.3.[51]

It follows, then, that as the resources available to members for legislative work decline and the size of the legislative workload increases, the time and attention available to members for scrutinizing a bill drops. Indeed, in view of these developments, some congressional scholars opine that Congress is "elect[ing] to 'lobotomize' its internal committee and support agency (e.g., GAO, CBO, etc.) capacity in favor of allocating more staff to leadership and district offices to support reelection goals."[52]

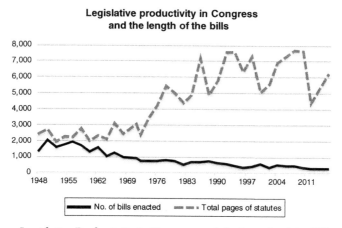

FIGURE 7.3 Legislative Productivity in Congress and the Length of the Bills over Time
Created based on the dataset published on Brookings Institution's website, Vital Statistics on Congress, ch. 6 (May 2018), available at www.brookings.edu/multi-chapter-report/vital-statistics-on-congress/#cancel

These resource limitations also provide a partial explanation for why members and their staff rarely read or discuss the text of bills themselves. Consistent with Linde's observations nearly half a century ago, congressional staff concede that "Members don't read text. Most committee staff don't read text. Everyone else is working off [the section-by-section] summaries [in the legislative history] ... The very best members don't even read the text, they all just read summaries."[53] In effect, given the practical restrictions of being in Congress today, congressmen and their staffs just don't have enough time to read all the material in the legislation they're passing.

Incentives to Invest in Understanding Bills. But what of the benefits to individual members for doing this difficult processing work? Won't members who take on incomprehensible laws be regarded as heroes by their constituents? Won't there be strong incentives for a few members to read and process information in order to maintain power?

In today's highly partisan Congress, however, this good Samaritan activity seems unlikely. Remember our speaker – the advocate for a bill – is a powerful member of Congress. In cases in which the bill is sponsored by a rank-and-file member's own party, the benefits to pointing out the flaws, particularly in a fragile, complicated bill, are likely low. Party loyalty is considered essential to congressional survival.[54] Moreover, when the member is not involved in the drafting process, well-intended scrutiny of the bill may be regarded as hostile rather than collegial. Party leaders may not appreciate efforts to document legislative incoherence, which in turn requires readjustments that may not survive constituent pressures. There would thus seem – in general – to be few benefits associated with sticking one's neck out within one's party to offer improvements, particularly those of the legal and technical nature.

But what if a congressman (and her party) opposes the bill? Wouldn't that be a perfect opportunity to point out incoherence? Indeed, as we've seen, the opposition is quick to point out when legislation is incomprehensible. But at the same time, we've also observed how this opposition is not always (or perhaps often) successful.[55] Even when buoyed with considerable media attention, some of these major incomprehensible laws manage to pass both houses nevertheless. It remains to be seen why this happens. Perhaps pointing out the incomprehensibility of a bill, standing alone, isn't enough to doom it in the political process. The losing party may even be poised to capitalize on the inevitable (and predicted) problems that arise post-enactment once an incomprehensible law is passed. By deploying these "I told you so" strategies, members may ultimately gain the political high ground, even when they lose the vote.[56]

Opportunity Costs. Up until now we have assumed a best case – namely that rank-and-file members will invest a reasonable amount of effort into understanding bills and contribute meaningfully to legislative deliberations. Yet in truth, at least some rank-and-file members may favor constituency services and reelection campaigns over their legislative responsibilities.[57] If the rank-and-file behave this way, the problem may not be just deficient speaker incentives, but also deficient audience incentives. We return to these audience incentives in our reform. But for the analysis that follows, we assume rank-and-file members *will* make a reasonable effort to understand the bills, engage in the legislative process vigorously, and vote responsibly. Since this best-case assumption presents the greatest challenge to our argument, it provides a way to further simplify our analysis.

Summary. In brief, the analysis so far has underscored the limited benefits and high costs to an individual member (and, to some extent, the institution of Congress itself) to scrutinize legislation for comprehensibility and coherence. As a result, our audience will generally have a limited capacity to process and understand complicated bills as well as face few incentives to do this resource-intensive work.

However, not all congressional audiences are created equally. In particular, when a bill goes through committee, the benefits to the rank-and-file member on that committee for scrutinizing the bill increase, sometimes significantly. Members of the legislative committee may be more motivated to invest resources into making sense of a bill because they bear some responsibility for ensuring the quality of the final product. (We discuss later how changing practices in Congress appear to be making this role less important, however.)

Together the aggregate evidence nevertheless supports the unfortunate fact that rank-and-file congressional members are "receiving one-sided information to a greater degree and are spending less time learning about potential solutions" relative to the past.[58] This disparity of resources and information processing does not bode well in general, but suggests particular worries for complicated bills, especially those that do not originate in a single committee.

B *Powerful Party Leaders and Sponsors as Speaker*

The speaker (again, *not* the Speaker of the House) in our analysis is a powerful party leader or chair supporting the bill and/or drafting it. These speakers enjoy considerable advantages in processing the substance of complex bills relative to other members, or at least in understanding some of the policy choices that lie behind the bill. As "managers" of the bill, speakers also have a fuller appreciation of the steps (and possibilities for slippage) involved in drafting the bill text that may not be evident to rank and file.[59] On the benefits side, such speakers stand to reap – in a subset of legislative settings – benefits to bill passage, even in cases where the law is incomprehensible at the time of passage and remains unintelligible.

Superior Processing Capacity. With respect to processing capabilities, our speakers have access to vastly more resources for processing information in a bill as compared to the normal rank-and-file members of Congress. Some of this superior capability is due to the speaker's role as bill-drafter or promoter, which places him in a superior position with respect to crafting the policy vision behind the legislation.[60]

Equally important is the much greater endowment of congressional staff and resources that these powerful members enjoy relative to rank-and-file members. While leaders have always enjoyed greater staff and resources compared to rank-and-file congressional members, the centralization of resources to a few, limited members has grown severalfold over the last few decades. In a 2010 study, the Congressional Research Service (CRS) found that staff working for leadership rose by more than 250 to 340 percent between 1979 and 2009 as compared to much more modest increases for rank-and-file members, who place most of the increased staff in district offices.[61]

Limited Benefits to Cooperative Communication in Some Legislative Settings. However, speakers do not merely enjoy greater resources to assess the comprehensibility of the bills relative to members; they also enjoy periodic benefits from shepherding incomprehensible legislation through the legislative process.

First and foremost, in today's legislative climate getting *any* legislation through the process is a triumph over "congressional gridlock." Leaders can tout the virtues of a passed bill, particularly for important topics such as health care, chemical regulation, or tax reform. Moreover, whether a particular passed law is "incomprehensible" is difficult to measure. As just discussed, critics must invest considerable energies in identifying incoherent features and might find it difficult to make this particular problem newsworthy. The public, for example, may not be concerned (and could even be relieved) to learn that an unwieldy bill does little more than kick the controversy down the road to agencies and courts. Incoherent laws may also offer some resourceful stakeholders the ability to wage war against implementing agencies, where they may enjoy greater power.[62]

Second, incomprehensible laws sometimes make it easier for leaders to keep the party together.[63] This unity is particularly necessary as a result of the well-documented trend of increasing polarization and partisanship within Congress. As Thomas Mann and Norman Ornstein explain, "The parties have become [increasingly] ideologically polarized, tribalized, and strategically partisan"[64] and can become "virulently adversarial" in many of their dealings.[65] See Figure 7.4. Incomprehensible laws, then, provide a way to keep members in line with the political party.

In *Legislating in the Dark*, Curry traces in detail the ways that information costs (which in large part consist of processing costs) allow congressional leaders to retain control over rank-and-file members. These leaders can craft the bills on behalf of their party, but establish processes – limited in time and extremely high in

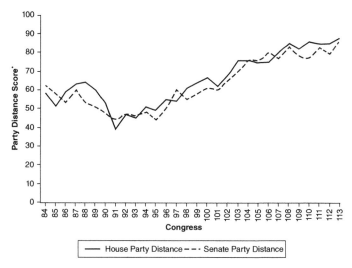

FIGURE 7.4 Distance between the Parties on Partisan Votes, 1955–2014
Barbara Sinclair, *Unorthodox Lawmaking: New Legislative Processes in the US Congress* Figure 6.1, at 144
(C.Q. Press, 5th ed, 2016) © Used with permission from Sage Publications

processing requirements – that virtually ensure that most of the members of their party will not be able to make sense of the law itself, much less trace its implications in the existing legislative landscape.[66] By "keeping [rank-and-file members] in the dark, leaders undermine the quality of legislative deliberations and dyadic representation in the House of Representatives."[67] Speakers, in other words, can use incomprehensibility as a proverbial stick – smacking rank-and-file members to keep them in line and ensure they don't get hold of too much congressional power.

Third and finally, given the collective aspect of congressional action, speakers and party leaders can often evade blame when incomprehensible laws are ultimately passed. Bills change as a result of negotiations and compromise; is the end product the sponsor's or drafter's fault? Safety in numbers may not only spare members from responsibility for legislative incoherence but also spare our speaker from the stigma associated with sponsoring incomprehensible laws.

Putting these pieces together, it makes sense why some legislation might not just pass in spite of but *because* of its incomprehensibility. In an era of high partisan debate and deadlock, incomprehensible laws are sometimes the only kind of law that most people can agree on.

The main question, however, remains: Why don't existing legislative processes and related checks institute strong incentives for speakers to ensure laws are comprehensible to rank-and-file members? In other words: Why does the law *allow* this incomprehensibility to go unchecked?

III COMPREHENSION ASYMMETRIES IN LEGISLATIVE PROCESS

We now turn to explore these existing practices and procedures in Congress with an eye to how well they help to encourage cooperative communication in legislative deliberations.

Before delving into more detailed procedures, however, our investigation begins on a sour note: There are no explicit requirements within Congress that require sponsors to craft bills that are coherent or accessible. At no point in a bill's life – from initial drafting all the way to the final vote – is there a procedural step that checks to ensure that the bill is reasonably understandable to other members of Congress, or even to the bill's sponsors and promoters. Thus, if all congressmen voting "yea" on a complex bill concede they have no earthly idea what they were voting on, no congressional rule or procedure is violated, and the resulting law is perfectly legal.

A number of authors have expressed concern about the lack of systematic checks on legislative coherence.[68] In his writing in 1963, Judge Friendly attributed the occasional passage of incoherent laws to the absence of these kinds of internal review mechanisms within Congress.[69] In his study of Congress's passage of the Truth in Lending Act, for example, Ed Rubin discusses at length the absence of methods and processes to ensure competent policy analysis with Congress.[70]

This absence of a formal check on incomprehensible legislation is not a particularly good omen for the analysis to come. But in an institution as complex as Congress, there are undoubtedly other practices and procedures at work that could encourage cooperative communications between speakers and their audience. It is to these more intricate procedures and practices we now turn.

The investigation begins with an analysis of the incentives of the conscientious Rule-Follower sponsoring a bill. We then explore the net incentives of the scheming Rule-Bender who seeks to enlarge his sphere of power by exploiting gaps in process.

A *Rule-Followers*

At first blush, one would imagine Rule-Following bill-drafters to be eager for rigorous, informed deliberation by congressional colleagues. However, we will see in the analysis that follows that ingrained procedures and requirements in Congress may actually impede Rule-Followers in their efforts to produce a bill that is reasonably accessible to fellow congressmen.

Some of these procedural impediments not only undermine the audience's understanding of the bill but can impede speakers themselves from fully comprehending a bill's meaning and implications. There are in fact two distinct challenges for dedicated Rule-Followers in cooperatively communicating. First and perhaps most challenging, the Rule-Followers themselves are beholden to law-text drafters and other congressional staff to adequately capture the policy vision and put it into legal language.[71] The Rule-Followers thus experience comprehension asymmetries of their own with respect to the drafters of legal text who have a superior grasp of the bill. Second, the Rule-Followers then must cooperatively communicate their knowledge (including their lack of understanding of the intricacies of the legal text) to rank-and-file in the course of persuading them to vote in favor of the bill.

Under both circumstances, the rank-and-file may not be fully apprised of the contents of the bill.

1 Bill-Drafting

Our tour of legislative processes begins at the earliest life stage of a bill – the drafting process – and identifies several challenges that can impede the ability of Rule-Followers to ensure the bill is reasonably comprehensible. Current congressional practice (within which the Rule-Follower operates) tends to both disperse and fragment the drafting process, which allows a number of different entities to become involved in crafting the basic terms of a bill. As a result, the bill may become more complicated and unwieldy.

A DELEGATED AND FRAGMENTED AUTHORSHIP

Since the Rule-Following speakers in our analysis are typically the powerful advocates of a bill, we would assume the basic conventions of authorship and attribution would serve as a powerful disciplining force to ensure resulting bills are of high quality. A speaker would not want to propose, much less support, a bill that is incoherent in important respects.

Yet, it turns out that even the most conscientious, Rule-Following speakers typically do not draft their own bills, and some may not read them carefully once drafted. The true bill-drafters in Congress generally consist instead of an assortment of interest groups, administrative agencies, committee staff, and the staff in Congress's Office of Legislative Counsel. Sometimes each of these groups has a hand in drafting a bill, and in other instances only one of these characters is the actual author. But in many cases, bills will be drafted by someone other than the sponsors and their personal staff.

The resulting delegation of authorship, as a matter of institutional practice, leads to attenuated control as well as potentially significant fragmentation in the drafting process that may cause even the Rule-Followers themselves to sometimes be unfamiliar with the precise terms of the bill they are introducing. Yet despite these challenges, "there is currently no mechanism for coordinating drafting behavior" in Congress among these various drafting sources.[72] Atiyah and Summers conclude, "This lack of centralization in the drafting of federal legislation in America is itself the cause of many problems arising from the use of legislation as a source of law."[73]

Risks of incoherent bills, along with other quality control problems, appear to be at their worst when private parties and agencies serve as the primary drafters.[74] Commentators note that these lay drafters (especially private parties) can be particularly inexpert in legislative drafting, and yet some evidence suggests these private parties may well draft the majority of bills introduced into Congress.[75] Private parties also have their own axes to grind that may impact the text in subtle ways that even the sponsor may not fully appreciate or even notice. Despite these risks, externally prepared bills are not always (or perhaps often) reviewed or edited by Congress's centralized Office of Legislative Counsel.[76]

Almost all of the remaining bills are drafted in-house by the staff in congressional committees and by Congress's Legislative Counsel Office. Congressional committees generally have counsel on staff who are able to do the fine-grained work of legislative drafting; this specialist might take the first crack at drafting major bills. For its part, the Legislative Counsel Office consists of a nonpartisan group of expert lawyers whose primary job is to translate a sponsor's policies into legislative text. Because of their expertise, there is widespread agreement that the existence of this Legislative Counsel Office improves the coherence and legal rigor of the resulting bill. Indeed, even expert counsel in committees may engage this Office to check and fine-tune their own drafting efforts. But, given the attenuation between sponsor and drafting, there are also reasons to expect that in some cases the resulting "disconnect between text and policy"[77] will create room for errors and sometimes increase the processing costs needed to understand a bill.

This disjointed legislative drafting process can lead to a number of possible misunderstandings and sources of inflated processing costs in the resulting legislation. First, there are multiple steps in the assembly line in drafting a bill. According to Gluck and Bressman, staffers who work for members or sometimes even committees typically prepare policy bullet points or outlines that the lawyers in the Legislative Counsel's office turn into statutory text.[78] The members, then, convey the policies to staff who convey the policies to the Legislative Counsel who then turn the policies into draft legislation. But the necessary feedback loop that closes the circle – namely sponsor scrutiny of the final product – is sometimes and perhaps almost always absent. In the Gluck and Bressman survey, for example, the "non-Legislative Counsel staffers told us that they often are not capable of confirming that the text that Legislative Counsel drafts reflects their intention."[79] Gluck and Bressman found multi-layered problems: "Our ordinary counsels reported that the difficulties of understanding technical statutory language and of tracking the numerous statutory cross-references and amendments to preexisting legislation make penetrating the language that Legislative Counsel generates challenging even for staffers who are lawyers."[80]

There also does not appear to be close oversight of the legislative drafting by the Rule-Followers or their staff, at least in some cases. Gluck and Bressman conclude, "Our findings cast doubt on whether members or high-level staff read, much less are able to decipher, all of the textual details."[81] As one staffer conceded: "Leg. Counsel rewrites it and sometimes changes it. It's kind of like translating the Bible." Another remarked that "Legislative Counsel drafts, and the staffer doesn't have the law degree or expertise to evaluate what Legislative Counsel did."[82]

Second, and further complicating the role of these nonpartisan drafters in the crafting of a bill, is the fragmentation and variation within the Legislative Counsel's office itself. Apparently, the disjointed committee jurisdictions within Congress are mirrored in similar silos in the staff working for Legislative Counsel. Those working in the Counsel office concede that the fragmentation leads to very different drafting practices, word choices, and even the role that the Counsel plays in a given topic area. For example, in some areas, Legislative Counsel play a major role in text drafting, but not in others.[83] The role of Legislative Counsel also varies depending on the source of the originating text or policy. As noted, in cases where private parties draft the statute, as one example, Legislative Counsel play a less central role than in cases where they prepare the first draft from scratch.[84]

Third, it is common practice for Rule-Follower sponsors to typically draft a single statute with multiple audiences in mind, and this fact can further complicate the internal coherence of a bill. One Legislative Counsel staffer reports that the professional office is used to draft the technical parts of the statute, but most statutes contain other more expressive messages directed at constituencies (or sometimes drafted by them). For these portions of a bill, Legislative Counsel is not involved in the drafting process.[85] Thus a statute can be sliced into pieces with each piece drafted by a different author and directed to a different audience (e.g., court versus industry benefactor) and written with different communicative goals in mind (the latter being clear communication and the former being accurate rendition of the details, such as they are).[86]

B FRAGMENTED COMMITTEE JURISDICTION

The fragmentation introduced into bill-drafting by turf-conscious committees has been a long-standing problem in Congress that may also adversely impact the coherence and comprehensibility of some of the Rule-Follower's bills.[87] Gluck and Bressman observe, based on their surveys, that "the division of Congress into committees creates drafting 'silos' that exacerbate drafting fragmentation and also 'turf' consciousness that incentivizes drafting to protect jurisdiction."[88]

In particular, survey participants report that "committees draft statutes to keep matters within their own jurisdiction, even if doing so requires contorted language and not the 'ordinary' language that courts presume drafters use."[89] Fifteen percent of the participants volunteered that "committees go out of their way to draft statutes so that agencies within their jurisdiction will implement them."[90] This is the case even when the "fit is unclear."[91] One survey respondent elaborated that "'Committee jurisdiction is really important to how stuff gets drafted … It affects general policy approaches, leads to contorted ways of talking about things in legislation … you try to phrase the policy to keep it in your committee.'"[92]

Different committees also have different practices, use terms differently, and diverge in the types of staff they hire and their role in drafting.[93] None of these divergences necessarily will lead to more incoherent and incomprehensible laws.

But the fact that there are so many varying practices with staffs playing different roles creates still more opportunities for confusion that might be expressed in the resulting statutory texts. As one staff survey participant observed, "some members don't use lawyers in drafting and it's more sloppy."[94]

2 Adjusting Bills to Achieve Better CBO Scores

The Rule-Follower's bill must also provide a "Congressional Budget Office" score as a bill leaves committee, but this requirement can create pressure on the Rule-Follower to adjust the bill in ways that can make the bill less coherent and accessible. More specifically, Section 402 of the Congressional Budget and Impoundment Control Act of 1974 requires the Congressional Budget Office to develop a cost estimate for every bill passing through committee, except bills originating within appropriations committees.[95] The score provides ready information to all congressional members on the approximate costs involved in implementing the bill. In theory, then, the score places a highly accessible "price tag" on all bills, including those that are unwieldy or otherwise incomprehensible.

There is some preliminary evidence that this well-intended effort to identify the financial implications of a bill can take a toll on drafting practices. In order to keep a bill on or below the target amount, Rule-Followers may inadvertently produce a bill that becomes more convoluted. Coherence takes a back seat to obtaining an impressive CBO number. In Gluck and Bressman's study, for example, survey participants reported that they "routinely change the bill text to bring legislation within a budgetary goal."[96] One respondent even volunteered that the budget score can affect how much detail to put into legislation versus leaving the issues ambiguous.[97] Other commenters report other forms of gaming of the CBO process in order to manipulate the budget score.[98]

3 Post-Committee Amendments

As the legislation-crafting process proceeds, Rule-Followers lose more and more control over the coherence of their bill as members take advantage of the opportunity to amend bills on the floor. In some cases, unlimited amendments are allowed.[99] In fact, "amending marathons" are not uncommon. "[S]ince amendments may make a bill more broadly attractive or at least give the sponsors of successful amendments a greater stake in the legislation's enactment" ... "[t]he adoption of floor amendments may enhance a bill's chances of ultimate legislative success."[100] Barbara Sinclair even found "[a]mending marathons are [in fact] associated with legislative success. Bills subject to ten or more Senate amendments decided by roll call votes are more likely to pass the Senate and more likely to become law than are other measures."[101]

Yet while this amending activity does help gain buy-in and can sometimes add useful adjustments, at the same time, unrestricted amendments also seem capable of compromising the coherence and textual integrity of a bill. Committee and party leaders do sometimes attempt to anticipate and placate disgruntled senators in advance before the bill reaches the floor (taking the form of post-committee adjustments), but this anticipatory work is not always successful.[102] Either way, the resulting amending activity may place significant pressure on the internal coherence of a bill by introducing various ad hoc compromises inserted after the fact to make the bill more politically palatable.

4 Negotiations and Compromise

Most challenging for the Rule-Followers, however, is the effect of inevitable, informal legislative deliberations and negotiations on the coherence of the emerging bill. The multiple steps (or "obstacle course")[103] that a bill must pass through means that "even those working on the statutes themselves cannot always predict whether they will be able to touch, or fix, them later in the process."[104] In some (but not all cases), rather than a deliberative process that over time produces an increasingly coherent piece of legislation, the realities of legislative bartering and negotiation can lead to the opposite – a type of Mr. Potato-head statute with each interest adding their own appendage to the legislation.

The adverse effects of this necessary compromise on comprehensibility have been of continuing concern to congressional scholars. In 1987, Atiyah and Summers noted how the imperative of compromise in Congress leads to legislation that can often be both confusing and inconsistent.[105] Melnick similarly observed that the fragmented process in Congress, coupled with the challenges of reaching agreement on controversial issues, cause "many" statutes to "lack coherence, fail to resolve controversies, or even incorporate inconsistent requirements."[106] Kagan observes that although American statutes have always been "less carefully drafted and hence less coherent than those of the British Parliament . . . in an era of divided government and weak political party unity, American legislation has gotten worse." The statutes are "painfully stitched together by shifting issue-specific coalitions."[107] Graetz observes in the tax context how unconstrained congressional negotiations "create[] the lack of a coherent vision of tax equity. This, coupled with [the tax law's] complexity, has made the tax code unstable."[108] And, in his empirical work on complexity in legislation, Curry finds a positive correlation between bills that attract substantial interest from lobbyists and bill complexity, with a coefficient that is statistically significant.[109]

There are at least two more specific sets of challenges that arise for Rule-Followers as their bills are subject to these negotiations. Each challenge threatens to complicate a bill and thus increase the processing costs required for other rank-and-file members to make sense of the draft legislation.

A FAVORED WORDS AND "SAUSAGE-Y" BILLS

In Gluck and Bressman's study, the art of compromise can sometimes lead to the insertion of key words that a particular member of Congress or engaged constituency demands. These words often do not serve to illuminate but instead complicate the meaning and implications of the law. One interviewee noted, for example, that "sometimes the lists [of words] are in there to satisfy groups, certain phrases are needed to satisfy political interests and they might overlap."[110] Rule-Followers may nevertheless opt for these compromises because the insertion of favored items or "gimmies" to pacify some opponents helps grease the wheels for bill passage.

Yet, the coherence and precision of bills can be compromised when words are selected to make various constituencies happy rather than arrive at a coherent legislative statement. These compromises over word choice create possible sources of inconsistency not only within but also between statutes. For example, only 9 percent of the respondents in Gluck's and Bressman's sample reported that "drafters often or always intend for terms to apply consistently across statutes that are unrelated by subject matter."[111] One legislative staffer nicely sums up this incremental compromise approach and its impact on the comprehensibility of the resulting legislation:

> We've been working on this bill very hard recently and I was talking to somebody . . . and he was saying, "okay, alright, so we're done with the policy part of it, now let's do the politics part of it." And . . . I knew exactly what he was saying . . . Okay, now here we are talking about "can you put this in? Will X buy it? Will Y buy it? Will Z buy it? No, Z won't buy it. Okay forget it. Can we word it like this? No. Why? Okay, Y won't buy that, but Z will." And so you go through that period and what I think is that if you actually have enough time to do that, you can kind of – it's still sausage, but you can kind of get it to work. When you have to do it at the last minute, especially on these bills that are really complicated . . . when you start doing that in the last minute, it's just, it's bad.[112]

B EXCESSIVE AMBIGUITY

Another coping mechanism used by Rule-Followers to avoid deadlock in negotiations is to replace precise terms with select ambiguous terms. The use of this tactic, however, tends to make it more difficult for rank-and-file members to understand a bill and its implications. In *The Devil Is in the Details*, Rachel VanSickle-Ward finds that "on a high-profile issue, legislators and executive actors often choose ambiguity as a political strategy to achieve compromise."[113] Ambiguity also helps avoid opposition from high-stakes groups who might object to specific language. Rather, "leaving 'loopholes,' 'flexibility,' or 'wiggle room'" is a safer legislative course.[114] VanSickle-Ward even shows that the number of times ambiguous terms are used increases when the vote on an issue is likely to be close and/or the issue being discussed is highly salient.[115] (Lower salient issues can typically be hammered out with more clarity because the stakes are lower; contention on these issues actually facilitates specificity.)[116] Of course, ambiguity does not always succeed; sometimes the issues are deadlocked and the bill fails.[117] But when controversial legislation passes in a sharply divided Congress, significant ambiguities in the legislation are likely.

Ambiguity does not translate directly to incomprehensibility.[118] But in some cases, ambiguity could be considered a first cousin since the use of ambiguous terms increases processing costs, particularly when it involves some uncertainty and complexity with regard to what a law means. One state legislator in VanSickle-Ward's study summed it up this way: "[Ambiguous language means] you're not hurting anybody's feelings and you're not causing anyone to say '[explicative] I'm not going to vote for that,' whereas they can say 'well … it means this,' and they can walk off feeling good and the other person walks away thinking it means the exact opposite."[119]

B *Rule-Benders*

Rule-Benders – again, the party leaders and committee chairs that sponsor or are the driving force behind bills – will use incomprehensibility to expand their power base and gain control over the rank-and-file. As long as legislative processes do not sanction or even call attention to incomprehensible bills, Rule-Benders will find a way to use this neglect to their advantage.

1 The Curry Study

In *Legislating in the Dark*, James Curry traces a variety of ways that powerful congressional leaders exploit comprehension asymmetries in the House to gain greater control over rank-and-file members. These tactics include negotiating behind closed doors while keeping the legislative language secret up until the very last minute, changing the legislation immediately before its consideration, and manipulating the complexity of the legislative language itself.[120]

The resulting tactics help Rule-Benders leverage greater party loyalty on legislation. Specifically, because members cannot gain independent information to understand the bills, they line up behind party leaders and find it more difficult to defect.[121] Even the basic policy vision behind the law can be communicated to rank-and-file members in ways that are not accessible or accurate. And leaders can do this precisely because rank-and-file members lack the time and expertise to check those representations against the bill's text.

Incomprehensibility also impedes those who seek to oppose the bill from gaining purchase on the bill's content. This is particularly true when complex bills are rushed through the system. One frustrated minority leader staffer observed:

Where we can be given notice of a bill, and sometimes a pretty substantial bill, that is coming to the floor the next day, we get that notice the night prior, sometimes at midnight or something like that. In that case we're really scrambling. So the information that we are coming up with, one, we don't have access to it, two, we don't have time.[122]

Curry's quantitative analysis in fact reveals strong correlations between complex bills and sponsorship by powerful leaders in the House. While this does not imply that powerful leaders actively sit down and attempt to make laws more incomprehensible, it could suggest that leaders are attracted to or do not hesitate to make bills more complex since these bills carry some advantages in bringing discipline to the rank-and-file. Curry concludes from his analysis that "majority leadership priority bills [were] . . . significantly more complex than other bills . . . by almost one-third of a standard deviation."[123] Curry's analysis also reveals that bill complexity is increasing over time,[124] although this observation does not cut across all legislative areas.

Curry also finds that this incomprehensibility matters; the resulting bill complexity can and does adversely affect the audience's ability to understand a bill. In some legislative settings, "the information encompassing their [rank-and-file members'] worlds is crushing and cacophonous. The challenge for them is not simply to accrue information but to identify the useful information within their time and resource constraints."[125] One member observed that understanding a bill that is being rushed is "like going to a neurosurgeon and asking for brain surgery and him saying it will take ten hours and you asking him if he can do it in thirty minutes."[126] Another member noted that even when "[t]here was usually enough time [to read the bills] . . . it was like reading a computer program. The language is dense and hard to understand."[127]

Finally, and most relevant to the Rule-Bender categorization, is some evidence that these maneuvers are deployed deliberately.[128] Among the techniques Curry identifies for keeping members' processing costs high are:

- "[P]ackag[ing] legislation in an omnibus bill that is hundreds of pages long, deals with a multitude of issues, and is time consuming for rank-and-file lawmakers to process"[129]
- "[D]raft[ing] legislation to be more difficult to read, using more technical jargon than is necessary, writing provisions in a way that is less than straightforward, or burying the lead by including significant provisions toward the end."[130]
- Making last-minute changes to bills that are not recorded in track change and are inserted into non-searchable PDFs.[131]
- Restricting release of the bill to the public so that members cannot consult expert stakeholders for input.[132]
- Controlling the release of bills so there is no time for amendments or negotiations on terms before it reaches the House floor.[133]

Some Rule-Benders even fess up to the occasional use of these exploitive tactics, particularly with regard to withholding an accessible summary of how a bill is likely to work in practice. One staff from a party leader conceded using these tricks but argued they were ultimately harmless; "unless you are a committee staffer that wrote the damn thing" members won't understand the implications of the bill even if they read it. "So this whole 'read the bill' stuff is almost a little bit disingenuous, because reading five lines referencing some part of the code isn't going to help you at all."[134] As a result, members on both sides of the aisle find themselves dependent on sponsors and party leaders to explain the "big stuff" about what the bill will actually do in practice.[135]

The target audience appears well aware of at least some of these exploitive tactics. One rank-and-file staffer aptly summarized how his own party uses incomprehensibility to gain control over the vote:

> There will be some information given out about the bill that is more detailed and less accessible. On things they might not want you to understand because you might vote against it, they will be less clear. And on things that they are full-throatily behind they will be more clear.[136]

Even attentive members – those who are especially interested in a given area of legislative activity – sometimes find themselves unable to muster the resources to participate. As Curry notes, "Even if a few skeptical lawmakers do allocate the time necessary to scrutinize the information legislative leaders give them" and find that legislation problematic, "these efforts will have consequences only if these skeptical lawmakers have the resources, contacts, and clout to convince a significant number of their colleagues that their leaders are misleading them."[137]

As a result, because they are adrift in a sea of unprocessed information, most members find they must resort to looking for "proxies" to determine how to vote and when to support legislation. Those proxies – not coincidentally – are in large part the same chairs and leaders who attempt to exploit information-processing costs in order to gain the trust of the rank-and-file members.[138] As one rank-and-file member interviewed for Curry's study ultimately conceded:

> People would say, "You mean you don't understand every vote you take?" Well certainly I don't! No way! There's not enough time! Even my staff, as good as they were. So you find credible members on the other committees. And staff would find other staff that they trusted.[139]

Yet relying on these proxies for legislative guidance does not always work in advancing the goals of individual rank-and-file members.[140] Curry's case studies reveal instances in which members who vote the party line in favor of a convoluted law later discover that the bill conflicts with their own district's unique interests. In one case, for example, party leaders advanced a purportedly benign bill calling for an EPA/NAS study of the effects of using ethanol in vehicles.[141] But the detailed provisions in the bill (not summarized in the sponsor's memo) effectively ensured the study would kill EPA's plans to use ethanol. This in turn undermined a large economic base in some congressional districts. However, based on the skewed information, Midwestern rank-and-file members who would normally oppose the bill unwittingly supported it.[142]

"In short, leaders can use their information advantages to persuade lawmakers, in part because lawmakers are persuadable."[143] The result is a concentration of power in a few leaders, with greater polarization between the parties. In fact, based on his quantitative analyses, Curry concludes, "Bill complexity has the most robust effect on partisanship, with every test indicating that more complexity results in more partisanship."[144]

2 Unorthodox Practices

Rule-Benders may also take advantage of the opportunity to bypass established congressional procedures intended to enhance deliberation and cooperative communication by utilizing a variety of "unorthodox practices." Taking advantage of these unorthodox practices puts the rank-and-file at an even greater disadvantage in understanding the terms of bills and hence may grease the wheels for bill passage by controlling deliberations. And Barbara Sinclair found that these efforts pay off; for bills "subject to two or more special procedures and practices in both chambers, 78 percent were successful; at the other extreme, if subject to none in either chamber [hence following the conventional path], only 48 percent were successful."[145]

While Sinclair identifies a number of unorthodox practices in use today by Congress,[146] there are two in particular that tend to exacerbate existing comprehension asymmetries.

A ECLIPSING AND BYPASSING COMMITTEES

Historically, congressional committees were used to provide opportunities for a subset of the rank-and-file to engage more deeply in the focused review and fine-tuning of draft legislation.[147] One prominent congressman from the middle of the last century was quoted as asserting that "'95 percent of all the legislation that becomes law passed the Congress in the shape that it came from our committees." He continued, "if our committee work is sloppy . . . our legislation in 95 percent of the cases will be bad and inadequate as well."[148]

Particularly over the last few decades, however, the power of committees has been eclipsed by increasingly powerful party leaders. Two changes deserve particular note in this regard. First, and in contrast to past practices, the majority party in committee sometimes operates as a unified block. Sinclair reports, for example, that while "[t]he rules allow the minority to offer amendments . . . consideration is perfunctory and all are voted down, with the majority voting in lockstep."[149] This eclipsing of minority views does not occur for all legislation. But legislation that sparks "high partisan polarization" can trigger these divides that leave the minority effectively cut out of the deliberative picture.[150] The result is less opportunity (and hence incentive) for the rank-and-file to invest scarce resources in understanding a bill. This is particularly true for minority members, but could impact all members to some extent. Thus, while committees still do not operate as a rubber stamp for leaders, commenters note how this party dominance has caused the committees' influence to wane as compared with the heydays of "committee government."[151]

Second, Rule-Benders sometimes manage to bypass the committee altogether, foreclosing this important opportunity for select rank-and-file members to engage more meaningfully with a bill. Statistics from the 112th Congress reveal that 41 percent of the bills did not go through committees of either the Senate or the House. Sinclair reports that "in the Congresses of the 1960s through the 1980s for which data are available, the committee was bypassed in the Senate on 7 percent of major measures; for the 103rd through 110th Congresses, the average increased to 26 percent; and from 2009 to 2014, it was 52 percent."[152] See Figure 7.5. Perhaps not surprisingly, as their services are bypassed, the deliberative work of the committees declines accordingly. Ornstein reports that the number of committee and subcommittee meetings dropped in half from the 1960s to the early 2000s.[153]

The conference committee – deployed to iron out the House and Senate differences – is also regularly bypassed in this new world of "unorthodox

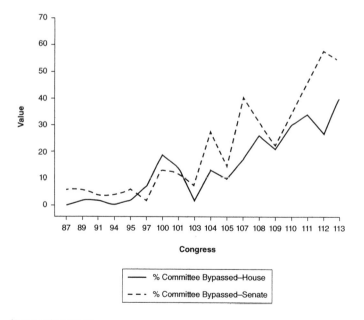

FIGURE 7.5 Percentage of Major Legislation on which the Committee of Jurisdiction Was Bypassed

Barbara Sinclair, *Unorthodox Lawmaking: New Legislative Processes in the US Congress* Figure 6.3 at 151 (C.Q. Press, 5th ed., 2016) © Used with permission from Sage Publications lawmaking." In the first year of the 112th Congress (2011–12), out of 91 total measures that went through both houses, only three ended up in a conference committee. "[T]he rest were worked out by leadership deals, special legislative processes such as reconciliation, or 'preconference' – a process in which differences are negotiated behind the scenes by staff, and then each chamber passes the amendments necessary to make the bills identical without going through conference."[154]

When the committee process is bypassed, it reduces the scrutiny that rank-and-file members can provide to bills. The minority is particularly handicapped, not only because of processing costs, but also the lack of opportunities for deliberation. Sinclair observes that "[s]ince the mid-1990s the minority party has to a large extent been excluded from decision making at the prefloor – and often also at the post-passage – stage on the most highly visible major legislation in the House."[155] And, while some deliberation can occur on the floor, the combination of highly complex legislation and restrictive rules at least in the House make the possibility of mean-ingful deliberation effectively illusory.[156]

B THE RISE OF OMNIBUS BILLS

Another increasingly unorthodox practice used by Rule-Benders that was "rare" before the 1980s is the bundling of single-subject bills together in a large omnibus bill.[157] These bills are "usually highly complex and long" precisely because each omnibus bill addresses "numerous and not necessarily related subjects, issues, and programs."[158] Omnibus bills can be huge, easily stretching to more than 1,000 pages.[159] An example is illustrated in Figure 7.6.

Omnibus bills are typically created by the party leaders to overcome gridlock that might otherwise block individual legislative proposals.[160] By combining different legis-lative proposals, an omnibus bill helps increase buy-in since more members will see something in it they like. Omnibus bills can also increase buy-in because members are not sure what is in the legislation. In these bills, "party and committee leaders can package or bury controversial provisions in one massive bill to be voted up or down."[161]

As a general matter, omnibus bills are considered to be much less transparent, lack legislative history, and are difficult to understand.[162] Given the rank-and-file members' higher processing costs associated with understanding and evaluating the merits of an omnibus bill, it is perhaps not surprising that these bills tend "to be adopted with little debate or scrutiny."[163] Indeed, typically "[o]mnibus legislating moves lawmaking behind closed doors. Rank-and-file members are given few if any opportunities to change the final package. More errors, mistakes and waste may creep into the final legislation as a result."[164]

Omnibus bills dramatically raise members' processing costs, but precisely because they are so blatant with respect to limiting congressional deliberations, omnibus bills are also relatively unusual. They are most common in extreme settings, for example, when leaders can utilize end-of-session pressures and the fear of a government shutdown to force the adoption of the package with minimal debate. In the leaders' view, "it's the only way to push a budget through the gridlocked Senate floor."[165]

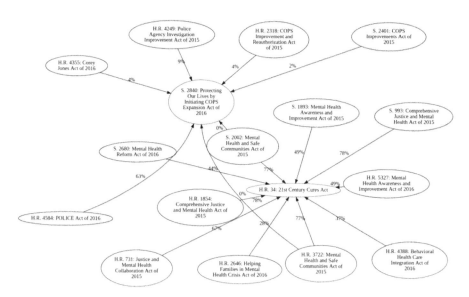

FIGURE 7.6 Mapping Omnibus Legislation: Provisions from 15 Separate Bills Were Merged into Two Bills that Congress Ultimately Enacted

Joshua Tauberer, "How a Complex Network of Bills Becomes a Law: Introducing a New Data Analysis of Text Incorporation!" *Government Track*, Jan. 7, 2017, available at https://medium.com/@govtrack/how-a-complex-network-of-bills-becomes-a-law-9972b9624d36

3 Public Choice Theory

The possibility that Rule-Benders might promote statutes, even when they do not fully understand them themselves, is at least partly explained by long-standing public choice theories of congressional behavior. In his classic 1987 article, McNollgast hypothesized that one means Congress uses to control policy is through "stacking the deck" procedurally to benefit favored constituencies in subsequent agency rule-makings.[166] McNollgast noted that the use of these procedural delegations increases in heated controversies. "[A] high level of conflict among congressmen creates an incentive to delegate increasingly large regulatory scope to an administrative agency" with procedures that at the very least are likely to slow agency progress.[167]

In the case of incomprehensible laws, the use of this "deck-stacking" technique can be both more subtle and devious. Rather than inserting terms into a law that will advance the interests of favored constituencies during implementation, the goal of this technique is to promote incomprehensible laws that are likely – by their very nature – to encounter substantial delays and implementation challenges. Incomprehensible legislation may, in fact, be more effective than procedural "deck-stacking" in settings where regulatory inaction is beneficial to influential stakeholders.

Indeed, a very clever Rule-Bender can take this public choice strategy further by tossing in a handful of favorable substantive provisions to appease the thinly financed opposition. As long as the law is replete with contradictions and unresolved

complexities, it will likely face a long and tortured path during implementation, and the bones thrown to the opposition will not materialize in practice.
Yet the speakers have significantly more insight into the extent of this internal
incomprehensibility and can fool the rank-and-file into placing more confidence in the bill than is actually warranted.[168] Moreover, and consistent with
Fiorina's 1982 "shift the blame" theory, incomprehensible laws can allow
Congress to gain credit in the short-term by overcoming gridlock and shifting
blame in the long-term if constituents lose battles during the agency's
implementation.[169]

Box 7.1 Comprehension Asymmetries in Legislative Process

The Rule-Follower Party Leader

Why are some processing costs passed
through to rank-and-file members rather than
internalized by the bill drafters?

- Bill drafting is institutionally fragmented in ways that leave even the speakers unable to process some bill text.
- Bills may need to be adjusted to obtain better CBO scores, even though the terms of the bill can become more complex as a result.
- Post-committee amendments are outside the control of the sponsors.
- Negotiations and compromise can complicate the bill.

AND

- There is no requirement that bills be comprehensible, so why invest the effort unless it becomes essential to passage?

The Rule-Bender Sponsor or Party Leader

How can the processing limitations of rank-
and-file members be overloaded in a way that
shifts control to sponsors and leaders?

- Utilize unorthodox practices, like bypassing committee and omnibus bills.
- Take advantage of rank-and-file members' limited processing ability by expanding the size and complexity of a bill.
- Make last-minute changes to bills that are not recorded accessibly.
- Limit the time available to review a bill.

4 Summary

In sum, the ability of Rule-Bending congressional leaders to profit from comprehension asymmetries resonates with both theory and evidence. As Curry summarizes, "[L]egislative leaders can exercise impressive influence over congressional policymaking by using their procedural prerogatives to exploit the asymmetrical possession of information within the chamber."[170]

Moreover, as more attentive groups are kept in the dark, the diversity of views and engagement drops and a few high stakes leaders dominate the deliberations. "By restricting information and accelerating the legislative process, leaders are minimizing the voices and influence on policymaking of representatives, interests, and ultimately constituents. The process becomes decisively top-down, driven by the goals and interests of those in leadership posts."[171]

Fortunately, Curry's research suggests this incomprehensibility occurs primarily in high priority, partisan bills, particularly when a party leader's power is threatened by other leaders or constituencies.[172] This is in part because the strategy is neither costless nor certain; in some cases, rank and file members do fight these strategies. Curry's study also reveals that many members are generally suspicious of the information that leaders provide.[173] With that said, because members have finite time and resources, they must pick the bills over which to spend time and effort to appease their suspicions. In the remaining cases they are generally at the mercy of the leaders' skewed information.

IV DOES INCOMPREHENSIBLE LAWMAKING MATTER?

Before discussing reform possibilities, we consider several important reasons why the problem of incomprehensible lawmaking may be best left alone. Most obvious, the legislative process is exceedingly complicated. Adjusting this one incentive for cooperative communication may upend even more important incentives within lawmaking, setting into motion a series of unintended consequences. While we ultimately introduce several preliminary reform ideas for purposes of discussion, the objections cataloged subsequently underscore the importance of proceeding both cautiously and conservatively.

A *Maybe Incomprehensible Laws Are Rare*

Several strands of evidence suggest that incomprehensible laws might be only a minor annoyance, and if so, any reforms to address incomprehensible laws would equate to using a "missile to kill a mouse."[174] First and foremost, since there are clear reputational costs for sponsors in particular and Congress in general to pass incomprehensible laws, these costs should generally suffice to discipline the prevalence of incomprehensible laws. Past media reports and internal sanctions suggest very high costs to sponsors and party leaders who resort to these practices. Political scientists reiterate the significant, informal sanctions in place to penalize the advocates of complicated bills, at least for omnibus legislation.[175] Sinclair also notes that leaders are aware that ramming omnibus bills through the process can generate a great deal of hostility from within the party. As a result, incomprehensible laws may be passed only in "extraordinary" circumstances.[176]

Second and as noted, there are multiple well-established opportunities in place to check legislative incoherence. These traditional legislative processes include multiple review steps that can serve to sharpen both the policy and the text of the bills. By requiring sponsors to "opt out" of conventional processes, the existing legislative system adequately constructs a default that favors coherent legislation.

Third, powerful interest groups and engaged agencies will also dedicate energy to improve the comprehensibility of a bill when it inures to their interest. Private parties who succeed in extracting benefits from a bill will be particularly eager to shore up the rigor of that language to protect their bequest. Agencies will similarly find reason to engage in the legislative process to ensure the delegations are at least coherent. In his recent study of the agencies' role in legislation, for example, Christopher Walker discusses how Congress regularly solicits the regulatory agencies for technical drafting assistance. Agencies report that even when they do not support the legislation, they devote considerable resources toward weighing in at a micro-level to minimize downstream damage.[177]

Nevertheless, and despite these and other important checks in the system, there is a worrisome undercurrent running through the literature that suggests that the problem of incomprehensible legislation is significant enough to deserve closer scrutiny. Gluck and Bressman report a systemic "'passing the buck' feel to virtually all of our respondents' comments about Congress's obligations [to the courts] . . . but [they] did not seem incentivized to act on it."[178] Hellman notes that "[c]orrection of ambiguities and omissions in statutes already on the books has never ranked high among congressional priorities."[179] Until greater evidence is available to suggest that incomprehensible laws are anomalies that do not require attention, then, erring on the side of caution and continuing to explore the phenomenon seems in order.

B *Perhaps Coherent and Precise Laws Are Worse than Incomprehensible Laws*

In some cases, incomprehensible laws may actually be preferable to precise laws. Some scholars have noted the dangers of overly prescriptive laws that can become inflexible and quickly outdated. Pamela Gruber notes that an ambiguous bill allows for much-needed agency flexibility and may improve the quality of implementation downstream.[180] Barbara Sinclair similarly argues that there are tradeoffs in representativeness versus responsiveness. Shortfalls in the transparency of bills and deliberative processes may ultimately allow for stronger responsiveness.[181]

Yet arguments touting the advantages of legislative ambiguity and open-endedness do not go so far as to excuse the problematic features of laws that are incomprehensible to members themselves. When legislation is not just open-ended but top expert observers and members who invest the effort cannot understand the law at even the simplest level, the problems run much deeper than ensuring flexibility in the statutory text.

In any event, meaningful reforms do not need to solve the different puzzle of when or how to strike the appropriate balance between precision and ambiguity in law.[182] Rather, reforms can simply endeavor to tune up the speakers' incentive system so as to create more costs for legislative incoherence. Ultimately, the choice is still up to sponsors of whether the slightly greater costs to incomprehensibility (in light of the reforms) outweigh whatever benefits they gain from the strategy.

C *Is Some Law Better than No Law*

A number of authors suggest that when it comes to ambiguous statutes or even convoluted omnibus bills, the fact that *any* law passed at all is better than congressional inaction. In *Hitching a Ride*, Glen Krutz makes this exact argument. He places the use of omnibus legislation within a larger context and highlights both the efficiency and effectiveness of bundling legislation relative to the challenges of passing the laws piecemeal. Such an approach not only facilitates greater congressional action and power, but also provides Congress with useful leverage over the president.[183]

As a substantive matter, however, if a law is excessively convoluted and incoherent, it is not altogether clear that the resulting law *is* better than nothing. A convoluted law that does not identify the major problems or addresses them in an incoherent way creates significant opportunity costs (the incomprehensible law impedes the passage of a better law), as well as the likelihood of misdirecting implementation and downstream agency, judicial, and private resources in dead ends and wrong-headed directions. Convoluted laws also tend to increase the risk of losing the forest for the trees on overarching policy goals; individual legislative requirements can take precedence over the bigger picture that the legal program seeks to advance.[184] Moreover, in implementing these complex laws, resources are not only necessary to make sense of the requirements, but also cause inevitable confusion downstream that can lead to an even more protracted and expensive litigation and political controversy that can be addressed only by returning full circle to Congress.[185]

There are also important process costs associated with incoherent laws. When significant laws are passed by a Congress whose members do not actually understand the terms or implications of the bills they pass, then we will be relying on a deliberative process that rests power and policymaking expertise in a very small group of largely unaccountable individuals. Centralization of power in Congress may ultimately turn out to be a positive adaptation for avoiding deadlock in the early twenty-first century,[186] but centralization is not the same thing as requiring all other members to be in the dark about the law.

Incomprehensible laws also create inequities in democratic engagement. As laws become more incomprehensible, thinly financed lobbyists and watchdogs who cannot afford the processing costs will drop out. In his discussion of the deliberate inflation of processing costs by congressional leaders, Curry concludes, "While using informational tactics helps legislative leaders get their parties to overcome collective action problems ... it reduces, degrades, and sometimes eliminates individual lawmakers' ability to participate and to represent their constituents on questions before the chamber."[187]

V LEGISLATIVE REFORM

In the discussion that follows, we offer three proposals that endeavor to encourage cooperative communication in legislative deliberations. The first set of reforms creates speedbumps for incomprehensible laws while simultaneously providing benefits for speakers who draft more comprehensible legislation. The second set of reforms infuses subsidies and rewards into the process to defray the costs of processing for both busy Rule-Following speakers and disadvantaged audiences. Lastly, we propose a targeted adjustment to the amendment process that imposes greater accountability (and costs) for members who amend bills.

In addition to the important qualification that these reforms may ultimately prove premature or even unnecessary, we add two more notes of caution before proceeding. First, the proposals we advance are the result of an abstract, arm-chair analysis and are intended to jumpstart discussion. Our thinking is not constrained by the actual viability of the reforms; nor do we make a case that any given reform is necessary. Second, because of the delicate nature of legislative deliberations, our proposals take the form of carrots (voluntary rewards) rather than sticks (prescriptive rules or heavy sanctions).

A *Speedbumps to Discourage Incomprehensible Lawmaking*

Although the public costs from incomprehensible laws might be substantial, there is little motivation beyond the raw political process as described to discipline this activity. Ideally, then, some type of "day-of-reckoning" could be instituted as a checkpoint to assess the comprehensibility of each major bill. Members would face higher costs associated with sponsoring, amending, and voting on these laws once the incomprehensibility is documented and publicized.

1 A Day of Reckoning Review

The most extreme option is the creation of a day-of-reckoning (DOR) review of each bill destined for final passage into law. This DOR review would *not* "rate" a bill or give it a comprehensibility score, nor would it serve as a type of gatekeeping device to weed out convoluted bills. Instead, the review will simply make public – for members, sponsors, affected groups and the public at large – what the bill is, how it works, and major questions that remain with respect to its implementation. This public review thus creates an analysis that could either buoy up a legislative project (when it is done well) or create some stigma around a legislative project when there are a number of open questions and problematic provisions. Coupled with a 30-day "cool off" period that follows each DOR review, legislators could then react to serious problems, particularly those major problems that were not anticipated or noticed during deliberations.

This DOR review could be mandatory, for example applied to all bills that pass both houses, or it could be purely voluntary. If mandatory, the DOR review might apply to a subset of laws most at risk, for example those bills that are not rigorously vetted by committee or that otherwise lack conference or committee reports that explain the bills. Omnibus bills might, however, be exempted from DOR review since these bills, by definition, lack coherence and hence may be difficult to analyze in the manner proposed here.

If voluntary, a sponsor could elect to submit his or her bill to the day-of-reckoning (DOR) committee at key points in the process – e.g., before the bill moves to the floor – both in order to educate other members as to its attributes and perhaps also to provide some buffer against excessive amendments that affect the legislative proposal in significant ways. Indeed, perhaps a sponsor could submit the bill to the DOR twice – once before it enters the floor for debate, and again after it has been amended. This double look would help spotlight whether or how various amendments might have made the bill more incomprehensible in problematic ways.

To be successful, the DOR review must include several other key features, such as:

- *Bipartisan Expert Assessment.* The DOR review must be conducted by the most bipartisan, neutral committee possible. Designing such a committee is not easy. Studies of the now-defunct Office of Technology Assessment (OTA) and of the National Academies suggest that is nevertheless possible, at least when the survival of the office depends on being perceived as bipartisan.[188] As a preliminary matter, moreover, we believe for this same reason that the DOR review should be conducted in-house by staff who are the most motivated to be bipartisan. To ensure the designated staff are adequately critical, however, they might also be expected to solicit "peer review" from many top academic and related

experts in the field. In-house staff would, however, be ultimately responsible for analyzing and summarizing this input.

- *Timing.* This DOR committee would need to be fully primed with
  wheels greased so that the assessments can proceed expeditiously. Limits
  would need to be placed on the committee's review time, for example, a
  60-day cap. Congress may also need a set time (e.g., 30 days) to respond
  before the official legislative deliberations conclude.
- *Documents Reviewed.* There will be decisions about what documents this
  DOR committee will review. Surely, the bill will be first on the list.
  Other supporting documents might be useful as well, including a summary statement of the bill, explanations and supporting materials of the
  bill provided to other members, and other reasonably accessible documents that were widely available to members. If these supplemental
  materials contradict the bill in significant ways, that will be noted in
  the DOR review. On the other hand, if the bill is quite complicated yet
  members are not brought up to speed, that fact would be noted as well.

However it is structured, the end game of the DOR review is to create positive
incentives for more comprehensible legislation and member engagement. It is
hoped that as a result of this review, bill sponsors, originating committees, and those
actively amending the bill would encounter some rewards or, conversely, demerits
from the added oversight.

2 Document the Rigor of Deliberations

A different, although potentially complementary reform, is to establish a standardized way to track and document a bill's deliberative record. In a way that is roughly
analogous to the agencies, the principle is that stronger deliberations denote more
comprehensible or at least more robust engagement by the audience. Documenting
these features helps to reward this rich engagement, while spotlighting its absence in
other bills.

As with the DOR review, the deliberative record could be instituted as mandatory
or voluntary. Bills passed into law could each be accompanied by this record that
would document its key deliberative features. Alternatively, a sponsor could elect to
have a deliberative record prepared at any point in the process after the bill reaches
the floor. A sponsor might do this to advertise the attributes of a bill, for example.

A deliberative record would itemize – for each bill – the deliberative highlights,
such as the involvement of an originating committee in vetting the bill; the
availability of rigorous summaries and explanations to other members; the size
and amount of time the bill was shared with other members; the opportunities for
questions and exchanges with sponsors; the extent of committee or related peer
scrutiny, both formal and informal; the amendment history (discussed later); and
even the identity of the original bill-drafters and their role (e.g., private parties;

agencies), including Legislative Counsel. A neutral congressional office could produce the record, perhaps at a sponsors' request.

This report provides some useful information regarding the deliberative process underlying legislation. Lengthy bills that lack summary statements or cogent explanations, were drafted by interest groups, and were publicly available to other members for only a few days or even a few weeks, etc., would be supported by deliberative records that make them somewhat suspect. These bills could be compared and contrasted with similarly sized bills that have more impressive deliberative records because the bills were summarized with crisp, certifiably accurate summaries and explanations; were prepared by the Legislative Counsel's Office; were subject to multiple rounds of committee mark-up, hearings, and discussion; and moved through Congress over a longer period of time (e.g., months rather than weeks).

A deliberative record could be voluntarily produced or even produced by the opposition. Either way, a deliberative record creates a useful incentive for bill sponsors to engage their audiences in cooperative communication, providing a kind of crude signal of the "due process of lawmaking."[189] Sponsors of bills that are subjected to less deliberation and scrutiny may be held accountable for the impoverished deliberations. The deliberative record also could give useful, quick information to agencies and courts during downstream implementation.

Finally, the heated partisan climate in Congress might seize on this deliberative record as a signal of legislative integrity; members would compete to produce bills with the most impressive deliberative records. Rather than a race to the bottom in preparing bills that bypass congressional deliberations, such a measure of legislative virtue could create a race to the top. At the very least, the extent to which bills are subjected to rigorous internal review within Congress will become more salient to outsiders.

B *Subsidies and Rewards*

Subsidies that support efforts to make bills more comprehensible may be useful as well, particularly in cases where most of the problems are primarily the result of a lack of resources and time by the speaker.

1 Resources for Speakers

Even though speakers enjoy greater resources and capabilities to understand and communicate their bills to rank-and-file members, some of the legislative incomprehensibility likely occurs because the speakers themselves lack sufficient resources to do this expensive work. One reform simply provides sponsors with more resources to help them translate bills for rank-and-file members, including both the preparation of summaries and explanations as well as scrutinizing the bill text. These resources could also be available to speakers to track amendments and changes, so the sponsor (and others) can stay abreast of the coherence of the legislation as it moves through the obstacle course of legislative negotiations.

While providing earmarked grants is the most straightforward approach, even more useful might be the creation of a nonpartisan team of experts – perhaps within the Legislative Counsel Office – whose job it is to help a sponsor make his bill coherent and more accessible to other members. Ed Rubin has offered one sketch of what this type of congressional assistance might consist of with respect to the key components of legislation – goal definition, implementation, substantive terms for effectuating the law, and the collection of data to run and adjust the law.[190] His work thus provides a good start in this regard.

2 Resources for the Audience

Earmarked grants could also be available to members who struggle to make sense of important legislative proposals. Yet while even limited support will improve the situation, this reform standing alone seems inadequate to ensure the audience will always be able to keep up with the proposed legislation.

An expert office – perhaps the same office just proposed for the speaker – could provide an important resource for rank-and-file members seeking to understand a bill. Curry emphasizes the need to provide members with some assistance to balance the inequities in informational resources within Congress. Curry suggests:

> Lawmakers need access to expert information that does not come from political actors or offices with explicit agendas. Restoring and bolstering congressional support offices that can supply this would be a good first step, including revoking the ban on the Office of Technology Assessment and other legislative service organizations ... These organizations, banned by Speaker Gingrich in 1995, employed policy experts, produced reports on policy proposals, and answered lawmakers' inquiries. Dissolving them gave legislative leaders and interest groups even more power as sources of knowledge and policy information.[191]

Expert ombuds along the same lines as proposed for the agencies in Chapter 6 might provide a useful reinforcement as well. With adequate financing, this type of ombud could hold sponsors accountable for bills that are afflicted with excessive processing costs, while simultaneously helping disadvantaged audiences keep up with important legislation.

Thumbnail Sketch of Legislative Reform

1 Create added costs for incomprehensible laws by, for example, instituting a day of reckoning review and documenting impoverished deliberations.
2 Provide resources and rewards to both sponsors and the rank-and-file for processing complicated bills.
3 Track amendments to enhance accountability as bills move through the legislative process.

3 Rewards for Particularly Hardworking Audiences

At least some of the comprehension asymmetries in legislation may be the result of insufficient audience incentives, as well as perverse speaker incentives. We know that not all rank-and-file members will engage in legislative deliberations. Some rank-and-file will place most of their energies instead in attempting to get reelected, thus operating as free-riders on their more dedicated colleagues.

It is difficult to encourage all rank-and-file members to engage more rigorously in legislation, but it may be possible to reward a small subset of the rank-and-file who are already contributing to improve the quality of key legislation. With clear rewards, still more rank-and-file members might invest resources into understanding and engaging in these important legislative deliberations.

Partisanship already creates some rewards for investing in scrutinizing bills – the opposing party will gain some political benefits to halting, slowing, or weakening its opponent's bill. Within a party, however, there appear to be fewer incentives for rank-and-file to engage vigorously in deliberating over a bill that party leaders favor. And yet at some level, the greatest potential for improving legislation may ultimately lie within the party's own rank-and-file.

One means of shoring up audience incentives is the establishment of an official "deliberative credit," or similar reward, for individual members who play a meaningful role in the deliberations underlying a bill. Members making particularly valuable contributions would receive a "call-out" in the bill itself (listed under the names of the sponsors). This call-out distinguishes these more dedicated legislators from other rank-and-file who remain relatively unengaged. Legislators who are remiss in participating in legislative processes would thus have resumes with few credits; active, hardworking legislators would enjoy multiple credits that showcase their legislative commitment. Moreover, because a member's name will appear on the bill as a vigorous participant (although not as a co-sponsor), he or she will presumably take more responsibility for ensuring the quality of the legislation.

Providing this attribution for individual, hardworking members could be left to the discretion of the speaker, although to prevent cronyism, the speaker should be required to provide evidence of significant contributions. It may even be helpful to create an appeal process when a member believes that his contribution should have been acknowledged as a "valued deliberator," but he wasn't given that credit. The more rigorously this reward is administered, the more valued it will become as a signal of legislative good-citizenship. It may even facilitate, rather than detract from, a member's reelection efforts.

Grants or "free" expert staff, available on request as mentioned, could also be provided to members to do this deliberative work. Thus, dedicated members could leverage congressional resources to get assistance and yet earn credit at the same time.

Of course, not all rank-and-file members will respond to these incentives, and it is possible that few will. The overarching idea, however, is to provide still more resources and rewards that shift the rank-and-file members' energies toward engaging in legislative deliberations. Those who do this work should be rewarded publicly; those who ride on their coattails should face some stigma by comparison.

C *Creating Greater Accountability for the Amendment Process*

One final proposal endeavors to create more accountability for the amendment process. There are at least two distinct features of the existing amendment process that could be improved.

The first reform simply seeks to ensure that the audience understands – even in the most technical sense – how the amendment fits into the preexisting legislation. In many areas of Congress, rather than provide a red-line version of the legislation that places the proposed amendments in context, the bare amendments are itemized in the proposed bill. See Figure 7.7. Readers must locate the original legislation and

```
 6 SEC.    4.    CHEMICAL    ASSESSMENT    FRAMEWORK;
 7               PRIORITIZATION SCREENING; TESTING.
 8        (a) IN GENERAL.—Section 4 (15 U.S.C. 2603) is
 9 amended—
10            (1) in the heading, by striking "TESTING OF
11        CHEMICAL  SUBSTANCES  AND  MIXTURES"  and
12        inserting  "CHEMICAL  ASSESSMENT  FRAME-
13        WORK;  PRIORITIZATION  SCREENING;  TEST-
14        ING".
15            (2) by redesignating subsection (e) as sub-
16        section (l);
17            (3) in subsection (l) (as so redesignated)—
18                (A) by striking "rule" each place it ap-
19            pears and inserting "rule, testing consent
20            agreement, or order";
21                (B) by striking "under subsection (a)"
22            each place it appears and inserting "under this
23            subsection"; and
24                (C) in paragraph (1)(B), by striking "rule-
25            making"; and
```

FIGURE 7.7 Excerpt from S.1009, The Chemical Safety Improvement Act, 113th Cong. (Nov. 2013)

create their own red-line or similar mark-up to understand the text that is being changed. The sponsors do not provide this information.

The reform here is simple. Rather than allow these "cut-and-bite amendments," Congress should require the "amendments-in-context" style of presenting draft legislation.[192] This method "adds a visible indication of what has changed using strike and insert notation," essentially like a red-lined document in Microsoft Word. Accordingly, the sponsor would provide a red-line that shows how the amendment fits with the earlier law, thus lowering the audience's processing costs almost instantly.

The second reform focuses not on lowering the unnecessarily inflated processing costs to the audience, but on encouraging those proposing an amendment to an existing bill to take responsibility for their changes. If an amendment impairs the coherence or comprehensibility of a bill in significant ways, the member introducing that amendment should be identified easily. Accordingly, authorship of each amendment to a bill should be tracked, just as sponsorship for the bill itself.

This attribution for successful amendments to bills is not currently recorded in a user-friendly way. In theory, one can identify a particular amending member's hand in a final law by piecing together the congressional history of the bill and individual amendments. In practice, however, this is difficult and laborious work.

Our second reform would thus provide some enhanced accountability for members amending bills by providing one version of the final law in a track-changed, annotated form. This form would identify – by name – each of the members amending the bill and their contributions. If the amendments were also changed, then the elaborate track change would note that as well.

There have already been proposals for this kind of change to the existing amendment system within Congress.[193] For example, a 2016 bill (that did not make it out of the committee) proposed: "In the operation of the Congress.gov website, the Librarian of Congress shall ensure that each version of a bill or resolution which is made available for viewing on the website is presented in a manner which permits the viewer to follow and track online, within the same document, any changes made from previous versions of the bill or resolution."[194] Obviously, there are inevitable details that remain to be worked out; still, this more specific reform should increase accountability for amending activities, particularly when it positions a bill to be more, rather than less, incomprehensible.

VI CONCLUSION

Thankfully, incomprehensibility seems to afflict only a small subset of the laws that are passed. For this subset of laws, however, comprehension asymmetries and speaker incentives appear to explain in part why these laws are so difficult to understand. Moreover, our findings show that existing legislative rules and procedures sometimes exacerbate, rather than counteract, incomprehensible lawmaking.

In particular, our study of speaker incentives spotlights a number of troubling legal processes and procedures. These findings suggest that however reform is accomplished, legislative practices should be adjusted so that they provide sponsors and powerful party leaders with greater incentives for cooperative communication with rank-and-file members.

PART III

Reform

8

A Blueprint for Reform

Fallingwater, the famous Frank Lloyd Wright home that straddles a river, is a masterpiece of modern architecture. Millions of visitors come to admire it each year. But Fallingwater's future was once in jeopardy. Decades of water continuously pounding against its foundation was taking its toll. "Fallingwater is falling down," reporters joked.

In response, those dedicated to the preservation of Fallingwater took immediate action and hired engineers, architects, and other specialists to diagnose the problem and suggest a solution. The structure of Fallingwater, these experts concluded, was simply not strong enough to stand up to the elements. Piece by piece, engineers took the house apart and rebuilt the foundation with stronger materials. The reconstruction cost five times more than the original building, but few doubted that it was worth it.

In hindsight, the wear and tear caused by a rushing river pounding the foundation seems easy to anticipate. Wright in fact did account for some of this stress in his design. But the extent of the problem far outstripped the predictions. As the owner's son observed, the magnitude of the river's force on "Fallingwater w[as] not foreseen; neither were those (from side to side) in early skyscrapers, yet these are now accepted as normal."[1]

Today, the architecture of a number of important legal programs faces an analogous moment of truth, as a torrent of unprocessed information continues to flood into a number of vital legal programs. While a hundred years ago, when information was comparatively scarce, the volume and velocity of unprocessed information did not impose risks to the stability of our institutions, now this torrent emerges as a central consideration in legal design. One of the critical elements to the structural stability of a legal program is effective communication between parties. Yet in a number of institutional settings, legal architects have ignored this seemingly obvious goal. They underestimate the ways that speakers may fail to communicate in reasonably comprehensible ways. And equally problematic, they underestimate the challenges that some target audiences face in attempting to understand the abstruse, voluminous information that is handed over to them.

Indeed, rather than curbing the inclination of actors to submit unprocessed information, some programs actually encourage this excessive information.

Like the engineer called in to investigate Fallingwater, we have looked at the foundation underlying various legal programs to assess their viability for the conditions in which they operate. And, like Fallingwater, from this investigation we have isolated multiple legal programs that fail a basic structural test.

The current legal architecture is unstable because it encourages a much greater torrent of information than is necessary to resolve social problems. Both the volume and intensity of this deluge comes, in part, from the way we have designed the rules. Speakers who otherwise are fully capable of communicating clearly are relieved of responsibility for doing so and sometimes even perversely encouraged to become incomprehensible. Our investigation thus spotlights an important way that this instability in our legal architecture is different from the design challenges facing Fallingwater. To be stable, Frank Lloyd Wright's building must merely withstand the exogenous force of water that inevitably comes from constructing a home in the middle of a swiftly moving river. In the legal programs we have surveyed, the problem runs deeper and the deluge is partly self-inflicted.

Since the basic architecture of a number of important legal programs is inadequate, legal reform is imperative. This chapter begins the necessary conversation about the repairs that must be made. First, we briefly refresh the findings in the prior chapters to gain a more systemic, bird's-eye view of the nature of existing design problems. We then extract more general principles for reform based on the individual proposals offered in all six of the chapters in Part II. The reform discussion in this final chapter offers a kind of meta-analysis of how we might think about broader institutional reform going forward. This is particularly important since there are reasons to believe that the design problems are not limited to the six legal programs surveyed in Part II.[2] Finally, in the last section we attempt to spark a preliminary conversation about whether, in addition to improving the design of individual legal programs, the overarching methods for designing legal programs need to be changed as well.

I FINDINGS

Our basic argument is a simple one: Meaningful communication is essential to the effective functioning of a number of legal programs and should be factored into the legal design of these programs. If the imperative of ensuring cooperative communication is not accounted for – for example, if participants are bewildered and overwhelmed because speakers are perversely encouraged to inundate them with details without being held responsible for ensuring the comprehensibility of those details – then a central feature of institutional design is unstable and the legal program is at risk of collapse.

The resultant social costs from these mis-designed systems are substantial. Consumers are regularly "phished" and "phooled" in markets where firms compete – not over quality or price – but over exploitive tactics that take advantage of the consumers' limitations.[3] Financial entities find ways to turn a profit by creating ever more complex and risky structures that, as we saw in 2008, can sometimes fail precisely because they escape scrutiny from regulators and market investors.[4] Inventors of weak inventions face better odds of obtaining a patent when they play information games with the patent examiners, including drafting convoluted applications that tax the examiners' limited time and energy; the inventors then use the undeserved claim to block other inventors from that creative space in ways that undermine rather than advance innovation.[5] Chemical manufacturers produce and sell tens of thousands of chemicals that they have never analyzed for long-term safety (according to public records), while impeding agencies from doing these same assessments by swamping them with input of dubious value. The market for chemicals thus does not include competition over the long-term safety of chemicals, despite laws that promised the public these protections.[6] Agencies and legislators both learn that the legal system is sometimes kindest to their work when their public rules and laws are incomprehensible. Critics drop away as a result of the excessive processing costs, while lawmakers and regulators gain credit for at least taking some action, even though nobody may really understand what that action is. The accountability of government institutions suffers, leading to what one commenter considers a "crisis" of legitimacy.[7]

At a general level, the imperative of rigorous communication as a necessary ingredient for institutional design is unassailable. Markets and governmental processes function well only when there is rigorous and diverse engagement between speakers and their audiences. In these programs, a meaningful conversation between two parties is generally the end game. Civil society fundamentally rests on an effort to facilitate and protect this vibrant exchange.

But a closer look at a number of legal programs reveals that, in endeavoring to lay the groundwork for the sharing of *all* information, we have stopped short of pinning down the central objective of communication itself. Information needs to be shared. But it also needs to be understandable.

Our redesign tracks, in broad strokes, the renovation of Fallingwater. Fallingwater lacked adequate support against the river, and so later engineers carefully designed ways to shore up the structure to withstand the force of the water. Similarly, legal architects must now put in place strong requirements to ensure cooperative communication between speakers and their audiences, despite the roaring torrent of information flowing through the system. We must keep in mind that our legal systems are designed by humans to advance social goals. The tsunami of unprocessed information that undermines the effective functioning of these programs is a problem of design. It results from how we have chosen to structure our legal programs and is not outside our control.

Until speakers are required to communicate meaningfully with their target audience, halfhearted gestures to bolster audience understanding are likely to fail. Speakers will remain incomprehensible until their incentives are changed.

We have grounded this common-sense claim with evidence from wide-ranging legal programs that purport to improve the efficiency and effectiveness of both markets and democratic processes. Despite obvious and dramatic differences between these programs, the aggregate evidence spotlights the recurring neglect of cooperative communication in legal design. Before moving on to more specific reforms, we briefly refresh this evidence.

Consumer Law (Chapter 4). Prominent economists and legal analysts observe significant pockets of market failure in some complex consumer markets. Rather than making informed choices, consumers in markets as wide-ranging as credit cards, mortgages, insurance, mobile phone, drugs, and even food find themselves misled by sellers. In these settings, sellers who devise the most manipulative sales tactics often enjoy a competitive edge. And, on the audience side, the most vulnerable consumers (those with the fewest resources and most limited expertise for processing information) tend to be the most affected by this market failure.

In Chapter 4, we recounted the law's contribution to these dysfunctional consumer markets. Under existing law, sellers must divulge all information relevant to the transaction to the audience, but there are often few corresponding legal requirements that demand that this information also be comprehensible. For example, Bar-Gill observes that the mortgage agreements written for the poorest homeowners are even *more* difficult to understand than those written for middle class groups.[8] The resulting contracts leave plenty of room for sellers to exploit their audience's limitations to gain market advantages. In the words of top economists, firms will compete in "phishing for fools."[9]

Financial Regulation (Chapter 5A). A number of scholars document how financial products are sometimes too complex for even the CEOs of the firms offering these products to understand. Yet the prospect of short-term profits leads these firms to continue to market the products nonetheless. Indeed, this underlying ignorance may explain, in part, the turmoil we have experienced in complex financial markets over the last few decades.

Legal regulation endeavors to force financial entities to disclose various details of their transactions to others, but it stops short of requiring regulated entities to actually master the key information about their operations and financial risks themselves. Regulated parties instead must simply comply with prescriptive disclosure requirements. What is even worse, these legal requirements tend to tolerate or even encourage information dumping by financial entities to ensure that key facts are not withheld. As a result, some firms rationally over-comply, submitting all potentially relevant information just to be safe, without adequately processing the information or its implications themselves. Other strategic actors go even farther and exploit the mis-design of this legal program by structuring needlessly complex disclosures or transactions to obscure possible long-term risks that might compromise high-payoff, short-term ventures.

Patent Allocation (Chapter 5B). The patent process awards a "large number" of undeserving patents.[10] While the social consequences of these invalid patents are less dramatic than some of the other problems discussed in this book, they are by no means unimportant. When an undeserving patent is issued, it impedes innovation, not only because other inventors avoid the inventive space for fear of preemption, but also because some first-to-discover inventors zealously guard their patent claim through expensive infringement litigation.[11]

Legal scholars converge on the same conclusion – a poorly designed legal process is to blame for undeserving patents. And what is one of the most serious problems with this legal design? Applicants for patents (speakers) are allowed to shift the processing costs needed to understand their inventions to underfunded patent examiners (audience). Since the patent process allows appeals *only* for patent rejections, and not wrongful patent approvals, the examiners' incentives are clear. Examiners that approve applications are less vulnerable to legal challenge and may even be rewarded by management for their expeditious reviews. Because processing costs are legally the examiner's responsibility, moreover, inventors can increase the likelihood that applications will be approved by obfuscating basic features of their inventions.

Chemical Protection (Chapter 5C). Despite more than 40 years of regulation, the chemical market is characterized by poorly understood chemicals that have unknown long-term effects on health and the environment. The resulting ignorance regarding chemical safety makes it effectively impossible for agencies to set minimal safety standards, encourage innovation in safer products, or foster a competitive chemical market.

Since manufacturers develop these chemical products, they have superior capabilities – relative to agencies and intermediaries – to evaluate the long-term risks of their chemicals. They are also well positioned as a financial matter to do this assessment work. Yet, despite the manufacturers' advantages in processing the long-term risks of chemical products, the legal system places this burden on regulators. In the current regulatory system, manufacturers are, with only a few exceptions, absolved of responsibility for assessing the long-term safety of their chemical products. Their responsibilities end once they share their raw, unprocessed data with regulators or, in rare cases, conduct several additional toxicity tests at the behest of agency officials. Some manufacturers may even exploit this backwards regulatory design and inundate regulators with superfluous or unreliable technical information in the hope of throwing them off the trail.

Administrative Process (Chapter 6). The lack of administrative legitimacy, particularly with respect to agency accountability, is a source of continuing concern across party lines. There is strong evidence of excessive industry influence in regulatory decisions, despite the crafting of legal processes that are intentionally designed to tie agency accountability to public participation. Critics point out the hyperlexis of a regulatory state that produces more numerous and convoluted rules than can be understood.[12] And scholars observe the public's cynicism regarding both the competence and legitimacy of many federal agencies today. As Richard Fallon observes, "administrative agencies are widely believed to face a serious, even alarming, sociological legitimacy deficit."[3]

However, rather than insist that agency proposals be communicated comprehensibly to affected groups, administrative law generally ignores this critical requirement. And, what's worse, the incentives for comprehensiveness, documentation, record-creating, and the like tend to discourage both agencies and stakeholders from investing in meaningful communications. For example, on the stakeholder side, the law encourages affected groups to submit information that will "create a record" and "preserve arguments for appeal," but there are no limits on this information nor requirements that the information be capable of being reasonably processed by the agency. The agency faces similar, perverse incentives with respect to cooperative communication. The agency must promulgate proposals for comment, but the law does not require these proposals to be reasonably comprehensible to affected parties. Indeed, the agency appreciates that comprehensible rules tend to generate *more* work, litigation, and political interference. These two groups – stakeholders and agencies – instead take turns loading more and more information into the process. As a result, some rules become increasingly unwieldy, making the underlying choices so unintelligible that smart, democratic decisions are compromised or not made at all.

Legislation (Chapter 7). A similar fate surrounds some pockets of legislative decision-making. Congress can and sometimes does pass legislation that few, if any, members understand. The purpose, implications, and even goals of a bill may be effectively inscrutable and the bill itself fundamentally incoherent.

The design of legislative processes allows the passage of incomprehensible legislation in settings where Congress is pressured to "do something," and yet there is little chance of agreement on what that "something" is. A number of procedural rules allow and sometimes tacitly encourage powerful bill-drafters to create enormous, convoluted bills that they can ram through Congress when the conditions are right.

The resulting incomprehensible laws undermine both the integrity and the effectiveness of our lawmaking system. Incomprehensible laws can obscure the need for effective legislative action, allowing problems to fester. Moreover, difficulties in interpreting incoherent laws can result in substantial delay or even halt their implementation as agency decisions are challenged in perpetual reverse-and-remand feedback loops. Judicial review becomes unpredictable in settings where bill-drafters themselves lacked not only discernable "intent" for the legislation, but may have had contradicting purposes and messages.

Our conclusion is that through all of this, comprehension asymmetries weave, like a single unifying thread. Each of these unstable legal programs aggravate existing comprehension asymmetries by placing incentives on privileged speakers to shift high processing costs to their disadvantaged audience, rather than to take responsibility for cooperative communication.

II LESSONS FOR A REFORMED BLUEPRINT

If it is true that there is a systematic neglect of meaningful communication in a number of important legal programs, what do we do? In this section we extract from our case studies several overarching, general lessons to guide reform. After locking down several basic objectives for redesign, we can then move on to the more tentative exercise of suggesting repairs to specific parts of the system.

Our findings offer the following overarching lesson for future reform: In the design of a legal system, the speaker must have strong net incentives (benefits must outweigh costs) to communicate key messages to the target audience in a comprehensible way.

If the speakers benefit from an audience that is kept in the dark, and these same speakers are spared responsibility for being comprehensible, then the communicative terrain is unlikely to correct on its own. Comprehension asymmetries seldom, if ever, are resolved merely by attempts to shore up a highly disadvantaged audience's processing capacity. A motivated speaker will continue to be incomprehensible as long as there are benefits to this behavior. A motivated speaker will also stay one step ahead of audience efforts to increase its processing capabilities, as long as doing so serves the speaker's self-interest.

As noted in Chapter 3, this problematic structure is not universal across all legal programs. In some settings, such as appellate arguments, the audiences (judges) are just as capable of processing complex information as the speakers (advocates), and thus the speakers' communicative incentives are not crucial to the effectiveness of the process. In other settings – for example, lawyers' arguments before a jury – speakers are highly motivated to communicate their case clearly and succinctly. The speakers' success in these programs depends on connecting with their audience. And, in still others, speakers and audiences are well-matched, making the shifting of excess processing costs to the audience potentially inefficient but not necessarily detrimental to the integrity of the legal process. Comprehension asymmetries are simply not an important factor in the structure of these legal programs.

But in some settings (what we called the "problem quadrant" in Chapter 3), the speakers' net incentives for cooperative communication are missing and audiences are less equipped to process information than their speakers. It is here that comprehension asymmetries become important. In this quadrant, legal programs must be carefully designed to encourage meaningful communication from speaker to audience.

From this more general lesson, several more discrete lessons also emerge for reform:

Lesson #1: Information processing can be costly. Therefore, when there are few rewards for communicating comprehensibly in the market or law, speakers in a variety of legally regulated settings will tend to shift process-ing costs to their audience. As long as the adverse consequences of incomprehensibility fall mainly on the audience, speakers will naturally seek to shift these costs. Remember our inventors who apply for patents discussed in Chapter 5B? It is difficult to articulate the precise specifica-tions and value of an invention in relation to prior discoveries. Because the law effectively relieves inventors from doing this work and assumes the best about the public value of their invention, inventors will tend to shift responsibility for developing clear descriptions of the public value of their discoveries to patent examiners.

Lesson #2: Some speakers may actively exploit their audiences' information-processing limitations to advance their own self-interest. In some settings, a speaker will not only save expenses by skimping on cooperative com-munication but will benefit from keeping the audience in the dark. In these cases, the audience's processing load might not only be unjusti-fiably high, but the speaker might deliberately inflate the audience's processing costs. For example, crafty lenders can slip legally mandated disclosures into the middle of a stack of convoluted forms they require a consumer to sign, as part of an effort to overwhelm and confuse the consumer. For these lenders, incomprehensibility provides a means to manipulate an audience without violating transparency or "full disclos-ure" requirements.

In cases where speakers are not motivated to communicate with the audience in a meaningful way, comprehension asymmetries will not go away on their own. And if speakers actually profit from shifting process-ing costs to its audience, the equilibrium will tend toward greater and greater speaker–audience asymmetries.

Lesson #3: Comprehension asymmetries vary in different legal settings, and legal reform must take this variation into account. Despite some overarch-ing principles for reform, it is also important to account for the variation between legal programs with respect to comprehension asymmetries. This variation will affect how reforms should be structured. At least three different types of comprehension asymmetries emerge from the case studies, each of which requires a slightly different set of corrective reforms.

Simple Comprehension Asymmetries. In some settings – and complex transactions in the consumer market are a paradigmatic case – speakers understand the key risks but are reluctant to share this information with their audience. These speakers typically enjoy substantial resource, expertise, and stake differentials that provide them with advantages relative to their audience in processing information. As discussed in Chapter 4, to reverse speakers' resistance to cooperative communication, speakers must be required to prove that their communications are comprehensible to the target audience.

Complex Comprehension Asymmetries. In highly complex settings, there is a risk that the speakers themselves lack incentives to master the information needed to understand reality, much less make it comprehensible to others. Operating in ignorance – for example, of the long-term fragility of financial transactions or the long-term risks of chemical products – may be more cost-effective for a speaker than spending time trying to understand this reality. As discussed in Chapters 5A, 5B, and 5C, to head off this set of challenges, legal reformers must encourage speakers to master all relevant information themselves, before communicating it. Then the speakers must be required (again) to ensure that the key messages are communicated to the target audience in an accurate and reasonably comprehensible way.

Comprehension Asymmetries in Government Processes. Ensuring greater comprehensibility of messages is not costless; and yet, in the two scenarios just listed, incomprehensibility benefits only speaker, with resultant high costs to the audience. By shifting processing costs to their audiences, speakers save communication expenses and can even manipulate audiences to advance the speakers' self-interested ends. Reform must thus force these speakers to internalize their processing costs – to assess and communicate significant risks as a condition to doing business.

In governmental settings, however, requiring public officials to invest in greater comprehensibility may divert scarce resources and attention from other public goals – such as rigorous expert analysis or expedient decisions. Because of these opportunity costs, the ultimate determination of whether comprehensibility should become a priority should be left to the governmental decision-maker. As discussed in Chapters 6 and 7, reform should provide the speaker with heightened incentives for comprehensibility but should not elevate comprehensibility above other, equally important public decision-making objectives.

III SPECIFIC REFORMS

With these general principles under our belt, we now turn to crafting more specific blueprints for reform. Piecing together the program-specific reforms presented at the close of each of the chapters in Part II, we take a step back and outline several meta-reforms. These meta-reforms extract the essential elements from the program-specific reforms so that they can be applied to a broader array of legal programs. If, for example, we discover that portions of tax law or pharmaceutical regulation also suffer from these same types of comprehension asymmetries, how might we begin to conceive of potential reform? This section offers a preliminary set of guidelines to make progress in answering this question.

As the individual chapters in Part II reveal, not all failing legal programs share the same types of pathologies. The three categories of troubled legal programs just discussed need to be treated separately for purposes of reform. We thus offer three separate blueprints for reform that are tailored to the unique features of these different types of legal programs.

A *Simple Comprehension Asymmetries*

The easiest legal programs to reform, at least in the abstract, are those in which the speaker has processed the information but faces few benefits to ensuring the audience can understand key information. In this case, the speaker will be inclined to cut corners and simply shift all costs of processing the message to the audience (usually the public at large). The speaker may even deliberately confuse the audience. Incomprehensibility in this context then becomes a tool the speaker uses for manipulating and deceiving the audience to achieve an outcome that serves the speaker's interests.

To address this incentives problem, the law must require the speaker to bear the burden of ensuring meaningful communication at the outset. Contrary to current law, which expects the audience to root out incomprehensibility, under the reforms proposed here, it is the speaker's responsibility to establish that his communications are comprehensible.

The most straightforward means to this end is to require speakers – as a condition to operating in the market – to establish that their communications are comprehensible to reasonable or median members of the target audience. Until speakers can establish that their communication – say a contract – is comprehensible, they cannot conduct their activity.

This take-no-prisoners approach to incomprehensibility can be instituted at either of two different points in a transaction. In an ex ante – before the communication – approach, the speaker bears the burden of proving that his communication was designed to be comprehensible before selling a product or operating in the market.[14] This legal intervention generally takes the form of a regulatory requirement.

An ex post or after-the-fact approach would institute the intervention after the transaction, typically through litigation. A plaintiff, for example, would be entitled to a claim of incomprehensibility by alleging in good faith that a communication central to the transaction was confusing to a reasonable or median audience member and that there was no public record of the speaker doing his due diligence to ensure the comprehensibility of the message. The speaker would be required to rebut this allegation with evidence of his reasonable effort to ensure the communication was comprehensible, including by testing it on consumers and refining it based on the resulting feedback. If speakers fail to rebut the allegation of incomprehensibility, the audience-victim would ideally collect sufficient damages and penalties to reverse the speaker's incentives in the future.[15]

To ensure adequate private enforcement, added sanctions may be needed, such as punitive fines. Bounties may also be useful to encourage victimized audiences to hold speakers accountable. Public enforcement of this ex post approach, for example by the FTC and CFPD, will also likely be important to supplement private enforcement.

B Complex Comprehension Asymmetries

Requiring speakers to be comprehensible does little good if the speakers themselves are not inclined to make sense of relevant information. In some complex settings, however, ignorance really is bliss. Do inventors want to learn that their invention is not unique? Or is it better to file an application and hope that the examiner doesn't notice the faulty claims to originality? Does a chemical manufacturer really want to learn about the adverse effects of its chemical on hormone systems? What if it can be reasonably sure that others will not make the causal connection? The manufacturer's incentives are all the stronger since partial information could trigger a rash of tort litigation that would be difficult to curtail.

In some complex settings, speakers are not naturally inclined to understand all the relevant information, much less communicate it to others. And yet, compared to the target audience, the speaker is vastly better situated to do this work.

When the speaker is poised to opt for ignorance, simply requiring that speakers be comprehensible falls well short of the mark. The remedial tools for this set of complex comprehension asymmetries must place incentives on speakers not only for comprehensible messages but for gaining an understanding of the complex reality as well. The needed reform thus targets two separate incentives: first, speakers must be convinced to invest in understanding the nature of the risks of their activities; and second, speakers must be motivated to explain those risks to his target audience. Each of these alternatives is discussed in turn.

1 Incentives for Comprehending Reality

With regard to the first, more difficult goal – ensuring that the speaker processes and makes sense of the key information – Henry Hu's pioneering work provides the most promising approach to reversing speaker incentives.[16] Hu proposes that speakers should be required to provide a more diverse information portfolio to regulators and intermediaries, perhaps as a prerequisite to operating in the market. These multiple information tools analyze reality in different ways and through different frames of reference. Without multiple representations of reality prescribed in advance, the actor can locate the most favorable snapshot of reality and deprive the audience of a richer understanding of the assumptions and limitations of that favored perspective.

Hu offers a number of specific suggestions for how to diversify the information portfolio in financial regulation to force speakers to analyze financial arrangements more rigorously. One type of new mandated information, for example, would require financial actors to run several computational models designed by government regulators to assess the stability of financial arrangements. A related informational requirement would allow the actor to develop his own models and analysis, but these models would be benchmarked using standardized data to allow for cross-comparisons between competitor firms. Hu also proposes that firms must supply various types of "pure information" to allow the audience to check their representations.

We also added a proposal that would require the speaker to summarize the gist of this more diverse information portfolio. The speaker would thus provide an accessible synopsis of the most significant risks and related information that its target audience would be interested in learning. A final addendum would require a procedural pedigree for all information and representations – explaining how the data was collected, how the analysis was run, the extent of rigorous peer review and scrutiny, and the independence of the analysts conducting the project.

There are other permutations of ensuring a diverse information portfolio that could be designed and required. The key is to identify multiple, rigorous ways that the speaker *must* explain the reality of his activities and risks to the audience. The hope is that these overlapping, relatively rigid representation requirements begin to constrain speaker discretion at the foundational stage of information collection and analysis.

Consider, as an illustration, how this proposal might apply to reform chemical regulation. Rather than shift all costs of understanding the long-term risks of a chemical to the regulators, the chemical manufacturer would be required to provide several basic assessments of the existing scientific information pertaining to a chemical's risks as a condition to doing business. First, the manufacturer would be required to conduct multiple risk assessments using agency-constructed computational models. Second, the manufacturer could voluntarily create its own models to assess long-term chemical risks. But these models would need to be fully described and benchmarked using agency-prepared, standardized data. Finally, the manufacturer would be required to provide a crisp narrative summary explaining what is known about the long-term risks of the chemical as compared to competitor products. In all cases, the manufacturer would be required to document how the assessments were prepared, ideally by employing highly qualified, independent scientists and peer reviewers. These assessments would be mandatory; either chemical manufacturers would provide them prior to selling their chemicals, or manufacturers could be held legally responsible after the fact in private and public enforcement when the assessments have not been prepared adequately. Either way, the penalties for violating the assessment requirements would be designed to alter manufacturer behavior in favor of cooperative communication.

2 Incentives for Comprehensible Representations of Reality

Speakers would then be held responsible for cooperatively communicating this information. Default rules would assign all costs of audience confusion on the speaker. Unclear passages or terms should be interpreted against the speaker's interest. Doing so will help to ensure that speakers are motivated to communicate in a cooperative way.

Box 8.1 Key Elements of Legal Reform of Comprehension Asymmetries

Key Elements of Private Law Reform for Simple Comprehension Asymmetries

1 Institute a "comprehension rule" that places the burden on the actor to establish cooperative communication.
2 Deploy both public and private enforcement of the requirement.

Key Elements of Regulatory Reform for Complex Comprehension Asymmetries

1 Require actor/speaker to provide multiple robust representations of its activities, including a narrative summary.
2 Information representations must also include a pedigree explaining how the information was collected and synthesized.
3 Communicate information cooperatively to the target audience.
4 Enlist public and private enforcement of requirements.

Key Elements of Reforms for Comprehension Asymmetries in Public Deliberations

1 Create rewards for comprehensible communications.
2 Create mechanisms for documenting the rigor and balance of deliberations.
3 Make adjustments to current doctrines and rules that tolerate or encourage incomprehensibility (e.g., tracking amendments; exhaustion of remedies doctrine).

For example, if a patent applicant drafts a claim that is ambiguous with respect to the nature or scope of the invention, the narrowest, most limited interpretation of the invention will become the default interpretation used by examiners and courts. Additionally, if the examiner cannot make sense of a patent application, the application can be rejected on this basis alone.[17] In making this rejection, the examiner would not carry any burden of establishing the incomprehensibility beyond a good faith allegation; the burden of justifying the comprehensibility of the patent claim would fall on the inventor. The inventor's description, in other words, will be viewed skeptically and all doubts resolved against it.

To add further incentives, any extra administrative costs incurred by the examiner to process an application would be borne by the applicant. Iterative or protracted discussions to resolve questions about incomprehensible applications for a patent would require compensation of the examiner. Processing costs could no longer be shifted to the Patent and Trademark Office without consequence.

3 Private Sector Reinforcements

In some legal settings, incentives for comprehensibility could also be reinforced by tapping into market competition. Once success in the market turns on rigorous self-assessments, firms will compete to win. There are at least two ways to tap into competitive pressures in this regard.

First, government prizes could be meted out for speakers that demonstrate that their transaction, invention, or chemical (or other contribution) involves comparatively lower risks than competitors (assuming this showing is both rigorous and comprehensible). Legal processes that offer a prize – like a license – to the best product or patent application (submitted among competitors) – could trigger a race to the top in terms of rigorous and comprehensible applications.

Second, to leverage market pressures, the regulator could actively solicit comments on each application from a speaker's competitors. Competitors could then use this opportunity to point out various details or risks that remain unassessed or under-specified in the application (e.g., are incomprehensible). With the burden of assessing and communicating risks now placed on speakers, this added scrutiny may convince agencies to reject or restrict the scope of an application. As long as competitors are motivated to invest energy into this comment period (which seems likely in some settings), the resulting adversarial pressure should increase a speaker's incentives for cooperative communication in anticipation of the added critical oversight.

Implementing this proposal in chemical regulation, for example, would require the agency to provide a regulatory license for a product only after a manufacturer can establish that its chemical is reasonably safe for a particular use, as compared to all competitors. Competitors would be invited to comment on this submission and would be highly motivated to look critically at it. Indeed, from a competitive standpoint, competitors might be worried that if the manufacturer's application prevails, it will produce adverse information about the relative safety or their own products.

Third, a variation of the competitive-based model could be applied in regulatory processes in which there is not a natural balance of adversaries. Prizes could be awarded for the most rigorous and constructive, but skeptical, comments on a patent claim or agency rule by members of the public or independent experts.

Finally, market intermediaries could also be established or subsidized to provide this kind of competition-based assessment. Karen Schulz, for example, discusses several intermediaries in the consumer market (Mint.com and Billshrink.com) that "process consumer financial data compiled from multiple savings, checking, and credit card accounts to inform consumer finance decisions, such as which cellular telephone package best suits their calling data at the most affordable price."[18] The extent to which these intermediaries can genuinely exert enough pressure to incentivize speakers to provide accurate and accessible messages will depend on their own processing capacity relative to the speakers, however.

C Comprehension Asymmetries in Public Deliberations

A different challenge arises in improving the incentives for comprehensible communications in public decision-making processes. While government decision-makers could benefit from stronger incentives for comprehensibility, there are also tradeoffs associated with elevating comprehensibility in public processes. For example, we saw in the legislative process in Chapter 7 that some of the incomprehensibility in bills or rules may result from last-minute, valuable compromises. Requiring comprehensibility could put a stop to these constructive adjustments. Moreover, some participants might abuse a comprehensibility requirement to strategically block progress in legislation and regulation.

With these dangers out in the open, we suggest some added nudges and related adjustments that may encourage agencies, congressmen, and even private participants to be more inclined toward cooperative communication in at least some deliberative settings. While we might not be able to construct a total reform by implementing these suggestions, we can at least begin tipping the needle back toward instituting greater incentives for comprehensibility.

1 Eliminate Legal Benefits to Incomprehensibility

At least in the administrative setting, the courts have unwittingly produced some direct rewards for agencies that draft incomprehensible rules and, similarly, for stakeholders who submit incomprehensibly detailed comments. Remember that under the exhaustion of remedies doctrine, if participants cannot make heads nor tails of an agency proposal and therefore do not file comments, the agency is off the hook, both in responding to comments and worrying about downstream litigation. Somewhat similarly, on the stakeholder side, if a commenter databombs the agency with formal comments in the hopes of slowing down or confusing the agency, the agency is nonetheless required to "consider" all of this input, regardless of whether the comments are reasonably coherent.

These doctrines should be adjusted to remove the benefits to speakers of being incomprehensible. A commenter who can establish that a rule was unreasonably difficult to process should not be barred from litigating it later. On the flip side, if an agency receives convoluted criticisms from a stakeholder (e.g., a 30-page comment with no summary, organization, reliable support for key points, etc.), then the agency should be able to argue that the stakeholder waived his opportunity to offer reasonably intelligible input.

Determining the point at which a rule or a set of comments reaches this "incomprehensibility" threshold will likely be slippery for the litigants and courts. To err on the side of under-enforcing this new requirement, it may be best to start with a high burden on the challenger – such as requiring proof that the rule or comment was "wholly inadequate" in communicating the key points for a reasonable target audience.

There do not appear to be parallel suggestions for Congress on this problematic aspect of legal design. The one possible avenue of congressional deliberation reform worth exploring more fully would be altering the permissive approach to legislative amendments, since this may be exploited by Rule-Benders eager to throw a wrench in a bill. While the Congressional Record details amendments and their authors, the public (and other congressmen) must invest considerable effort in determining which members are responsible for which portion of text in a final law. Thus, for all practical purposes, Rule-Benders could infuse a law with incomprehensible twists and turns, but leave few fingerprints. To counteract this opportunity, a tracking system could be devised to identify, in red-line and with annotations, each contribution made by various members to a final law throughout the amendment process.

2 Enhance the Benefits for Comprehensibility

In both administrative and legislative systems, the speakers (or drafters) of a subset of complicated rules and bills do not recoup their investments in making a proposal readily comprehensible to their target audience. The adjustments suggested here attempt to increase the benefits to speakers who are making the effort to engage in meaningful communication.

A REWARD AGENCIES FOR COMPREHENSIBILITY

If the thrust of much administrative scholarship is correct, agencies appear to be motivated to reduce the threat of unpredictable judicial challenges to final rules. Litigation drains agency resources from other endeavors. Even anticipating the risks of litigation can divert time and energy if the agency attempts to make its rules bulletproof in response.

Our proposed reform would calibrate the deference the agency receives in judicial review to the comprehensibility of its rules. The more comprehensible the agency's rulemaking – including the entire process of engaging stakeholders – the higher the judicial deference. A court need only be content that the agency has not committed a "clear error" when a rule satisfies this comprehensibility test. Active, effective deliberations signal a decision process that is working and does not require as much oversight from the courts.

Courts (and agencies), however, must be able to measure or document that a particular rule meets some floor of "comprehensibility" to earn this particular reward. While it is tempting to revert to a laundry list of prescriptive requirements, the key, as we have learned, is to place this overarching incentive in the speaker's lap. The agency (speaker) should be granted deference for comprehensible rules only when the agency can convince the court that the agency's decision process and reasons for a rule are understandable and accessible to the reasonable target audience. (We assume, at a minimum, that the audience has access to a lawyer able to dedicate 10 hours to representation on a rule.)

In litigation, this reform proposal would work as a type of affirmative defense. If the agency is sued, it could argue that it is entitled to greater deference because of the comprehensibility of its rule. The agency would then provide evidence to support the comprehensibility assertion, leaving it to the court to determine whether the agency should enjoy this particular judicially bestowed reward of greater discretion. If so, then all claims would be reviewed under a "clearly erroneous" standard.

B REWARD CONGRESSIONAL SPONSORS FOR COMPREHENSIBILITY

Judicial review operates as a type of day of reckoning for agencies that has no parallel in Congress. To create a benefit for comprehensible laws (and a stigma for convoluted laws) without creating a rigid requirement, we propose a "Day of Reckoning" (DOR) review in Congress. The idea of this DOR review, which would likely only be applied to a subset of legislation, is to solicit an independent, expert analysis of how the bill works and what it accomplishes (as drafted) and to identify any major questions that might arise in implementation, especially questions that could come from vague, ambiguous, or incomprehensible language.

The DOR review would be conducted by a congressional expert office, perhaps consisting of a subset of experienced staff from the General Accounting Office (CAO), who would conduct an abbreviated but intensive analysis of a bill. This office would need to be supremely bipartisan and deeply fearful of being labeled as biased by either party.

The expert reviewers would summarize, in their view, what the bill sets out to do, specify the problem it seeks to solve, and identify questions about its operation based on the text. To take full account of the sponsor, committee, and other members' efforts to engage seriously in the terms of the bill, the submission for the DOR review could include not only the bill itself but the significant summaries and other materials prepared to explain the bill to other members of Congress. To conduct this review, the expert office would also solicit help from top experts in the field, but the office staff would be ultimately responsible for collating reviews and compiling the ultimate analysis. The focus would be on only the most significant features of the bill; nitpicking would be explicitly outside the scope of the review.

The DOR review must occur quickly, however. A 45 day review, with a 30-day "cool down" (allowing for resulting debate and amendments in Congress), would provide some useful analysis without bogging down the legislative process significantly. The DOR review could occur at different points in time, but it might be much more cost-effective for this review to occur after a bill passes both houses (and before it enters conference committee, if this occurs). In essence, the DOR review offers a type of peer review function, providing one last hard review and giving Congress the needed time to correct any glaring defects or missteps, as well as putting the rest of the country on notice of significant problems in the legislation.

The primary benefits of the DOR proposal, therefore, are likely to arise from its deterrent effect. If the comprehensibility of a law becomes salient, then this feature will be taken more seriously earlier in the drafting and amendment process. Comprehensible laws, by contrast, may provide sponsors and other participants with political rewards.

C CREATE A "DELIBERATIVE RECORD" TO REWARD DELIBERATIONS IN AGEN-
CIES AND CONGRESS

A different kind of reward could arise from establishing a formal metric that documents the rigor of the regulatory and legislative deliberations themselves in what we call a "Deliberative Record." In general, richer and fuller deliberations from diverse parties improve the comprehensibility of an end product.

In substance, this Deliberative Record would capture the nature of the deliberations on a bill or rule. Who are the authors of the text? What types of educational materials and background documents were available to bring the target audiences up to speed on the purpose of the bill or rule? Were diverse experts and attentive groups involved in the legislative or agency deliberations, and if so, how engaged were they? How was the proposal changed, when, and by whom? Is there evidence that some affected parties were *not* engaged in the deliberations?

For example, in administrative law a Deliberative Record could require agencies to provide relevant deliberative information in a format that permits cross-comparisons between agencies and between rules. Agencies would also be required to narratively summarize the Deliberative Record to capture all important features of the deliberations, including those that might be overlooked by a formal template. Some coordinating institution – perhaps the White House Office of Information and Regulatory Affairs (OIRA) – could ensure that this deliberative record is compiled for all rules and that agencies provide this information in a readily digestible format.

In Congress, the deliberative records could be maintained, or at least audited, by the same kind of "neutral" congressional expert office that we proposed above to help with the DOR review. This office could establish the relevant parameters and means of validating information, as well as providing sponsors and committees with the opportunity to summarize the integrity of the bill's deliberations in their own words.

Ideally, if it functions as intended, the Deliberative Record would factor into the audience's assessment of the quality of a proposal. We have already suggested a way in which rigorous deliberations could inform judicial review. And in Congress, it is possible to imagine how partisans might compete over demonstrating their commitment to rigorous deliberation. Using the Deliberative Record, participants could point out stark contrasts between complicated bills that have been reviewed by many members and committees over a period of months versus "incomprehensible" bills that are complex, are available for review for an unreasonably short period of time, and provide members with little opportunity for meaningful analysis. Tracking the authorship of the bill also provides useful information to the target audience's understanding of the bill; a bill drafted by the tobacco lobby might be scrutinized more carefully than a bill drafted by an elected member of Congress.

There are dangers to this approach, of course. A Deliberative Record could be misunderstood or used in misleading ways against bills or rules that, in fact, reflect rigorous deliberation. To check these dangers, continuous oversight and adjustments of the proposal will be necessary. The overarching goal is to produce benefits for speakers who actually engage the full range of affected and interested parties when developing their proposals.

3 Provide Subsidies for Comprehensibility

As noted throughout the analysis, some incomprehensibility in agencies and Congress is the result of well-meaning corner-cutting. Cooperative communication of complicated issues takes resources and effort. If this effort is not required, then other priorities will take precedence. But if targeted resources *are* available for making communications more comprehensible (and we bracket where these resources might come from), at least some speakers and audiences might take advantage of this subsidy to improve the comprehensibility of their communications.

A RESOURCES FOR SPEAKERS

Rule-Followers might be eager to apply for grants that allow their communications to be more comprehensible. This type of grant could even be open-ended, available not simply for text-smoothing but for developing educational materials, outreach, and informative background analyses that document the nature of the problem or issues at stake and the proposal's role in addressing them.

If monies were dedicated to improving comprehensibility and some agencies and congressional staff took advantage of these resources, their leadership might create more pressure on those speakers who forgo the assistance. Incomprehensible laws will begin to stick out, and critics might wonder why sponsors and agencies did not make the added, subsidized effort at improving the comprehensibility of particularly convoluted projects.

Securing resources for this proposal is an obvious challenge. There will be constituencies – the existing well-endowed actors – who might actively oppose a project that finances this kind of work. But, in general, it seems sufficiently benign and nonpartisan that at least a pilot project instituted by Congress providing these types of grants might be feasible.

B RESOURCES FOR AUDIENCES

Target audiences with limited processing capacity could be subsidized in this same way. This kind of grant system for administrative process and congressional work may have more opposition (particularly in administrative process), but the idea is the same. Those target audiences with the most limitations in making sense of proposals and bills would be subsidized, so they can engage with speakers meaningfully and effectively. In agencies, this funding would go to the most thinly financed groups; in Congress, the funding would be available to rank-and-file members with fewer resources than party leaders.

In addition to a grant process, publicly funded public ombuds or watchdogs could be established to represent interests that are otherwise unrepresented in particularly complicated bills and rules. When the conditions are right – for example, the ombuds have ample resources and are not compromised by politics – ombuds can help provide more diverse perspectives and scrutiny to policy proposals.[19] In congressional deliberations, members of Congress who lack the resources to keep up but who might be adversely impacted by a legislative proposal would be able to deploy these public translators to help make sense of draft legislation, or even simply document that a bill is too convoluted to allow for rigorous deliberation in the first place.

As noted throughout, however, while the deployment of both ombuds and subsidies can help provide fortification against speaker incomprehensibility, these tools should not be regarded as a substitute for ensuring that speakers face strong incentives for cooperative communication. Every forward step the audience takes can be thwarted by speakers who develop new ways to increase the processing costs for their audiences. Thus, this reform may be effective only when comprehension asymmetries are relatively small and the speakers' incentives to exploit disadvantaged audiences are low.

IV INSTITUTIONAL PROCESSES WRIT LARGE

Thus far we have focused on ways that the substantive rules codified in regulation, contracts, and government procedures could be adjusted to take comprehension asymmetries into account. In this brief closing section we pause to consider whether there are also lessons to be learned from *how* the institutional process itself is structured. We explore the meta-design, in other words, of how we develop these rules and procedural requirements.

Recall that not *all* legal programs suffer from this inattention to processing costs in their basic design or structure. In Chapter 3, we discussed how common law areas such as tort tend to be more focused on ensuring that speakers communicate meaningfully with their audience. Excessive processing costs and accompanying comprehension asymmetries are one of the central challenges that these particular legal programs seek to address. From a comparative perspective, we have also noted in passing how comprehension asymmetries are sometimes better accounted for in the design of legal counterpoint programs abroad. The European Union's (EU's) administrative process rules, for example, are more attentive to creating incentives for rigorous communication among participants.[20] In those processes, the EU Commission (which is roughly equivalent to US agencies) is required to solicit diverse views from all affected parties and is expected to provide summaries and accessible descriptions. Limits are also placed on the number and extent of comments. The stakeholders' perverse incentives for inundating the EU Commission are comparatively lower as well since, among other things, there is no judicial review and thus no corresponding incentive to "create a record" for every conceivable complaint.[21]

What might explain these system-wide differences among legal programs? Why are some legal programs designed in ways that insist on meaningful communication, while others neglect this seemingly obvious objective? From a high altitude, one explanation might be the pressures placed on the legal architects themselves. In the tort system, judges devise common law rules that – first and foremost – comport with common sense and reasonable sensibilities. The wisdom of the rules is benchmarked against grounded, case-by-case tests, not only for the litigants and defendants bound by the common law, but also by the juries who apply them. Indeed, when the rules drift too far from common sense, we see juries actually adjusting or nullifying the legal rules in ways that sometimes lead judges to overhaul the legal requirements themselves.[22]

And, while it is beyond the scope of this book to delve into comparative law, it is worth taking note that some processes in the European Union – particularly the development of rules that bind member states – may be similarly sensitive to the need for rigorous communication and deliberation because of the very different situation that this centralized regulatory body occupies as compared to the United States.[23] In Europe, centralized government is limited by the willingness of the member states to accede to it. If the rules are incomprehensible to member states, then the member states are at some, albeit limited, risk of refusing to support the rule, particularly if it comes up for a vote.[24] EU rulemaking generally may be more accessible to participants, then, because the legitimacy and authority of the centralized Commission depends on assent from member states.

By contrast, the unstable programs we investigate in Chapters 4–8 usually (but not always) occur in political processes where powerful affected private groups play a prominent role in legal design.[25] The legal architect must please, or at least stay on the right side of, this influential constituency. For example, the significant role that regulated entities play in the legal design of financial regulation, patents, and chemical regulation is legendary.[26] These groups enjoy a distinct advantage over thinly financed and poorly organized groups because they have more resources to engage in the process and a greater financial stake in how the process works.[27] If comprehension asymmetries primarily benefit these rich, influential constituents (who typically overlap our advantaged speakers in many programs), then these constituents will not only be happy to sweep the problem under the rug but will actively oppose reform.

As long as the privileged constituents are the primary beneficiaries of these mis-designed systems, then, we would seem to face a political impasse. The legal architect understands that probing into this structural instability and tinkering with repair work will get him into trouble.

But that is where our more holistic investigation of the legal system pays off. If we, like the engineers at Fallingwater, can identify a specific foundational element that is unstable across numerous, different legal programs, then the remedial work becomes both more vital and more focused. A structural view of the legal system can help identify features that, once rectified, can correct system-wide instabilities.

Once this foundational weakness becomes apparent, we can no longer look the other way; comprehension asymmetries exist and they help explain why so many of these legal programs are incomprehensible to the audiences they intend to benefit. Reversing a speaker's incentives so that the speaker's success in the future depends on cooperative communication fortifies a legal program against a deluge of unprocessed information. Of course the details are challenging, the work is not easy, and once in place this structural repair will not fix everything that is wrong with these programs. But like any renovation, priorities are necessary. And the evidence suggests that this particular repair project may be capable of going a long way toward improving the integrity and function of a number of legal programs.

Once the diagnosis and choices are crystallized in this way, it also alters the collective action picture. Rather than an invisible, structural instability that savvy participants obscure from view, we have a visible and serious foundational problem that can be understood and appreciated without a great investment of effort. Lowering the processing costs to understand the problem brings in more and more affected audiences who can now rally behind the needed renovation work. It is not only vulnerable consumers who lose from this particular design flaw. Expert investors, agencies, powerful congressmen, and various competitors may join as protagonists to repair this structural deficiency across legal programs.

Mancur Olson's concept of collective action instructs us that when institutional problems are split in too fine-grained a way and are too difficult to understand, the ability to organize a vigorous group to offset a powerful and well-funded minority is unlikely or at least will be temporary.[28] The tyranny of small decisions – of attempting to tackle design problems one at a time and often without the benefit of a more systemic view – operates to further obscure the underlying problem. We certainly have seen those predictions play out in the rolling waves of disappointments in reform areas as diverse as disclosures, patents, regulation, and governmental processes over time.

If the more systemic problem of comprehension asymmetries is exposed, along with the damage it is doing throughout our legal system, then perhaps the battlefield can change. Identifying and reforming comprehension asymmetries – as a larger *cause célèbre* – reshuffles the players so that the otherwise dispersed have-nots share a specific blueprint for structural reform, while the haves are left scrambling to find commonalities that will allow them to oppose this newly united front. Indeed, precisely because legal programs are siloed and fragmented, the powerful stakeholders that have successfully fended off meaningful reform will now be at a disadvantage.

A new, system-wide institutional blueprint may thus offer hope on several levels. Stronger foundational elements can be isolated and devised to place primary responsibility on actors for communicating the risks of their activities. Government processes can be renovated so that vigorous deliberation becomes a benefit for regulators and legislators, rather than a liability, in the making of important public decisions. And like-minded reformers, currently dispersed throughout fragmented legal systems, can be unified to rally around a common blueprint and ensure that institutional renovations are faithful to the key specifications.

V CONCLUSION

Like Fallingwater, our legal system is a treasure that requires constant tending and care. And like Fallingwater, the structure is no longer able to weather the environment it was built to withstand.

It is time to revisit the largely unexamined assumptions that support the architecture of important legal programs. By developing a conceptual probe using comprehension asymmetries, we illuminate one important structural element that appears unstable.

The ending to this story is positioned to be a happy one. The evidence recounted here suggests that perhaps we *can* comprehend some incomprehensibility after all. And once it is comprehended, we can begin the important work of eradicating it.

Notes

1 INTRODUCTION

1 Herbert A. Simon, *Administrative Behavior: A Study of Decisionmaking Processes in Administrative Organizations* 242–43 (Free Press, 4th ed., 1997).
2 As each chapter in Part II reveals, albeit in different ways, that the issues are sufficiently complex that various nonprofit and market intermediaries are generally unable to close the gap in communication between speaker and audience.
3 Omri Ben-Shahar and Carl E. Schneider, *More Than You Wanted to Know: The Failure of Mandated Disclosure* chs. 1–3 (Princeton, 2014).
4 See Chapter 4.
5 See, e.g., George Akerlof and Robert Shiller, *Phishing for Phools: The Economics of Manipulation and Deception* xii (Princeton, 2015).
6 Lauren E. Willis, "The Consumer Financial Protection Bureau and the Quest for Consumer Comprehension," 3 *Russell Sage Foundation Journal of the Social Sciences* 74, 74 (2017).
7 See Chapter 5C.
8 See Chapter 5B.
9 See Chapter 7.

2 MODELING COMPREHENSION ASYMMETRIES

1 Simon, 1997, at 208.
2 Louis Phlips, *The Economics of Imperfect Information* 3 (Cambridge, 1988); Joseph E. Stiglitz, "The Contributions of the Economics of Information to Twentieth Century Economics," 115 *Quarterly Journal of Economics* 1441, 1461 (2000).
3 Ian Ayres and Robert Gertner, "Filling Gaps in Incomplete Contracts: An Economic Theory of Default Rules," 99 *Yale Law Journal* 87, 91 (1989).
4 Simon, 1997, 242–43.
5 Mark Andrejevic, *Infoglut: How Too Much Information Is Changing the Way We Think and Know* 10 (Routledge, 2013).

6 Id. at 10.
7 Louis D. Brandeis, "What Publicity Can Do," *Harper's Weekly*, Dec. 20, 1913, reprinted in Louis D. Brandeis, *Other People's Money and How the Bankers Use It* 92, 92 (1914); see also Andrejevic, 2013, at 10.
8 This history is described in detail in James Gleick, *The Information: A History, A Theory, A Flood* (Pantheon, 2011).
9 Nate Silver, *The Signal and the Noise: The Art and Science of Prediction* 3 (Penguin, 2012).
10 David Shenk, *Data Smog: Surviving the Information Glut* 38 (Harper, 1997).
11 Eli Noam, "Visions of the Media Age: Taming the Information Monster," paper presented at the Third Annual Colloquium, Alfred Herrhausen Society for International Dialogue, June 16/17, 1995, Frankfurt am Main, Germany, 3, available at www.citi.columbia.edu/ elinoam/articles/infomonster.htm.
12 Andrejevic, 2013, at 10.
13 Id. at 7.
14 Simon, 1997, at 242–43.
15 Id. at 242.
16 Cf. Neil K. Komesar, *Imperfect Alternatives: Choosing Institutions in Law, Economics, and Public Policy* 8 (Chicago 1994).
17 Simon, 1997, at 226; Noam, 1995, at 1.
18 Noam, 1995, at 2.
19 For a general discussion of these effects geared toward a popular audience, see Shenk, 1997, ch. 2.
20 See Siegfried Streufert and Michael J. Driver, "Conceptual Structure, Information Load, and Perceptual Complexity," 3 *Psychonomic Science* 249, 250 (1965).
21 See, e.g., Robert S. Owen, "Clarifying the Simple Assumption of the Information Load Paradigm," in 19 *Advances in Consumer Research Volume* 770, 773 (John F. Sherry, Jr. and Brian Sternthal, eds. 1992).
22 Shenk, 1997, at 101.
23 Andrejevic, 2013, at 8.
24 Id. at 15.
25 Mark Casson, *Information and Organization: A New Perspective on the Theory of the Firm* (Oxford, 1997). In his book, however, information is treated as a straightforward asset, id. at 4, 274, 277, 296. The possibility that there is a concavity to information in some settings is not explored, even though Casson does discuss processing costs and notes their role in contributing to transaction costs more generally. Id. at 279, 294.
26 Henry E. Smith, "The Language of Property: Form, Context, and Audience," 55 *Stanford Law Review* 1105, 1140 (2003).
27 Cynthia R. Farina and Mary J. Newhart, *Rulemaking 2.0: Understanding and Getting Better Public Participation* 19 (IBM Center for The Business of Government 201) (describing how to address this problem, but noting that solutions entail resources).
28 Chapters 3–7 provide numerous doctrines and legal policies that do exactly this.
29 Shenk, 1997, at 28 (citing Jaako Lehtonen), 30, and 31.
30 As the analyses in Part II reveal, we identify a "reasonable or median" target audience member rather than suggest that communications must be comprehensible to every single member of the audience.

31 See, e.g., Jim Suchan, "The Effect of High-Impact Writing on Decision Making within a Public Sector Bureaucracy," 35 *The Journal of Business Communication* 299 (1998).

32 Komesar, 1994, at 7.

33 We bracket the infinite regress that can sometimes happen when even an attentive and resourceful member of the audience attempts to extract a message, but the processing costs are unexpectedly high so that this audience member is never able to decode the message. This does not change our analysis, but it does reveal that in some cases incomprehensibility may be so pervasive that it effectively blocks all communications.

34 The "additional costs that must be incurred because of the strategic behavior of privately informed economic agents can be viewed as one category of . . . transaction costs." Jean-Jacques Laffont and David Martimort, *The Theory of Incentives: The Principal Agent Model* 3 (Princeton, 2002); see also Casson, 1997, at 33–34, 279 (placing processing costs in the larger bucket of transaction costs).

35 Stiglitz argues that imperfections in information are not subsumed within the larger set of transaction costs but is a separate and distinct category of problems. Stiglitz, 2002, at 472.

36 This concept of communication as having a "speaker" and "audience" draws from basic fundamental schemas in both information and communication theory. See conceptual frameworks in James L. Kinneavy, *A Theory of Discourse: The Aims of Discourse* 19 (Norton, 1971); Claude E. Shannon and Warren Weaver, *The Mathematical Theory of Communication* 7 (Illinois, 1971).

37 Simon, 1997, at 227.

38 Ines Macho-Stadler and J. David Perez-Castrillo, *An Introduction to the Economics of Information: Incentives and Contracts* 187 (Oxford, 2001).

39 Bruce M. Owen and Ronald Braeutigam, *The Regulation Game: Strategic Use of the Administrative Process* 4 (Ballinger, 1978).

40 These processing limitations are considered in behavioral economics. See Amos Tversky and Daniel Kahneman, "Judgment under Uncertainty: Heuristics and Biases," 185 *Science* 1124 (1974) and the enormous literature that path-breaking seven-page article spawned, including from Tversky and Kahneman themselves. Features such as cognitive dissonance explored in behaviorial economics, for example, generally fall well outside the types of processing limitations we discuss in this book.

41 See, e.g., the introductory example in Chapter 4.

42 See, e.g., Margaret Jane Radin, *Boilerplate: The Fine Print, Vanishing Rights, and the Rule of Law* 148–50, 219–20 (Princeton, 2012) (critically discussing some of these proposals).

43 E.g., Dodd-Frank Act, § 1032(b)(2)(A); Cynthia R. Farina, Mary J. Newhart, and Cheryl Blake, "The Problem with Words: Plain Language and Public Participation in Rulemaking," 83 *The George Washington Law Review* 1358, 1373–79 (2015).

44 See Ben-Shahar and Schneider, 2014, at 185–90 (critically discussing these proposals).

45 See generally id.

46 Archon Fung, Mary Graham, and David Weil, *Full Disclosure: The Perils and Promise of Transparency* (Cambridge, 2007).

47 See, e.g., Shenk, 1997, at 62.

48 As he explains, the technological optimist "anticipates a world in which control over the tremendous amount of information generated by interactive devices is concentrated in the

hands of the few who use it to sort, manage, and manipulate." Andrejevic, 2013, at 17; see also id. at 54–55.

49 Smith, 2003, at 1149–50 (describing significant variations in audiences with respect to processing information).

50 Yet, even if technology can solve these challenges, the first step (the one we spotlight throughout this book) remains the same; the privileged speaker must have strong, unfailing incentives to successfully communicate key messages to the target audience and to ensure that all technological tools deliver on that promise.

51 For example, Mark Andrejevic's insightful analysis of the problem ends with elaborate reforms that seek to supplement audience capabilities. Andrejevic, 2013.

52 Kinneavy, 1971, at 1–2 (focusing on the aim of the communication); Shannon and Weaver, 1998, at 31 (attempting to optimize the process of data transfer to minimize errors in transmission); see also James Herrick, *The History and Theory of Rhetoric: An Introduction* 8–9, 200–04 (Allyn and Bacon, 3rd ed., 2004).

53 E.g., Maureen E. Brady, "The Forgotten History of Metes and Bounds," 128 *Yale Law Journal* 872 (2019) (documenting cooperative communication among experts in property law).

3 THE IMPLICATIONS OF COMPREHENSION ASYMMETRIES FOR THE LAW

1 See, e.g., Oliver Wendell Holmes, *The Path of the Law* 6 (Little, Brown, 2012) (reprinted from 10 *Harv. L. Rev.* 457–58 (1896)).

2 Arthur Leff, *Swindling and Selling* 12, 110, 117–18, 130 (Free Press, 1976).

3 In his book on lying and deception, Thomas Carson identifies these two intentional techniques as separate but overlapping within philosophical studies. Deception involves manipulating the audience's understanding but without making a false statement. "Keeping the audience in the dark" is a separate technique that is distinguished from deception since it does not move the audience to a predetermined misunderstanding; indeed, the actor himself may be in the dark and simply prefer that this ignorance be perpetuated across the board. Thomas L. Carson, *Lying and Deception: Theory and Practice* 46 (Oxford, 2010). But in some cases, keeping someone in the dark converges with deception and even lying. Id. at 54.

4 Deception need not involve making a false statement . . . or making statements of any sort." Carson, 2010, at 4.

5 Edward J. Balleisen, *Fraud: An American History from Barnum to Madoff* 38 (Princeton, 2017).

6 Id. at 22.

7 Karen Bradshaw Schulz calls this larger tactic of "inundat[ing] consumers with junk information to hide bad facts" "information flooding." Karen Bradshaw Schulz, "Information Flooding," 48 *Indiana Law Review* 755, 758 (2015).

8 Urban Dictionary, available at www.urbandictionary.com/define.php?term=databomb.

9 Id.

10 Owen and Braeutigam, 1978, at 4.

11 Id. at 4.

12 William Lutz, *Double-Speak* 5 (Harpercollins, 1989).

13 www.nps.gov/features/eise/jrranger/quotes2.htm.

14 Willis, 2017, at 79.

15 Deceptions often involve the use of weasel words or the exploitation of ambiguities. Deceptions in the abstract then involve some types of manipulations of processing costs. For examples, see Lutz, 1989, at 16–17, 46–48, 82; Brooks Jackson and Kathleen Hall Jamieson, *Unspun: Finding Facts in a World of Disinformation* ch. 3 (Random House, 2007); Gerald E. Jones, *How to Lie with Charts* (BookSurge 2d ed., 2006). For simplicity, however, we focus on those tricks that can be traced more directly to the inflation of some processing costs and the lowering of others.

16 Bar-Gill, 2012.

17 A search of the term in the patent literature on August 2, 2017 yielded 44 articles that use the term.

18 Dan L. Burk and Mark A. Lemley, "Fence Posts or Sign Posts? Rethinking Patent Claim Construction," 157 *University of Pennsylvania Law Review* 1743, 1788, n.169, 1798 (2009).

19 Id. at 1788, n.169.

20 "Lawyers are paid to interpret language – whether in statutes, contracts, or patent claims – in ways that serve their clients' interests. And they are, as a general matter, quite good at it." Id. at 1752.

21 This arises under the inequitable conduct doctrine created by the courts in the 1920s and is described in Chapter 5B.

22 Brief for the ABA as Amicus Curiae in *Therasense, Inc.* at 11 (June 17, 2010).

23 Even within a legal program, the identification of the target audience can vary depending on the overarching policy goals. The target audience in technical rulemakings discussed in Chapter 6, for example, necessarily includes the full range of affected stakeholders, including those representing the diffuse public affected by a rule. Yet choices must still be made in specifying the outer limits of expertise and resources of these participants. Similarly, in consumer markets, the target audience is typically considered to be the median consumer participating in a given market, but again, as discussed in Chapter 4, this formulation is not the only option. It is inevitable that judgments must be made in specifying the target audience for the purposes of analysis.

24 Note again that we assume away parallel information asymmetries in these cases.

25 See, e.g., Bernard Lo and Marilyn Jane Field, *Conflict of Interest in Medical Research, Education, and Practice.* (National Acad. Press, 2009) (documenting conflicts resulting from financial incentives from pharmaceutical companies); Jason Shafrin, "Operating on Commission: Analyzing How Physician Financial Incentives Affect Surgery Rates," 19 *Health Economics* 562 (2010) (correlating certain fee arrangements for physicians with significantly greater rates of surgery).

26 Smith, 2003, at 1113.

27 Id. at 1163.

28 Virtually every article providing tips for appellate brief writing emphasizes the need for being as succinct as possible and for sharpening arguments to make them accessible to the busy judicial panel. See, e.g., Shari M. Oberg and Daniel C. Brubaker, "Supreme Review," 87 *Michigan Business Journal* 30, 33 (2008); Michael J. Traft, "Special Consider-ations in Appellate Briefs," in 1 *Appellate Practice in Massachusetts* ch. 14, § 14.1 (2008).

29 See, e.g., Fed. R. Evid. § 403; see also Dale A. Nance, "The Best Evidence Principle," 73 *Iowa Law Review* 227, 229 (1988).

30 Mauricio J. Alvarez et al., "'It will be your duty. . . .:' The Psychology of Criminal Jury Instructions," 1 *Advances in Psychology and Law* 119, 125 (M.K. Miller & B.H. Bornstein eds.) (Springer, 2016); id. at 120, 121, 150; Dennis J. Devine, *Jury Decision Making: The State of the Science* 55–56, 57 (NYU, 2012).

31 A relatively sizable and diverse literature reinforces how the incentives are currently tipped in the exactly wrong direction. For example, public-choice theories predict that political officials benefit by designing overcomplicated regulatory systems that benefit certain well-financed constituencies. Peter H. Schuck, "Legal Complexity: Some Causes, Conse-quences, and Cures," 42 *Duke Law Journal* 1, 26 (1992) (observing that the beneficiaries of complex laws include "groups that are relatively well equipped to cope with complexity and for whom complexity can create a competitive advantage").

32 Within the legal community, the implications of processing costs for the functioning of various legal programs has received little attention. One author – Jean Nicolas Druey at the University of St. Gallen, Switzerland – has written about the need for legal anticipa-tion and accommodation of processing costs, but his work has not been translated into English. See, e.g., Jean Nicolas Druey, "Information als Gegenstand des Rechts," Schulthess: Zurich and Nomos: Baden-Baden, 1995; Jean Nicolas Druey, "Daten-Schmutz" – Rechtliche Ansatzpunkte zum Problem der ber-Information, in: Festschrift zum 65. Geburtstag von Mario M. Pedrazzini. – Bern, 1990, at 379–96. English summaries of his work suggest that Druey currently focuses primarily on ways the legal system might better accommodate the audience's resultant overload; his work appears to dedicate less attention to the speakers' incentives. See, e.g., "Information Overload," avail-able at https://blogs.harvard.edu/ugasser/2004/10/08/information-overload-a-legal-perspective-part-i/; ugasser, https://blogs.harvard.edu/ugasser/2004/10/18/information-overload-a-legal-per spective-part-ii/.

33 While this approach may sound expensive, there are many proposals for doing just that in the chapters ahead and these proposals by and large seem relatively feasible.

34 See discussion of the financial market in Chapter 5A.

35 Henry C. Hu, "Disclosure Universes and Modes of Information: Banks, Innovation, and Divergent Regulatory Quests," 31 *Yale Journal on Regulation* 565, 634 (2014).

4 COMPREHENSION ASYMMETRIES AND CONSUMER PROTECTION LAW

1 Adapted after John M. Broder, "Warning: Maybe Too Much of a Good Thing," *New York Times*, Mar. 5, 1997.

2 Emery v. American General Finance, Inc., 71 F.3d 1343, 1346 (5th Cir. 1995).

3 Id. at 1346.

4 Id. at 1347. Posner continued "[N]othing has been 'set aside' for her. '[W]e could write your check on the spot. Or, call ahead and I'll have the check waiting for you.' Yes – along with a few forms to sign whereby for only $1,200 payable over three years at an even higher monthly rate than your present loan . . . you can have a meager $200 now." Id.

5 Id. at 1347.

6 "We were not reassured when at the oral argument American General Finance's lawyer was unable to tell us what it cost Verna Emery to obtain the $200 through a refinancing compared to what it would have cost her had the company simply made her a separate loan for that amount." Id.

7 Id. at 1351.

8 Id. at 1346.

9 William C. Whitford, "The Functions of Disclosure Regulation in Consumer Transactions," 1973 *Wisconsin Law Review* 400, 439 (1973) (underscoring the role of persuasion in effective consumer disclosures).

10 See generally Bar-Gill, 2012.

11 Akerlof and Shiller, 2015, at xii.

12 See Chapter 2.

13 Omri Ben-Shahar, "The Myth of the 'Opportunity to Read' in Contract Law," 5 *European Review of Contract Law* 1, 15 (2009).

14 Willis, 2017, at 76 (citations omitted).

15 Bar-Gill, 2012, at 21.

16 Tess Wilkinson-Ryan, "The Perverse Consequences of Disclosing Standard Terms," 103 *Cornell Law Review* 117, 121 (2017). Specifically, "subjects believed policies embedded in contract were more likely to be legally enforceable, judged those policies as more fair, and imagined that they would be less likely to challenge those policies in court." As a result, they felt more bound and less likely to challenge the provisions, regardless of their actual fairness or unfair burdens. Id. at 164.

17 See generally Bar-Gill, 2012.

18 Akerlof and Shiller, 2015, at 168–69.

19 Alan Schwartz and Louis Wilde call these persistent consumers, who sometimes protect nonsearchers from overreaching firms, to be "pecuniary externalities." Alan Schwartz and Louis L. Wilde, "Intervening in Markets on the Basis of Imperfect Information: A Legal and Economic Analysis," 127 *University of Pennsylvania Law Review* 630, 638 (1979); cf. Omri Ben-Shahar and Lior Jacob Strahilevitz, "Interpreting Contracts via Surveys and Experiments," 92 *New York University Law Review* 1753, 1803 (2017) (observing from empirical work on consumer understanding that "if heterogeneity of the response data in our sample shows us anything, it is that individual judgments and responses can be quirky and mystifying, but majoritarian judgments about contractual meaning are comprehensible").

20 Shmuel I. Becher, "Asymmetric Information in Consumer Contracts: The Challenge That Is Yet to Be Met," 45 *American Business Law Journal* 723, 736–53 (2008) (critically discussing this argument).

21 Oren Bar-Gill and Elizabeth Warren, "Making Credit Safer," 157 *University of Pennsylvania Law Review* 1, 7–56 (2008).

22 Yannis Bakos, Florencia Marotta-Wurgler, and David R. Trossen, "Does Anyone Read the Fine Print? Consumer Attention to Standard-Form Contracts," 43 *Journal of Legal Studies* 1 (2014).

23 Schwartz and Wilde, 1979, at 663, 665.

24 Bar-Gill and Warren, 2008, at 22.

25 See, e.g., Bar-Gill, 2012, at 18–19, 36 n.37 (citing multiple sources); but see Ben-Shahar and Schneider, 2014, at 185–90 (touting the benefits of intermediaries).

26 Anna Gelpern, Mitu Gulati, and Jeromin Zettelmeyer, "If Boilerplate Could Talk: The Work of Standard Terms in Sovereign Bond Contracts," *Law and Social Inquiry* (forthcoming 2018).

27 See generally Akerlof and Shiller, 2015; Bar-Gill, 2012.

28 Bar-Gill and Warren, 2008, at 23–25.

29 Akerlof and Shiller, 2015, at 164–65.

30 1 E. Allan Farnsworth, *Farnsworth on Contracts* § 3.6 (Aspen, 2004).

31 See generally Tal Kastner, "The Persisting Ideal of Agreement in an Age of Boilerplate," 35 *Law & Social Inquiry* 793, 820 (2010) (discussing a "new turn" in contract law with contracts of adhesion, boilerplate, and a departure from the old way of thinking about contracts focused on informed agreements, but concluding that some "ideal of agreement" remains even in this new world of contract as a foundational principle).

32 Farnsworth, 2004, at 440.

33 All-Ways Logistics, Inc. v. USA Truck, Inc. 583 F.3d 511, 516 (8th Cir. 2009); Bristol West Ins. Co. v. Wawanesa Mut. Ins. Co., 570 F.3d 461, 464 (1st Cir. 2009); Sargent Constr. Co. Inc. v. State Auto Ins. Co., 23 F.3d 1324 (8th Cir. 1994).

34 E.g., Michelle Boardman, "Contra Profernentem: The Allure of Ambiguous Boilerplate," 104 *Michigan Law Review* 1105, 1111 (2006).

35 U.C.C. § 2–314.

36 W. David Slawson, "Contractual Discretionary Power: A Law to Prevent Deceptive Contracting by Standard Form," 2006 *Michigan State Law Review* 863.

37 Ben-Shahar and Strahilevitz, 2017, at 1756–57.

38 Id. at 1757; see also id. at 1792–93.

39 See, e.g., Anderson v. Southeastern Fidelity Ins. Co., 307 S.E.2d 499, 500 (Ga. 1983) ("an ambiguity in a document should be construed against its draftsman. 'If the construction is doubtful, that which goes most strongly against the party executing the instrument or undertaking the obligation is generally to be preferred'"); North Gate Corp. v. National FoodStores, Inc., 140 N.W.2d 744, 747 (Wis. 1966) ("Where various meanings can be given a term, the term is to be strictly construed against the draftsman of the contract.").

40 WashU Law, at https://onlinelaw.wustl.edu/blog/why-are-u-s-contracts-so-long/.

41 "[O]ne of the most time-honored maxims of contract interpretation is that a contract is to be interpreted *contra proferentem* (against its author or profferer)." E. Allan Farnsworth, *Contracts: Cases and Materials* 437 (Aspen, 8th Edition 2013). The rule is also underscored in the Restatement (Second) of Contracts, which says "in choosing among the reasonable meanings of a promise or agreement or a term thereof, that meaning is generally preferred which operates against the party who supplies the words or from whom a writing otherwise proceeds." *Restatement 2d of Contracts,* § 206.

42 DiTommaso v. Union Cent. Life Ins. Co., No. 89–6323, 1991 WL 124601, at *2, 1991 USDist. LEXIS 9159, at *5 (E.D.Pa. July 3, 1991).

43 Eric Posner, "The Parol Evidence Rule, the Plain Meaning Rule, and the Principles of Contractual Interpretation," 146 *University of Pennsylvania Law Review* 533, 535 (1998).

44 Id. at 534–35.

45 Farnsworth, 2004, at § 7.12, 314–15.

46 Karen Eggleston, Eric A. Posner, Richard Zeckhauser, "The Design and Interpretation of Contracts: Why Complexity Matters," 95 *Northwestern University Law Review* 91, 104 (2000).

47 Id. at 105–06.

48 See, e.g., *Restatement (Third) of Torts: Products Liability* § 2(c).

49 W. Kip Viscusi, "Individual Rationality, Hazard Warnings, and the Foundations of Tort Law," 48 *Rutgers Law Review* 625, 628 (1996).

50 Eggleston, Posner, and Zeckhauser, 2000, at 94–97.

51 Claire A. Hill and Christopher King, "How Do German Contracts Do as Much with Fewer Words," 79 *Chicago-Kent Law Review* 889, 894 (2004).

52 https://hbr.org/2018/01/the-case-for-plain-language-contracts.

53 Slawson notes how these doctrines, however, are unevenly applied across the courts. Slawson, 2006, at 863.

54 See, e.g., Margaret Jane Radin, *Boilerplate: The Fine Print, Vanishing Rights, and the Rule of Law* 84 (Princeton, 2012) (citing Lieb). The test is that "[t]he objectively reasonable expectations of the applicants and intended beneficiaries regarding the terms of insurance contracts will be honored even though painstaking study of the policy provisions would have negated those expectations." Robert E. Keeton, "Insurance Law Rights at Variance with Policy Provisions: Part Two," 83 *Harvard Law Review* 961, 967 (1970).

55 Ben-Shahar, 2009, at 8.

56 Ben-Shahar and Schneider, 2014, at 164 (citing Kohn v. American Metal Climax, Inc., 322 F Supp 1331, 1362–63 (E.D. Pa. 1971)).

57 See, e.g., Thomas J. Rueter and Joshua H. Roberts, "Pennsylvania's Reasonable Expectations Doctrine: The Third Circuit's Perspective," 45 *Villanova Law Review* 581, 587–89 (2000).

58 Eggleston, Posner, and Zeckhauser, 2000, at 97.

59 Charles N. Knapp, "Is There a 'Duty to Read'?" in *Revisiting the Contracts Scholarship of Stewart Macaulay* 316 (Jean Braucher et al. eds.) (Hart, 2013).

60 Radin, 2012, at 40–41.

61 Bibbs v. House of Blues New Orleans Restaurant Corp., 2011 WL 183873, *5 (ED La.) cited in Knapp, 2013.

62 Restatement Section 211 attempts to counteract the ability of drafters to obscure key terms through boilerplate by striking down those terms that lie beyond the range of consumers' reasonable expectations. Wayne R. Barnes, "Towards a Fairer Model of Consumer Assent to Standard Form Contracts: In Defense of Restatement Subsection 221(3)," 82 *Washington Law Review* 227 (2007); see also Ian Ayres and Alan Schwarz, "The No-Reading Problem in Consumer Contract Law," 66 *Stanford Law Review* 545, 560 (2014). But few courts have applied Section 211 because of the challenges of identifying what constitutes a "reasonable" expectation. As discussed later, however, considerable progress is being made toward this same goal by providing constructive incentives for contract drafters.

63 See, e.g., Williams v. First Gov't Mortgage & Investors Corp., 225 F.3d 738, 744–51 (D.C. Cir. 2000); Nevarez v. O'Connor Chevrolet, Inc., 303 F. Supp.2d 927, 936 (N.D. Ill. 2004); Turner v. Beneficial Corp., 242 F.3d 1023 (11th Cir. 2001), Rugumbwa v. Betten Motor Sales, 200 F.R.D. 358, 364–65 (W.D. Mich. 2001).

64 Slawson, 2006, at 858–61.

65 See, e.g., Rodriguez v. Raymours Furniture Co., 93 A.3d 760, 767 (N.J. Superior Ct. App. Div. 2014).

66 Slawson, 2006, at 858–59.

67 E. Allan Farnsworth, "Developments in Contract Law during the 1980s: The Top Ten," 41 *Case Western Reserve Law Review* 203, 222 (1990).

68 Colleen McCollough, Note, "Unconscionability as a Coherent Legal Concept," 164 *University of Pennsylvania Law Review* 779, 786, 805–06 (2016).

69 Colleen McCollough argues that the unconscionability doctrine is evolving to a broader standard that requires that contracts be understandable. Id. at 807. In the future, she argues, speakers may understand that if they have "reason to believe that a reasonable person in the shoes of the offeree would not know the meaning of the terms in the contract," they cannot impose those terms as a legal matter. Id. at 815–16. Her set of cases cited as evidence of this gradual move are not that compelling, however. One case involved an arbitration clause at a car dealership that nobody apparently could understand, including the car dealers themselves. Basulto v. Hialeah Automotive, 141 So.3d 1145, 1152 (Fla. 2014). Another case rejected an unconscionability claim in part because the contract was considered "understandable," but the court does not indicate the converse – namely that if the contract had been difficult to understand, it would have been unconscionable. Indeed, the court indicates great reluctance to void a contract on these grounds. See, e.g., Energy Home, Div. of Sehi v. Peay, 406 S.W.3d 828, 836 (Ky. 2013).

70 Charles R. Calleros, "US Unconscionability and Article 1171 of the New French Civil Code: Achieving Balance in Statutory Regulation and Judicial Intervention," 45 *Georgia Journal of International & Comparative Law* 259, 277 (2017).

71 Hazel Glenn Beh, "Curing the Infirmities of the Unconscionability Doctrine," 66 *Hastings Law Journal* 1011, 1021 (2015).

72 Russell A. Hakes, "Focusing on the Realities of the Contracting Process – An Essential Step to Achieve Justice in Contract Enforcement," 12 *Delaware Law Review* 95, 110 (2011).

73 There are parallel doctrines to unconscionability in subfields that go further and provide stronger incentives for speakers to ensure the significant messages are spotlighted for consumers, but they, too, fall short of considering the contract from the perspective of the audience. In contract law, for example, any limits on a warranty must be "conspicuous." U.C.C. § 2–316. However, and again like unconscionability assessments, the courts still generally evaluate compliance by studying the contract text itself. Even the "reasonable expectation" doctrine in insurance law, which seeks to protect consumers from incomprehensible contracts, is generally deemed satisfied as long as the "unexpected" terms are clearly written and ideally highlighted. Slawson, 2006, at 863. Judges who enforce the doctrine tend to limit its application to contracts in which the written terms are vague or inconspicuous. Id.

74 Id. at 860.

75 Alan Rau, "Everything You Really Need to Know about 'Separability' in Seventeen Simple Propositions," 14 *The American Review of International Arbitration* 182, 189 (2004) (citing "Note, Medical Malpractice Arbitration: A Patient's Perspective," 61 *Washington University Law Review* 123, 148 n.198 (1983)).

76 Bar-Gill, 2012, at 237.

77 Ben-Shahar and Schneider, 2014, at 24–25.

78 Id. at 25.

79 Radin, 2012; Lauren E. Willis, "Performance-Based Consumer Law," 82 *University of Chicago Law Review* 1309, 1389, and n.285 (2015).

80 Ben-Shahar and Schneider, 2014, at 83–84.
81 Id. at 84.
82 These authors suggest the possibility that boilerplate contracts can serve in some settings "as a cartel-facilitating tool, an anticompetitive signaling device, or a tool for creating the appearance of a fair contract, rather than to merely extract surplus from uninformed consumers." David Gilo and Ariel Porat, "The Hidden Roles of Boilerplate and Standard-form Contracts: Strategic Imposition of Transaction Costs, Segmentation of Consumers, and Anticompetitive Effects," 104 *Michigan Law Review* 983, 1030 (2006).
83 Id. at 1005–06.
84 Id. at 1007.
85 Id. at 1008.
86 For a detailed discussion of various adverse consumer consequences that flow from this fine print, see David Cay Johnston, *The Fine Print* (Portfolio, 2012).
87 Clever drafters can also craft the contracts so that the important "losses" to consumers are offset, in writing, by other benefits that are likely of less value but make the overall contract appear fair. So a dry cleaning company may disclaim liability for losses above a threshold amount but offer in boilerplate the option of purchasing low-cost insurance for these higher losses for a fee. When the contract is challenged, the drafter could claim that in its entirety the contract is both fair and efficient. Yet the reality is that consumers will remain unaware of these legally relevant benefits. Gilo and Porat, 2006, at 1015.
88 Bar-Gill, 2012, at 19–20.
89 Id. at 20.
90 Id. at 158.
91 Id. at 229.
92 Id. at 66 (citing an industry representative).
93 Id. at 53.
94 Id. at 94 (quoting David Evans and Richard Schmalensee).
95 Id. at 208 (quoting billshrink.com).
96 Id. at 227.
97 Id. at 52.
98 Lauren E. Willis, "Decisionmaking and the Limits of Disclosure: The Problem of Predatory Lending: Price," 65 *Maryland Law Review* 707, 807 (2006).
99 Bar-Gill and Warren, 2008, at 23–24 (describing these practices in detail).
100 Willis, 2017, at 80 (describing specific tactics and examples of this targeting over time).
101 Willis, 2006, at 770.
102 Id. at 786; see also Bar-Gill and Warren, 2008, at 22, 31 (discussing similar discriminatory practices).
103 For a detailed discussion of the enhanced complexity of mortgages in general and subprime in particular, see Bar-Gill, 2012, at 141–45 and 158–59.
104 Id. at 163–64.
105 Rodriguez v. Raymours Furniture Co., 93 A.3d 760, 766 (N.J. Super. Ct. App. Div. 2014).
106 Slawson, 2006, at 859–60.
107 McCollough, 2016, at 785 ("Besides criticizing unconscionability's vagueness, most scholarship ignores the doctrine, thereby failing to connect with the tools courts have to respond to such contracts").

108 Jeffrey C. Bright, "Unilateral Attorney's Fees Clauses: A Proposal to Shift to the Golden Rule," 61 *Drake Law Review* 85 (2012).

109 U.C.C. § 2–302.

110 See, e.g., Frank Luchak, "Consumer Contracts and Class Actions," Duane Morris. Available at www.duanemorris.com/articles/static/luchak_njlawyer_0411.pdf. See also AT&T Mobility v. Concepcion, 563 US 333, 365 (2011).

111 Consumer Financial Protection Bureau (CFPB), *Arbitration Study: Report to Congress 2015*, Section 1 pgs. 9–10 (Mar. 2015).

112 Id. at Section 5 at pgs. 6–7 ("If the parties settle their arbitration dispute, for example, only in very rare circumstances are the terms of settlement available. In fact, for most arbitration disputes reviewers cannot even determine the type of outcome reached.").

113 Id. at Section 1 at pgs. 9–10.

114 Epic Systems Corp. v. Lewis, 584 US 1612 (2018).

115 CFPB, 2015, at Section 2 at pgs. 8–9, 12–13, 16–17, 20–21.

116 Akerlof and Shiller, 2015, at 168-69.

117 See, e.g., Thomas McGarity and Wendy Wagner, *Bending Science: How Special Interests Corrupt Public Health Research* 121–23 (Harvard, 2008).

118 Dodd-Frank § 1023(a).

119 Martin Bishop, "Regulatory: Unfair, Deceptive, or Abusive Acts or Practices. Amorphous New Statutory Provisions Create Serious Compliance Risks," *Inside Counsel*, July 27, 2011. See, e.g., Dodd-Frank § 1053(b).

120 Dodd-Frank also requires the CFPB to dedicate resources to improving consumer literacy and providing counseling services. Dodd-Frank, § 1013(d).

121 Dodd-Frank Act, § 1032(b)(2)(A).

122 Ben-Shahar and Schneider, 2012, at 122.

123 5 U.S.C. §§ 1601 et seq.

124 The Real Estate Settlement Procedures Act, 12 U.S.C. §§ 2601 et seq., and the Home Ownership and Equity Protection Act, Pub. L. No. 103–325, 108 Stat. 2190 (1994).

125 Oren Bar-Gill and Ryan Bubb, "Credit Card Pricing: The CARD Act and Beyond," 97 *Cornell Law Review* 967, 989–1003 (2012).

126 Ben-Shahar and Schneider, 2012, at 122–24.

127 See Table 2.1 in Fung et al., 2007, at 21–23.

128 Ben-Shahar and Schneider, 2014, at 50–51 (describing legislative efforts that involved a series of unsuccessful disclosures as a result of the mortgage crisis).

129 See, e.g., id. at 59, 86–87.

130 Willis, 2017, at 74. Karen Schulz also discusses this problem with disclosures in her article on "Information Flooding." See, e.g., Schulz, 2015, at 775 (arguing that "the failure of mandatory disclosure is caused by corporations' ability to innovate around disclosure laws as soon as they are passed" and observing this is accomplished in part by "deliberately overwhelming consumer with too much information").

131 Kevin Haeberle and M. Todd Henderson, "Making a Market for Corporate Disclosure," 35 *Yale Journal on Regulation* 383, 387 (2018).

132 This discussion is drawn from Fung et al., 2007, at 72.

133 Daniel E. Ho, "Fudging the Nudge: Information Disclosure and Restaurant Grading," 122 *Yale Law Journal* 574, 595 (2012) (also noting the diversion of scarce government

resources to inspections and grading disputes, with no apparent improvement in public health and foodborne illness rates).

134 Mary Graham and Catherine Miller, "Disclosure of Toxic Releases in the United States," in *Industrial Transformation* (Theo de Bruijn and Vicki Norberg-Bohm eds.) (MIT, 2005); Lori Bennear, "Strategic Response to Regulatory Thresholds: Evidence from the Massachusetts Toxics Use Reduction Act" (2005), available at http://people .duke.edu/~lds5/papers/Strategic_Response_To_Regulatory_Thresholds.pdf.

135 David Dranove et al., "Is More Information Better? The Effects of 'Report Cards' on Health Care Providers," 111 *Journal of Political Economy* 555 (2003).

136 Lauren Willis exposes a veritable smorgasboard of ways that sellers can and regularly do bypass disclosures. Willis, 2017, at 1322. Fung et al. similarly chart a variety of tactics that regulated parties use to avoid communicating meaningfully with consumers, while still complying with disclosure requirements. Fung et al., 2007, at Table. 4.4 at pages 75–76 (see the second to the last column).

137 Willis, 2006, at 790 (quoting Jay Finkelman, an expert psychologist hired as an expert in financial litigation).

138 Schultz, 2015, at 777.

139 Id. (footnotes omitted).

140 Captain Crunch contains 12g sugar/serving; Kashi Go-Lean contains 13 g sugar/serving. The GMO claims also proved to be problematic. See, e.g., Nick Meyer, "A Box of Kashi Cereal Was Put under the Microscope. What They Found Is Even Worse Than Anyone Thought," AltHealth Works, Aug. 6, 2015, available at http://althealthworks.com/7226/a-box-of-this-healthy-cereal-was-put-under-the-microscope-what-they-found-is-even-worse-than-the-unhealthy-stuff/; see also Willis, 2015, at 1325–26 (also discussing this tactic in the food industry).

141 Id. at 1327.

142 Aaron Rutkoff, "Restaurant Makes Best out of 'B' Grade," *The Wall Street Journal* (Sept. 17, 2010).

143 Ho, 2012, at 631 (quoting comment on *New York Times* blog).

144 Bar-Gill, 2012, at 96–97 (citing literature on this point).

145 Willis, 2015, at 1328.

146 Id. at 1327.

147 Id.

148 Id. at 1327–28.

149 Elena Fagotto and Archon Fung, "Too Much Information," *Boston Review*, Aug. 17, 2015.

150 David A. Westbrook, "Corporation Law After Enron: The Possibility of a Capitalist Reimagination," 92 *Georgia Law Journal* 61, 88–90 (2003); John R. Kroger, "Enron, Fraud, and Securities Reform: An Enron Prosecutor's Perspective," 76 *University of Colorado Law Review* 57, 61–62 (2005).

151 The Sarbanes-Oxley Act of 2002, Pub L. 107–204, 116 Stat. 745.

152 Willis, 2015, at 1330; see also Ben-Shahar and Schneider, 2014, at 51.

153 Ho, 2012, at 586, n.70 (citing *The Wall St Journal*).

154 Id. at 595.

155 Id. at 624.

156 Willis, 2015, at 1315.
157 See generally Bryan M. Haynes, Anne Hampton Andrews, and C. Reade Jacob, Jr., "Compelled Commercial Speech: The Food and Drug Administration's Effort to Smoke Out the Tobacco Industry through Graphic Warning Labels," 68 *Food and Drug Law Journal* 329 (2013); see also Kellie Combs and Albert Cacozza, "Drug Promotion in the Post-*Caronia* World," *Food and Drug Law Institute, Update,* Mar./Apr. 2013, at 14.
158 See generally Haynes et al., 2013.
159 Robert Post and Amanda Shanor, "Adam Smith's First Amendment," 128 *Harvard Law Review Forum* 165, 170–72 (2015).
160 Virginia State Bd. of Pharmacy v. Virginia Citizens Consumer Council, Inc., 425 US 748, 757 (1976).
161 Id. at 771–72 ("The First Amendment, as we construe it today, does not prohibit the State from insuring that the stream of commercial information flows cleanly as well as freely").
162 Central Hudson Gas & Electric Corp. v. Public Service Commission, 447 US 557 (1980).
163 44 Liquormart, Inc. v. Rhode Island, 517 US 484, 511 (1996).
164 Post and Shanor, 2015, at 172.
165 Id. at 175.
166 Akerlof and Shiller, 2015.
167 Sorrell v. IMS Health Inc., 131 S. Ct. 2653 (2011).
168 Id. at 2671 (emphasis added). In *Sorrell,* the Supreme Court invalidated a Vermont law that sought to restrict the distribution of data regarding doctor's prescribing practices that could be used by pharmaceutical companies to target sales.
169 E.g., Akerlof and Shiller, 2015.
170 Fung et al., 2007, at 112, seem to reach similar conclusions, although their analysis is focused more on the ability of the audience to use disclosures and less on the incentives of the speakers. See id. at 173–75 (listing the conditions for success of transparency policies, none of which hinge on altering disclosure incentives). The user-focus leads them to conclude that both mortgage lending and nutritional labeling will be areas where the disclosures are more likely to be successful, id. at 113, despite potential recalcitrance of the most powerful participants in those arenas.
171 Alan D. Mathios, "The Impact of Mandatory Disclosure Laws on Product Choices: An Analysis of the Salad Dressing Market," 43 *Journal of Law and Economics* 651 (2000).
172 Fung et al., 2007, at 3–4.
173 Willis, 2017, at 82.
174 A number of authors discuss the underlying problem of how contracts are not comprehensible to target audiences, but their solutions begin with a focus on how to adjust contract rules to better accomodate the audience's processing limits with little to no focused attention on altering the speakers' perverse incentives. Ben-Shahar and Schneider, 2014, rest their argument about the failure of disclosures on the limitations – in time, interest, and aptitude – of consumers. Id. at 11–13. Fung et al. conclude that the success of disclosures depends on providing usable information to the audience. Fung et al., 2007, at 11. Ayres and Schwarz, while crafting a reform that alters incentives, take as their starting point the implications of contract law for the reasonable consumer/audience; they seek to remedy that problem first. See, e.g., Ayres and Schwarz, 2014, at 551–52 (acknowledging the audience-focused starting point for their reform and proposing "that

the expectations of representative consumers should be sufficient to satisfy the knowledge prerequisite for informed consent"). The primary focus of Radin's important investigation of boilerplate is on its adverse consequences to consumers in particular and democratic society more generally. Radin, 2012.

175 Hakes, 2011, at 112–18 (advocating that contracts be treated differently with interpretive principles depending on whether the signator is represented and bargaining occurs on the terms).

176 This approach was apparently suggested by the ALI in Restatement section 211, but courts have not embraced the proposal. Radin, 2012, at 84. See also Lior Strahilevitz and Matthew Kugler, "Is Privacy Policy Language Irrelevant to Consumers?" 45 *The Journal of Legal Studies* S69 (2016) (discussing this approach for privacy contractual terms).

177 Willis, 2017, at 75.

178 See, e.g., id. at 79 (offering examples).

179 Id. at 75.

180 Willis, 2015, at 1334–41.

181 Willis, 2017.

182 Id. at 88.

183 Id. at 90.

184 A number of commenters suggest that this set of contracts should be treated differently. See generally Hakes, 2011. Radin even suggests that contracts of adhesion with consumers perhaps should not be treated like contracts at all. See, e.g., Margaret Jane Radin, "The Deformation of Contract in the Information Society," 37 *Oxford Journal of Legal Studies* 505 (2017).

185 Ayres and Schwartz's position is that courts should not enforce "terms that a substantial number of consumers believe are more favorable to them than the terms actually are," and this result sometimes follows in contract law from the duty to read doctrine. Ayres and Schwartz, 2014, at 605.

186 Id. at 552.

187 Id. at 562. They suggest that the methods should meet the minimum standards set by the FTC, for example. Id. at 585–86.

188 Id. at 606. That learning, moreover, must document "which of their terms [consumers] optimistically mistake, and to correct those mistakes with vivid warnings." Id.

189 Strahilevitz also proposed this reform in resolving privacy policy disputes. Strahilevitz and Kugler, 2016. In this context, the authors suggest that "consumer contract interpretation would become a question of fact rather than a question of law. Where a consensus emerges among consumers as to the contours of a deal, this consensus understanding [revealed by empirical evidence] would become the contract's meaning." Such a test puts the onus on the companies to design their policies and contracts in ways that successfully "inform consumers about what the companies are doing and why they are doing it." Id. at S89.

190 Ben-Shahar and Strahilevitz, 2017, at 1802.

191 See generally id.

192 Ayres and Schwartz, 2014, at 606.

193 Willis, 2015, at 1334–41.

194 Willis, 2017, at 75.

195 Willis, 2015, at 1334–41.

196 In the context of privacy policies, for example, the FTC examines the transaction from the perspective of a reasonable consumer, taking "consumers as it finds them, full of preexisting expectations, contextual norms, and cognitive limitations, and prohibiting companies from exploiting these assumptions and rational ignorance." Daniel J. Solove and Woodrow Hartzog, "The FTC and the New Common Law of Privacy," 114 *Columbia Law Review* 583, 667 (2014).

197 The FTC apparently does use industry best practices in assessing infringements on consumer privacy as well, although how the best practices are identified actually vary by context. See, e.g., id. at 626–27.

198 Jean Braucher and Angela Littwin, "Examination as a Method of Consumer Protection," 87 *Temple Law Review* 807 (2015).

199 Willis, 2017.

200 Fung et al., Ben-Shahar and Schneider, and Bar-Gill all converge on the potential use of intermediaries to rectify some of the disclosure problems. See, e.g., Ben-Shahar and Schneider, 2014, at ch. 12; Fung et al., 2007, at 123–25; and Bar-Gill, 2012, at 33–35.

201 At least one company already fills the niche of providing employers with a service to employees to navigate the complicated, legally incomprehensible employment system of benefits, insurance, leave policies, etc. See, e.g., Jellyvision for employers, which "provides personalized interactive explanations [of various employee benefit options] based in behavioral science," available at www.jellyvision.com/.

202 Fung et al., 2007, at 124.

203 Radin, 2012, at 193–94.

204 Ethan J. Leib and Zev J. Eigen, "Consumer Form Contracting in the Age of Mechanical Reproduction: The Unread and the Undead," 2017 *University of Illinois Law Review* 65, 105 (2017).

205 Radin, 2012, at 182. In the EU, differing presumptions (including that some provisions are patently illegal) are applied to different categories of clauses found in various consumer contracts. Id. at 227–240.

206 See, e.g., Bar-Gill, 2012, at 4, 111–12.

207 Willis, 2017, at 91.

5A COMPREHENSION ASYMMETRIES IN FINANCIAL REGULATION

1 Monica Langley, "Inside J.P. Morgan's Blunder," *The Wall Street Journal*, May 12, 2012.

2 Hu, 2014, at 634; Henry C. Hu, "Financial Innovation and Governance Mechanisms: The Evolution of Decoupling and Transparency," 79 *Business Lawyer* 347, 387 (2015).

3 Malcolm Gladwell, "Open Secrets," *The New Yorker* 44, 49 (Jan. 8, 2007).

4 Id.

5 Henry C. Hu, "Too Complex to Depict?: Innovation, 'Pure Information,' and the SEC Disclosure Paradigm," 90 *Texas Law Review* 1601, 1614 (2012); Troy A. Paredes, "Blinded by the Light: Information Overload and its Consequences for Securities Regulation," 81 *Washington University Law Quarterly* 417, 423 (2003).

6 H. Comm. On Interstate and Foreign Commerce, 95th Cong., Report of the Advisory Committee on Corporate Disclosure to the Securities and Exchange Commission at D-6 (Comm. Print 1977).

7 See, e.g., Basic v. Levinson, 485 US 224 (1988) (memorializing this presumption in the fraud-on-the-market theory that presumes market prices encapsulate all available information).

8 Hu, 2012, at 1618; Erik R. Sirri, "SEC Regulation of Investment Banks: Testimony before the Financial Crisis Inquiry Commission," May 5, 2010, Washington, D.C., available at https://fraser.stlouisfed.org/files/docs/historical/fct/fcic/fcic_testimony_sirri_20100505.pdf.

9 SEC, Investor Bulletin: Private Placements under Regulation D, at www.sec.gov/oiea/investor-alerts-bulletins/ib_privateplacements.html.

10 Robert F. Weber, "New Governance, Financial Regulation, and Challenges to Legitimacy: The Example of the Internal Models Approach to Capital Adequacy Regulation," 62 *Administrative Law Review* 783, 811–12 (2010).

11 Hu, 2012, at 1618–20 (documenting this recent history).

12 Paredes, 2003, at 418; see also Hu, 2014, at 596 (describing SEC's enhancement of the MD&A disclosures in part as a response to the Lehman Brothers' obfuscation and ultimate collapse).

13 Hu, 2014, at 586.

14 Plain English Disclosure, Securities Act Release No. 7497, Exchange Act Release No. 39,593, 63 Fed. Reg. 6370 (1998).

15 Paredes, 2003, at 476.

16 Hu, 2015, at 387.

17 See, e.g., Langley, 2012; cf. Henry Hu, "Misunderstood Derivatives: The Causes of Informational Failure and the Promise of Regulatory Incrementalism," 102 *Yale Law Journal* 1457, 1493 (1993).

18 Id. at 1492.

19 In the words of the Delaware state court, "the discretion granted directors and managers allows them to maximize shareholder value in the long term by taking risks without the debilitating fear that they will be held personally liable if the company experiences losses." In Re Citigroup Inc. Shareholder Derivative Litigation, 964 A 2d 106 (Del Ch 2009).

20 Hu, 1993, at 1493.

21 Id.

22 Id.

23 As Hu summarizes, "[u]nfortunately ... the social costs of bank failure are far greater than the private costs." Id. at 1495

24 Id.

25 Nolan McCarty, "Complexity, Capacity, and Capture," in *Preventing Regulatory Capture: Special Interest Influence and How to Limit it* 99, 102 (Daniel Carpenter and David A. Moss, eds.) (Cambridge, 2013).

26 Steven L. Schwarcz, "Intrinsic Imbalance: The Impact of Income Disparity on Financial Regulation," 78 *Law and Contemporary Problems* 97, 101, 106 (2015).

27 See, e.g., Ted Kaufman, "Set up to Fail: Dodd-Frank Leaves Bank Regulators Overwhelmed, Underfunded," *Forbes,* July 19, 2013.

28 Jim Angel, "Financial Regulation a 'Bureaucratic Mess' Thanks to Dodd Frank," *The Hill*, Dec. 13, 2016.

29 Schwarcz, 2015, at 105–06; Kevin L. Young, Tim Marple, and James Heilman, "Beyond the Revolving Door: Advocacy Behavior and Social Distance to Financial Regulators," 19 *Business and Politics* 327 (2017). One empirical study concluded that comments made

by regulated parties did not enjoy an advantage in the SEC's rulemaking effort. David C. Nixon, Robert M. Howard, and Jeff R. DeWitt, "With Friends Like These: Rule-Making Comment Submissions to the Securities and Exchange Commission," 12 *Journal of Public Administration Research and Theory* 59 (2002). This study provides some counter-evidence for traditional forms of industry influence and capture, but it is limited to rules promulgated in 1998 and thus is only a limited source of information in this regard.

30 Schwarcz, 2015 at 105–06.

31 Project on Government Oversight, *Dangerous Liaisons: Revolving Door at SEC Creates Risk of Regulatory Capture* at appendix A, tables 3A and 3B (listing "top recruiters of SEC Alumni") and appendix B (tracing "SEC Revolving Door Career Paths") (Feb. 11, 2013).

32 James Kwak, "Cultural Capture and the Financial Crisis," in *Preventing Regulatory Capture: Special Interest Influence and How to Limit It* 71 (Daniel Carpenter and David A. Moss, eds.) (Cambridge, 2013).

33 Kathryn Judge, "Fragmentation Nodes: A Study in Complexity, Financial Innovation, and Systemic Risk," 64 *Stanford Law Review* 657, 692 (2012).

34 Hu, 1993, at 1494 (citing *Forbes* article).

35 Schwarcz, 2015, at 107.

36 Hu, 2012, at 1652. Note, however, that KPMG is a company that makes a living as an intermediary providing translation services.

37 Paredes, 2003, at 418.

38 Id. at 429.

39 Id.

40 Id. at 430.

41 Rachel E. Silverman, "GE to Change Its Practices of Disclosure," *TheWall Street Journal*, Feb. 20, 2002, A3 (quoted in Paredes, 2003, at 430).

42 Henry Hu notes that some "banks' public reports are now some three hundred pages long, yet some prominent investment managers refuse to invest in such banks on the grounds that they do not understand what's in the black box." "Rethinking the Nature of Information: Henry Hu Discusses How Complexity and Innovation Mandate Radical Changes in Disclosure," *UT Law Magazine*, Dec. 12., 2012, available at https://law.utexas.edu/news/2012/12/12/rethinking-the-nature-of-information/.

43 Hu, 2014, at 572.

44 Id. at 571.

45 Paredes, 2003, at 425–26. The MD&A also requires the disclosure of known changes or uncertainties that could have a material impact on the registrant's business and other forward-looking statements – a text-based requirement that requires judgment and is difficult to compare with other entities. Id.

46 Id. at 426.

47 Id. at 418.

48 Financial Stability Forum, "Report of the Financial Stability Forum on Enhancing Market and Institutional Resilience" 1 (2008).

49 1 CFA Inst., "User Perspectives on Financial Instrument Risk Disclosures under International Financial Reporting Standards (IFRS)" 1 (2011).

50 Singer, quoted in Hu, 2014, at 571.

51 Transcript of Financial Disclosure and Auditor Oversight Roundtables, Panel 1, at 6 (Improving Financial Disclosure), Mar. 4, 2002, available at www.sec.gov/spotlight/round tables/accountround030402.htm#panel1.

52 Tim Loughran and Bill Mcdonald, "Regulation and Financial Disclosure: The Impact of Plain English," 45 *Journal of Regulatory Economics* 94, 96 (2014).

53 Dodd-Frank Act, § 932 (q).

54 Id. at § 14A(b).

55 Id. at §§ 1462(j) and 1463(k).

56 Gladwell, 2007, at 50.

57 Hu, 2012, at 1638–39.

58 As Henry Hu notes, with respect to contractual language alone: "[a]n investor would either have to hire formidable legal and financial talent to plow through the (often highly complex) contractual provisions, or retain the services of a third party who tries to engage in that task on behalf of multiple clients." Id. at 1642.

59 Hu, 2012, at 1640.

60 Id. at 1641 (citing Rubin and Tucker Letter).

61 Id.

62 Id. at 1637–41.

63 Id. at 1626, 1625.

64 Id. at 1634–35 (discussing these types of problems in the ABS market).

65 Hu, 2014, at 596–601.

66 Id. at 598–99.

67 Id. at 613 (describing these requirements).

68 The requirements of the Management Discussion and Analysis (MD&A) section of the SEC's Financial Reporting Manual are designed to facilitate meaningful communication and synthesis of the data to various expert audiences. Specifically, the "MD&A is a narrative explanation of the financial statements and other statistical data that the registrant believes will enhance a reader's understanding of its financial condition, changes in financial condition and results of operation." It is intended "[t]o provide a narrative explanation of a company's financial statements that enables investors to see the company through the eyes of management." Management's Discussion and Analysis of Financial Position and Results of Operations § 9110.1, available at www.sec.gov/corpfin/cf-manual/topic-9. Yet the MD&A also necessarily reserves sufficient flexibility to management to enable them to game the accessibility of these narrative statements using the various incomprehensibility tactics discussed in this book.

69 Hu, 2014, at 626 ("dealers may fail to invest enough in fully understanding the true characteristics of their complex products"); Weber, 2010, at 737 (observing that "banks currently are able to externalize the costs of their complexity onto taxpayers").

70 Gladwell, 2007, at 53.

71 Sony Kapoor, in Andrea Orr, "Too Complex to Regulate?: Commentary," Economic Policy Institute (June 8, 2009), available at www.epi.org/publication/too_complex_to_regulate/.

72 Judge, 2012, at 688.

73 Id. at 689.

74 Hu, 2012, at 1637 (quoting industry observers Robert Coughlin and Ripley Hastings).

75 Robert Weber, "Structural Regulation as Antidote to Complexity Capture," 49 *American Business Law Journal* 643, 645 (2012).

76 Judge, 2012, at 676.

77 Id. at 676.

78 Id. at 691.

79 Hendrik Hakenes and Isabel Schnabel, "Regulatory Capture by Sophistication," Nov. 28, 2014, at 24, available at www.econstor.eu/bitstream/10419/79991/1/VfS_2013_pid_164.pdf.

80 Id. at 3–5 (the model is also applied to Pillar II of the Basel Accord and the Volcker Rule and regulatory decisions regarding the choice of bank closure versus bailouts).

81 Id. at 4.

82 Robert Johnson, prior managing director of Soros Fund Management and chief economist for the Senate Banking and Budget Committee, in Andrea Orr, "Too Complex to Regulate?: Commentary," Economic Policy Institute (June 8, 2009), available at www.epi.org/publication/too_complex_to_regulate/.

83 Judge, 2012, at 667.

84 Weber, 2012, at 704.

85 Hu, 2015, at 383.

86 In any reform, specifying the identity of the speaker and audience is critical. It helps create a baseline, bilateral structure that decreases the opportunities for complex communication chains to create noise and sources of error as the messages are transmitted. Judge, 2012, at 720. It also provides a benchmark against which the accessibility of the communications can be assessed; the goal is to ensure information is reasonably understandable to the target audience.

87 Hu, 2014, at 571.

88 Hu, 2015, at 381.

89 Hu, 2014, at 578.

90 Id. at 654.

91 For diagrams illustrating the analytical framework's three modes of information, see id. at 576 (descriptive mode), 579 (transfer mode), and 582 (hybrid mode).

92 Id. at 636.

93 See Hu, 2012; Hu, 2014; Hu, 2015.

94 Id. at 654.

95 Id. at 654–55.

96 Note, too, that this approach is not the same as the ineffective disclosure templates used in the consumer market since Hu's framework involves a "diversified portfolio of informational sources." Id. at 654.

97 Id. at 583.

98 Id. at 578–80.

99 Id. at 639–42 (on the potential as well as the limitations of the transfer mode, including with respect to the demands placed on market participants).

100 Id. at 580–83.

101 Id. at 650–54.

102 Id. at 650.

103 Id. at 637.

104 Id. at 651, 652.

105 Lawrence G. Baxter, "Betting Big: Value, Caution and Accountability in an Era of Ultra-Large Banking," 31 *Review of Banking & Financial Law* 765 (2012).
106 Hu, 2014, at 651.
107 Id. at 653.
108 Id. at 654 (citing Basel Commission on Banking Supervision) (2013).
109 Id. at 638.
110 See, e.g., Brett McDonnell and Daniel Schwarcz, "Regulatory Contrarians," 89 *North Carolina Law Review* 1629, 1662, 1670 (2011).
111 See, e.g., Schwarcz, 2015, at 106–07; Glenn Blackmon and Richard Zeckhauser, "Fragile Commitments and the Regulatory Process," 9 *Yale Journal on Regulation* 73, 104 (1992); Paul L. Joskow and Richard Schmalensee, "Incentive Regulation for Electric Utilities," 4 *Yale Journal on Regulation* 1, 18 (1986).

5B COMPREHENSION ASYMMETRIES IN THE LAW OF PATENTS

1 See, e.g., Wesley M. Cohen et al., "Protecting Their Intellectual Assets: Appropriability Conditions and Why U.S. Manufacturing Firms Patent (or Not)," 17 (Nat'l Bureau of Econ. Research, Working Paper No. 7552, 2000), available at www.nber.org/papers/w7552 (82 percent of survey respondents list as a reason for patenting "blocking rival patents on related innovations").
2 Michael Frakes and Melissa Wasserman, "Decreasing the Patent Office's Incentives to Grant Invalid Patents" 5 (The Hamilton Project, Brookings) (Dec. 2017b).
3 See, e.g., Adam B. Jaffe and Josh Lerner, *Innovation and Its Discontents: How Our Broken Patent System is Endangering Innovation and Progress, and What to Do about It* (Princeton, 2004).
4 Mark Lemley and Bhaven Sampat, "Is the Patent Office a Rubber Stamp?" 58 *Emory Law Journal* 181 (2009).
5 Jaffe and Lerner, 2004, at 143 (noting that the definition of an "important" invention is one "that is successfully patented in all three of the world's major patent-granting jurisdictions").
6 James Bessen and Michael J. Meurer, *Patent Failure: How Judges, Bureaucrats, and Lawyers Put Innovators at Risk* 10 (Princeton, 2008) (citing White v. Dunbar, 119 U.S. 47, 51 (1886)).
7 Christopher A. Cotropia, Mark Lemley, and Bhaven Sampat, "Do Applicant Patent Citations Matter," 42 *Research Policy* 844, 845 (2013) (citing American Intellectual Property Law Association, 2011, for the $5 million figure, which includes numerous experts that are inevitably needed in this type of litigation.).
8 Wasserman and Frakes, 2017b, at 2.
9 John M. Golden, "Proliferating Patents and Patent Law's 'Cost Disease,'" 51 *Houston Law Review* 455, 476 (2013). The result is a human-labor bottleneck that is growing worse over time. Indeed, it is not only the rising number of applications but their increased complexity – both in substance and in the number of claims – that flood the system. John R. Allison and Mark A. Lemley, "The Growing Complexity of the United States Patent System," 82 *Boston University Law Review* 77, 79 (2002) ("By almost any measure – subject matter, time in prosecution, number of prior art references cited, number of claims, number of

continuation applications filed, number of inventors – the patents issued in the late 1990s are more complex than those issued in the 1970s"); Golden, 2013, at 477–78.

10 Jaffe and Lerner, 2004, at 34–35. Even if "non-operative" is a bit harsh, as we will see, there are multiple reinforcing reasons why the examination process puts the audience-examiner at a significant processing disadvantage relative to the applicant.

11 R. Polk Wagner, "Understanding Patent-Quality Mechanisms," 157 *University of Pennsylvania Law Review* 2135, 2154–55 (2009).

12 Golden, 2013, at 459.

13 Id. at 489.

14 37 C.F.R § 1.56.

15 Sean B. Seymore, "Uninformative Patents," 55 *Houston Law Review* 377, 387 (2017).

16 35 U.S.C. § 112(a).

17 R. P. Wagner, 2009, at 2150 (citing the PTO's own acknowledgment of this fact in the MDEP).

18 Improperly granted patents can be challenged by third parties under various mechanisms, including the inter parties review provisions, 35 U.S.C. §§ 31 et seq., and the Blonder-Tongue estoppel, 402 U.S. 313 (1971). But these challenges raised post-grant to invalid patents are likely to be limited as compared to the inventor's appeal of a wrongly denied patent. This is primarily because the challengers for wrongly approved patents are third parties who generally have less at stake than the patent grantee.

19 Jonathan Masur, "Patent Inflation," 121 *Yale Law Journal* 470, 474 (2011). Masur also argues that the nature of federal appellate review serves only to further expand the scope of what may be patented. Id. at 475.

20 The customer reference is still used in some areas of the PTO. See, e.g., www.uspto.gov/patents-application-process/applying-online/getting-started-new-users.

21 Doug Lichtman and Mark A. Lemley, "Rethinking the Presumption of Validity," 60 *Stanford Law Review* 45, 47 (2007).

22 "Under that doctrine, courts are obligated to defer to the PTO's initial determination that an invention qualifies for patent protection unless the defendant can show by 'clear and convincing' evidence that the PTO erred." Id. at 47.

23 In cases of patent rejections or even negotiations, the examiner at points becomes the "speaker" and the conversation is flipped. There may be incentives for the examiner, in this speaker role, to also exploit some comprehension asymmetries in ways that aren't wholly dissimilar to those considered for agency-speakers in Chapter 6. Yet for purposes here, we avoid getting into this level of complicated detail lest it distract from our focus on the applicant's incentives.

24 Cotropia et al., 2013, at 845; Michael Frakes and Melissa Wasserman, "Is the Time Allocated to Review Patent Applications Inducing Examiners to Grant Invalid Patents?: Evidence from Micro-Level Application Data," 99 *The Review of Economics and Statistics* 550, 552 (2017a); Nat'l Research Council for the Nat'l Academies, *A Patent System for the 21st Century* 147 (Stephen A. Merrill et al., eds.) (NAS, 2004) (this estimate excludes the time spent on RCEs).

25 GAO, Testimony: "U.S. Patent and Trademark Office Hiring Efforts Are Not Sufficient to Reduce the Patent Application Backlog" 3 (2008) ("70 percent of patent examiners reported working unpaid overtime during the past year in order to meet their production goals").

26 Id. at 8.
27 Id. at 9.
28 Michael Frakes and Melissa Wasserman, 2017a, at 550.
29 Melissa Wasserman, "The PTO's Asymmetric Incentives: Pressure to Expand Substantive Patent Law," 72 *Ohio State Law Journal* 379, 385–86 (2011).
30 Jaffe and Learner, 2004, at 136.
31 Frakes and Wasserman, 2017b, at 6.
32 Cecil D. Quillen, Jr. and Ogden H. Webster, "Continuing Patent Applications and Performance of the U.S. Patent and Trademark Office," 11 *Federal Circuit Bar Journal* 1, 14 (2002).
33 Frakes and Wasserman, 2017b, at 5; Arti Rai, "Growing Pains in the Administrative State: The Patent Office's Troubled Quest for Managerial Control," 157 *University of Pennsylvania Law Review* 2051, 2062–63 (2009).
34 Wasserman, 2011, at 409–10.
35 Additionally, at an individual level, there will be inevitable variation among examiners. For example, one study reports that younger examiners may actually react to the insufficient time in ways that lead to excessive patent claim denials. Wasserman, 2011, at 385–86. For our purposes, however, we simply take note of the fact that the aggregate picture yields a process that tips toward premature patent approval by the PTO, particularly in cases where processing costs make learning of the embedded weaknesses of an application difficult.
36 Masur, 2011, at 476.
37 Golden, 2013, at 493.
38 Id. at 495.
39 Sean B. Seymore, "Patent Asymmetries," 49 *UC Davis Law Review* 963, 991–92, 995 (2016).
40 Tun-Jen Chiang and Lawrence Solum, "The Interpretation-Construction Distinction in Patent Law," 123 *Yale Law Journal* 530, 589–90 (2013).
41 Oskar Livak, "Finding Invention," 40 *Florida State University Law Review* 57, 58–59 (2012).
42 E.g., Seymore, 2017.
43 See also R. P. Wagner, 2009, at 2137 (making this argument).
44 35 U.S.C. § 112(a); see also Manual of Patent Examination and Procedure (MPEP) § 2162–64.
45 35 U.S.C. § 112(a) (forming the basis of rejection); 37 C.F.R. § 1.113 (laying out the requirements for making a final office action).
46 MPEP § 608.01(m).
47 See generally MPEP § 600.
48 Recent empirical studies report Section 112(a) rejections ranging from about 4 to 12% of all rejections. E.g., Quiang Lu, et al., "USPTO Patent Prosecution Data," Nov. 2017, at Table 2, pg. 34, https://patentlyo.com/media/2017/11/USPTO-Patent-Prosecution-Research-Data_Unlocking-Office-Action-Traits-1.pdf (finding that 4.3% of claim rejections from 2008 to 2017 were Section 112(a) rejections); James Cosgrove, "112 Rejections: Where they are Found and How Applicants Handle Them," IPWatchdog, May 9, 2017, at https://www.ipwatchdog.com/2017/05/09/112-rejections-applicants-handle/id=82668/ (finding that 11.7% of office actions from 2005 to 2014 included Section 112(a) rejections). These statistics may even

overstate rejection rates. Section 112(a) includes three distinct grounds for rejection (written description, enablement, and best mode). *E.g.* MPEP § 2161. Only some of the first two kinds of Section 112(a) rejections are of interest here. Further, both studies lump data (e.g., aggregating non-final and final rejection rates) in ways that may overstate the extent of final Section 112(a) rejections based on issues of clarity. See also R.P.Wagner, 2009, at 2150.

49 In re Wertheim, 541 F.2d 257, 263 (CCPA 1976); see also MPEP § 2162–63.

50 Lu, et al., 2017, at 4–5.

51 See, e.g., Stephen Schott, "An Appeal to the New Patent Office Director: Repeal the Single Sentence Rule," *Patently-O* 2009, available at http://patentlyo.com/patent/2009/09/an-appeal-to-the-new-patent-office-director-repeal-the-single-sentence-rule.html.

52 Id.

53 37 C.F.R. § 1.56(a)(1).

54 *Therasense*, 649 F.3d 1276, 1288 (Fed. Circ. 2013); see also 35 U.S.C. § 32 (describing the PTO's power to call for a hearing to investigate attorney misconduct).

55 See 37 C.F.R. §§ 1.56(a) and 11.18.

56 *Therasense*, 649 F.3d at 1306.

57 Id. at 1285.

58 Id. at 1287–88.

59 Christian Mammen, "Controlling the 'Plague': Reforming the Doctrine of Inequitable Conduct," 24 *Berkeley Technical Law Journal* 1329, 1358 (2009).

60 *Therasense*, 649 F.3d at 1289 (citing ABA Section of Intellectual Property Law, "A Section White Paper: Agenda for 21st Century Patent Reform" 2 (2009)).

61 *Therasense*, 649 F.3d at 1289.

62 Id. (citing Brief for the United States as Amicus Curiae at 17 and Brief of the Biotechnology Industry Organization as Amicus Curiae at 7).

63 Cotropia et al., 2013, at 848, n.13.

64 Id. at 848 (quoting Popp et al., (2004) at 13). The authors also quote an examiner who observes that "The trend today seems to be toward more and more extensive IDSes, usually with less and less relevant art cited." Id. at 848.

65 Brief for the ABA as Amicus Curiae in *Therasense, Inc.* at 11 (June 17, 2010).

66 Rai, 2009, at 2075–76.

67 Dennis Crouch, "Information Disclosure: Less is More for PTO?" *Patently-O*, Sept. 17, 2008, available at www.patentlyo.com/patent/2008/09/information-dis.html.

68 *Therasense*, 649 F.3d at 1306.

69 Id. at 1290–91.

70 E.g., KSR Int'l Co. v. Teleflex Inc., 550 U.S. 398, 399 (2007); Atlas Powder Co. v. E.I. du Pont De Nemours & Co., 750 F.2d 1569, 1576 (Fed. Cir. 1984); Dan L. Burk and Mark A. Lemley, "Is Patent Law Technology-Specific?" 17 *Berkeley Technical Law Journal* 1155, 1185–96 (2002).

71 Burk and Lemley, 2009, at 1745.

72 Id. at 1745.

73 Id. at 1754.

74 Id. at 1756.

75 A successful malpractice claim can provide the inventor with the recovery of lost profits on the unpatented invention. E.g., Panduit Corp. v. Stahlen Bros. Fibre Works, Inc., 575 F.2d 1152, 1156 (6th Cir. 1978).

76 Burk and Lemley, 2009, at 1753–54.
77 John M. Golden, "Redundancy: When Law Repeats Itself," 94 *Texas Law Review* 629 (2016).
78 Id. at 677.
79 Id. at 677–78 (citing David Pressman, *Patent it Yourself* 245 (Richard Stim ed., 13th ed.) (Nolo, 2008)).
80 Russ Krajec, "What Does a Good Patent Application Look Like?" (undated), available at www.blueironip.com/good-patent-application-look-like/.
81 R. P. Wagner, 2009, at 2149.
82 Burk and Lemley, 2009, at 1753.
83 Bob DeMatteis, Andy Gibbs, and Michael Neustel, *The Patent Writer: How to Write Successful Patent Applications* 107 (Square One, 2006).
84 Chiang and Solum acknowledge that this deliberate ambiguity can occur in claim-drafting in theory, but doubt that it will occur very often in practice because it requires the inventor to "bamboozle" the examiner. Chiang and Solum, 2013, at 589–92. Yet the limited processing costs of the examiner, particularly nearing the end of the examination period, create precisely the right conditions for this type of deliberate trickery.
85 Bessen and Meurer, 2008, at 57; Burk and Lemley, 2009, at 1752–53 (2009); R. P. Wagner, 2009, at 2149, 2151, n.39.
86 MPEP § 707.05 provides that with respect to the citation of references, "The examiner must consider all the prior art references (alone and in combination) cited in the application or reexamination, including those cited by the applicant in a properly submitted Information Disclosure Statement."
87 Brief of Amicus Curiae Boston Patent Law Association in *Therasense*, available at 2010 WL 3390226 (citing 71 Fed. Reg. 38808, 38809 (2006)).
88 Brief for the ABA as Amicus Curiae in *Therasense*, at 10–11 (June 17, 2010).
89 Cotropia et al., 2013, at 845. Of course, this important legal feature of the IDS can also be leveraged by the Examiner to insist that the IDSs are easily searchable. The Examiner can thus reclaim at least some of her time from the applicant by insisting on IDSs that can be reviewed more easily.
90 Frakes and Wasserman, 2017b, at 12.
91 Frakes and Wasserman, 2017a, at 551.
92 Frakes and Wasserman, 2017b, at 6.
93 37 C.F.R. § 1.114; see also MPEP § 706.07(h).
94 Frakes and Wasserman, 2017b, at 6.
95 See Michael D. Frakes and Melissa F. Wasserman, "Does the U.S. Patent and Trademark Office Grant Too Many Bad Patents?: Evidence from a Quasi-Experiment," 67 *Stanford Law Review* 613 (2015).
96 "Patent Examiner Count System," available at www.uspto.gov/patent/initiatives/patent-examiner-count-system ("RCEs are currently placed on the examiner's Regular Amended docket, which means that examiners have two months from the date the RCE is forwarded to them in order to act on the application"); see also Hussein Akhavannik, BakerHostetler, "USPTO Practice" at 6, available at www.aipla.org/committees/committee_pages/Patent-Agents/Committee%20Documents/USPTO%20Count%20System%20Presentation.pdf (discussing how to game the RCE process).

97 Frakes and Wasserman, 2015.

98 Quillen and Webster, 2002, at 14.

99 Frakes and Wasserman, 2017b, at 14.

100 If examiners spend most of their time on RCEs, they may fall behind on "normal" cases. For an overview of the intricate performance criteria for an examiner's workflow (including allocations for the review of "new"/"amended"/"special new" (which includes RCEs) applications), see USPTO, "Examination Time and the Production System," available at www.uspto.gov/sites/default/files/documents/Examination%20Time%20and%20the%20Production%20System.pdf.

101 Frakes and Wasserman, 2015, at 1762.

102 John Golden in fact discusses how applicants strategically "pepper their applications with a multiplicity of claims" using distinct terms in an effort to inflate the scope of their patent. Golden, 2016, at 680; see also Burk and Lemley, 2009, at 1754.

103 Masur, 2011, at 506.

104 Frakes and Wasserman, 2017a, at 560.

105 R. P. Wagner, 2009, at 2146, 2149.

106 Id. at 2137.

107 Compare European disclosure requirements, see, e.g., EP 1830225 A1 (Espacenet), with U.S. requirements; see. e.g., 13/602,680 (Public Pair); see also Brian Cronin, "The Quest for Patent Quality: European Inventive Step and US Obviousness," Dec. 21, 2016, *IPWatchdog*, available at www.ipwatchdog.com/2016/12/21/patent-quality-european-inventive-step-us-obviousness/id=75860/.

108 35 U.S.C. § 112.

109 Polk Wagner offers a similar type of reform, although it is not clear what the legal effect of the PTO's "more thorough claim-construction analyses" would be. See R. P. Wagner, 2009, at 2166.

110 Cosgrove, 2017 (reporting higher success of RCEs for 112(a) rejections as compared to other types of rejections).

111 35 U.S.C. § 122(e)(1).

112 Lichtman and Lemley, 2007, at 49.

113 The application could be placed on the existing "special new" docket that fast-tracks select applications, for example.

114 R. P. Wagner, 2009, at 2167.

115 35 U.S.C. § 112(c).

116 Brief for the Biotechnology Industry Organization and the Pharmaceutical Research and Manufacturers of America as Amici Curiae Supporting Appellee and Affirmance of the Lower Court Decision at 14, Marine Polymer Techs., Inc. v. Hemcon, Inc., 672 F.3d 1350 (Fed. Cir. 2012) (cited in Mercado, 2013, at 570).

117 Raymond A. Mercado, "Ensuring the Integrity of Administrative Challenges to Patents: Lessons from Reexamination," 14 *Columbia Science & Technology Law Review* 558, 590–91 (2013).

118 Id. at 594 (quoting respondents in study).

119 Id. at 595 (citing PTO, Changes to Implement Inter Parties Review Proceedings, 77 Fed. Reg. 7041, 7051 (2012)).

120 Cf. Chiang and Solum, 2013 (proposing a more elaborate and complete version of this general idea).

121 Dan L. Burk and Mark A. Lemley, "Quantum Patent Mechanics," 9 *Lewis and Clark Law Review* 29, 30 (2005).
122 Golden, 2016.

5C COMPREHENSION ASYMMETRIES IN CHEMICAL REGULATION

1 See, e.g., John S. Applegate, "The Government Role in Scientific Research: Who Should Bridge the Data Gap in Chemical Regulation?" in *Rescuing Science from Politics* 255, 268 (Wendy Wagner and Rena Steinzor, eds.) (Cambridge, 2006).
2 See National Research Council, *Toxicity Testing: Strategies to Determine Needs and Priorities* 60, 151–63 (NAS, 1984).
3 Environmental Defense Fund, "Toxic Ignorance: The Continuing Absence of Basic Health Testing for Top-Selling Chemicals in the United States" (1997); Environmental Protection Agency, Office of Pollution Prevention and Toxics, "What Do We Really Know about the Safety of High Production Volume Chemicals?" 22 *Chemical Regulation Reporter* (BNA) 261 (1998).
4 National Research Council, *Toxicity Testing in the 21st Century: A Vision and a Strategy* (NAS, 2007).
5 But see Bernard Goldstein, "Risk Assessment of Environmental Chemicals: If It Ain't Broke . . ." 31 *Risk Analysis* 1356, 1357 (2011) (highlighting the delay involved in these risk assessments).
6 See, e.g., GAO, Observations on the Toxic Substances Control Act and EPA Implementation 13 (June 2013); Office of Technology Assessment, US Congress, No. OTA-BP-ENV-166, Screening and Testing of Chemicals in Commerce 11 (1995) (reporting a 1994 GAO finding that in the 19-year history of TSCA implementation, the EPA had reviewed only about 2 percent of the chemicals then existing in commerce).
7 For an insightful analysis of the uncertain risks associated with shale gas development that parallels the analysis in this chapter, see Bernard D. Goldstein et al., "Challenges of Unconventional Shale Gas Development: So What's the Rush," 27 *Notre Dame Journal of Law, Ethics, & Public Policy* 149, 182 (2013).
8 Bryan Walsh, "Officials Don't Really Know How Dangerous the Chemical Spilled in West Virginia Is," *Time*, Jan. 14, 2014.
9 Id.
10 Center for Science and Environment, "The Bhopal Diaster," in *State of India's Environment 1984–1985* at 207 (1985).
11 Janet Wilson and Oladele A. Ogunseitan, "A Call for Better Toxics Policy Reform," 59 *Environment: Science and Policy for Sustainable Development* 30, 31 (2017).
12 Tiffany Hsu, "Johnson & Johnson Told to Pay $4.7 Billion in Baby Powder Lawsuit," *New York Times*, 7/12/2018, available at www.nytimes.com/2018/07/12/business/johnson-johnson-talcum-powder.html.
13 E.g., Gulf South Insulation v. CPSC, 701 F.2d 1137 (5th Circ. 1983); GAO, Consumer Product Safety Commission: Challenges and Options for Responding to New and Emerging Risks (Oct. 2014); see also a similar but even more serious story on hazardous paint strippers. Jamie Hopkins, "The Government Isn't Regulating a Deadly Pain Stripper, so Retailers Are Instead," *Slate*, Dec. 14, 2018.
14 E.g., Kathleen Kreiss, "Recognizing Occupational Effects on Diacetyl: What Can We Learn from This History?" 388 *Toxicology* 48 (2017); OSHA, Flavorings-Related Lung

Disease, at www.osha.gov/SLTC/flavoringlung/index.html (acknowledging that no standards are in place for these workplace risks); see also Thomas O. McGarity et al., Center for Progressive Reform, "Workers at Risk: Regulatory Dysfunction at OSHA" 16 (2010), www.progressivereform.org/articles/osha_1003.pdf.

15 US GAO, Report No. GAO-05-458, "Chemical Regulation: Options Exist to Improve EPA's Ability to Assess Health Risks and Manage Its Chemical Review Program" 18 (2005).

16 Noah M. Sachs, "Jumping the Pond: Transnational Law and the Future of Chemical Regulation," 62 *Vanderbilt Law Review* 1817, 1830 (2009).

17 Watershed Protection & Development Review Department, City of Austin, *The Coal Tar Facts: Coal Tar Sealant Fact Sheet* (2004), available at http://ci.austin.tx.us/watershed/downloads/coaltarfacts.pdf.

18 See, e.g., Wendy E. Wagner, "Racing to the Top: How Regulation Can Be Used to Create Incentives for Industry to Improve Environmental Quality," 29 *Journal of Land Use and Environmental Law* 1, 2–3 (2014) (recounting this story with accompanying articles).

19 Id.

20 15 U.S.C. § 2604(d)(1).

21 US GAO, 2005, at 12.

22 Id. at 17–18; Richard Denison, "A Primer on the New Toxic Substances Control Act (TSCA) and What Led to It," EDF Health at 3 (Apr. 2017).

23 See, e.g., 15 U.S.C. §§ 2603(a) and 2607; see also Wendy Wagner, "Using Competition-Based Regulation to Bridge the Toxics Data Gap," 83 *Indiana Law Journal* 629, 631–37 (2008).

24 15 U.S.C. §§ 2603 (a)(3) and (4) and (b), 2603(b); John S. Applegate, "The Perils of Unreasonable Risk: Information Regulatory Policy and Toxic Substances Control," 91 *Columbia Law Review* 261, 310–13 (1991).

25 E.g., Chem. Mfrs. Ass'n v. EPA, 859 F.2d 977, 984 (D.C. Cir. 1988) (holding that the EPA must establish a "more-than-theoretical" probability of an unreasonable risk in order to require additional testing).

26 15 U.S.C. § 2607(e).

27 See generally Wendy E. Wagner, "Choosing Ignorance in the Manufacture of Toxic Products," 82 *Cornell Law Review* 773, 798–802 (1997).

28 See, e.g., US EPA Use of Quantitative Structure-Activity Relationship and Category Approaches in Profiling Hazards of Industrial Chemicals (6/26/08), available at www.epa.gov/sites/production/files/2014-08/documents/usepa_use_of_qsar_and_category_approaches_juno8.pdf.

29 Mary L. Lyndon, "Secrecy and Innovation in Tort Law and Regulation," 23 *New Mexico Law Review* 1, 34–35 (1993).

30 Applegate, 1991, at 299.

31 National Research Council, 1984, at 120.

32 This reality is in fact contemplated by the substantial risk reporting requirements, which include oral communications and related information that come to the manufacturer post-marketing. See, e.g., 43 Fed. Reg. 1111–12. Manufacturers' notorious success in keeping some of this post-market information sealed from public view further underscores the extent of manufacturers' privileged access to firsthand information regarding chemical

risks. Wendy Wagner and David Michaels, "Equal Treatment for Regulatory Science: Extending the Controls Governing the Quality of Public Research to Private Research," 30 *American Journal of Law & Medicine* 119, 126–28 (2004); Kathleen M. Roberts, Section 8 – Procedures for Reporting and Recordkeeping Requirements, in *New TSCA: A Guide to the Lautenberg Chemical Safety Act and Its Implementation* 155–56 (Lynn L. Bergeson and Charles M. Auer, eds. 2017).

33 Mary L. Lyndon, "Tort Law and Technology," 12 *Yale Journal on Regulation* 137, 150 (1995).

34 George Eads and Peter Reuter, *Designing Safer Products: Corporate Responses to Product Liability Law and Regulation* 53–54, n.2 (Rand, 1983).

35 Applegate, 1991, at 317.

36 See, e.g., NRC, 2007.

37 See generally Wagner, 2008, at 635 (summarizing the literature on this point).

38 Cynthia A. Williams, "Corporate Law and the Internal Point of View in Legal Theory: A Tale of Two Trajectories," 75 *Fordham Law Review* 1629, 1648 (2006).

39 See, e.g., Timur Kuran and Cass R. Sunstein, "Availability Cascades and Risk Regulation," 51 *Stanford Law Review* 683, 733 (1999).

40 See, e.g., Andrew Caesar-Gordon, "Lessons to Learn from a Product Recall," *PR Week,* Oct. 28, 2015.

41 Wagner, 1997, at 790–96.

42 Id.

43 Id.; Carl Cranor, *Legally Poisoned: How the Law Puts Us at Risk from Toxicants* (Harvard, 2011).

44 However, note that even for new chemicals, manufacturers may sometimes find the lure of possible short-term profits outweighs indeterminant, long-term risks and will forgo all but the lowest cost toxicity assessments. This under-testing has been documented on nanotechnology products, for example. See, e.g., Georgia Miller and Fern Wickson, "Risk Analysis of Nanomaterials: Exposing Nanotechnology's Naked Emperor," 32 *Review of Policy Research* 485 (2015).

45 See generally Wagner, 1997; Wagner, 2008.

46 Mary L. Lyndon, "Information Economics and Chemical Toxicity: Designing Laws to Produce and Use Data," 87 *Michigan Law Review* 1795, 1814 n.72 (1989).

47 See, e.g., Wagner, 2008, at 630 n.8.

48 See, e.g., id. at 632.

49 See, e.g., Sheldon Krimsky, "The Unsteady State and Inertia of Chemical Regulation under the US Toxic Substances Control Act," 15 *PLoS Biol* (12) (2017): e2002404. https://doi.org/10.1371/journal.pbio.2002404.

50 GAO, *Chemical Assessments: Challenges Remain with EPA's Integrated Risk Information System* 6 (Dec. 2011). They report that "as of December 2007, most of the ongoing assessments being conducted at that time had been in process for more than 5 years and that some assessments of key chemicals – chemicals that are likely to cause cancer or other significant health effects – had been in process even longer." Id. at 2. The Obama Administration did not make a noticeable dent in this pervasive inactivity. See, e.g., David Heath, "EPA Still Slow to Study Toxic Chemicals, Despite Obama Pledge," *Time,* Jan. 23, 2015.

51 See, e.g., NRC, 2007.
52 See, e.g., Thomas McGarity, "The Internal Structure of EPA Rulemaking," 54 *Law & Contemporary Problems* 57 (1991).
53 See also infra Part II.B.1.
54 See, e.g., 15 U.S.C. §§ 2603 and 2607.
55 Only CBI-cleared officials can view this classified information. 15 U.S.C. § 2613(a); Julie Yang, Note, "Confidential Business Information Reform under the Toxic Substances Control Act," 2 *Environmental Law* 219, 232 (1995).
56 See, e.g., Wagner, 2014, at 8–9.
57 15 U.S.C. § 2604(d)(1)(B) & (C).
58 Notification requirements demand immediate reporting by manufacturers of any information that suggests substantial risks to health and the environment from exposure to a chemical. 15 U.S.C. § 2607(e), 2607(c). In order to ensure they are in compliance with these post-market information disclosure requirements, Rule-Followers again will be inclined to diligently send every piece of research, complaint, or data along to the agency, regardless of its veracity. See, e.g., Roberts, 2017, at 155–56 (reporting on enforcement cases brought for violations of the substantial risk reporting requirements).
59 43 Fed. Reg. 1112; TSCA Section 8(e) Reporting Guide at 7.
60 The EPA in fact emphasizes that the substantial risk information need not establish conclusively that seriousness or the probability of the risk. EPA, TSCA Section 8(e) Reporting Guide at 2.
61 EPA, Reporting a TSCA Chemical Substantial Risk Notice, available at www.epa.gov/assessing-and-managing-chemicals-under-tsca/reporting-tsca-chemical-substantial-risk-notice; 43 Fed. Reg. 11111.
62 Wagner and Michaels, 2004, at 131.
63 Id. at 130.
64 Id. at 129–32.
65 As noted, the 2017 amendments to TSCA provide numerous new opportunities for Rule-Followers to dedicate resources to these critiques of agency analyses, but the amendments also provide the Rule-Follower with even greater incentives to make the effort. If, after considering the comments, the EPA ultimately determines that a chemical does not present an "unreasonable risk," that decision becomes the law of the land. 15 U.S.C. § 2617(a)(1)(B). States and localities are no longer allowed to regulate the chemical. Thus, Rule-Followers will be even more eager to provide input at every step since the result not only eliminates federal regulation but state restrictions as well.
66 See an elaborated discussion of this APA incentive in Chapter 6.
67 Wagner and Michaels, 2004, at 145, n.158.
68 Id. at 145–46; McGarity and Wagner, 2008, at 200.
69 See also the EPA's own summary of how it analyzes and prioritizes existing chemicals, which makes no mention of using the incoming 8(e) disclosures. See, e.g., www.epa.gov/assessing-and-managing-chemicals-under-tsca.
70 McGarity and Wagner, 2008, at ch. 4.
71 Id.
72 For more than 30 pages of "tricks" along these lines, see id.

73 Id.
74 See Valerio Gennaro and Lorenzo Tomatis, "Business Bias: How Epidemiologic Studies May Underestimate or Fail to Detect Increased Risks of Cancer and Other Diseases," 11 *International Journal of Occupational and Environmental Health* 356 (2005); David S. Egilman and Marion Billings, "Abuse of Epidemiology: Automobile Manufacturers Manufacture a Defense to Asbestos Liability," 11 *International Journal of Occupational and Environmental Health* 360 (2005).
75 McGarity and Wagner, 2008, ch. 4.
76 "One in Three Scientists Confesses to Having Sinned," 435 *Nature* 718 (2005); Rick Weiss, "Many Scientists Admit to Misconduct," *Washington Post*, June 9, 2005, at A3.
77 David Michaels, *Doubt is Their Product: How Industry's Assault on Science Threatens Your Health* (Oxford 2008); Naomi Oreskes and Erik M. Conway, *Merchants of Doubt: How a Handful of Scientists Obscured the Truth on Issues from Tobacco Smoke to Global Warming* (Bloomsbury, 2009); Devra Davis, *When Smoke Ran Like Water: Tales of Environmental Deception and the Battle against Pollution* (Basic, 2002); Gerard E. Markowitz and David Rosner, *Deceit and Denial: The Deadly Politics of Industrial Pollution* (U. Calif., 2003); McGarity and Wagner, 2008; Robert R. Kuehn, "Scientific Speech: Protecting the Right of Environmental Scientists to Express Professional Opinions," 35 *Environmental Law Reporter* 10857 (2005).
78 Justin E. Bekelman, Yan Li, and Cary P. Gross, "Scope and Impact of Financial Conflicts of Interest in Biomedical Research," 289 *JAMA* 454 (2003).
79 Danielle Ivory, "EPA Relies on Industry-Backed Studies to Assess Health Risks of Widely Used Herbicide," *Scientific American* (July 28, 2010), available at www.scientificamerican.com/article/epa-atrazine-herbicide/?print=true.
80 Id.
81 For example, in response to the EPA's registration review, Syngenta submitted three lengthy comments just in 2016; one comment contained 13 files. See, e.g., EPA-HQ-OPP-2013–0266-0925; see also EPA-HQ-OPP-2013–0266-0303; EPA-HQ-OPP-2013–0266-0299.
82 Ivory, 2010.
83 Id.
84 Wagner and Michaels, 2004, at 129–34.
85 Id.; see also 15 U.S.C. §§ 2613(b)(3)(C)(ii), 14(e)(1), and 14(g)(1).
86 The new 2017 amendments to TSCA did not change this approach for some sets of trade secret claims. 15 U.S.C. § 2603(c)(2).
87 15 U.S.C. § 2613(g)(1)(C).
88 Environmental Working Group, "Off the Books: More Secret Chemicals" (May 9, 2016).
89 Wagner and Michaels, 2004, at 134; Hampshire Research Associates, Inc., "Influence of CBI Requirements on TSCA Implementation" (1992).
90 General Accounting Office, "Toxic Substances Control Act: Legislative Changes Could Make the Act More Effective," GAO/RCED-94-103, at 56 (Sept. 26, 1994).
91 Center for Effective Government, "A Citizen's Platform for Our Environmental Right-to-Know" (2001).
92 See infra Part III.
93 James Landis, "Report on Regulatory Agencies to the President-Elect" 51 (1960).

94 For example, the EPA's risk assessment of formaldehyde – a well-known human carcinogen – has been ongoing for 18 years as of 2018. GAO, "Chemical Assessments: Challenges Remain with EPA's Integrated Risk Information System" 2 (Dec. 2011).
95 Sheila Jasanoff, "Research Subpoenas and the Sociology of Knowledge," 59 *Law & Contemporary Problems* 95, 98–100 (1996).
96 Id.
97 Marcus Munafo et al., "A Manifesto for Reproducible Science," 1 *Nature Human Behavior* 1, 2 (2017).
98 Stuart Shapiro, "Can Analysis of Policy Decisions Spur Participation?" 2018 *Journal of Benefit-Cost Analysis* 1, 23.
99 See generally Thomas McGarity, "Daubert and the Proper Role for the Courts in Health, Safety, and Environmental Regulation," 95 *American Journal of Public Health*, Supplement 1, S92 (2005).
100 McGarity and Wagner, 2008, at 154.
101 Gulf South Insulation v. CPSC, 701 F.2d 1137, 1146 (5th Circ. 1983).
102 See generally Wendy Wagner, "The 'Bad Science' Fiction: Reclaiming the Debate over the Role of Science in Public Health and Environmental Regulation," 66 *Law & Contemporary Problems*, Autumn 2003, 63.
103 Id.
104 See Competitive Enterprise Institute, Petitions to Cease Dissemination of the National Assessment on Climate Change, Feb. 20, 2003.
105 See Wendy Wagner, Testimony on S. 1009: The Chemical Safety Improvement Act, Energy & Commerce Committee's Subcommittee on Environment and the Economy, US House of Representatives, Nov. 13, 2013, available at http://progressivereform.org/articles/Wagner-House-Hrg_11122013.pdf (pointing out some of these attachment points in the bill).
106 Corrosion Proof Fittings v. EPA, 947 F.2d 1201, 1215 (5th Cir. 1991).
107 Irving J. Selikoff, et al., "Asbestos Exposure and Neoplasia," 188 *JAMA* 22 (1964).
108 Corrosion Proof, 947 F.2d at 1215.
109 See, e.g., Wagner, 2014, at 5.
110 Id.
111 Summary of 1812 Battle of Lake Erie, available at www.historynet.com/war-of-1812-battle-of-lake-erie-oliver-perrys-miraculous-victory.htm.
112 Denison, 2017, at 9–11.
113 15 U.S.C. § 2605(b).
114 Oscar Hernandez and Charles Auer, "Key Science Concepts," in *New TSCA: A Guide to the Lautenberg Chemical Safety Act and Its Implementation* 24–25, 26, 31 (Lynn L. Bergeson and Charles M. Auer, eds.) (ABA, 2017) (highlighting three new types of findings the EPA must make in each chemical assessment); Dennison, 2017, at 9–11; Wilson and Ogunseitan, 2017, at 31.
115 Dennison, 2017, at 4–5.
116 15 U.S.C. § 2607(b); see also Dennison, 2017, at 9.
117 15 U.S.C. §§ 2605(b)(1), (b)(2)(C), and 2618(a)(1)(C).
118 15 U.S.C. § 2605(b)(2) and (4).
119 15 U.S.C. § 2605(b)(4)(D); EPA, Procedures for Chemical Risk Evaluation under the Amended TSCA: Proposed Rule, 82 Fed. Reg. 7562 (2017).

120 15 U.S.C. § 2605(b)(3)(H).

121 Id. at § 2605(i)(2).

122 Id. at § 2605(b)(4)(F)(i) through (v).

123 Id. at § 2605(b)(4)(ii).

124 Id. at § 2605(b)(4)(iv).

125 Id. at § 2604(a)(3); see also Denison, 2017, at 6.

126 Id. at § 2625(h).

127 Id. at § 2625(j)(1)–(5).

128 Id. at § 2603(a)(3) and (4).

129 Id. at § 2613(c)(3); this is a change from the old TSCA, see Denison, 2017, at 7; Wagner and Michaels, 2004, at 129–35 (2004).

130 Brady Dennis, "Trump Budget Seeks 23 Percent Cut at EPA, Eliminating Dozens of Programs," *Washington Post*, Feb. 12, 2018.

131 Hu, 2014, at 636.

132 Existing, overbroad trade secret claims may also need to be reviewed to ensure there are not unjustified constraints on public access to some of the information.

133 15 U.S.C. § 2604(d).

134 The representations that we propose at this point involve relatively rigid, standardized methods for extracting information from individual studies and for inserting data directly into the same, simple models. Implementing the approach, ideally, would entail an estimated burden of less than a half-hour per dataset or study to format the information in terms the models can accept.

135 National Research Council, *Models in Environmental Regulatory Decision Making* 172–76 (NAS, 2007).

136 Once the universe of available research exceeds 200 studies, for example, there would be a presumption of collective model-building by all affected manufacturers.

137 FIFRA, 7 U.S.C. §§ 136–136y (2000); Thomas O. McGarity and Sidney A. Shapiro, "The Trade Secret Status of Health and Safety Testing Information: Reforming Agency Disclosure Policies," 93 *Harvard Law Review* 837, 874–82 (1980).

138 Hu, 2014, at 636.

139 The new TSCA "conditions of use" requirements could help identify what constitutes a "major use" of a chemical.

140 For a slightly different but parallel reform, see Wagner, 2014.

141 The agency may need to conduct representations for dozens of standard, non-chemical alternatives for manufacturers to use for this set of comparisons.

142 In some cases, the EPA might use other existing authorities to take action against some chemicals based on these representations, but how that is done falls outside the scope of this proposal. For more specific legal suggestions along these lines, see Wagner, 2014.

143 See, e.g., National Research Council, *Review of the Environmental Protection Agency's Draft IRIS Assessment of Formaldehyde* (NAS, 2011).

144 Richard R. Nelson and Disney G. Winter, *An Evolutionary Theory of Economic Change* 259–60 (Belknap, 1982).

145 See, e.g., Brett McDonnell and Daniel Schwarcz, "Regulatory Contrarians," 89 *North Carolina Law Review* 1629, 1672 (2011).

146 REACH (EC 1907/2006); see also Alex Scott, "Chemical Firms Rush to Meet Final REACH Regulation Deadline," 96 *Chemical and Engineering News*, May 24, 2018.

147 REACH does require manufacturers of extremely hazardous chemicals to justify the continued marketing of their products against the available substitutes, but our proposal applies to all chemicals, not just the worst ones. REACH, Art. 58(1).

148 Cf. Wagner, 2008, at 638–39 (discussing the long history of manufacturer opposition to meaningful chemical regulation reform).

149 While the manufacturers preparing these comparative risk assessments will not have access to the representations from nonparticipating competitors, the agency could provide methods for how a manufacturer could make these comparative assessments on their own, touting the comparative advantages of the chemicals as among the safest in a use category.

150 Wagner, 2008, at 640–48.

6 COMPREHENSION ASYMMETRIES IN ADMINISTRATIVE PROCESS

1 E.g., Edward Rubin, "It's Time to Make the Administrative Procedure Act Administrative," 89 *Cornell Law Review* 95, 101 (2003); Louis J. Virelli III, "Scientific Peer Review and Administrative Legitimacy," 61 *Administrative Law Review* 723, 751–53 (2009); Michael Sant' Ambrogio and Glen Staszewski, "Public Engagement with Agency Rulemaking," Final Report for ACUS, Nov. 19, 2018, available at www.acus.gov/sites/default/files/documents/Public%20Engagement%20in%20Rulemaking%20Final%20Report.pdf.

2 E.g., Joseph Sax, *Defending the Environment: A Handbook for Citizen Action* (Knopf, 1972); Lynton Caldwell, "The National Environmental Policy Act: Retrospect and Prospect," 6 *Environmental Law Reporter* 50,030 (1976); Ralph Nader, "Freedom from Information: The Act and the Agencies," 5 *Harvard Civil Rights–Civil Liberties Law Review* 1 (1970).

3 Freedom of Information Act, 5 U.S.C. § 552 (2006).

4 Federal Advisory Committee Act, 5 U.S.C. app. §§ 1–16 (2006).

5 Government in the Sunshine Act, 5 U.S.C. § 552b (2006).

6 Negotiated Rulemaking Act, 5 U.S.C. §§ 561–70 (2006).

7 See Richard B. Stewart, "The Reformation of American Administrative Law," 88 *Harvard Law Review* 1669, 1723, 1748 (1975).

8 Justice Brandeis's phrase, "sunlight is said to be the best of disinfectants," see Louis D. Brandeis, "What Publicity Can Do," *Harper's Weekly*, Dec. 20, 1913, has been repeated almost like a mantra in some administrative law and regulatory circles.

9 Carol M. Rose, "Rethinking Environmental Controls: Management Strategies for Common Resources," 1991 *Duke Law Journal* 1, 1.

10 Eric W. Orts, "Reflexive Environmental Law," 89 *Northwestern Law Review* 1227, 1228 (1995); see generally Cynthia R. Farina, Mary J. Newhart, and Cheryl Blake, "The Problem with Words: Plain Language and Public Participation in Rulemaking," 83 *The George Washington Law Review* 1358, 1365 (2015) (observing this phenomenon).

11 Farina, Newhart, and Blake, 2015, at 1365.

12 See Wendy E. Wagner, "Administrative Law, Filter Failure, and Information Capture," 59 *Duke Law Journal* 1321, 1331–34 (2010) (making this general argument).

13 Michael D. Reagan, *Regulation: The Politics of Policy* 8 (Foresman, 1987).

14 Michael Stokes Paulsen, "The Most Dangerous Branch: Executive Power to Say What the Law Is," 83 *Georgetown Law Journal* 217, 224 (1994); see also Frank B. Cross, "Shattering the Fragile Case for Judicial Review of Rulemaking," 85 *Virginia Law Review* 1243, 1297 (1999).

15 Mark Seidenfeld, "A Civic Republican Justification for the Bureaucratic State," 105 *Harvard Law Review* 1511, 1541 (1992).

16 E.g., Virelli, 2009, at 751–53.

17 Pasky Pascual et al., "Making Method Visible: Improving the Quality of Science-Based Regulation," 2 *Michigan Journal of Administrative and Environmental Law* 429 (2013).

18 Stewart, 1975; Rubin, 2003, at 101.

19 Jerry L. Mashaw, "Small Things like Reasons Are Put in a Jar: Reason and Legitimacy in the Administrative State," 70 *Fordham Law Review* 17, 24 (2001).

20 Seidenfeld, 1992, at 1518.

21 Id.; 5 U.S.C. § 551 et seq.

22 Id. at § 553(c).

23 Id. at § 706(2)(a).

24 Reuel E. Schiller, "The Era of Deference: Courts, Expertise, and the Emergence of New Deal Administrative Law," 106 *Michigan Law Review* 399, 417 (2007); see also H. George Frederickson, et al., *The Public Administration Theory Primer* 44–45 (Westview 2d ed., 2012).

25 Stewart, 1975.

26 "Report of the Attorney General's Committee on Administrative Procedure in Government Agencies" 103 (Washington, D.C. 1941).

27 Peter L. Strauss, "From Expertise to Politics: The Transformation of American Rulemaking," 31 *Wake Forest Law Review* 745, 773–74 (1996).

28 Farina, Newhart, and Blake, 2015, at 1369–79 (describing this history).

29 Id. at 1373–79 (describing the series of legal mandates requiring plain English).

30 Id. at 1396.

31 E.g., James Salzman and J. B. Ruhl, "Mozart and the Red Queen: The Problem of Regulatory Accretion in the Administrative State," 91 *Georgetown Law Journal* 757 (2003); cf. Thomas J. Donohue, president & CEO, US Chamber of Commerce, "The Regulatory Tsunami – How a Tidal Wave of Regulations Is Drowning America" (Oct. 7, 2010), available at www.uschamber.com/press/speeches/2010/regulatory-tsunamihow-tidal-wave-regulations-drowning-america.

32 Informal interview with anonymous public interest litigator involved in litigation against EPA's air toxic rules in the 1990s, May 29, 2009 (interview in Chicago, IL).

33 Sidney Shapiro et al., "The Enlightenment of Administrative Law: Looking Inside the Agency for Legitimacy," 47 *Wake Forest Law Review* 463, 491–502 (2012).

34 Wendy Wagner et al., "Rulemaking in the Shade: An Empirical Study of EPA's Air Toxic Emission Standards," 63 *Administrative Law Review* 99, 145 (2011) (reporting that average EPA HAPs rules were 39 pages in the Federal Register, including the preamble).

35 Kimberly D. Krawiec, "Don't 'Screw Joe the Plummer': The Sausage-Making of Financial Reform," 55 *Arizona Law Review* 53–103 (2013).

36 Id. at 71.

37 Id. at 86, Table 2.

38 Id. at 98, Table 8.
39 Cary Coglianese, "Challenging the Rules: Litigation and Bargaining in the Administrative Process," U. of Michigan Dissertation, unpublished, 51 (1994).
40 James Q. Wilson, *Bureaucracy: What Government Agencies Do and Why They Do It* 283 (Basic, 1991).
41 E.g., Patrick McLaughlin and Richard Williams, Why We Need Regulatory Reform in Two Charts (May 27, 2014), available at http://mercatus.org/publication/why-we-need-regulatory-reform-two-charts; Salzman and Ruhl, 2003, at 775.
42 Florida Peach Growers Ass'n v. Department of Labor, 489 F.2d 120, 129 (5th Cir. 1974).
43 Aqua Slide 'N' Dive Corp. v. CPSC, 569 F.2d 831, 837 (5th Cir. 1978).
44 Natural Resources Defense Council, Inc. v. SEC, 606 F.2d 1031, 1052 (D.C. Cir. 1979).
45 See Lynn Blais, Thomas McGarity, and Wendy Wagner, "Draft Preliminary Report to TCEQ on Enforcement against Air Toxics Hotspots in Texas" (12/31/2002) (on file with author) (citing TCEQ memoranda also on file with author).
46 The investigation was financed by the Texas Council of Environmental Quality (TCEQ) using an EPA grant. See Id.
47 EPA, Proposed Rule: National Emission Standards for Hazardous Air Pollutants for Source Categories; Organic Hazardous Air Pollutants from the Synthetic Organic Chemical Manufacturing Industry and Seven Other Processes, 57 Fed. Reg. 62608, 62618 (1992) (describing Method 21).
48 40 C.F.R. § 63.120(a)(1).
49 Id. at § 63.120(a).
50 Id. at § 63.123(c).
51 Wagner, 2010, at 1349–50.
52 Id.
53 Id. at 1350.
54 See Table of rulemakings at www.epa.gov/stationary-sources-air-pollution/synthetic-organic-chemical-manufacturing-industry-organic-national.
55 59 Fed.Reg. 19402, 19436, 19444 (1994).
56 Id. at 19436.
57 See William T. Gormley, Jr., "Regulatory Issue Networks in a Federal System," 18 *Polity* 595, 607 (1986). Although Richard Stewart's concerns were more far ranging, he raised this particular problem as well throughout his seminal article. Stewart, 1975, at 1767–70.
58 See James Q. Wilson, *The Politics of Regulation* 367 (Basic, 1980) (providing four quadrants where interest group pressures vary substantially from one quadrant to another).
59 See infra Part 3 (discussing imbalances in participation in some rules).
60 Farina identifies four categories of participants. Farina and Newhart, Rulemaking 2.0 (undated), available at https://scholarship.law.cornell.edu/ceri/15/. The first consists of "sophisticated stakeholders," which include high stakes regulated parties and in some settings might also include well-organized NGOS. The second category – missing stakeholders – are directly affected but may be impeded from participation due to a lack of expertise and resources. The third and fourth categories (unaffiliated experts and interested members of the public) are less essential to ensuring vigorous participation, although by no means are they wholly peripheral, either. For purposes of this article, however, references to the "public" include all three of these absent categories. Since directly

affected groups vary from rule to rule and may not be well organized or organized at all, they are drawn from the larger population by virtue of the impacts of the rule on them. Yet, they are still part of the larger "public," broadly defined.

61 See, e.g., Gormley, 1986; Wilson, 1980; Farina and Newhart, Rulemaking 2.0, undated, at 6, 12; Farina, Newhart, and Blake, 2015, at 1362–63.

62 See, e.g., Farina and Newhart, Rulemaking 2.0, undated, at 11; Miriam Seifter, "Second-Order Participation in Administrative Law," 63 *UCLA Law Review* 1300, 1306–07, 1315 (2016); Wendy Wagner, The Government's Use and Abuse of Environmental Nonprofit Organizations as Representatives of the Citizenry (unpublished paper prepared for the ARNOVA conference, New Orleans, LA – Nov. 18, 2000).

63 Stuart Shapiro, 2018, at 6.

64 See generally Farina, Newhart, and Blake, 2015, 1364–66.

65 See Rena Steinzor and Sidney Shapiro, *Special Interests, Government, and Threats to Health, Safety, and the Environment* 65–67 (Chicago, 2010).

66 Stuart Shapiro, 2018, at 6.

67 5 U.S.C. § 706.

68 Steinzor and Shapiro, 2010, at 65–67.

69 See, e.g., Wagner, 2010, at 1345–47.

70 Indeed, Coglianese found in his study of EPA hazardous waste rules that "[o]ne reason groups select or settle issues is that the court imposes page limits on briefs and a time limit on oral argument." Coglianese, 1994, at 114.

71 See, e.g., Seifter, 2016, at 1315; Farina and Newhart, Rulemaking 2.0, undated, at 11; Farina, Newhart, and Blake, 2015, at 1362–63.

72 Stuart Shapiro, 2018, at 6.

73 See generally Farina, Newhart, and Blake, 2015, at 1362–63, 1373.

74 Wagner, 2010, at 1396–1403 (providing an overview of the commentary on these problems).

75 Mashaw, 2001, at 25.

76 5 U.S.C. § 553(c).

77 Cynthia R. Farina, "Rulemaking in 140 Characters or Less: Social Networking and Public Participation in Rulemaking," 31 *Pace Law Review* 382, 419–20 (2011) (observing that the "requirement to accept public comments has never been understood as an affirmative, inquisitorial duty to seek out members of all affected groups and ensure a broadly representative range of participation").

78 For a fuller exposition of this argument, see Wendy Wagner, "The Missing Link in Citizen Participation in US Administrative Process," 3 Accueil – Les Editions de l'MO-DEV (online Journal) (2016), available at http://ojs.imodev.org/index.php/RICO/article/view/47/126.

79 Needless to say, since the focus is exclusively on administrative process, the scope of this analysis does not consider many other important forms of citizen participation – in the political process, in reinforcing enforcement cases, in impacting agency priorities and framing of priorities and decisions, and in local or nonlegal community decision processes or collective action.

80 See Ralph L. Keeney, *Value-Focused Thinking* vii–ix, 29–30, 44–51 (Harvard, 1992) (highlighting the benefits of value-focused thinking and discussing how neglecting a

universal map of the goals, problems, and possible solutions can result in wrongheaded decisions).

81 Farina, Newhart and Blake, 2015, at 1362–63.

82 5 U.S.C. § 553(c).

83 1 Richard J. Pierce, Jr. *Administrative Law Treatise* §7.4 at 445 (5th ed., 2010).

84 Rosemary O'Leary, "The Impact of Federal Court Decisions on the Policies and Administration of the US Environmental Protection Agency," 41 *Administrative Law Review* 549, 562 (1989).

85 Ethyl Corp. v. EPA, 541 F.2d 1, 40 (D.C. Cir. 1976) (Leventhal concurring and arguing for "hard look" review).

86 Industrial Union Dept., AFL-CIO v. Hodgson, 499 F.2d 467, 475 (D.C. Cir. 1974).

87 Pierce, 2010, at §7.4.

88 Id. at §7.1.

89 Richard J. Pierce, Jr., "Waiting for Vermont Yankee III, IV, and V? A Response to Beermann and Lawson," 75 *George Washington Law Review* 902, 920 (2007).

90 O'Leary, 1989, at 566.

91 Richard B. Stewart, "Vermont Yankee and the Evolution of Administrative Procedure," 91 *Harvard Law Review* 1805, 1812 (1978).

92 Sheila Jasanoff, *Science at the Bar: Science and Technology in American Law* 91 (Harvard, 1997); R. Shep Melnick, *Regulation and the Courts: The Case of the Clean Air Act* 356 (Brookings, 1983).

93 See generally Robert Kagan, *Adversarial Legalism: The American Way of Law* 223, 225 (Harvard, 2003).

94 Jerry L. Mashaw, *Greed, Chaos, and Governance: Using Public Choice to Improve Public Law* 181 (Yale, 1999).

95 Pierce, 2010, § 7.4 at 449–50 (discussing how *State Farm* requires an agency to respond to all comments and criticisms and the resultant adverse effects that it has on the agency).

96 R. Shep Melnick, "Administrative Law and Bureaucratic Reality," 44 *Administrative Law Review* 245, 247 (1992).

97 Id.

98 E.g., Shell Oil Co. v. EPA, 950 F.2d 741, 757–63 (D.C. Cir. 1991).

99 William F. West, "Formal Procedures, Informal Processes, Accountability and Responsiveness in Bureaucratic Policy Making: An Institutional Policy Analysis," 64 *Public Administration Review* 66 (2004); see also Natural Resources Defense Council v. USEPA, 595 F. Supp. 1255, 1262 (S.D.N.Y. 1984) ("I agree that the negotiated programs without rulemaking cannot be sanctioned under TSCA, though negotiation [solely with industry] to determine appropriate test protocols as well as other relevant criteria certainly is not only permissible but indeed preferable to blind, often impractical, bureaucratic blundering").

100 Krawiec, 2013, at 71, 73; Wagner et al., 2011, at 125.

101 See Coglianese, 1994, at 14.

102 See, e.g., Wagner et al., 2011.

103 Liz Fisher, Pasky Pascual, and Wendy Wagner, "Rethinking Judicial Review of Expert Agencies," 93 *Texas Law Review* 1681, 1714–15 (2015).

104 Id.

105 Id.

106 Pierce, 2010, at 596, 604, 680.

107 For discussions of the large role that both the president and Congress play in the substance of agency rulemakings in the US, see Daniel A. Farber and Anne Joseph O'Connell, "The Lost World of Administrative Law," 92 *Texas Law Review* 1137 (2014) (discussing the important role of the president in intervening in regulations); Thomas O. McGarity, "Administrative Law as Blood Sport: Policy Erosion in a Highly Partisan Age," 61 *Duke Law Journal* 1671 (2012) (describing the same for Congress).

108 While both Congress and the president are also "audiences" within the deliberative dialog for agency rules (and at some points even speakers) we treat them separately because their legal roles are quite different.

109 McGarity, 2012, at 1678.

110 Nina A. Mendelson, "Disclosing 'Political' Oversight of Agency Decision Making," 108 *Michigan Law Review* 1127, 1157 (2010).

111 Thomas O. McGarity, "Presidential Control of Regulatory Agency Decisionmaking," 36 *American University Law Review* 443, 455–56 (1987).

112 Thomas McGarity and Wendy Wagner, "Deregulation using Stealth 'Science' Strategies," *Duke Law Journal* (forthcoming 2019).

113 Id., Curtis W. Copeland, "Length of Rule Reviews by the Office of Information and Regulatory Affairs," A Study for ACUS, at 16, 24, 36–37 (2013).

114 Id.

115 McGarity and Wagner, 2019 (discussing American Farm Bureau Federation v. EPA, 559 F.3d 512 (D.C. Cir. 2009)).

116 McGarity, 2012, at 1711–12, 1733.

117 See generally Wagner, 2015; Simon F. Haeder and Susan Webb Yackee, "Influence and the Administrative Process: Lobbying the US President's Office of Management and Budget," 109 *American Political Science Review* 507 (2015).

118 Jennifer Nou, "Agency Self-Insulation Under Presidential Review," 126 *Harvard Law Review* 1755, 1771 (2013).

119 Id. at 1793.

120 Id.

121 McGarity, 2012, at 1681 (quoting Levitt).

122 Melnick, 1983, at 322.

123 McGarity, 2013, at 1712; Nou, 2013, at 1764.

124 E.g., Elena Kagan, "Presidential Administration," 114 *Harvard Law Review* 2245 (2001).

125 Farber and O'Connell, 2014, at 1140–41.

126 McKart v. United States, 395 US 185 (1969).

127 Andrea Bear Field and Kathy E. B. Robb, "EPA Rulemakings: Views from Inside and Outside," 5 *Natural Resources and Environment*, Summer 5, 9–10 (1995).

128 Coglianese, 1994, at 112. Another attorney conceded that the appellate brief was unsuccessful in part because the brief writers had failed to do an adequate job of controlling information excess: The brief "was so filled with so many issues of such a technical nature that I think we got lost in explaining basically how simple this one [issue] was." Id. at 111 (alteration in original).

129 E.g., NRDC v. Thomas, 805 F.2d 410 (D.C. Cir. 1986).

130 McKart v. United States, 395 US 185 (1969).

131 Marcia R. Gelpe, "Exhaustion of Administrative Remedies: Lessons from Environmental Cases," 53 *George Washington Law Review* 1 (1985); see also Clean Air Act, 42 U.S.C. § 7606(d)(7)(B) ("Only an objection to a rule or procedure which was raised with reasonable specificity during the period for public comment (including any public hearing) may be raised during judicial review" with limited exceptions).

132 Patrick Schmidt, "Pursuing Regulatory Relief: Strategic Participation and Litigation in US OSHA Rulemaking," 4 *Business and Politics* 71 (2002).

133 See id. at 77.

134 E.g., Portland Cement Ass'n v. Ruckelshaus, 486 F.2d 375, 394 (D.C. Cir. 1973).

135 Field and Robb, 1995, at 9–10.

136 5 U.S.C. at § 553(c).

137 E.g., Pierce, 2010, at §7.4.

138 Stuart Shapiro, 2018, at 6.

139 See, e.g., Strengthening Transparency in Regulatory Science, 83 Fed. Reg. 18768 (2018); E. S. Pruitt, "Back-to-Basics Process for Revising National Ambient Air Quality Standards" (EPA, May 9, 2018).

140 Robinson Meyer, "Scott Pruitt's New Rule Could Completely Transform the EPA," *The Atlantic*, Apr. 25, 2018.

141 See, e.g., Devon Hall, "New EPA Rule Would Force People to Choose between Privacy and Health," *CNN Opinion*, July 31, 2018, available at www.cnn.com/2018/07/31/opinions/epa-regulation-threatens-privacy-health-hall/index.html. For general discussions of these approaches, see, e.g., Chris Mooney, *The Republican War on Science* (New York: Basic Books, 2005).

142 See, e.g., Wendy E. Wagner, "The Clean Air Interstate Rule's Regulatory Impact Analysis: Advocacy Dressed Up as Policy Analysis," in *Reforming Regulatory Impact Analysis* 56 (Richard Morgenstern et al. eds., 2009) (observing that in one major Regulatory Impact Analysis conducted by the EPA, the EPA considered only one regulatory alternative against the agency's preferred proposal).

143 E.g., EPA, Strengthening Transparency in Regulatory Science, 83 Fed. Reg. 18768, 18770 n.9 (2018) (providing an illustration of this tactic; note that the authors of those reports, including Wagner, later pointed out that the citation was not accurate).

144 If one selects any EPA or OSHA final rule at random in the Federal Register, one is likely to find a section entitled something like "significant changes to the proposed rule" that itemizes the most important comments and the agency's responses. This section generally details these issues in no particular order and will not provide readers with explanations that link together or put those concerns in context. For a sample of the high processing costs associated with these explanations of agency response to significant comments, see Wendy Wagner, "Revisiting the Impact of Judicial Review on Agency Rulemaking: An Empirical Investigation," 53 *William and Mary Law Review* 1717, 1780 (2012) (providing a sample); see also supra at Part II.

145 E.g., Wagner, 1995.

146 If one selects any EPA proposed rule at random in the Federal Register, one is likely to find this assertion to be true. See also Bipartisan Policy Ctr., "Improving the Use of Science in Regulatory Policy" 15–16 (2009) (noting the problem in the course of advocating reform).

147 James Landis, "Report on Regulatory Agencies to the President-Elect" 71 (1960).

148 Louis L. Jaffe, "The Effective Limits of the Administrative Process: A Reevaluation," 67 *Harvard Law Review* 11–5, 1113–19 (1954); Louis L. Jaffe, "Federal Regulatory Agencies in Perspective: Administrative Limitations in a Political Setting," 11 *Boston College Industrial & Commercial Law Review* 565, 566 (1970).

149 O'Leary, 1989, at 549.

150 Owen and Braeutigam, 1978, at 4.

151 Id.

152 Id. at 4. These techniques can also be deployed in more adversarial settings to overcome the opposition's efforts. For example, "If another party has supplied damaging information, it is important to supply contrary information in as technical a form as possible so that a hearing is necessary to settle the issues of 'fact.'" Id. The authors even advise the regulated parties to deploy decentralized information systems so that officials can be selected who can testify truthfully on what they know, but be carefully protected from other, conflicting or damaging sources of information. Id.

153 Coglianese, 1994, at 52.

154 42 U.S.C. § 4321 et seq.

155 Stuart Shapiro, 2018, at 16 (noting how this incomprehensibility of EISs is sometimes the case).

156 Council on Environmental Quality, "The National Environmental Policy Act: A Study of Its Effectiveness after Twenty-Five Years" (1997); see also Stuart Shapiro, 2018, at 16.

157 Stuart Shapiro, 2018, at 8 (citing Karkkainen).

158 See Mark Seidenfeld, "A Table of Requirements for Federal Administrative Rulemaking," 27 *Florida State University Law Review* 533 (2000).

159 See generally Stuart Shapiro, 2018.

160 See, e.g., Christopher Carrigan and Stuart Shapiro, "What's Wrong with the Back of the Envelope? A Call for Simple (and Timely) Benefit-Cost Analysis," 11 *Regulation and Governance* 203 (2016); Winston Harrington, Lisa Heinzerling, and Richard D. Morgenstern, "What We Learned," in *Reforming Regulatory Impact Analysis* 226 (Winston Harrington, Lisa Heinzerling, and Richard D. Morgenstern eds.) (RFF, 2009) (observing, based on the chapter case studies, that "RIAs have become huge, dense documents that are almost impenetrable to all but those with training in the relevant technical fields . . . [but that] even to the well-trained eye, RIAs are often opaque"); Stuart Shapiro, 2018, at 6, 16.

161 Farina, Newhart, and Blake, 2015, at 1365; Stuart Shapiro, 2018, at 6.

162 Farina, Newhart, and Blake, 2015, at 221–25.

163 See Martin Shapiro, "On Predicting the Future of Administrative Law," 6 *Regulation* 18 (1982); Shapiro, 2018, at 23.

164 Jennifer Shkabatur, "Transparency with(out) Accountability: Open Government in the United States," 31 *Yale Law and Policy Review* 79, 81 (2012).

165 See Maureen L. Cropper et al., "The Determinants of Pesticide Regulation: A Statistical Analysis of EPA Decision Making," 100 *Journal of Political Economy* 175, 178, 187 (1992) (examining interest group engagement in pesticide registrations between 1975 and 1989 and finding environmentalists participated in 49 percent of the cancellations); Marissa Martino Golden, "Interest Groups in the Rule-Making Process: Who Participates?

Whose Voices Get Heard?" 8 *Journal of Public Administration Research & Theory* 245, 253–54 (1998) (studying eight rules promulgated by the EPA and NHTSA, using content analysis to determine who participates and influences federal regulations, and finding no citizen engagement in five of the eight rules); Jason W. Yackee and Susan W. Yackee, "A Bias toward Business? Assessing Interest Group Influence on the Bureaucracy," 68 *Journal of Politics* 128, 131, 133 (2006) (studying 40 lower-salience rulemakings promulgated by four different federal agencies and finding that business interests submitted 57 percent of comments, whereas nonbusiness or nongovernmental organizations submitted 22 percent of comments, of which 6 percent came from public interest groups); Cary Coglianese, 1994, at 73, tbl. 2–2 (finding that businesses participated in 96 percent of rules and that national environmental groups participated in 44 percent); Wagner et al., *Rulemaking in the Shade*, 2011, at 128 (discovering that public interest groups participated in notice and comment for less than half (48 percent) of the rules setting emission standards for hazardous air pollutants from major categories of industry).

166 Yackee and Yackee, 2006; Wagner et al., 2011.
167 See generally Ronald G. Shaiko, *Voices and Echoes for the Environment: Public Interest Representation in the 1990s and Beyond* 152 (Columbia, 1999) (table on policy-relevant content in 77–78 communications of 5 national nonprofits with overall policy content ranging from 8.4 percent to 67.0 percent and specific policy content ranging from 2.2 percent to 45.9 percent) depending on the nonprofit); id. at 165 (table on policy-relevant content in 91–92 communications of same 4 national nonprofits with overall policy content ranging from 9.1 percent to 59.2 percent and specific policy content ranging from 2.7 percent to 31.8 percent). Shaiko concludes that there has been a marked decline in the communication from leaders to members and that, as a result, "[I]t will become increasingly difficult for organized interest groups to mobilize grassroots activists if they continue to diminish the role of communicating policy from leadership to membership in a timely fashion." Id. at 173.
168 Robert Putnam, *Bowling Alone* 160 (Simon and Schuster, 2000).
169 See Seifter, 2016, at 1333–50.
170 Cf. Steven P. Croley, *Regulation and Public Interests: The Possibility of Good Regulatory Government* 305 (Princeton, 2008) (arguing that APA processes stave off rent-seekers and keep regulatory outcomes more public benefitting).
171 E.g., Simon, 1997, at 242 (observing how many "systems were not designed to conserve the critical scarce resource – the attention of managers – and they tended to ignore the fact that the information most important to top managers comes mainly from external sources and not from the internal records that were immediately accessible for mechanized processing").
172 James Q. Wilson, *Bureaucracy: What Government Agencies Do and Why They Do It* 115 (Basic Books, 1991).
173 Rubin, 2003, at 103.
174 Wilson, 1991, at 283 (expressing concern and quoting others with the concern that the threat of judicial review will cause agencies to resist change or take risks on policies, "especially those that embody novel ideas or approaches").
175 O'Leary, 1989, at 549. Stewart worried – even in the early years of the interest representation model – that "[j]udicialization of agency procedures and the expansion of

participation rights may ... aggravate the tendency for the agency to assume a passive role, focusing on the unique character of each controversy in order to reach an ad hoc accommodation of the particular constellation of interests present." Stewart, 1975, at 1773. Stewart also gestured to the added possibility that the ad hoc analysis might not take into account all of the interests affected. Id. at 1789.

176 Schiller recounts how in the New Deal, agencies were supposed to serve "as a counter-weight to the incredible power wielded by large corporations ... The administrative state equalized the playing field by placing the government on the side of the people rather than having it simply act as a neutral 'umpire' in a dispute between two unequal parties." Reuel E. Schiller, 2007, at 429; see also Melnick, 1983, at 76–80, 129–35, 157–62, and 261–269 (discussing cases where courts emphasized the agency's role was to protect public health and the environment).

177 Christopher J. Bosso, *Pesticides and Politics: The Life Cycle of a Public Issue* 255 (Pittsburgh, 1987).

178 Schuck, 1992, at 22.

179 Orts, 1995, at 1241.

180 See Thomas O. McGarity, "Some Thoughts on 'Deossifying' the Rulemaking Process," 41 *Duke Law Journal* 1385, 1387 (1992). For a visual representation of the growth of environmental regulations from 1972 to 2008, see www.law.drake.edu/facStaff/docs/T_40_compared.JPG (last visited Jan. 1, 2010) (provided by Jerry Anderson, Drake Law School).

181 Croley, 2008, at 160.

182 Sidney Shapiro, et al., "The Enlightenment of Administrative Law: Looking Inside the Agency for Legitimacy," 47 *Wake Forest Law Review* 463, 491–501 (2012).

183 See also Gabriel Markoff, "The Invisible Barrier: Issue Exhaustion as a Threat to Pluralism in Administrative Rulemaking," 90 *Texas Law Review* 1065, 1065–66 (2012).

184 See Wagner, 2010, at 1419–22 (making some parallel reform suggestions).

185 See, e.g., Mossville Environmental Action Now v. EPA, 370 F.3d 1232, 1238–39 (D.C. Cir. 2004) (comments made by state not specific enough to support appeal).

186 See, e.g., Wagner, 2010, at 1406–14 (offering parallel recommendations).

187 This tracks the logic of Chevron v. NRDC, 467 US 837 (1984).

188 Louis J. Virelli III, "Deconstructing Arbitrary and Capricious Review," 92 *North Carolina Law Review* 721 (2014).

189 Id. at 738.

190 Id.

191 Jacob Gersen and Adrian Vermeule, "Thin Rationality Review," 114 *Michigan Law Review* 1355, 1402 (2016).

192 Virelli, 2014, at 765.

193 Id.

194 Mashaw, 2001, at 34.

195 Virelli, 2014, at 765–66; see also id. at 765–79 (elaborating in detail on this observation).

196 See, e.g., Mashaw, 2001, at 29, 33–35 (gesturing toward this larger goal of meaningful rulemaking deliberations in administrative law).

197 Gersen and Vermeule, 2016, at 1396.

198 E.g., McGarity and Wagner, 2019 (discussing this approach in the reform).

199 This showing comports with what Virelli calls the "input quality" and "research scope" features of hard look review. Virelli, 2014, at 745–52.

200 This showing overlaps several categories (including input quality and research scope), but is centered most directly in Virelli's "reason giving" prong of first-order hard look review. Id., at 743–44.

201 This showing is consistent with the "record building" feature of first-order hard look review identified by id., at 740–42.

202 This showing covers all four grounds of first-order review as the agency explains how it created a record, solicited input, defined the scope of its research, and provided reasons as a result of this process. See generally id., at 737–52.

203 E.g., American Farm Bureau Federation v. EPA, 559 F.3d 512 (D.C. Cir. 2009).

204 This is in fact an approach that has been advocated somewhat tangentially by Richard Pierce and Judge Kavanaugh in a dissenting opinion. Richard Pierce, "A Comparison of the Cultures and Performance of a Modern Agency and a Nineteenth-Century Agency," in *Administrative Law from the Inside Out: Essays on Themes in the Work of Jerry L. Mashaw* 322, 343–44 (Nicholas R. Parrillo ed.) (Yale, 2017); American Radio Relay League, Inc. v. FCC, 524 F.3d 227, 248 (2008) (J. Kavanaugh, dissenting).

205 Cf., Stijn Smismans, "Regulatory Procedure and Participation in the European Union," in *Comparative Law and Regulation* 129 (Francesca Bignami and David Zaring eds.) (Elgar, 2016).

206 Cf. Virelli, 2009, at 748–49.

207 Mississippi v. EPA, 744 F.3d 1334, 1358–62 (D.C. Cir. 2013).

208 Cf. IDEA, State of Democracy Assessment Framework in Germany, at www.idea.int/sod-assessments/approach/sod/ (providing an elaborate framework for assessing, among other things, the link between governmental processes and citizen perceptions of meaningful opportunities for participation in those processes).

209 See, e.g., Wagner, The Missing Link, 2016, at § 3 (making these suggestions).

210 See, e.g., Spencer Overton, "The Participation Interest," 100 *Georgetown Law Journal* 1259 (2012).

211 For an excellent overview of this topic, see Daniel Schwarcz, "Preventing Capture through Consumer Empowerment Programs: Some Evidence from Insurance Regulation," in *Preventing Regulatory Capture* 365, 368 (Daniel Carpenter and David A. Moss eds.) (Cambridge, 2014).

212 See David J. Arkush, "Direct Republicanism in the Administrative Process," 81 *George Washington Law Review* 1458 (2013); Hannah J. Wiseman, "Negotiated Rulemaking and New Risks: A Rail Safety Case Study," 7 *Wake Forest Journal of Law and Policy* 207 (2017); see also Sant' Ambrogio and Staszewski, 2018 (making other suggestions).

213 The agencies in the EU are required to actively solicit this type of engagement. See, e.g., Wagner, 2016, at 109.

214 Seifter, 2016, at 1337.

215 For a general sketch of this proposal, see Neil Komesar and Wendy Wagner, "Essay: The Administrative Process from the Bottom Up: Reflections on the Role, if Any, for Judicial Review," 69 *Administrative Law Review* 891, 944–48 (2017).

216 The Small Business Regulatory Enforcement Fairness Act of 1996 was based in part on a concern that information excesses precluded the smaller businesses from keeping up with bigger competitors in the provision of regulation. Pub. L. No. 104–121, 1996 U.S.C.C.A.N. (110 Stat.) 857 (to be codified in scattered sections of 5 U.S.C., 15 U.S.C., and 28 U.S.C.). The Act, among other things, provides small businesses with an agency ombud and related advocates to help protect their interests. See also Regulatory Flexibility Act, 5 U.S.C. § 601, as amended (providing comprehensive reviews of regulatory activities to consider impacts of rules on small businesses).

217 Thomas O. Sargentich, "Recent Developments: Regulatory Reform and the 104th Congress: The Small Business Regulatory Enforcement Fairness Act," 48 *Administrative Law Review* 123, 124–25 (1997).

218 E.g., Komesar and Wagner, 2017, at 945–46 (summarizing the literature on this particular risk).

7 COMPREHENSION ASYMMETRIES IN LEGISLATIVE PROCESS

1 15 U.S.C. §§2601–2697.

2 Frank R. Lautenberg Chemical Safety for the 21st Century Act, H.R. 2576, 114th Congress (2016). See also Chapter 5C.

3 Jonathan D. Salant, "US House Passes Lautenberg Chemical Safety Bill," *New Jersey Politics*, May 24, 2016, available at www.nj.com/politics/index.ssf/2016/05/us_house_passes_lautenberg_chemical_safety_bill.html.

4 Timony Cama, "Senate Passes Overhaul of Chemical Safety Rules," *The Hill*, Dec. 17, 2015, available at http://thehill.com/policy/energy-environment/263680-senate-passes-chemical-safety-reform.

5 See Chapter 5C for an overview of the intricacies of this legislation.

6 See Chapter 5C.

7 For example, the EPA can put the burden on the manufacturer to test "high priority" chemicals, but the agency can only impose this requirement through a convoluted process. Beyond these internal contradictions are terms that are so general that they permit almost complete discretion, such as the ability to bypass the strongest features of the risk assessment by excluding "legacy" uses. See, e.g., Annie Sneed, "Trump's EPA May Be Weakening Chemical Safety Law," *Scientific American*, Aug. 16, 2017.

8 Attachment points are the arguments that can be raised to legally challenge an agency decision. In the new Lautenberg Act, these attachment points include a series of scientific quality requirements imposed on EPA's risk assessments. See discussion of 2017 legislation in Chapter 5C.

9 James M. Curry, *Legislating in the Dark: Information and Power in the House of Representatives* 2 (U Chi., 2015).

10 See House roll call vote at http://clerk.house.gov/evs/2005/roll108.xml; Senate roll call vote at www.senate.gov/legislative/LIS/roll_call_lists/roll_call_vote_cfm.cfm?congress=109&session=1&vote=00044.

11 Jean Braucher, "The Challenge to the Bench and the Bar Presented by the Bankruptcy Act: Resistance Need Not Be Futile," 2007 *University of Illinois Law Review* 93, 100.

12 Henry L. Sommer, "Trying to Make Sense out of Nonsense," 79 *American Bankruptcy Law Journal* 191, 192 (2005).

13 Braucher, 2007, at 96.

14 Sommer, 2005, at 193.

15 Brannon Denning and Brooks Smith, "Uneasy Riders: The Case for a Truth-in-Legislation Amendment," 1999 *Utah Law Review* 957, 959 (1999).

16 Id. at 959 (citing John Godfrey, "House Passes Spending Bill Despite Jeers," *Washington Times*, Oct. 21, 1998, at A1 (reporting legislative reaction to spending bill)).

17 Id. at 959 (citing George Haber, "House Passes Spending Bill: Massive Omnibus Measure Larded with Pet Projects," *Washington Post*, Oct. 21, 1998, at A1).

18 Id. at 960.

19 Jack O'Brien, "Ron Johnson on Senate Healthcare Bill: Leadership Wants 'to Jam this Thing Through,'" *Washington Examiner* (Aug. 25, 2017).

20 McCain's Speech on the Senate Floor, CNN (July 25, 2017), available at www.cnn.com/2017/07/25/politics/john-mccain-speech-full-text-senate/index.html.

21 The House version is 468 pages in pdf. See, e.g., H.R.1., 115th Cong., 1st Session, available at www.congress.gov/bill/115th-congress/house-bill/1/text.

22 John Cassidy, "The Republican Tax Strategy: Speed, Subterfuge, and Diversion," *The New Yorker* (Nov. 17, 2017), available at www.newyorker.com/news/our-columnists/the-republican-tax-strategy-speed-subterfuge-and-diversion.

23 Harry Edwards, "The Role of a Judge in Modern Society: Some Reflections on Current Practice in Federal Appellate Adjudication," 32 *Cleveland State Law Review* 385, 424–25 (1983–84).

24 Id.

25 Henry J. Friendly, "The Gap in Lawmaking – Judges Who Can't and Legislators Who Won't," 63 *Columbia Law Review* 787, 792 (1963).

26 Id.

27 Ruth Bader Ginsburg, "A Plea for Legislative Review," 60 *Southern California Law Review* 995, 996 (1987) (citing Justice Scalia in Sharp v. Weinberger, 798 F.2d 1521, 1522).

28 Id. at 996, 997.

29 Ruth Bader Ginsburg and Peter Huber, "The Intercircuit Committee," 100 *Harvard Law Review* 1417, 1420, 1421 (1987).

30 Id. at 1417.

31 Curry, 2015, at 2.

32 Id.

33 Id. at 3.

34 Lisa Schultz Bressman and Abbe R. Gluck, "Statutory Interpretation from the Inside – An Empirical Study of Congressional Drafting, Delegation, and the Cannons: Part II," 66 *Stanford Law Review* 725, 733 (2014).

35 Id. at 729.

36 Ginsburg, 1987, at 996.

37 Friendly, 1963, at 793–94.

38 The ACA, for example, includes more than 40 provisions that require the implementation of regulations and the text is exceedingly long – spanning more than 900 pages. Curtis W. Copeland, Cong. Research Serv., R41180, "Regulations Pursuant to the Patient

Protection and Affordable Care Act (PPACA)," at Summary (2010), available at http:// geoffdavis.house.gov/UploadedFiles/Regulations_Pursuant_to_the_Patient_Protection.pdf. It is rumored that one "staffer who took a copy home as a souvenir after the Senate passed it on Christmas Eve 2009 had to remove it from his luggage or face an excess-baggage charge." "Legislative Verbosity, Outrageous Bills," *The Economist* (Nov. 23, 2103), available at www.economist.com/news/united-states/21590368-why-congress-writes-such-long-laws-outrageous-bills. In upholding the constitutionality of the ACA in King v. Burwell, Chief Justice Roberts, writing for the majority, expressed frustration with the excessive complexity and incoherence of the statute, observing that "the Act does not reflect the type of care and deliberation that one might expect of such significant legislation." 135 S. Ct. 2480, 2493 (2015).These deficiencies, according to the Court, were at least partly attributable to problematic legislative processes, which included a secretive drafting process and the disregard for standard deliberative procedures in a way that ultimately "limited opportunities for debate and amendment." Id.

39 The Dodd-Frank Wall Street Reform and Consumer Protection Act might also be identified by some observers as "incomprehensible" despite its very elaborate (e.g., dozens of hearings in each of the House and Senate) deliberative history, www.llsdc .org/dodd-frank-legislative-history. The final statute weighs in at 848 pages, which "is 23 times longer than Glass-Steagall, the reform that followed the Wall Street crash of 1929" and more than 2-1/2 times the size of "all the laws passed by Congress during its first five years ... [in] getting the new government under way." Felix Frankfurter, "Some Reflections on the Reading of Statutes," 47 *Columbia Law Review* 527, 527 (1947). The Dodd-Frank Act is also exceedingly complex. For its implementation, it "requires a minimum of 243 rules for its implementation," Curtis W. Copeland, Cong. Research Serv., R41380, "The Dodd-Frank Wall Street Reform and Consumer Protection Act: Regulations to Be Issued by The consumer Financial Protection Bureau" 3 (2010), available at www.fas.org/sgp/crs/misc/R41380.pdf, and some of these regulations are hundreds of pages long. The resulting legal complexity embedded and created by the statute is daunting. "Just one bit [of the statute], the 'Volcker rule,' which aims to curb risky proprietary trading by banks, includes 383 questions that break down into 1,420 subquestions." Timekeeper, "Over-regulated America," *The Economist* (Feb. 18, 2012).

40 With respect to the ACA, for example, Peggy Noonan, a political commentator, criticized ACA because the bill "was 2,000 pages of impenetrable paragraphs – real word-clots, word-slabs – accompanied by long lines of swimming numbers." Peter Wilson, "The Affordable Care Act is Not 'Incomprehensible,'" *The American Thinker*, Nov. 18, 2013, available at www.americanthinker.com/articles/2013/11/the_affordable_care_act_is_not_incomprehen sible.html. Michelle Bachman (R-MN) complained that there was not enough time to review the ever-changing bill. At times, only a few days were available for members to read a 1000+ page document. Angie Holman, "Speed-Reading the Health Care Reform Bill," *Politifact*, Oct. 7, 2009, available at www.politifact.com/truth o meter/article/2009/oct/07/ speed-reading-health-care-reform-bill/. And the then-House Judiciary Committee Chairman John Conyers (D-MI) lamented: "What good is reading the bill if it's a thousand pages and you don't have two days and two lawyers to find out what it means after you read the bill?" Victoria McGrane, "Read the Bill? It might Not Help," *Politico*, Sept. 8, 2009,

available at www.politico.com/story/2009/09/read-the-bill-it-might-not-help-026846. Efforts to repeal the ACA met with much of the same criticism. See, e.g., Olivia Beavers, "GOP Senator Defends Time to Read Senate Tax Bill before Vote," *The Hill*, Dec. 3, 2017, available at http://thehill.com/homenews/sunday-talk-shows/362986-gop-sen-says-there-was-plenty-of-time-to-read-tax-bill-before-vote; Rebecca Savransky, "Senate Dem: Passing ObamaCare a 'Very Different Process' than GOP Plan," *The Hill*, June 12, 2017, available at http://thehill.com/homenews/senate/337380-senate-dem-passing-obamacare-a-very-dif ferent-process-than-gop-plan.

After Dodd-Frank was passed, it also received criticisms about its unjustified incomprehensibility. In 2014, Rep. Jeb Hensarling, chairman of the House Financial Services Committee, observed: "With all due respect to its authors and admirers, Dodd-Frank stands as a monument to the arrogance and hubris of man in that its answer to incomprehensible complexity is yet more incomprehensible complexity." Press Release: Hensarling: Dodd-Frank Results in Less Freedom, Less Opportunity and a Less Dynamic Economy, July 16, 2014, available at https://financialservices.house.gov/news/documentsin gle.aspx?DocumentID=388236.

41 Hans A. Linde, "Due Process of Lawmaking," 55 *Nebraska Law Review* 197, 224 (1976).
42 Id.
43 Id.
44 Id. at 226.
45 Id.
46 For more recent data, go to www.brookings.edu/wp-content/uploads/2017/01/vitalstats_ ch6_full.pdf.
47 Russell W. Mills and Jennifer L. Selin, "Don't Sweat the Details! Enhancing Congressional Committee Expertise through the Use of Detailees," 42 *Legislative Studies Quarterly* 611, 612 (2017).
48 Id. at 616.
49 Id. at 616–17.
50 This is based on the total number of bills enacted and the total number of words in those bills. Available from https://medium.com/@govtrack/how-a-complex-network-of-bills-becomes-a-law-9972b9624d36.
51 "Legislative Verbosity: Outrageous Bills," *The Economist*, Nov. 23, 2013.
52 Mills and Selin, 2017, at 612 (citing others).
53 Abbe R. Gluck and Lisa Schultz Bressman, "Statutory Interpretation from the Inside – An Empirical Study of Congressional Drafting, Delegation, and the Cannons: Part I," 65 *Stanford Law Review* 901, 972–73 (2013) (quoting a congressional staffer).
54 Thomas Mann and Norman Ornstein, *It's Even Worse than It Looks/Was*, at xiv (Basic, 2012).
55 E.g., Part 1 of this chapter referencing these accounts.
56 E.g., Peggy Starr, "Fleming on Not Reading 10,535 Pages of Obamacare Regs: 'They're Incomprehensible,'" Oct. 15, 2013, available at www.cnsnews.com/news/article/ penny-starr/fleming-not-reading-10535-pages-obamacare-regs-they-re-incomprehensible ("An average person even with a law degree or a medical degree like me can't understand them [the regulations passed under Obamacare]," Fleming said. "They're incomprehensible."); see also Orrin Hatch, "The Road to Responsible Financial Reform," *Deseret News*

(Mar. 10, 2018), available at www.deseretnews.com/article/900012617/orrin-hatch-the-road-to-responsible-financial-reform.html.

57 Jonathan Lewallen, Sean M. Theriault, and Bryan D. Jones, "Congressional Dysfunction: An Information Processing Perspective," 10 *Regulation and Governance* 179, 181–83 (2015); R. Erik Peterson et al., CRS 7–5700, "House of Representatives and Senate Staff Levels in Member, Committee, Leadership, and Other Offices, 1977–2010" at 15 (2010).

58 Lewallen, Theriault, and Jones, 2015, at 179.

59 Jesse Cross, "The Staffer's Error Doctrine," 56 *Harvard Journal on Legislation* 101 (2018a).

60 Id.

61 Peterson, 2010, at 9 and 14.

62 See Public Choice Theory, supra Section II.B.3. of this chapter.

63 Curry, 2015, at 135.

64 Mann and Ornstein, 2012, at xiv.

65 Id. at xiv–xv.

66 Curry, 2015, at 2.

67 Id. at 4.

68 E.g., Ginsburg, 1987.

69 Friendly, 1963, at 792–93.

70 Edward L. Rubin, "Legislative Methodology: Some Lessons from the Truth-in-Lending Act," 80 *Georgetown Law Journal* 236, 278–29 (1991).

71 Jesse M. Cross, "When Congress Should Ignore Statutory Text," __ *George Mason Law Review* __ (forthcoming 2018b) [at 8].

72 Gluck and Bressman, 2013, at 1024.

73 P. S. Atiyah and Robert S. Summers, *Form and Substance in Anglo-American Law* 320 (Clarendon, 1987).

74 Id.; Gluck and Bressman, 2013; see also Baucher, 2007; Sommer, 2005.

75 John M. Kernochan, *The Legislative Process* 8 (Foundation, 1999) (reporting that more than half of the federal legislation originates outside of Congress and congressional staff).

76 Atiyah and Summers, 1987, at 320; Bressman and Gluck, 2014, at 737–47.

77 Bressman and Gluck, 2014, at 737.

78 Id. at 740.

79 Id. at 743.

80 Id.

81 Id. at 742.

82 Id. at 743 (quoting congressional staff members).

83 Id. at 747.

84 Id.

85 Cross, 2018b, [at 4].

86 Id. at [7]. (As "legislators attempt to use expressive rhetoric in order to placate interest groups' needs by addressing them in non-operative statutory text ... [they] seek to address them in a matter that creates opportunities elsewhere in statutes to direct courts via enforceable rules that are more public regarding.")

87 See generally Richard F. Fenno, Jr., *Congressmen in Committees* (Calif. 1973); David C. King, *Turf Wars: How Congressional Committees Claim Jurisdiction* (Chicago, 1997).

88 Bressman and Gluck, 2014, at 747–48.

89 Id. at 753.

90 Id.

91 Id. at 754.

92 Id. at 754–55.

93 Id. at 750–53.

94 Id. at 752–53.

95 2 U.S.C. § 653.

96 Bressman and Gluck, 2014, at 764.

97 Id.

98 E.g., Robert Saldin, "Gaming the Congressional Budget Office," *National Affairs* (Fall 2014), available at www.nationalaffairs.com/publications/detail/gaming-the-congressional-budget-office.

99 E.g., Barbara Sinclair, *Unorthodox Lawmaking: New Legislative Processes in the US Congress* 88, 141 (C.Q. Press, 5th ed., 2016) (contrasting the Senate with the House).

100 Id. at 263.

101 Id.

102 Id. at 79, 149.

103 Atiyah and Summers, 1987, at 314.

104 Bressman and Gluck, 2014, at 763.

105 Atiyah and Summers, 1987, at 307–11.

106 Shep Melnick, *Between the Lines: Interpreting Welfare Rights* 11 (Brookings, 1994).

107 Kagan, 2001, at 49.

108 Michael J. Graetz, *The Decline [and Fall?] of the Income Tax* 136 (Norton, 1997).

109 Curry, 2015, at 115.

110 Gluck and Bressman, 2013, at 934 (quoting an interviewee in their study).

111 Id. at 936.

112 Rachel VanSickle-Ward, *The Devil Is in the Details: Understanding the Causes of Policy Specificity and Ambiguity* 71 (SUNY, 2014).

113 Id. at 150.

114 Id. at 53.

115 Id. at 147.

116 Id. at 5.

117 Id. at 32.

118 Note, however, that some detailed legislation could also be ambiguous, and thus ambiguous is not the opposite of detailed. For example, detailed legislation is ambiguous if it is framed in ways that lead to legal uncertainty.

119 Id. at 49 (quoting a state legislator).

120 Curry, 2015, at 3.

121 Id. at 135.

122 Id. at 93.

123 Id. at 113.

124 Id. at 116.

125 Id. at 47.

126 Id. at 103

127 Id. at 102.

128 Id. at 79.
129 Id. at 102.
130 Id. at 102.
131 Id. at 87.
132 Id. at 88.
133 Id. at 88–89, 91–92.
134 Id. at 103.
135 Id.
136 Id. at 66.
137 Id. at 34.
138 Id. at 27.
139 Id. at 49.
140 Id. at 38.
141 For an excellent example, see id. at 120–21.
142 Id. at 66–67.
143 Id. at 33.
144 Id. at 131.
145 Sinclair, 2016, at 261.
146 General tactics include the use of multiple committee referrals for a single bill; the development of omnibus (multi-subject) laws; bypassing committee; and allowing post-committee adjustments during legislative deliberations. See generally id.
147 David W. Rohde, "Committees and Policy Formulation," in *Institutions of American Democracy: The Legislative Branch* 202 (Paul Quirk and Sarah A. Binder eds.) (Oxford, 2005). This general statement must be conditioned on Fenno's important work that traces considerable variation between committees, however. Fenno, 1973.
148 Frankfurter, 1947, at 545 (quoting Representative Monroney).
149 Sinclair, 2016, at 18.
150 Id.
151 Rohde, 2005, at 206–07.
152 Sinclair, 2016, at 51.
153 Norman Ornstein, *Roll Call*, Mar. 7, 2006.
154 Bressman and Gluck, 2014, at 762.
155 Sinclair, 2016, at 267.
156 Id. at 268.
157 Id. at 114.
158 Id. at 115.
159 Denning and Smith, 1999, at 959; Peter Hanson, "Restoring Regular Order in Congressional Appropriations," *Economic Studies Discussion Paper*, Nov. 2015, at 1.
160 See generally Glen S. Krutz, *Hitching a Ride: Omnibus Legislating in the US Congress* at ch. 1 (Ohio, 2001).
161 Walter J. Oleszek, *Congressional Procedures and the Policy Process* 504 (CQ Press, 10th ed., 2015).
162 Bressman and Gluck, 2014, at 756–58.
163 Hanson, 2015, at 1.
164 Id. at 4.

165 Id. at 1.
166 Mathew D. McCubbins, Roger G. Noll, and Barry R. Weingast, "Administrative Procedures as Instruments of Political Control," 3 *Journal of Law, Economics, & Organization*
243, 272 (1987) (touting the flexibility and open-ended benefits of procedural control
through legislation) [hereafter McNollgast].
167 Mathew D. McCubbins, "The Legislative Design of Regulatory Structure," 29 *American
Journal of Political Science* 721, 740 (1985).
168 Id. at 731 (focusing on this feature).
169 E.g., Morris Fiorina, "Group Concentration and the Delegation of Legislative Authority"
at 21, CalTech Working Paper No. 438 (1982).
170 Curry, 2015, at 138.
171 Id. at 139.
172 Id. at 41.
173 Id. at 75.
174 Lucas v. South Carolina Coastal Council, 112 S. Ct. 2886, 2904 (1992) (Blackmun, J.,
dissenting).
175 See, e.g., Krutz, 2001, at 140.
176 Sinclair, 2016, at 257.
177 Christopher J. Walker, "Legislating in the Shadows," 165 *University of Pennsylvania Law
Review* 1377, 1389, 1391, 1395 (2017).
178 Bressman and Gluck, 2014, at 792.
179 Arthur D. Hellman, "Case Selection in the Burger Court: A Preliminary Inquiry," 60
Notre Dame Law Review 947, 995 (1985) (footnote omitted).
180 Judith Gruber, *Controlling Bureaucracies: Dilemmas in Democratic Governance*
(Calif. 1987).
181 Sinclair, 2016, at 272.
182 E.g., VanSickle-Ward, 2014, at 159 (similarly leaving the net costs and benefits of statutory
ambiguity for others to examine and consider).
183 Krutz, 2001, at 76, 138–39.
184 Id.
185 James Salzman and J. B. Ruhl, "Mozart and the Red Queen: The Problem of Regulatory
Accretion in the Administrative State," 91 *Georgetown Law Journal* 757, 806–13 (2003);
Michael Mandel and Diana G. Carew, "Regulatory Improvement Commission:
A Politically-Viable Approach to US Regulatory Reform" at 3 (May 2013) (Progressive
Policy Institute).
186 See, e.g., James M. Curry and Frances E. Lee, "Capacity in a Centralized Congress"
(draft of Feb. 15, 2018).
187 Curry, 2015, at 21.
188 Bruce Bimber, *The Politics of Expertise in Congress: The Rise and Fall of the Office of
Technology Assessment* 67 (SUNY, 1996).
189 Linde, 1976, at 242–47.
190 Rubin, 1991, at Part IV.
191 Curry, 2015, at 205.
192 XC-Admin, "Transparent Legislation Should Be Easy to Read," *LegisPro* (July 8, 2013),
available at https://xcential.com/transparent-legislation-should-be-easy-to-read/.

193 Jessica Yabsley, "Automatic Redlining for Legislation? Rep. Elise Stefanik Wants to Make It Happen," *Data Coalition*, July 14, 2016, available at www.datacoalition.org/automatic-redlining-for-legislation-rep-elise-stefanik-wants-to-make-it-happen/.

194 H. R. 5493, 114th Cong., 2d Sess.

8 A BLUEPRINT FOR REFORM

1 Criticism of Fallingwater, available at www.wright-house.com/frank-lloyd-wright/criticism_fallingwater.html (citing Kaufmann, Jr.).

2 Concerns about comprehension asymmetries and resultant breakdowns in communication are discussed in a variety of other legal fields as well, including: tax (see, e.g., "Current Tax Code Called 'Incomprehensible,'" accountingWEB, Apr. 18, 2006, available at www.accountingweb.com/tax/irs/current-tax-code-called-incomprehensible; Joshua D. Blank and Leigh Osofsky, "Simplexity: Plain Language and the Tax Law," 66 *Emory Law Journal* 189 (2017)); class action notices (see, e.g., Shannon R. Wheatman and Terri R. LeClercq, "Majority of Class Action Publication Notices Fail to Satisfy Rule 23 Requirements," 30 *The Review of Litigation* 53, 57 (2010)); criminal law (see, e.g., Richard Leo, "The Impact of Miranda Revisited," 86 *Journal of Criminial Law and Criminology* 621, 663 (1996)); and more generically as a problem of paperwork "sludge" that clogs up a number of public and private sector programs. See, e.g., Richard H. Thaler, "Nudge, Not Sludge," 361 *Science* 431 (2018).

3 See Chapter 4.

4 See Chapter 5A.

5 See Chapter 5B.

6 See Chapter 5C.

7 See Chapters 6 and 7.

8 Bar-Gill, 2012, at 141–45 and 158–59.

9 Akerlof and Shiller, 2015.

10 Frakes and Wasserman, 2017, at 5.

11 Id. at 2.

12 Thomas J. Donohue, president & CEO, US Chamber of Commerce, "'The Regulatory Tsunami – How a Tidal Wave of Regulations Is Drowning America" (Oct. 7, 2010), available at www.uschamber.com/speech/regulatory-tsunami-how-tidal-wave-regulations-drowning-america.

13 Richard H. Fallon, Jr., "Legitimacy and the Constitution," 118 *Harvard Law Review* 1787, 1844 (2005).

14 Willis, 2017.

15 E.g., Ayres and Schwartz, 2014; Ben-Shahar and Strahilevitz, 2017.

16 E.g., Hu, 2012; Hu, 2014; Hu, 2015.

17 35 U.S.C. § 112(a).

18 Schulz, 2017, at 789.

19 E.g., Komesar and Wagner, 2017, at 944–47 (discussing the use of public advocates in regulatory processes).

20 Stijn Smismans, "Regulatory Procedure and Participation at the European Union," in *Comparative Law and Regulation: Understanding the Global Regulatory Process* 129 (Francesca Bignami and David Zaring eds.) (Elgar, 2016); Wagner, 2016, at 109.

21 Smismans, 2016; Wagner, 2016.

22 Valerie P. Hans and Neil Vidmar, *Judging the Jury* 156–60 (Basic, 1986); Wagner, 1997, at 827.

23 Smismans, 2016.

24 See generally *EU Committees: Social Regulation, Law, and Politics* (Ellen Vos and Christian Joerges eds.) (Hart, 1999).

25 Because the dye was cast for contracts in the seventeenth and eighteenth centuries, consumer contracts also hits the common law in an orthogonal way that creates inertia even in the common law. See Chapter 4.

26 E.g., Thomas O. McGarity, *Freedom to Harm: The Lasting Legacy of the Laissez Faire Revival* (Yale, 2013).

27 Komesar, 1994.

28 Mancur Olson, *The Logic of Collective Action: Public Goods and the Theory of Groups* (Harvard, 1965).

Bibliography

Akerlof, George and Robert Shiller. *Phishing for Phools: The Economics of Manipulation and Deception* (Princeton, 2015).

Allison, John R. and Mark A. Lemley. "The Growing Complexity of the United States Patent System," 82 *Boston University Law Review* 77 (2002).

Andrejevic, Mark. *Infoglut: How Too Much Information Is Changing the Way We Think and Know* (Routledge, 2013).

Applegate, John S. "The Government Role in Scientific Research: Who Should Bridge the Data Gap in Chemical Regulation?" in *Rescuing Science from Politics* 255 (Wendy Wagner & Rena Steinzor, eds.) (Cambridge, 2006).

"The Perils of Unreasonable Risk: Information Regulatory Policy and Toxic Substances Control," 91 *Columbia Law Review* 261 (1991).

Atiyah, P. S. and Robert S. Summers. *Form and Substance in Anglo-American Law* (Clarendon, 1987).

Ayres, Ian and Robert Gertner. "Filling Gaps in Incomplete Contracts: An Economic Theory of Default Rules," 99 *Yale Law Journal* 87 (1989).

Ayres, Ian and Alan Schwarz. "The No-Reading Problem in Consumer Contract Law," 66 *Stanford Law Review* 545 (2014).

Bakos, Yannis, Florencia Marotta-Wurgler, and David R. Trossen. "Does Anyone Read the Fine Print? Consumer Attention to Standard-Form Contracts," 43 *The Journal of Legal Studies* 1 (2014).

Bar-Gill, Oren. *Seduction by Contract* (Oxford, 2012).

Bar-Gill, Oren and Ryan Bubb. "Credit Card Pricing: The Card Act and Beyond," 97 *Cornell Law Review* 967 (2012).

Bar-Gill, Oren and Elizabeth Warren. "Making Credit Safer," 157 *University of Pennsylvania Law Review* 1 (2008).

Barnes, Wayne R. "Towards a Fairer Model of Consumer Assent to Standard Form Contracts: In Defense of Restatement Subsection 221(3)," 82 *Washington Law Review* 227 (2007).

Baxter, Lawrence G. "Betting Big: Value, Caution and Accountability in an Era of Ultra-Large Banking," 31 *Review of Banking & Financial Law* 765 (2012).

Becher, Shmuel I. "Asymmetric Information in Consumer Contracts: The Challenge that Is Yet to Be Met," 45 *American Business Law Journal* 723 (2008).

Beh, Hazel Glenn. "Curing the Infirmities of the Unconscionability Doctrine," 66 *Hastings Law Journal* 1011 (2015).

Bekelman, Justin E., Yan Li, and Cary P. Gross. "Scope and Impact of Financial Conflicts of Interest in Biomedical Research," 289 JAMA 454 (2003).

Ben-Shahar, Omri. "The Myth of the 'Opportunity to Read' in Contract Law," 5 European Review of Contract Law 1 (2009).

Ben-Shahar, Omri and Carl E. Schneider. More Than You Wanted to Know: The Failure of Mandated Disclosure (Princeton, 2014).

Ben-Shahar, Omri and Lior Jacob Strahilevitz. "Interpreting Contracts via Surveys and Experiments," 92 New York University Law Review 1753 (2017).

Bessen, James and Michael J. Meurer. Patent Failure: How Judges, Bureaucrats, and Lawyers Put Innovators at Risk (Princeton, 2008).

Bimber, Bruce. The Politics of Expertise in Congress: The Rise and Fall of the Office of Technology Assessment (SUNY, 1996).

Bishop, Martin. "Regulatory: Unfair, Deceptive, or Abusive Acts or Practices. Amorphous New Statutory Provisions Create Serious Compliance Risks," Inside Counsel, July 27, 2011.

Blackmon, Glenn and Richard Zeckhauser. "Fragile Commitments and the Regulatory Process," 9 Yale Journal on Regulation 73 (1992).

Bosso, Christopher J. Pesticides and Politics: The Life Cycle of a Public Issue (Pittsburgh, 1987).

Brandeis, Louis D. "What Publicity Can Do," Harper's Weekly, Dec. 20, 1913.

Braucher, Jean. "The Challenge to the Bench and the Bar Presented by the Bankruptcy Act: Resistance Need Not Be Futile," 2007 University of Illinois Law Review 93.

Braucher, Jean and Angela Littwin. "Examination as a Method of Consumer Protection," 87 Temple Law Review 807 (2015).

Bressman, Lisa Schultz and Abbe R. Gluck. "Statutory Interpretation from the Inside – An Empirical Study of Congressional Drafting, Delegation, and the Cannons: Part II," 66 Stanford Law Review 725 (2014).

Bright, Jeffrey C. "Unilateral Attorney's Fees Clauses: A Proposal to Shift to the Golden Rule," 61 Drake Law Review 85 (2012).

Burk, Dan L. and Mark A. Lemley. "Fence Posts or Sign Posts? Rethinking Patent Claim Construction," 157 University of Pennsylvania Law Review 1743 (2009).

"Quantum Patent Mechanics," 9 Lewis and Clark Law Review 29 (2005).

Carrigan, Christopher and Stuart Shapiro. "What's Wrong with the Back of the Envelope? A Call for Simple (and Timely) Benefit-Cost Analysis," 11 Regulation and Governance 203 (2016).

Carson, Thomas L. Lying and Deception: Theory and Practice (Oxford, 2010).

Casson, Mark. Information and Organization: A New Perspective on the Theory of the Firm (Oxford, 1997).

Chiang, Tun-Jen and Lawrence Solum. "The Interpretation-Construction Distinction in Patent Law," 123 Yale Law Journal 530 (2013).

Coglianese, Cary. "Challenging the Rules: Litigation and Bargaining in the Administrative Process," University of Michigan Dissertation unpublished (1994).

Combs, Kellie and Albert Cacozza. "Drug Promotion in the Post-Caronia World," Food and Drug Law Institute, Update, Mar./Apr. 2013, at 14.

Consumer Financial Protection Bureau (CFPB). Arbitration Study: Report to Congress 2015 (Mar. 2015).

Cotropia, Christopher A., Mark Lemley, and Bhaven Sampat. "Do Applicant Patent Citations Matter," 42 Research Policy 844 (2013).

Croley, Steven P. *Regulation and Public Interests: The Possibility of Good Regulatory Government* (Princeton, 2008).

Cross, Frank B. "Shattering the Fragile Case for Judicial Review of Rulemaking," 85 *Virginia Law Review* 1243 (1999).

Cross, Jesse. "The Staffer's Error Doctrine," 56 *Harvard Journal on Legislation* 101 (2018a).

"When Courts Should Ignore Statutory Text," *George Mason Law Review* (forthcoming, 2018b).

Curry, James M. *Legislating in the Dark: Information and Power in the House of Representatives* (Chicago, 2015).

Davis, Devra. *When Smoke Ran Like Water: Tales of Environmental Deception and the Battle against Pollution* (Basic, 2002).

DeMatteis, Bob, Andy Gibbs, and Michael Neustel. *The Patent Writer: How to Write Successful Patent Applications* (Square One, 2006).

Denison, Richard. "A Primer on the New Toxic Substances Control Act (TSCA) and What Led to It," EDF Health (Apr. 2017).

Denning, Brannon and Brooks Smith. "Uneasy Riders: The Case for a Truth-in-Legislation Amendment," 1999 *Utah Law Review* 957 (1999).

Dranove, David, et al. "Is More Information Better? The Effects of 'Report Cards' on Health Care Providers," 111 *Journal of Political Economy* 555 (2003).

Edwards, Harry. "The Role of a Judge in Modern Society: Some Reflections on Current Practice in Federal Appellate Adjudication," 32 *Cleveland Stare Law Review* 385 (1983–84).

Eggleston, Karen, Eric A. Posner, and Richard Zeckhauser. "The Design and Interpretation of Contracts: Why Complexity Matters, 95 *Northwestern University Law Review* 91 (2000).

Egilman, David S. and Marion Billings. "Abuse of Epidemiology: Automobile Manufacturers Manufacture a Defense to Asbestos Liability," 11 *International Journal of Occupational and Environmental Health* 360 (2005).

Farber, Daniel R. and Anne Joseph O'Connell. "The Lost World of Administrative Law," 92 *Texas Law Review* 1137 (2014).

Farina, Cynthia R. "Rulemaking in 140 Characters or Less: Social Networking and Public Participation in Rulemaking," 31 *Pace Law Review* 382 (2011).

Farina, Cynthia R. and Mary J. Newhart. *Rulemaking 2.0: Understanding and Getting Better Public Participation* (IBM Center for The Business of Government 201) (undated).

Farina, Cynthia R., Mary J. Newhart, and Cheryl Blake. "The Problem with Words: Plain Language and Public Participation in Rulemaking," 83 *The George Washington Law Review* 1358 (2015).

Farnsworth, E. Allan. 1 *Farnsworth on Contracts* (Aspen, 3rd ed., 2004).

"Developments in Contract Law during the 1980's: The Top Ten," 41 *Case Western Reserve Law Review* 203 (1990).

Fenno, Richard F., Jr. *Congressmen in Committees* (Calif. 1973).

Field, Andrea Bear and Kathy E. B. Robb. "EPA Rulemakings: Views from Inside and Outside," 5 *Natural Resources and Environment*, Summer 5 (1995).

Fiorina, Morris P. and Roger G. Noll. "Voters, Bureaucrats and Legislators: A Rational Choice Perspective on the Growth of Bureaucracy," 9 *Journal of Public Economics* 239 (1978a).

"Voters, Legislators and Bureaucracy: Institutional Design in the Public Sector," 68 *American Economic Review* 256 (1978b).

Fisher, Liz, Pasky Pascual, and Wendy Wagner. "Rethinking Judicial Review of Expert Agencies," 93 *Texas Law Review* 1681 (2015).

Frankfurter, Felix. "Some Reflections on the Reading of Statutes," 47 *Columbia Law Review* 527 (1947).

Frakes, Michael and Melissa Wasserman. "Is the Time Allocated to Review Patent Applications Inducing Examiners to Grant Invalid Patents?: Evidence from Micro-Level Application Data," 99 *The Review of Economics and Statistics* 550 (2017a).

"Decreasing the Patent Office's Incentives to Grant Invalid Patents" (The Hamilton Project, Brookings) (Dec. 2017b).

"Does the U.S. Patent and Trademark Office Grant Too Many Bad Patents?: Evidence from a Quasi-Experiment," 67 *Stanford Law Review* 613 (2015).

Frederickson, H. George, et al. *The Public Administration Theory Primer* (Westview 2d ed., 2012).

Friendly, Henry J. "The Gap in Lawmaking – Judges Who Can't and Legislators Who Won't," 63 *Columbia Law Review* 787 (1963).

Fung, Archon, Mary Graham, and David Weil. *Full Disclosure: The Perils and Promise of Transparency* (Cambridge, 2007).

Gelpe, Marcia R. "Exhaustion of Administrative Remedies: Lessons from Environmental Cases," 53 *George Washington L. Rev.* 1 (1985).

Gennaro, Valerio and Lorenzo Tomatis. "Business Bias: How Epidemiologic Studies May Underestimate or Fail to Detect Increased Risks of Cancer and Other Diseases," 11 *International Journal of Occupational and Environmental Health* 356 (2005).

Gersen, Jacob and Adrian Vermeule. "Thin Rationality Review," 114 *Michigan Law Review* 1355 (2016).

Gilo, David and Ariel Porat. "The Hidden Roles of Boilerplate and Standard-form Contracts: Strategic Imposition of Transaction Costs, Segmentation of Consumers, and Anticompetitive Effects," 104 *Michigan Law Review* 983 (2006).

Ginsburg, Ruth Bader. "A Plea for Legislative Review," 60 *Southern California Law Review* 995 (1987).

Ginsburg, Ruth Bader and Peter Huber. "The Intercircuit Committee," 100 *Harvard Law Review* 1417 (1987).

Gladwell, Malcolm. "Open Secrets," *The New Yorker* 44 (Jan. 8. 2007).

Gleick, James. *The Information: A History, A Theory, A Flood* (Pantheon, 2011).

Gluck, Abbe R. "Congress, Statutory Interpretation, and the Failure of Formalism: the CBO Canon and Other Ways That Courts Can Improve on What They Are Already Trying to Do," 84 *University of Chicago Law Review* 177 (2017).

Gluck, Abbe R. and Lisa Schultz Bressman. "Statutory Interpretation from the Inside – An Empirical Study of Congressional Drafting, Delegation, and the Cannons: Part I," 65 *Stanford Law Review* 901 (2013).

Golden, John M. "Redundancy: When Law Repeats Itself," 94 *Texas Law Review* 629 (2016).

"Proliferating Patents and Patent Law's 'Cost Disease,'" 51 *Houston Law Review* 455 (2013).

Goldstein, Bernard D., et al. "Challenges of Unconventional Shale Gas Development: So What's the Rush," 27 *Notre Dame Journal of Law, Ethics, & Public Policy* 149 (2013).

Goldstein, Bernard. "Risk Assessment of Environmental Chemicals: If It Ain't Broke . .," 31 *Risk Analysis* 1356 (2011).

Gormley, William T., Jr. "Regulatory Issue Networks in a Federal System," 18 *Polity* 595 (1986).

Graetz, Michael J. *The Decline [and Fall?] of the Income Tax* (Norton, 1997).

Graham, Mary and Catherine Miller. "Disclosure of Toxic Releases in the United States," in *Industrial Transformation* (Theo de Bruijn & Vicki Norberg-Bohm, eds.) (MIT, 2005).

Haeberle, Kevin and M. Todd Henderson. "Making a Market for Corporate Disclosure," 35 *Yale Journal on Regulation* 383 (2018).

Haeder, Simon F. and Susan Webb Yackee. "Influence and the Administrative Process: Lobbying the U.S. President's Office of Management and Budget," 109 *American Political Science Review* 507 (2015).

Hakenes, Hendrik and Isabel Schnabel. "Regulatory Capture by Sophistication," Nov. 28, 2014, available at https://www.econstor.eu/bitstream/10419/79991/1/VfS_2013_pid_164.pdf.

Hakes, Russell A. "Focusing on the Realities of the Contracting Process – An Essential Step to Achieve Justice in Contract Enforcement," 12 *Delaware Law Review* 95 (2011).

Harrington, Winston, Lisa Heinzerling, and Richard D. Morgenstern. "What We Learned," in *Reforming Regulatory Impact Analysis* 226 (Winston Harrington, Lisa Heinzerling & Richard D. Morgenstern, eds.) (Routledge, 2009).

Haynes, Bryan M., Anne Hampton Andrews, and C. Reade Jacob, Jr., "Compelled Commercial Speech: The Food and Drug Administration's Effort to Smoke Out the Tobacco Industry through Graphic Warning Labels," 68 *Food and Drug Law Journal* 329 (2013).

Hernandez, Oscar and Charles Auer. "Key Science Concepts," in *New TSCA: A Guide to the Lautenberg Chemical Safety Act and Its Implementation* 24 (Lynn L. Bergeson & Charles M. Auer, eds.) (ABA, 2017).

Herrick, James. *The History and Theory of Rhetoric: An Introduction* (Allyn & Bacon, 3rd ed., 2004).

Holmes, Oliver Wendell. *The Path of the Law* (Little, Brown, 2012) (reprinted from 10 *Harvard Law Review* 457–58 (1896)).

Hill, Claire A. and Christopher King. "How Do German Contracts Do as Much with Fewer Words," 79 *Chicago-Kent Law Review* 889 (2004).

Ho, Daniel E. "Fudging the Nudge: Information Disclosure and Restaurant Grading," 122 *Yale Law Journal* 574 (2012).

Hu, Henry C. "Financial Innovation and Governance Mechanisms: The Evolution of Decoupling and Transparency," 79 *Business Lawyer* 347 (2015).

"Disclosure Universes and Modes of Information: Banks, Innovation, and Divergent Regulatory Quests," 31 *Yale Journal on Regulation* 565 (2014).

"Too Complex to Depict?: Innovation, 'Pure Information,' and the SEC Disclosure Paradigm," 90 *Texas Law Review* 1601 (2012).

"Misunderstood Derivatives: The Causes of Informational Failure and the Promise of Regulatory Incrementalism," 102 *Yale Law Journal* 1457 (1993).

Jackson, Brooks and Kathleen Hall Jamieson. *Unspun: Finding Facts in a World of Disinformation* (Random House, 2007).

Jaffe, Adam B. and Josh Lerner. *Innovation and Its Discontents: How our Broken Patent System is Endangering Innovation and Progress, and What to Do about it* (Princeton, 2004).

Jasanoff, Sheila. "Research Subpoenas and the Sociology of Knowledge," 59 *Law & Contemporary Problems* 95 (1996).

Science at the Bar: Science and Technology in American Law (Harvard, 1997).

Jones, Gerald E. *How to Lie with Charts* (BookSurge 2d ed., 2006).

Joskow, Paul L. and Richard Schmalensee. "Incentive Regulation for Electric Utilities," 4 *Yale Journal on Regulation* 1 (1986).

Judge, Kathryn. "Fragmentation Nodes: A Study in Complexity, Financial Innovation, and Systemic Risk," 64 *Stanford Law Review* 657 (2012).

Kagan, Robert. *Adversarial Legalism: The American Way of Law* (Harvard, 2001).

Kagan, Elena. "Presidential Administration," 114 *Harvard Law Review* 2245 (2001).

Kastner, Tal. "The Persisting Ideal of Agreement in an Age of Boilerplate," 35 *Law & Social Inquiry* 793 (2010).

Keeton, Robert E. "Insurance Law Rights at Variance with Policy Provisions: Part Two," 83 *Harv. L. Rev.* 961 (1970).

Kinneavy, James L. *A Theory of Discourse: The Aims of Discourse* (Norton, 1971).

Knapp, Charles N. "Is There a Duty to Read?" in *Revisiting the Contracts Scholarship of Stewart Macaulay* 316 (Jean Braucher, et al., eds.) (Hart, 2013).

Komesar, Neil K. *Imperfect Alternatives: Choosing Institutions in Law, Economics, and Public Policy* (Chicago, 1994).

Komesar, Neil and Wendy Wagner. "Essay: The Administrative Process from the Bottom Up: Reflections on the Role, if Any, for Judicial Review," 69 *Administrative Law Review* 891 (2017).

Krawiec, Kimberly D. "Don't 'Screw Joe the Plummer': The Sausage-Making of Financial Reform," 55 *Arizona Law Review* 53 (2013).

Kroger, John R. "Enron, Fraud, and Securities Reform: An Enron Prosecutor's Perspective," 76 *University of Colorado Law Review* 57 (2005).

Krutz, Glen S. *Hitching a Ride: Omnibus Legislating in the U.S. Congress* (Ohio, 2001).

Kuehn, Robert R. "Scientific Speech: Protecting the Right of Environmental Scientists to Express Professional Opinions," 35 *Environmental Law Reporter* 10857 (2005).

Kuran, Timur and Cass R. Sunstein, "Availability Cascades and Risk Regulation," 51 *Stanford Law Review* 683 (1999).

Kwak, James. "Cultural Capture and the Financial Crisis," in *Preventing Regulatory Capture: Special Interest Influence and How to Limit It* 71 (Daniel Carpenter & David A. Moss, eds.) (Cambridge, 2013).

Laffont, Jacques and David Martimort. *The Theory of Incentives: The Principal Agent Model* (Princeton, 2002).

Leff, Arthur. *Swindling and Selling* (Free Press, 1976).

Leib, Ethan J. and Zev J. Eigen. "Consumer Form Contracting in the Age of Mechanical Reproduction: The Unread and the Undead," 2017 *University of Illinois Law Review* 65 (2017).

Lemley, Mark and Bhaven Sampat. "Is the Patent Office a Rubber Stamp?" 58 *Emory Law Journal* 181 (2009).

Lewallen, Jonathan, Sean M. Theriault, and Bryan D. Jones. "Congressional Dysfunction: An Information Processing Perspective," 10 *Regulation and Governance* 179 (2016).

Lichtman, Doug and Mark A. Lemley. "Rethinking the Presumption of Validity," 60 *Stanford Law Review* 45 (2007).

Linde, Hans A. "Due Process of Lawmaking," 55 *Nebraska Law Review* 197 (1976).

Livak, Oskar. "Finding Invention," 40 *Florida State University Law Review* 57 (2012).

Lo, Bernard and Marilyn Jane Field. *Conflict of Interest in Medical Research, Education, and Practice* (National Acad. Press, 2009).

Loughran, Tim and Bill McDonald. "Regulation and Financial Disclosure: The Impact of Plain English," 45 *Journal of Regulatory Economics* 94 (2014).

Lutz, William. *Double-Speak* (HarperCollins, 1989).

Lyndon, Mary L. "Tort Law and Technology," 12 *Yale Journal on Regulation* 137 (1995).

"Secrecy and Innovation in Tort Law and Regulation," 23 *New Mexico Law Review* 1 (1993).

"Information Economics and Chemical Toxicity: Designing Laws to Produce and Use Data," 87 *Michigan Law Review* 1795 (1989).

Macey, Jon. "Promoting Public-Regarding Legislation through Statutory Interpretation: An Interest Group Model," 86 *Columbia Law Review* 223 (1986).

Macho-Stadler, Ines and J. David Perez-Castrillo. *An Introduction to the Economics of Information: Incentives and Contracts* (Oxford, 2001).

Mammen, Christian. "Controlling the 'Plague': Reforming the Doctrine of Inequitable Conduct," 24 *Berkeley Technology Law Journal* 1329 (2009).

Mann, Thomas and Norman Ornstein. *It's Even Worse than It Looks/Was* (Basic, 2012).

Markowitz, Gerard E. and David Rosner. *Deceit and Denial: The Deadly Politics of Industrial Pollution* (Calif., 2003).

Mashaw, Jerry L. "Small Things Like Reasons Are Put in a Jar: Reason and Legitimacy in the Administrative State," 70 *Fordham Law Review* 17 (2001).

Greed, Chaos, and Governance: Using Public Choice to Improve Public Law (Yale, 1999).

Masur, Jonathan. "Patent Inflation," 121 *Yale Law Journal* 470 (2011).

Mathios, Alan D. "The Impact of Mandatory Disclosure Laws on Product Choices: An Analysis of the Salad Dressing Market," 43 *Journal of Law and Economics* 651 (2000).

McCarty, Nolan. "Complexity, Capacity, and Capture," in *Preventing Regulatory Capture: Special Interest Influence and How to Limit it* 99 (Daniel Carpenter & David A. Moss, eds.) (Cambridge, 2013).

McCollough, Colleen. "Unconscionability as a Coherent Legal Concept," 164 *University of Pennsylvania Law Review* 779 (2016).

McDonnell, Brett and Daniel Schwarcz. "Regulatory Contrarians," 89 *North Carolina Law Review* 1629 (2011).

McGarity, Thomas O. *Freedom to Harm: The Lasting Legacy of the Laissez Faire Revival* (Yale, 2013).

"Administrative Law as Blood Sport: Policy Erosion in a Highly Partisan Age," 61 *Duke Law Journal* 1671 (2012).

"Daubert and the Proper Role for the Courts in Health, Safety, and Environmental Regulation," 95 *American Journal of Public Health*, Supplement 1, S92 (2005).

"Some Thoughts on 'Deossifying' the Rulemaking Process," 41 *Duke Law Journal* 1385 (1992).

"The Internal Structure of EPA Rulemaking," 54 *Law & Contemporary Problems* 57 (1991).

"Presidential Control of Regulatory Agency Decisionmaking," 36 *American University Law Review* 443 (1987).

McGarity, Thomas and Wendy Wagner. *Bending Science: How Special Interests Corrupt Public Health Research* (Harvard, 2008).

McCubbins, Mathew D. "The Legislative Design of Regulatory Structure," 29 *American Journal of Political Science* 721 (1985).

McCubbins, Mathew D., Roger G. Noll, and Barry R. Weingast[McNollgast]. "Administrative Procedures as Instruments of Political Control," 3 *Journal of Law, Economics, & Organization* 243 (1987).

Melnick, R. Shep. "Administrative Law and Bureaucratic Reality," 44 *Administrative Law Review* 245 (1992).

Regulation and the Courts: The Case of the Clean Air Act (Brookings, 1983).

Mendelson, Nina A. "Disclosing 'Political' Oversight of Agency Decision Making," 108 *Michigan Law Review* 1127 (2010).

Mercado, Raymond A. "Ensuring the Integrity of Administrative Challenges to Patents: Lessons from Reexamination," 14 *Columbia Science & Technology Law Review* 558 (2013).

Michaels, David. *Doubt is Their Product: How Industry's Assault on Science Threatens Your Health* (Oxford 2008).

Munafo, Marcus, et al. "A Manifesto for Reproducible Science," 1 *Nature Human Behavior* 1 (2017).

Mills, Russell W. and Jennifer L. Selin. "Don't Sweat the Details! Enhancing Congressional Committee Expertise through the Use of Detailees," 42 *Legislative Studies Quarterly* 611 (2017).

Nance, Dale A. "The Best Evidence Principle," 73 *Iowa Law Review* 227 (1988).

National Research Council. *Review of the Environmental Protection Agency's Draft IRIS Assessment of Formaldehyde* (NAS, 2011).

    Toxicity Testing in the 21st Century: A Vision and a Strategy (NAS, 2007).

    Toxicity Testing: Strategies to Determine Needs and Priorities (NAS, 1984).

Nixon, David C., Robert M. Howard, and Jeff R. DeWitt. "With Friends Like These: Rule-Making Comment Submissions to the Securities and Exchange Commission," 12 *Journal of Public Administration Research and Theory* 59 (2002).

Noam, Eli. "Visions of the Media Age: Taming the Information Monster," Paper presented at the Third Annual Colloquium, Alfred Herrhausen Society for International Dialogue, June 16/17, 1995, Frankfurt am Main, Germany.

Nou, Jennifer. "Agency Self-Insulation Under Presidential Review," 126 *Harvard Law Review* 1755 (2013).

Oberg, Shari M. and Daniel C. Brubaker. "Supreme Review," 87 *Michigan Business Journal* 30 (2008).

O'Leary, Rosemary. "The Impact of Federal Court Decisions on the Policies and Administration of the U.S. Environmental Protection Agency," 41 *Administrative Law Review* 549 (1989).

Oleszek, Walter J. *Congressional Procedures and the Policy Process* (CQ Press, 10th ed., 2015).

Oreskes, Naomi and Eric M. Conway. *Merchants of Doubt: How a Handful of Scientists Obscured the Truth on Issues from Tobacco Smoke to Global Warming* (Bloomsbury, 2009).

Orts, Eric W. "Reflexive Environmental Law," 89 *Northwestern Law Review* 1227 (1995).

Overton, Spencer. "The Participation Interest," 100 *Georgetown Law Journal* 1259 (2012).

Owen, Bruce M. and Ronald Braeutigam. *The Regulation Game: Strategic Use of the Administrative Process* (Ballinger, 1978).

Owen, Robert S. "Clarifying the Simple Assumption of the Information Load Paradigm," in 19 *Advances in Consumer Research Volume* 770 (John F. Sherry, Jr. and Brian Sternthal, eds.) (Assn. for Consumer Research, 1992).

Paredes, Troy A. "Blinded by the Light: Information Overload and its Consequences for Securities Regulation," 81 *Washington University Law Quarterly* 417 (2003).

Pascual, Pasky, et al. "Making Method Visible: Improving the Quality of Science-Based Regulation," 2 *Michigan Journal of Administrative and Environmental Law* 429 (2013).

Paulsen, Michael Stokes. "The Most Dangerous Branch: Executive Power to Say What the Law Is," 83 *Georgetown Law Journal* 217 (1994).

Pierce, Richard J., Jr. *Administrative Law Treatise* (5th ed., 2010).

    "Waiting for Vermont Yankee III, IV, and V? A Response to Beermann and Lawson," 75 *George Washington Law Review* 902 (2007).

Phlips, Louis. *The Economics of Imperfect Information* (Cambridge, 1988).

Post, Robert and Amanda Shanor. "Adam Smith's First Amendment," 128 *Harvard Law Review Forum* 165 (2015).

Powell, Mark R. *Science at EPA: Information in the Regulatory Process* (RFF, 1999).

Quillen, Cecil, D., Jr. and Ogden H. Webster. "Continuing Patent Applications and Performance of the U.S. Patent and Trademark Office," 11 *Federal Circuit Bar Journal* 1 (2002).

Radin, Margaret Jane. "The Deformation of Contract in the Information Society," 37 *Oxford Journal of Legal Studies* 505 (2017).

    Boilerplate: The Fine Print, Vanishing Rights, and the Rule of Law (Princeton, 2012).

Rai, Arti. "Growing Pains in the Administrative State: The Patent Office's Troubled Quest for Managerial Control," 157 *University of Pennsylvania Law Review* 2051 (2009).

Rau, Alan. "Everything You Really Need to Know about 'Separability' in Seventeen Simple Propositions," 14 *The American Review of International Arbitration* 182 (2004).

Rohde, David W. "Committees and Policy Formulation," in *Institutions of American Democracy: The Legislative Branch* 202 (Paul Quirk and Sarah A. Binder, eds.) (Oxford, 2005).

Robbins, Paul, John Hintz, and Sarah Moore. *Environment and Society: A Critical Introduction* (Wiley, 2d ed., 2014).

Roberts, Kathleen M. "Section 8 – Procedures for Reporting and Recordkeeping Requirements," in *New TSCA: A Guide to the Lautenberg Chemical Safety Act and Its Implementation* 155 (Lynn L. Bergeson & Charles M. Auer, eds.) (ABA, 2017).

Rubin, Edward. "It's Time to Make the Administrative Procedure Act Administrative," 89 *Cornell Law Review* 95 (2003).

    "Legislative Methodology: Some Lessons from the Truth-in-Lending Act," 80 *Georgetown Law Journal* 236 (1991).

Rueter, Thomas J. and Joshua H. Roberts. "Pennsylvania's Reasonable Expectations Doctrine: The Third Circuit's Perspective," 45 *Villanova Law Review* 581 (2000).

Sachs, Noah M. "Jumping the Pond: Transnational Law and the Future of Chemical Regulation," 62 *Vanderbilt Law Review* 1817 (2009).

Salzman, James and J. B. Ruhl. "Mozart and the Red Queen: The Problem of Regulatory Accretion in the Administrative State," 91 *Georgetown Law Journal* 757 (2003).

Sant' Ambrogio, Michael and Glen Staszewski. "Public Engagement with Agency Rulemaking," ACUS Final Report, Nov. 19, 2018, available at https://www.acus.gov/sites/default/files/documents/Public%20Engagement%20in%20Rulemaking%20Final%20Report.pdf.

Schiller, Reuel E. "The Era of Deference: Courts, Expertise, and the Emergence of New Deal Administrative Law," 106 *Michigan Law Review* 399 (2007).

Schmidt, Patrick. "Pursuing Regulatory Relief: Strategic Participation and Litigation in U.S. OSHA Rulemaking," 4 *Business and Politics* 71 (2002).

Schuck, Peter H. "Legal Complexity: Some Causes, Consequences, and Cures," 42 *Duke Law Journal* 1 (1992).

Schulz, Karen Bradshaw. "Information Flooding," 48 *Indiana Law Review* 755 (2015).

Schwarcz, Daniel. "Preventing Capture Through Consumer Empowerment Programs: Some Evidence from Insurance Regulation," in *Preventing Regulatory Capture* 365 (Daniel Carpenter & David A. Moss, eds.) (Cambridge, 2014).

Schwarcz, Steven L. "Intrinsic Imbalance: The Impact of Income Disparity on Financial Regulation," 78 *Law and Contemporary Problems* 97 (2015).

Schwartz, Alan and Louis L. Wilde. "Intervening in Markets on the Basis of Imperfect Information: A Legal and Economic Analysis," 127 *University of Pennsylvania Law Review* 630 (1979).

Seidenfeld, Mark. "A Table of Requirements for Federal Administrative Rulemaking," 27 *Florida State University Law Review* 533 (2000).
"A Civic Republican Justification for the Bureaucratic State," 105 *Harvard Law Review* 1511 (1992).
Seifter, Miriam. "Second-Order Participation in Administrative Law," 63 *UCLA Law Review* 1300 (2016).
Seymore, Sean B. "Uninformative Patents," 55 *Houston Law Review* 377 (2017).
Shafrin, Jason. "Operating on Commission: Analyzing How Physician Financial Incentives Affect Surgery Rates," 19 *Health Econonomics* 562 (2010).
Shaiko, Ronald G. *Voices and Echoes for the Environment: Public Interest Representation in the 1990s and Beyond* (Columbia, 1999).
Shannon, Claude E. and Warren Weaver. *The Mathematical Theory of Communication* (Illinois, 1971).
Shapiro, Martin. "On Predicting the Future of Administrative Law," 6 *Regulation* 18 (1982).
Shapiro, Sidney, et al. "The Enlightenment of Administrative Law: Looking Inside the Agency for Legitimacy," 47 *Wake Forest Law Review* 463 (2012).
Shapiro, Stuart. "Can Analysis of Policy Decisions Spur Participation?" 2018 *J. Benefit Cost Anal.* 1.
Shenk, David. *Data Smog: Surviving the Information Glut* (Harper, 1997).
Shkabatur, Jennifer. "Transparency with(out) Accountability: Open Government in the United States," 31 *Yale Law and Policy Review* 79 (2012).
Silver, Nate. *The Signal and the Noise: The Art and Science of Prediction* (Penguin, 2012).
Simon, Herbert A. *Administrative Behavior: A Study of Decisionmaking Processes in Administrative Organizations* (Free Press 4th ed., 1997).
Sinclair, Barbara. *Unorthodox Lawmaking: New Legislative Processes in the U.S. Congress* (C.Q. Press, 5th ed., 2016).
Slawson, W. David. "Contractual Discretionary Power: A Law to Prevent Deceptive Contracting by Standard Form," 2006 *Michigan State Law Review* 863.
Smismans, Stijn. "Regulatory Procedure and Participation at the European Union," in *Comparative Law and Regulation: Understanding the Global Regulatory Process* 129 (Francesca Bignami & David Zaring, eds.) (Elgar, 2016).
Smith, Henry E. "The Language of Property: Form, Context, and Audience," 55 *Stanford Law Review* 1105 (2003).
Solove, Daniel J. and Woodrow Hartzog. "The FTC and the New Common Law of Privacy," 114 *Columbia Law Review* 583 (2014).
Sommer, Henry L. "Trying to Make Sense out of Nonsense," 79 *American Bankruptcy Law Journal* 191 (2005).
Steinzor, Rena and Sidney Shapiro. *Special Interests, Government, and Threats to Health, Safety, and the Environment* (Chicago, 2010).
Stewart, Richard B. "Vermont Yankee and the Evolution of Administrative Procedure," 91 *Harvard Law Review* 1805 (1978).
"The Reformation of American Administrative Law," 88 *Harvard Law Review* 1669 (1975).
Stiglitz, Joseph E. "The Contributions of the Economics of Information to Twentieth Century Economics," 115 *Quarterly Journal of Economics* 1441 (2000).
Strahilevitz, Lior and Matthew Kugler. "Is Privacy Policy Language Irrelevant to Consumers?" 45 *The Journal of Legal Studies* S69 (2016).
Strauss, Peter L. "From Expertise to Politics: The Transformation of American Rulemaking," 31 *Wake Forest Law Review* 745 (1996).

Streufert, Siegfried and Michael J. Driver. "Conceptual Structure, Information Load, and Perceptual Complexity," 3 *Psychonomic Science* 249, 250 (1965).

Suchan, Jim. "The Effect of High-Impact Writing on Decision Making within a Public Sector Bureaucracy," 35 *The Journal of Business Communication* 299 (1998).

Thaler, Richard H. "Nudge, Not Sludge," 361 *Science* 431(2018).

Traft, Michael J. "Special Considerations in Appellate Briefs," 1 *Appellate Practice in Massachusetts* (2008).

Tversky, Amon and Daniel Kahneman. "Judgment under Uncertainty: Heuristics and Biases," 185 *Science* 1124 (1974).

U.S. GAO, Report No. GAO-05–458. "Chemical Regulation: Options Exist to Improve EPA's Ability to Assess Health Risks and Manage its Chemical Review Program" (2005).

VanSickle-Ward, Rachel. *The Devil is in the Details: Understanding the Causes of Policy Specificity and Ambiguity* (SUNY, 2014).

Virelli III, Louis J. "Deconstructing Arbitrary and Capricious Review," 92 *North Carolina Law Review* 721 (2014).

"Scientific Peer Review and Administrative Legitimacy," 61 *Administrative Law Review* 723 (2009).

Viscusi, W. Kip. "Individual Rationality, Hazard Warnings, and the Foundations of Tort Law," 48 *Rutgers Law Review* 625 (1996).

Wagner, R. Polk. "Understanding Patent-Quality Mechanisms," 157 *University of Pennsylvania Law Review* 2135 (2009).

Wagner, Wendy E. "Participation in Administrative Process," in *Comparative Law and Regulation: National, International, and Transnational Perspectives* 109 (Francesca Bignami & David Zaring, eds.) (Elgar, 2016).

"A Place for Agency Expertise: Reconciling Agency Expertise with Presidential Power," 115 *Columbia Law Review* 2019 (2015).

"Racing to the Top: How Regulation Can Be Used to Create Incentives for Industry to Improve Environmental Quality," 29 *Journal of Land Use and Environmental Law* 1 (2014).

"Administrative Law, Filter Failure, and Information Capture," 59 *Duke Law Journal.* 1321 (2010).

"The Clean Air Interstate Rule's Regulatory Impact Analysis: Advocacy Dressed Up as Policy Analysis," in *Reforming Regulatory Impact Analysis* 56 (Richard Morgenstern, et al., eds.) (RFF, 2009).

"Using Competition-Based Regulation to Bridge the Toxics Data Gap," 83 *Indiana Law Journal* 629 (2008).

"The 'Bad Science' Fiction: Reclaiming the Debate over the Role of Science in Public Health and Environmental Regulation," 66 *Law & Contemporary Problems*, Autumn 2003, at 63.

"Choosing Ignorance in the Manufacture of Toxic Products," 82 *Cornell Law Review* 773 (1997).

"The Science Charade in Toxic Risk Regulation," 95 *Columbia Law Review* 1613 (1995).

Wagner, Wendy E. and David Michaels. "Equal Treatment for Regulatory Science: Extending the Controls Governing the Quality of Public Research to Private Research," 30 *American Journal of Law & Medicine* 119 (2004).

Wagner, Wendy E., Katherine Barnes, and Lisa Peters. "Rulemaking in the Shade: An Empirical Study of EPA's Air Toxic Emission Standards," 63 *Administrative Law Review* 99 (2011).

Walker, Christopher J. "Legislating in the Shadows," 165 *University of Pennsylvania Law Review* 1377 (2017).

Wasserman, Melissa. "The PTO's Asymmetric Incentives: Pressure to Expand Substantive Patent Law," 72 *Ohio State Law Journal* 379 (2011).

Weber, Robert F. "Structural Regulation as Antidote to Complexity Capture," 49 *American Business Law Journal* 643 (2012).

"New Governance, Financial Regulation, and Challenges to Legitimacy: The Example of the Internal Models Approach to Capital Adequacy Regulation," 62 *Administrative Law Review* 783 (2010).

West, William F. "Formal Procedures, Informal Processes, Accountability and Responsiveness in Bureaucratic Policy Making: An Institutional Policy Analysis," 64 *Public Administration Review* 66 (2004).

Westbrook, David A. "Corporation Law After Enron: The Possibility of a Capitalist Reimagination," 92 *Georgetown Law Journal* 61(2003).

Whitford, William C. "The Functions of Disclosure Regulation in Consumer Transactions," 1973 *Wisconsin Law Review* 400.

Willis, Lauren E. "The Consumer Financial Protection Bureau and the Quest for Consumer Comprehension," 3 *Russell Sage Foundation Journal of the Social Sciences* 74 (2017).

"Performance-Based Consumer Law," 82 *University of Chicago Law Review* 1309 (2015).

"Decisionmaking and the Limits of Disclosure: The Problem of Predatory Lending: Price," 65 *Maryland Law Review* 707 (2006).

Wilson, James Q. *Bureaucracy: What Government Agencies Do and Why They Do It* (Basic, 1991).

The Politics of Regulation (Basic, 1980).

Wilson, Janet and Oladele A. Ogunseitan. "A Call for Better Toxics Policy Reform," 59 *Environment: Science and Policy for Sustainable Development* 30 (2017).

Yackee, Jason W. and Susan W. Yackee. "A Bias toward Business? Assessing Interest Group Influence on the Bureaucracy," 68 *Journal of Politics* 128 (2006).

Young, Kevin L., Tim Marple, and James Heilman. "Beyond the Revolving Door: Advocacy Behavior and Social Distance to Financial Regulators," 19 *Business and Politics* 327 (2017).

Index